RUSI

and

BRASSEY'S

Defence Yearbook 1985

Edited by

The Royal United Services Institute for Defence Studies

London

95th Year of Publication

BRASSEY'S DEFENCE PUBLISHERS

a member of the Pergamon Group

LONDON · OXFORD · WASHINGTON DC · NEW YORK

TORONTO · SYDNEY · PARIS · FRANKFURT

U.K. (Editorial)	Brassey's Defence Publishers Ltd., Maxwell House, 74 Worship Street, London EC2A 2EN
(Orders)	Brassey's Defence Publishers Ltd., Headington Hill Hall, Oxford OX3 0BW, England
U.S.A. (Editorial)	Pergamon-Brassey's International Defense Publishers, 1340 Old Chain Bridge Road, McLean, Virginia 22101, U.S.A.
(Orders)	Pergamon Press Inc., Maxwell House, Fairview Park, Elmsford, New York 10523, U.S.A.
CANADA	Pergamon Press Canada Ltd., Suite 104, 150 Consumers Road, Willowdale, Ontario M2J 1P9, Canada
AUSTRALIA	Pergamon Press (Aust.) Pty. Ltd., P.O. Box 544, Potts Point, N.S.W. 2011, Australia
FEDERAL REPUBLIC OF GERMANY	Pergamon Press GmbH, Hammerweg 6, D-6242 Kronberg-Taunus, Federal Republic of Germany

---

This edition 1985

Reprinted 1985

Library of Congress Catalog card no. 75–641843

British Library Cataloguing in Publication Data
Rusi and Brassey's defence yearbook.—1985
1. Armed Forces—Periodicals
I. Royal United Services Institute for Defence Studies
355′.005 U1

ISBN 0 08 031168 7 (Hard cover)
ISBN 0 08 031169 5 (Flexi cover)

Printed in Great Britain by A. Wheaton & Co. Ltd., Exeter

Contents

Part IV

Preface

THE Royal United Services Institute is now in its 153rd year, and is playing an ever-increasing role in the advancement of the science and literature of the Armed Forces, and in keeping the public informed on defence matters. The RUSI holds lectures and seminars on all aspects of national security, publishes a quarterly Journal and a monthly News Brief. Brassey's Yearbook is now in its 95th year, and has an established reputation as one of the most authoritative sources in the defence field. As the *RUSI/Brassey's Defence Yearbook,* it carries on the tradition of high standards in the breadth and quality of its contents. Such is the reputation which the Yearbook has earned that the Editors can enlist the support of contributors of the highest prestige and qualifications as the contents list so clearly indicates.

Setting the Scene

A New Age of Diplomacy?

Introduction

Earlier attempts at 'setting the scene' for forthcoming years have been titled 'Myths and Realities' and 'Imperatives and Incentives'. These phrases have sought to capture an underlying spirit, theme, or dynamic, across the field of defence and security issues. Towards the end of 1982 there was a sense of searching for idealistic goals; ephemeral aims which sometimes seemed to take little account of military, political and economic realities. A year later the mood had changed perhaps because of better public recognition of the parameters within which change might be possible. It could be said that constraints were imposing a brake on movement and there was thus a need to come to terms with the imperatives for further development whilst appreciating the sort of incentive which might be needed to prompt concession or movement.

This year there are glimmerings of hope in some areas of international relations and even in those issues where little or no improvement might be in prospect, there is increasing confidence that we might be able to manage them a little better. A new American administration seeking to make its mark with much less than four years in which to respond to the expressed wishes of its electorate and its allies. A Soviet Union trying to avoid 'a-new-leader-a-year' syndrome by strengthening its collective leadership in its transition to the next generation. And a more assertive Europe, in the West largely the result of American goadings; in the East, attempting to take advantage of the Kremlin's self-preoccupation to gain a little more freedom of action.

There are still many pressures and conflicts. The Iran-Iraq war rumbles on. There are occasional flare-ups of violence elsewhere, in Southern Africa, Central America, the Far East, and international terrorism presages even more frequent and violent attacks. Yet in all these areas there is the perceived need to contain the effects of such violence and, perhaps, to move towards greater stability. To improve international relations, to find peaceful solutions to problems and to manage difficulties when a satisfactory end is not in sight, calls for all the skills of the diplomatist. If a new age of diplomacy is in prospect then, at least in the West, a wider understanding is needed of the tools of diplomacy. Military power has its part to play, not just in its utility of pressure, real or perceived, or even as trade-offs at the conference table, but also in the recognition by the military themselves of the wider environment in which they operate and, ironically for what can be the brutal application of military force, the finesse they may be called upon to exhibit. On occasion, a rapier can be more effective than a bludgeon; a timely exercise more appropriate than actual operations; a task force over the horizon more constraining than direct involvement in a conflict.

East-West Relations

The Soviet View

On the highway from Moscow airport to the city there is a memorial at the side of the road to mark the limit of the Nazi advance in the Second World War. The effect can be imagined upon the people of the United Kingdom if a similar memorial existed close to the Hammersmith 'fly-over' on coming into London, or if Dulles airport outside Washington had been in hostile hands. Herein lies one of the roots of differing perceptions of national security. The communist system in the Soviet Union has not yet been in power for 70 years but it has twice had to rebuild large elements of its industrial capacity as well as its towns and villages, as a result of war. Whilst communist ideology has not lost its importance, the Russians are now critical of their own economic failures and weaknesses. Although the need for incentives might be accepted, this would strike at the very core of centralised control so they are now favouring 'a systems approach' to their problems and, possibly, the introduction of more flexible industrial units. The demands made upon the Soviet economy by military expenditure and the way this detracts from economic growth is well appreciated but, in Leninist terms, 'The Revolution is worthless if it cannot defend itself'.

The Soviet régime is a reactive and secretive one. It allows little scope for either incentive or imagination. Moreover, the Russians are a pragmatic people and their present low-grade welfare state satisfies their basic needs. It is also a system which can respond effectively, if faced by the threat of an aggressor, by belt-tightening over a protracted period. But this should not be overstated; there are consumer demands in the Soviet Union, people want cars, improved living conditions, better social services, and more and reliable consumer goods. Again in Marxist-Leninist terms, 'socialism can only prove its validity by its economic achievements'. This is not lost on the Politburo.

Andropov's death was mourned by the *Apparatchniks*, despite his short time as leader, because he offered the prospect of advancement on ability rather than seniority also and he wished to bring official pronouncements closer to reality. It was feared that President Chernenko would signal the return of the dead hand of Brezhnev. Initially, this seemed to be true but there are indications that some reforms are continuing and the most blatant offences of bribery and corruption are being punished. However, not only are President Chernenko's days numbered but so too are those of Marshal Ustinov and Mr Gromyko. The manoeuvring for advantage in the succession is evident. The Gorbechov and Romanov factions await the departure of the old guard. In any such struggle for power, the support of the military is a tremendous asset. Always subservient to the Party, its influence if not its power is to be reckoned with in the councils of the Politburo. Will the military thereby obtain a greater share of resources or will its growth be constrained by the need for economic development?

Whilst privately admitting that only the strong are able to be flexible in negotiation and have the confidence to make concessions, the Soviet Union claims that the United States is bent on a policy of superiority. It is fearful that America, which it sees at the heart of NATO, has no commitment to meaningful negotiations but rather seeks to assuage its allies and its own public opinion: that it only negotiates with Congress and the Europeans and not with the Russians. The Soviets believe that America is moving from a policy of 'mutually assured destruction' to one of assured survival; that this is evidenced by the contradictions in its negotiating stance of going ahead with the deployment of theatre nuclear weapons whilst involved in the INF negotiations, of developing the MX missile whilst taking part in the START negotiations, and developing binary weapons when claiming the need for a treaty to control chemical weapons. It is easy to dismiss these views as propaganda yet they are much voiced Soviet preoccupations.

So often, attempts to achieve a break-through in arms control by the Superpowers reflect a cyclical approach with one side out of phase with the other. Occasionally, endeavours become better synchronised and there is a coalescence of aims, albeit reflecting self-interest, which result in a measure of agreement. We could be approaching such a period in 1985. The incentive for the Soviets is to avoid the vast economic investment in the competition for weapons in outer-space. However, they also claim to seek proof of serious intent on the part of the United States to negotiate. The evidence which they seek is ratification of the Limited Test-Ban Treaty followed by a move towards a complete test-ban treaty; a moratorium on nuclear weapon development, particularly in space, whilst negotiations proceed; agreement on practical verification in the field of chemical weapons; and a no-first-use declaration. It would be foolhardy to accept such negotiating stand-points at their face-value. *Realpolitik* calls for hard bargaining from a position of strength. What is certain however is the importance of 'face' in the Russian character. Rhetorical up-braiding is counter-productive, the need for calm but resolute diplomacy is much more likely to succeed. Loudly to claim that increased military strength will force them back to the conference table is destined to achieve the opposite. What is needed is the recognition of mutual self-interest in curtailing the competition for arms, then moving cautiously and patiently towards that end without any palpable weakening in resolve or in military strength.

The US View

A new American administration takes office in 1985. It will have the opportunity of building on the increased confidence which Americans feel after four years of President Reagan. An economic turn-round, increased expenditure on defence, an increased authority in its foreign policy all command increased attention. The rhetoric of the 1980 presidential campaign has not been repeated in 1984: perhaps necessary for domestic reasons, the earlier statements worried friends and potential enemies alike. So did the first two years of the new administration as, seemingly, it sought to give effect to its electoral statements. Subsequently, it has sought to convince the Soviet Union, albeit at some prompting by its European allies, that it is committed to arms control and negotiation. It is 12 years since the US re-elected an incumbent President, it has been 24 years since such a re-elected president completed two full terms. To know with whom you are dealing and whether policies are likely to be consistent is of great importance to allies and adversaries. It has been repeated on many occasions that this is recognised by the Reagan administration and that the next term will see a continuation of the policies of the last two years, and carried out by a team very similar to the outgoing administration. The first measure of the intent of the new administration will be the selection of key appointments and the past statements and policies with which they have been associated. Nowhere will the interest be keener than in the Soviet Union itself, followed by America's allies in NATO. American defence policies will be measured, not only by the defence budget and policy statement in February, but by its development of the strategic defence initiative, its anti-satellite capability and its implications for the ABM treaty and furthermore, by its ability to harness emerging technology to those operational concepts it seeks to develop in the conventional field. All of these will have far-reaching effects; for example, will the US be able to sustain the projects upon which it has embarked over the last administration's period of greatly increased defence expenditure? What is particularly notable, however, is that both Superpowers now seem to be listening to what the other says rather than talking past each other to a wider audience.

Developments in the Middle East

The Gulf War

There has been recent and notable evidence of the deployment of US military power in the Middle East. First, in the direct involvement of land, sea and airforces in the Lebanon and then the deployment of the carrier task group off the Persian Gulf. This last reflected both a sense of responsibility and of restraint as its presence over the horizon, coupled with the AWACS operating from Saudi Arabia, encouraged the Gulf States but deterred Iran from precipitate actions. Nevertheless, the Iran-Iraq war continues to drag on with all sides, less perhaps the combatants themselves, seemingly content to let it do so. The Gulf States can remember the Baath Party of Iraq seeking to export its doctrines and bring the Gulf under its sway. They also see Iran as the centre of Islamic fundamentalism; the revolution which recognises no national frontiers. Western Europe and Japan, on the other-hand, seek to ensure that no one régime will control the oil lines of communication through the Gulf. Whilst also supporting the freedom of navigation, both Superpowers are performing a balancing act to avoid backing the loser in the war yet, at the same time, preventing the other Superpower from being hailed as the peace-maker or emerging as the predominant influence in the region.

Initially a war spawned by miscalculation, Iran with its great geographic area and larger population has lost the advantage of preponderant force over its adversary in the Gulf, as other Arab States and both the Superpowers have supported Iraq with arms and money. Denied resupply, and unable to achieve air superiority over the battle areas, Iran has little chance of gaining surprise and, even if it could break through the Iraqi defences, it would be unable to maintain the momentum of its attack as it lacks adequate logistic support. Iraq has long recognised that it cannot win the war; it now seeks to prevent Iran from becoming the victor and thus to drive it to the conference table. Despite his grip on the country, President Sadam Hussain appears to lack confidence in maintaining that control should casualties greatly increase. He has therefore adopted a largely defensive strategy, expending materiel rather than troops. His offensive actions seem confined to restricting reinforcement by sea to the Iranian forces and to stand-off attacks on Kharg Island in an endeavour to reduce Iran's currency-earning oil flow. This in turn prompts reprisals by Iran to discourage the Gulf states from supporting Iraq and to curtail its oil exports. With these pressures on both sides, military stalemate has resulted with only the occasional flare-up; these are likely to continue but at decreasing intervals. The situation might well be called a balance of military incompetence.

An assassin's bullet is always possible and, obviously, that could change the situation but probably not as dramatically as might be thought. Like the American hostage crisis when he belatedly realised that he had achieved all that was politically possible, Ayatollah Khomeini may save face by handing the problem of Iraq to the Majlis to resolve. In his demands that Iraq should accept culpability and pay vast reparations, some negotiated deal might be possible. If then the removal of Sadam Hussain is the only bar to peace then the Baath Party might seek to resolve that difficulty. The death of the Ayatollah would not necessarily presage peace as factions in Iran wrestle for power possibly preventing any endorsement of a peace plan. Thus the situation will drift on with occasional Iranian forays but neither side reducing its guard. New pipe lines will help Iraq to sell its oil but its debts to other Arab states are likely to constrain its earlier ambitious development plans for many years to come.

Developments in the Levant

The Iran-Iraq war might come to resemble the Arab-Israeli dispute by its protracted nature. However, there are now promising developments in the Levant. Elections in 1984 have brought to power a grand coalition in Israel to break the impasse of the Likud and Labour party being able to lead a coalition on their own. Seen as a means of unifying the country to face the desperate measures necessary to counter rampant inflation, there are fears that, with its diverse elements, it could become a government of paralysis. Such a development could become very serious indeed as it might increase the appeal of more extreme politicians and their desperate measures. Nevertheless efforts to disengage from Southern Lebanon, always consistent with maintaining the security of Israel from PLO attacks, will continue with the possibility of United Nations forces again policing the divide.

Syria, initially delighted with its greatly enhanced reputation in the area by bringing apparent peace to the warring Lebanese factions where America and Israel had failed, could be wearying in its efforts to produce a workable solution for Lebanon. Nevertheless, it seeks to exert its authority over the many disparate elements involved. Syria might well be content if it could induce the Israelis to withdraw from the Bekaa Valley, and thus deny them the leverage they enjoy over Damascus itself, whilst maintaining their own hold over the Lebanon. Jordan's support of Yasser Arafat and its diplomatic recognition once again, of Egypt along with its continuing support for Iraq, which is opposed to Syria, has not brought increased affection for King Hussein from President Assad. However, Amman's repeated rejection of the Camp David Accords efforts to compensate with a purchase of Soviet or Western European weapons after its failure to obtain American air defence missiles, is evidence of King Hussein's efforts to maintain Jordan's independence. He also very patently seeks to find a solution to the Palestinian problem. The prospects for such a solution look no nearer but at least the cement of rigid positions holding the mosaic together shows signs of cracking; perhaps the beginnings of some rearrangement might be possible.

Atlantic Alliance

Strains within the Alliance centre on East-West relations and the differing views of how to deal with the Russians; the question of 'burden-sharing', with some Americans emphatically believing that Europe is not paying its way in defence; and a review of operational concept with emerging technologies seen as giving a new dimension to the overall strategy of 'Flexibility in Response and Forward Defence'.

Arms Control

Progress in East-West relations and particularly arms control negotiations will largely depend upon the motivation, aims and objectives of the next American administration. Many strands go into the weaving of official policy and hence a need exists to appreciate the position of any particular spokesman in the wider political context. Nevertheless, the aim of President Reagan's new administration will be one of continuing his more recent policies in an endeavour to break the deadlock with the Soviet Union and to develop a dialogue leading to better relations.

In the field of arms control it is believed that there is a US commitment to reduce nuclear weapon stocks and to retard the competition for new offensive nuclear weapon systems, but only through verifiable agreements. Despite explanatory discussions at Foreign Minister level, there is little evidence yet of a positive Soviet response to proposals designed to reach an arms control agreement. It is to be hoped that Moscow has been preparing its position in order to enter into meaningful negotiations with the new American administration. It is unlikely that there will be a formal return to the Strategic Arms Reduction Treaty talks and the Intermediate-Range Nuclear Force talks in Geneva. Yet discussions on conventional defence measures, whilst no-one can deny their correlation with nuclear weapon talks, could be given a fresh impetus if so desired in the MBFR talks in Vienna and in attempts to enhance confidence-building measures in the follow-up talks to the Helsinki accords in Stockholm. If so called 'umbrella' talks, which are vague in what they cover, extend to nuclear weapons in space, then it must be hoped that, either concurrently or shortly thereafter, negotiations can be resumed on both strategic and theatre nuclear weapons: the format for the talks being determined by how the negotiations might best be managed. A further thrust should come from the 1985 Review Conference on the Non-Proliferation Treaty. The preparatory committee will hold its third meeting in April and the Review Conference itself is planned for September 1985.

In all these discussions Europe has interests and a role to play. If agreement can be approached in the area of strategic weapons then the question of the British and French strategic nuclear capability will need to be taken into account. Further, the continuing deployment of Pershing-II and Cruise missiles, and particularly the development of sea and air-launched Cruise missiles, will continue to hold the close interest of Western European governments. Some argue that the 1979 'twin-track' decision, on seeking substantive negotiations with the Soviet Union but going ahead with the deployment of modernised theatre nuclear weapons if agreement or reductions were not forthcoming, has provided tangible evidence of the strength and cohesion of the Alliance. Even whilst accepting this, some believe that in reaching the 1979 decision and then sustaining its implementation, NATO has eroded a great deal of its political strength and good-will and that this costly decision should not be repeated. These views further provoke American fears that the Europeans are not totally committed to their own defence.

The possibility of reaching an agreement on the banning of all chemical weapons is also one of concern to the Alliance. It was reported that there had been some movement in these negotiations and it only remained to determine a reasonable means of verification. Old arguments concerned with on-site inspections however brought these negotiations to a halt too. In these and in the START and INF talks, the USA kept its NATO allies fully informed. Similarly, in the MBFR talks and at the CDE negotiations in Stockholm, there is considerable consultation and cooperation within the Alliance. It is important that this is continued and consistency maintained by the West in their initiatives and proposals to the USSR across the whole arms control spectrum. In so doing, it is important that there is a military understanding of the arms control proposals and, ideally, that there is military involvement in the formulation of such proposals.

Burden-sharing

A prevalent view exists in the United States that Europe does not pay enough for its own defence, and that it fails to recognise the global responsibilities of the US and the additional costs that these incur. This came to a head with the introduction of the Nunn Amendment to the US Defence Authorisation Bill for Fiscal year 1985 which was introduced in June 1984. Despite being a strong advocate of NATO, Senator Sam Nunn's exasperation was apparent in his proposal to reduce the US troop ceiling of 326,414 in Europe by 30,000 a year, beginning in 1987, unless during the previous year the Europeans had increased their defence spending by 3 per cent in real terms, or increased their weapon stocks towards 30 days operational supplies, or provided aircraft shelters and support facilities required to support US reinforcing tactical aircraft, or in some other way had increased their conventional defence capability as sanctioned by SACEUR. If all three objectives were met there would be no troop reduction, if only one was met then the cut would be 20,000 troops and if two objectives had been attained then the cut would be only 10,000 men. The merits of such an approach have been the subject of much argument, not least in the belief that proper account of the European contribution to the NATO defence, including conscript forces, real-estate, and ready forces, had not been taken properly into account. Although the amendment was narrowly defeated in Congress, it is certain that similar proposals will be debated again in 1985. The concern of many Europeans at being subject to an annual review by Congress would then become a reality. Although Senator Nunn might have made his proposal in an endeavour to goad the Europeans to greater contributions in their common defence, he may also have unleashed an American reaction, based on superficial knowledge, which he might now have difficulty in controlling in the newly elected Congress. This could be dangerous for Alliance cohesion. After all, American forces are deployed in Europe to defend American interests as well as those of the European allies, and whilst their contribution is a very important one, in the end, it is the *collective* efforts of the Alliance which will provide the best counter to potential Soviet aggression.

Emerging Technology and NATO's Military Doctrine

In the field of emerging technology further transatlantic dissension has arisen. On the one hand, there is the American belief that in its trading with the Soviet Union and Eastern Europe, the Western allies have been transferring technological know-how, which has enhanced the military capability of the Warsaw Pact, as well as its industrial knowledge, at little investment cost to Moscow. Whilst this suspicion might be true in part, and measures have now been initiated to restrict technology transfer, it has been counter-balanced by the European irritation in thinking that investment in future weapon systems was being pressed upon them largely to satisfy US commercial interests. The European concern was that the American defence industries might build such a lead in emerging technology that their own industries would be subordinated to them to the detriment of European innovation, research and development and production. Understandably, the prospect of such a dependency is resented in Europe. However, unless the Europeans can coordinate their defence industries, with whom can the Americans deal, and how might the Europeans improve their own position? A fragmented European domestic market is certainly not the answer.

In terms of military doctrine there has always been an underlying tension between Europe and the United States. Europe, having witnessed the decimation of two World Wars, seeks a strategy which deters aggression without the prospect of a conventional conflict fought over its soil. America, on the other hand, is deeply concerned that should deterrence fail it should not be forced to cross the nuclear threshold early in a conflict, putting the continental US itself at risk in a strategic nuclear exchange. The US would therefore prefer to see a considerable increase in conventional capability sufficient to hold a conflict at that level for some time before the prospect of nuclear release. It is this perceived need, and a lack of response on the part of the Europeans to increase NATO conventional capability, which lies at the heart of the proposed Nunn amendment.

Flexibility in response and forward defence became the strategy for NATO in 1967 following the realisation that instant and massive nuclear retaliation to any attack was no longer credible. Whilst the keystone of the new strategy was that an aggressor must be convinced of NATO's readiness to use nuclear weapons if necessary, it was aimed first at meeting any aggression with direct defence, and then retaining the capability to escalate the conflict at NATO's choosing thereby enhancing deterrence. NATO's readiness to "go nuclear" was constant but the deterrent effect was further increased by the uncertainty of the timing and circumstances in which those weapons might be used, with the initiative to do so vested in the Alliance.

The application of the flexible response and forward defence strategy is again being called into question. It is argued that a strategy which depends upon the threatened use of nuclear weapons holds the seeds of its own incredibility when such use would prompt a nuclear exchange and the risk of mutual destruction for both sides. Doubts are also expressed that a political decision might not be forthcoming at a time of crisis in war to sanction the use of nuclear weapons. Moreover there is considerable public concern over this nuclear dependency and its implications should deterrence fail. These concerns have given rise to the need to increase the conventional forces of the Alliance, thereby giving evidence both of political will and military capability, and to extend any advantage which the West might enjoy in emerging technology.

Interest in emerging technology has centred on improved surveillance: command, control, communications and intelligence systems, and terminally guided munitions. Additional surveillance to detect enemy movement, and the ability to quickly sift, assimilate and react to such a mass of 'real-time' intelligence, is a long felt need and this is an area where considerable improvements have and are taking place. The means to hit key static targets, such as air fields and geographic choke points, with great accuracy, and a method of delivery which does not rely upon manned aircraft encroaching into densely defended areas, are also of great benefit. Terminally guided submunitions coupled with effective target acquisition, 'real-time' surveillance and enhanced communications, offer the prospect of being able to engage mobile targets too. It is these improvements which promise markedly increased effectiveness in NATO's conventional capability. When matched with improvement in barrier defence, including the ability to create tank-traps and to channel movement by the rapid laying of mine-fields, by shell, helicopter or aircraft, then the increased deterrent value of the flexible response and forward defence strategy becomes manifest.

There is considerable evidence to show that the Warsaw Pact is developing a concept of operations which with the echeloning of its forces, would enable it quickly to reinforce any breakthrough of NATO defences. The aim would then be to neutralise rear headquarters, the deployment of reserves and reinforcements and, by the speed of its movement, pre-empt a decision on the part of NATO to use nuclear weapons. There is still discussion over whether the Warsaw Pact has in fact designated particular formations, known as Operational Manoeuvre Groups, charged with the aim of specifically breaking through and creating havoc in the rear of NATO's defences: such groups being self-contained, of not less than divisional strength and including elements of all arms, highly mobile and logistically supported by helicopter. Others argue that the Soviet concept is to attack along the whole NATO front and, where a weakness is found, to drive additional formations through: such a manoeuvre has been likened to digging-in the prongs of a garden fork. In either event second echelon Warsaw Pact forces would seek to exploit any advantage. American forces have examined a series of possibilities to exploit their own conventional capabilities in Europe to counter the revised Soviet concept of operations. Terms like Follow On Forces Attack and Air Land Battle have been adopted to describe the new thinking. Improved surveillance, command and control arrangements and terminally guided submunitions from missile launchers, are held to offer the prospect of striking deep into Warsaw Pact territory against their rear echelon forces—perhaps even as far as the Western Military Districts of the Soviet Union.

Many doubts exist over the deep-strike concept. Some commentators question its feasibility. Locating tank concentrations 300km behind the East German frontier, taking immediate decisions on target allocation and acquisition are tasks that demand a very high proficiency in information handling and an efficient command system. Proponents argue that if NATO posed such a conventional threat, it would force the Soviet Union to expend scarce economic resources on its own rear area defences and thus reduce the threat of an attack against Western Europe. Such claims are countered by the need for the NATO Alliance first to improve its capability to withstand an initial Soviet attack; secondly, and building on that, NATO then needs to improve its capability to take on fixed targets, perhaps some 150km or more beyond the East German frontier. These capabilities would markedly improve NATO's deterrence posture and might restrain defence expenditure within realistic limits. The military has traditionally sought to take advantage of evolving technology. However, whilst the rate of technological development is increasing at an unprecedented rate, it cannot be suggested that new weapons in themselves offer a panacea. A lead in the competition for military advantage usually provokes a rapid counter-development.

Western Europe is well aware of the transatlantic differences within the Alliance and it is endeavouring to respond. Nevertheless the prospect of increased Western European defence expenditure, in competition with other social demands is most unlikely. The pressing need is therefore to make better use of joint European resources. In so doing, it is earnestly hoped that France will become more closely involved in the military aspects of the Alliance. This has prompted a positive response to the regeneration of the Western European Union when foreign and defence ministers will meet twice a year for discussions. This in itself will generate an expectation for tangible results and the harmonisation of defence and procurement policies would be a useful goal. The greatest challenges lie in the field of weapon procurement and the development of a European defence industry. A more forward looking and decisive Independent European Programme Group (IEPG) would be a help, with multinational defence-industrial consortia responding to the political lead. *Juste retour* may then take the form of off-set agreements, with the lead in some projects and a supporting role in others, thus retaining a measure of expertise, in desired areas.

United Kingdom Defence Issues

No longer formally committed to maintaining the annual 3 per cent real growth in defence expenditure, Michael Heseltine in 1984 embarked upon a reorganisation of the Ministry of Defence to improve efficiency in decision-making and to make better use of the resources allocated to defence. Few would argue with the need for an overall defence solution as opposed to one which satisfies single services. Even so, the timing and method of the reorganisation gave rise to much interest. Whether it should have been done at all and, if so, at this time, are now matters of no more than academic interest. If the reorganisation will bring marked improvements and economies, as opposed to a mere reshuffling and renaming of different parts of the MOD structure, is also open to doubt. Regrettably, whilst this country continued to play its part within NATO during 1984, the MOD reorganisation seems to have distracted the UK from taking initiatives in examining a variety of operational concepts, force structures and organisation within the Alliance. Hopefully the implementation of the reorganisation will not prevent the UK from taking the lead in some of these areas now, perhaps building on CDS's earlier review of certain strategic options.

The focus of public interest now is whether, at the present level of planned defence expenditure, we can maintain the four pillars of our national defence; that is our nuclear capability, the defence of the UK base, the commitment of our ground and air forces in Europe, and our maritime forces in the Channel and Eastern Atlantic. If present force levels are to be maintained, weapon and other logistic stocks increased to meet the needs of 'sustainability', and further improvements made in taking advantage of emerging technology, then the question of whether we can afford such levels of defence expenditure will no doubt continue to be asked. Officially, it is held that our present forces can be maintained and planned improvements achieved within the forecast allocation of resources for at least this decade. Of particular point is the replacement of our Polaris strategic nuclear system with the Trident II. Largely priced in dollars, the falling exchange level of the pound has brought consequent increases to the cost of Trident. In the argument over replacement of Polaris the wrong questions are usually asked. Should this country maintain a strategic nuclear deterrent at all? If so, then a ballistic missile system is almost certainly required. In this case, the proposed purchase and employment of Trident II has evident economic advantages. So far the present government is committed to it; if it were not, or it changed its mind, there would still be serious doubts that any money thereby saved would be spent on improving our conventional capability.

It is hoped that the resurgence of thinking on how the 1st British Corps best meets its tasks, and the review which this has prompted throughout Northern Army Group and the 2 Allied Tactical Air Force in Germany, will effectively spread to our NATO allies. The examination in the MOD of various strategies open to this country has re-affirmed our commitment to a credible deterrent posture based on a doctrine of 'flexible response and forward defence'. A similar review within NATO, and not tackled piecemeal by separate agencies, would seem to have considerable merit, not least in determining how evolving technology might enhance a credible deterrence strategy for the Alliance as a whole and the consequent NATO-wide operational concepts and requirements.

The UK almost had a fifth pillar in its defence policy, that of 'out-of-NATO-area' operations. Whilst this did not materialise, because of resource limitations, increased emphasis has been made upon 'joint warfare' in planning, training, and operations. With recognition of our responsibilities world-wide, this might be extended to prompt a further UK initiative with our European allies to achieve a tangible multinational capability which, if not formally structured, would at least have agreed concepts, developed and sustained by frequent exercises. It might also help to counter the American criticism that Europe is too inward looking and does not adequately support the US in meeting its global security responsibilities.

Conclusion

President Reagan, in his second term of office, is likely to be motivated by the wish that he should go down in history as the initiator of a new period of peace and stability. Having made America stronger and increased her self-confidence, the prospects for negotiations between the Super Powers and of better East-West relations should now be improved. What is more open to question is whether the Soviet Union, with its own hierarchy albeit more settled but still in a period of transition and with a longer view of world events, will be able to respond to American initiatives. In the Middle East, there are signs that Israel and its Arab neighbours are more inclined to seek a negotiated solution to their difficulties. Even in the Iran/Iraq War there is the recognition that if neither side can win, each could certainly. There might be a glimmer of hope that Ayatollah Khomeini will see advantage in some form of mediation even if he, personally, opts out as he did in the American hostage crisis. Should this not occur, it is unlikely that intense protracted operations will continue. Elsewhere in the world too, in Central America, Southern Africa and in the Far East, recent events point to a search for a settlement by diplomatic rather than direct military means.

Within the Atlantic Alliance, though efforts will be made to improve cohesion, further transatlantic strains are developing. The American belief that Europe is not doing enough in its own defence has political ramifications, not least the prospect of a congressional task-master measuring European endeavours! Whilst every effort must be made to avoid misunderstandings there is no room for European complacency; we must make better use of our joint defence resources. There is also an urgent need to harmonise views on a re-examination of the military doctrine of the Alliance, how it may best be implemented and where evolving technology might best support it. Frank discussion between friends is required to ensure that differing views, national difficulties, and the competition for resources, do not develop into crises which further strain the Alliance and thus detract from its value and credibility in the eyes of the public. If there is a wider recognition of the constraints upon a nation or group of nations in the exercise of power, then it is to be hoped that such a positive understanding will be further developed. If the raw use of military force is thereby constrained, and its more sophisticated utility better appreciated, then the prospects for a period of greater stability are improved. Dialogue has many forms and public posturing seldom brings a positive response. If a new age of diplomacy is in prospect, between both friends and potential adversaries, then it is important that the military element underpinning such relations is understood by the diplomat, the politician and, not least, by the military itself.

November 1984 David Bolton

Part I — The Year Ahead

Perspectives of the World Scene: British Defence Issues in the Year Ahead

SIR FRANK COOPER, GCB, CMG

Lately Permanent Under-Secretary of State, Ministry of Defence, and now Consultant to the RUSI

The articles in this series originated in lectures on The Year Ahead given at the RUSI from January to March 1984

THE PUBLICATION of *RUSI Brassey's Defence Yearbook* is becoming the signal for the emergence of Nostradamuses and other seers and soothsayers of equally doubtful repute. Moreover, attempts at prophesying the future are likely, if past experience is any guide, to be a matter of chance. Having said this by way of disclaimer, I shall plunge in — but not before taking a brief look back at 1983.

One can certainly look back at 1983 as having many unpleasant surprises in terms of defence and foreign issues. Spies, terrorists and guerrillas were active in many parts of the world. War and near wars spanned much of the globe. We have only to remind ourselves of the Lebanon, Israel and Syria, Iran and Iraq, the internecine warfare within the Palestine Liberation Organisation, Cambodia, Kampuchea, Angola, Chad, El Salvador, Nicaragua, Honduras, Costa Rica, Panama — to mention some of the violence that can readily be recalled. There were many surprises too — ethnic riots in Sri Lanka, Cyprus, events in Grenada and the shooting down of the South Korean airliner, not to mention the violation of Japanese air space by four Soviet aircraft only a few days later. It was not a good year for order and stability. It was a year when much that was unexpected happened. It reminds us once again that the unexpected and the unforeseen are likely to rank high as issues in 1984, and that in terms of defending the rule of law, the world seems to be moving backwards rather than forwards. It is also a reminder to us and to all who write and speak about defence issues that Europe is happily one of the safest places to live in the whole world and has been for many years past. This suggests to me that from our narrow British point of view, we must ensure that it continues to be as safe in the future, and that we are not to be put off by empty and irresponsible vapourings — from whatever source they come.

The two main political parties have spelled out to us all the main British defence issues as they see them. The present Secretary of State for Defence, speaking at the RUSI's Annual Conference in June 1983 repeated the Government's devotion to Britain's four main defence contributions. Let me remind you briefly what he said. 'First there is the defence of the United Kingdom base. This is a vital task which has been neglected in the past.' Second he said that, so far as the Central Front in Europe was concerned, we would continue to provide our land and air forces. Third, at sea in the Eastern Atlantic and Channel, our strong maritime forces would continue to be modernised. Fourth, that we would continue to provide a UK strategic nuclear force. Michael Heseltine emphasised that our main focus would be on NATO, to which 90 per cent of our effort was devoted, but that we must be prepared to be innovative and ready for the unforeseen outside the NATO area. He saw continuing improvement in our capabilities there in the interests of promoting peace and stability, but rightly, in my view, said we could no longer aspire to the role of international policeman. He went out of his way to say that he did not see any fundamental shifts in our national strategic priorities over the next five years. Finally he said that he had a particular interest in arms control and made it clear that in his view, progress could come only from a position of strength and not from one of weakness, and in the management of defence where he intended to pursue a policy of value for money. He emphasised the need for competition and dual sourcing.

The leader of the Labour Party, Mr Neil Kinnock, has already been particularly active in 1984. He has repeated his Party's intention to withdraw from nuclear weaponry and to remove United States' bases from the United Kingdom. He foresaw these commitments being sustained into the next election, together with one to send back Cruise missiles to the United States and suspend the Trident missile programme.

He went on to make it plain that Labour remained pledged to maintaining and improving Britain's modern, conventional defences within NATO but that, to secure that end, 'we cannot engage in the expenses and risks that go with trying to sustain ourselves as a nuclear power'. He suggested that, as a result of implementing these policies, we should get 'an accelerated response from the Soviet Union on force reductions'.

Thus, there is a good part of the agenda laid out. Two issues which will be high on it are those concerned with nuclear matters and with arms control.

Nuclear Issues

Clearly, and in my view absolutely rightly, the British Government will sustain the British independent strategic nuclear deterrent. Conversely, there will be continuing opposition to this and to the progressive deployment of Cruise missiles in the United Kingdom if there is no change in East/West relations in this particular area. It is, incidentally, important to recognise that 31 December 1983 was one watershed, there are others. Moreover, it seems to me essential to take a balanced view. Arms talks failed but NATO remained cohesive whilst the initial deployment of Pershing and Cruise missiles took place. This was a considerable achievement, but it is right to take a balanced view of it and not regard deployment as a major triumph for the West.

On the other hand, it would be wrong to regard that deployment as more or less militarily necessary than was the Soviet Union's widespread production and deployment of SS–20s and other modernised missiles. In many ways these questions are more of politics than of defence, and more of will than of need. The fact remains — regrettable though it may be — that in defence (as in many walks of life), weakness leads to disaster. The fact is, and still remains, that the Soviet Union, the CND and, apparently some parts of the Labour Party, are pursuing a common policy. This can be expressed quite simply as seeking to stop the deployment and installation of nuclear weapons in Western Europe. I find it difficult to see the net result of this — if it were ever successful, which I trust it will not be — other than a major triumph for the Soviet Union, and that its net effect would be dangerously destabilising.

Nevertheless, I am sure that we can all agree that there are far too many nuclear weapons in both the East and West. I am sure too that we can all agree that every effort needs to be made to pursue productive methods of arms control and arms limitation.

Arms Control

I start from a firmly held belief that successive British Governments have paid far too little attention to this area, coupled with the equally strongly held belief that it is an essential part of our national security policy. I also take the view that activity, let alone thinking, in this area is not the monopoly of either the United States or the Soviet Union. We in Europe are in the front line and we have a continuing and distinctive interest which we should identify and pursue positively. Moreover, the position is going to get more difficult and more complex every year as technology continues to expand and all kinds of new weapons, whether nuclear or conventional, emerge.

There is a genuine need for a great deal more work to be done in this area, in this country and in conjunction with our European allies. The subject has never been particularly attractive to politicians. It is exceptionally difficult to understand. It needs a great deal of continuous hard work. It does not come particularly naturally but it is much too important to go by default, let alone be governed by the normal tribal war cries 'for this' or 'against that'.

Furthermore, there are some very serious questions to be asked. If one asks the most simple question, namely: 'Are there too many nuclear weapons, and particularly, too many in Europe?' Then I think there would be an almost universal answer that both sides have too many. How do we go from here?

One of the most important issues, to my mind, is (given the changing nature of weapons and the ever-diminishing time for real decision-taking), the question of command, control and procedures. This issue has been generally ignored and is actually crucial to us here in Britain and indeed to Europe and the rest of the world. If the armouries of the East and West are going to be filled with guided missiles of one kind or another (which I think is likely), the whole problem of timing, recognition and decision-making is going to become even more acute. There are few ground rules, and those that do exist are out of date. How do you tell if this is your friendly, conventional missile approaching, or a rather nasty, unfriendly nuclear missile which is due to arrive in a minute or so? This is a serious question, seriously put.

We seem to have become mesmerised by numbers, but ought we not to be thinking more in terms of operational characteristics and capabilities? For example, would it be sensible, over a period of time (I think it would be at least ten years) to try and confine nuclear weapons in the missile field to ballistic systems? Would it be equally sensible — and not least against a background of technological developments, to move to a situation where Cruise missiles remained sub-sonic and during the 1990s became non-nuclear? Again, is there not merit in seeking the complete abolition of short-range battlefield nuclear weapons? I do not think that this would do anything other than enhance our safety and reduce the risk of nuclear exchange.

These are all matters which are crucial British defence issues. I would like to see the year ahead being a year in which we demonstrate publicly our real interest in these matters. I would like to see a year in which we really invested a substantial amount of intelligent effort into solving problems of this kind. I would like to see the setting up of some small group or agency which would provide both an intelligent and practical base for policy in this area. It is totally insufficient simply to divide into camps, those 'for' and 'against', as this will lead nowhere other than to increase over the years the risk to us all. The present situation is strategically unsound.

There are obviously other areas in which we can and should concentrate. The obvious one is chemical weapons where the Russians have very large stocks and yet this seems of little concern — particularly to those outside the Government. Perhaps this concern will increase as a consequence of casualties in Iran apparently inflicted by chemical warfare.

Lastly, I suggest there is a need for much more broadly based international dialogue. Clearly we need to make a continuous and major effort with the United States. Both Government and Opposition need to understand the issues much more clearly and debate them much more seriously than hitherto. I regard much political comment as an insult to the British people and lacking in real care about our future. Above all I think the need for us to discuss these matters seriously with our European allies and with other countries in Europe is one of major importance.

As far as our European allies are concerned, I see no reason for the United States and the Soviet Union to be allowed to be in a position where they debate our future without our views being clearly known and clearly heard.

As far as other countries in Europe are concerned, and despite all that has gone before, the sooner we re-establish a continuing and effective dialogue with countries in the Eastern block — at all levels and not merely the political level — the better.

For some years past, there have been far too many sticks and stones in evidence and not enough dialogue. One of the paradoxes of the modern world is that the easier and quicker communications become, the more difficult it is to achieve a genuine understanding and a meeting of minds. This does seem to me to require not only much more widespread and convincing discussion and debate here and with our allies — a point to which I shall return at the end — but also with others.

The Soviet Union is a largely closed society. So too are other members of the Eastern bloc — but to a lesser degree. In comparison Western societies are much more open. What useful purpose is now served by an excessively restricted dialogue which is over-formalised? It seems to me positively dangerous. I hope 1984 will see a significant increase in dialogue and that this should, certainly with some of the Warsaw Pact countries, include defence links and exchanges.

Peace and security are too dangerous to be left exclusively to politicians and diplomats. Surely we should now encourage more broadly based debates between the defence communities of East and West. I also suggest we should be contemplating on an increasing scale reinstating exchanges of visits between our defence forces. We need to gain an insight and understanding of the East and vice-versa, not least in the military area. Defence exchanges and visits would make sense and are relevant particularly when account is properly taken of the totally different nature of our differing societies.

Beyond the NATO area

The issues here tend to be political — in almost every meaning of that word — which sometimes have a greater or lesser defence content. In a number of cases issues are already visible.

The Falkland Islands raise essentially political questions but there is a strong defence connection. It is, in my view, encouraging that messages have been emanating from both London and Buenos Aires which, despite the basic difficulties, have demonstrated a wish for movement. One very much hopes that this movement will take place. There is, I suggest, every reason not to delay. There is a new civilian government in the Argentine and a government in Britain with a large majority. The cost in lives, as well as resources, of 1982 is still fresh in all memories, including those of the Falkland islanders. Momentum is needed.

It is in the defence interest that there should be political movement of a constructive and honourable kind. The nettle has to be firmly grasped. The currently unavoidable expense of defending the Falkland Islands is not a productive use of national or defence resources. For the future this expenditure will inevitably be a successful Treasury target to ensure that as soon as possible it is carried within a net defence budget.

Hong Kong too is a political issue. The Chinese have said that they wish to see the outline of the future regime agreed by the autumn of 1984. Again, one very much hopes that this agreement will be reached in the belief that it is more likely to produce a stable situation in the area. In the shorter term instability would have unhappy consequences for defence. In the longer term stability will inevitably have happier consequences for Britain's defence responsibilities in Hong Kong.

The other issue clearly on the 1984 agenda is the future of the Lebanon. It seems to me that the small British contingent did an outstanding job and handled itself with great professional skill. Yet there is no gainsaying the fact that it was at risk each day because of circumstances over which neither it nor any Government had much control.

In my view it was wrong in the first place to have sent a British contingent, not because of the very high risks involved but because the aim was unclear, policy was obscure and the ability to influence — let alone control — the political situation small. Having said that, it must be right not to consider withdrawal until regional diplomatic negotiation has had a reasonable chance to establish a situation where a further large-scale bloodbath is not inevitable.

Britain still has residual defence responsibility for a number of territories around the world. True, Brunei is no longer directly one of them but Belize is still actively with us and I would hazard the thought that we shall be fortunate if the Caribbean is totally without defence interest in 1984.

Britain and the West as a whole have a direct interest in the future of Iran and Iraq, of the Gulf, and indeed in Central America. Again, these are essentially political and economic issues but there are possible defence repercussions, some of which could involve defence in one way or another.

It is absolutely right that Britain cannot and should not aspire to the role of international policeman. It is also, I suggest, absolutely right that Britain in conjunction with our allies, including the European allies who have much at risk, should seek to establish a common policy and programme of action wherever possible. This is better done outside NATO than within it. In addition, for a small investment Britain can play a considerable defence role in the field of military training and in taking part in joint exercises for which clearly identified British forces are needed.

It would be profitable in my view if the year ahead could see a little more effort put into these issues in terms of clarifying policies, practical action and resource allocation.

Maritime Policy

I have used the words maritime policy deliberately because it is much more than the Royal Navy. The traumas of the ship building industry in this country are there for all to see. Most of our goods are imported and exported by sea. This is the mode of conveyance of some 98 per cent of some 157 million tonnes of imports and 108 million tonnes of exports. There is an increasing awareness of the drastic fall off in the amount of merchant shipping sailing under the British flag with British seamen. There is also awareness of the vast increase in the flags of convenience shipping, particularly Liberia and Panama, whose crews owe allegiance to no one. It is not sufficient to explain all this by crew costs because the UK's crew costs are less than those of West Germany and surprisingly, well under half those of Japan, though crew costs of flags of convenience ships are about half of Britain's.

There are, however, some major naval questions. Do we plan on the basis that we have convoys and, if so, when and what will they carry? Do we plan on independent sailings? Are there enough merchant ships? Is it possible to obtain those merchant ships quickly and be assured they have loyal crews? Are the real costs of naval vessels going to continue rising? Do we expect the Royal Navy to be half its present size in another 20 years? The reduction was even greater in the last 20 years.

There are major issues here, including major defence areas and one would like to see them examined and explained.

Resources and Management

There is no particular reason to assume that money should be a major problem during 1984. This is not to say that 'noises off' will not be heard in the usual volume from both the Treasury and the Ministry of Defence. But as long as both departments keep a grip on expenditure then in the short term no acute problems will arise. Similarly, for people apart from in a very limited number of areas, there should be no major problems about service manpower.

Reducing Civil Service manpower is still a centre piece of the present Government's overall strategy. Much has been achieved and indeed, since the Ministry of Defence was set up in its present form in 1964, then over a 28 year period, civilian manpower has been cut by 230,000 — well over half. There is more to cut, apart from the results of privatisation, but we are entering an era of diminishing returns. There is still, however, a good deal of scope for the reduction of military, procurement and other overheads in all these areas. Results should be with us during 1984. We look forward to them.

Procurement

The central issues about defence procurement remain largely untouched: the continuing rise in real costs from one generation of equipment to another; the continuing fall-off in the quantities of equipment that the services buy; the shortage of logistic support: the continuing explosion of technical knowledge and, consequently, the ever widening choice of weapons systems and defence equipment, and the appallingly bad ratio between initial investment comparing research and development and expenditure with that of production and repair.

There is the question, as yet unresolved, as to what can and should be done. Should we buy more abroad? Should we cooperate with our allies to a greater extent and, if so, should emphasis be on cooperating with the other side of the Atlantic or with Europe? Should we cut back on the number of capabilities that we acquire? Should we reduce the amount spent on research and development? These are immensely complicated issues which have a deep impact on both defence and industry. They, together with individual decisions about equipment, should be a major defence issue in the coming year.

Credibility and Confidence

Finally, I would like to return to the general question of defence policy. It seems to me that there is generally good support in this country for defence and a considerable awareness of the Soviet threat and the lack of stability in the world as a whole. Yet there is a great deal of questioning and uncertainty. People do not seem to be convinced either that all the policies are right or that they are both comprehensible and sensible.

There are many reasons for doubts of this kind: the unsettled state of the world that some see as an over vigorous United States' reaction to events; the arguments about nuclear weapons; the failure of arms talks; a general lack of progress in arms limitation; the bizarre absences of the late Mr Andropov, and the extraordinary way in which Mr Chernenko arrived on the international scene.

There does seem to be an urgent need for a re-statement of defence policies. NATO is urgently in need of a policy review and the arrival of a new Secretary General seems a good time to set one in motion. It should be set in hand now, quickly. The case for a much clearer statement of British defence policy and attitudes to various issues is also required and again, the fact that there is now a Secretary of State who, perhaps, could have a long run in the post, seems as good a time as any to set such a review in motion. This all the more so because resources pressures, though always with us, are not particularly pressing in the short term. A good deal more effort needs to be put into explanation and communication with the various defence issues being brought out more into the open and a clear justification set out for particular policies.

Recently, that wise and eminently readable man, Sam Brittan, wrote an article from an economic point of view in the *Financial Times.* It was called 'The Future Has Not Yet Happened'. He started by mentioning that a Nobel Prize winner could not recall any economist making a fortune, or even a living, out of forecasting the future, though he could think of many who had done very well by selling their forecasts! He went on to say that the most important thing to say about the future was that it has not yet happened and the next most important thing is that it can be implemented by human action. These are not only wise words but true ones. They seem to me to be both the *alpha* and *omega* of the way we should look at defence issues in the year ahead. Above all, I would plead for optimism, realism and dialogue. There is a tremendous need for a positive approach and for Britain to play the part which we all know it is capable of playing.

Prospects for the Alliance

GEORGE WALDEN, CMG, MP

This was given at the RUSI on Wednesday, 18 January 1984. George Walden was the former PPS to Lord Carrington and Dr David Owen and the Member of Parliament for Buckingham

I SHOULD admit that I am not a strategist. So the only basis on which I can contribute is as a defrocked diplomat, who has seen something of life in communist countries; or as a relatively new politician—which I suppose is not much of a recommendation at all.

William Wordsworth was not a strategist either. But he said something very wise about the Alliance when he wrote: "we murder to dissect". NATO has been dissected often, and eagerly. The fact that it is not even a corpse has not put anyone off. If this dissection goes on at the present rate, it soon will be!

I hope to be able to apply some healing balm to some of the wounds.

ATLANTIC PARADOXES

But let me stress immediately that I do not intend to minimise the problems the Alliance faces. These are indeed severe. To make matters worse, they frequently take the form of paradoxes. Let me list some:

- The purpose of the intermediate nuclear force modernisation in Europe was to prevent de-coupling from the United States. Today we are told that this is precisely what it has achieved: Europe is now safe for a limited nuclear exchange.
- We are also told that the theory of flexible response has become inflexibility in practice, now that the Russians have drawn abreast with America in strategic weapons. The answer is for Europe to build up her conventional weaponry —presumably to make defence even more expensive, and war more thinkable.
- Then we are told too that American forces in Europe no longer serve any useful purpose, and that their removal would galvanise Europe into taking her own defence

seriously. But others claim that it would galvanise some countries into an accommodation with Moscow—especially when seen in the light of paradoxes number one and two.

With all its contradictions, NATO is the only Alliance we have got. It has been said that 'strategic ambiguity is a fact of life in Europe'; and also that American protection of Europe is based on 'doctrinal confusion and pragmatic success'. I have read the manuals, and can confirm the point about confusion—not always in my own mind, but sometimes, I suspect, in the text too.

If we have our theoretical uncertainties, so do the Russians. When we debate the so-called 'window of vulnerability', we should remember what it feels like to watch from Moscow the political disintegration of the major buffer state between you and the West, in Poland. Some windows of vulnerability look closer to the ground, and therefore more inviting than others. It depends on your angle of vision.

I repeat, I do not underestimate the reality of our problems, or the need for intensive reflection. But I sometimes wonder what purpose is served by probing these paradoxes to the limit. And I am certain that no purpose is served—and much damage done—by encouraging public opinion, by over-frequent or incautious statements, to probe the ultimate paradox of nuclear weapons themselves. These weapons exist in order never to be used. I know that this is an intellectual simplification—that they cannot not be used unless we are ready to use them. But the political reality is, for once, the higher reality.

A Sense of Disproportion

De-coupling is a fashionable concept. But it takes many forms. It is easy to de-couple strategy from politics; to de-couple abstract military mathematics from common sense; and to de-couple defence spending from public support.

I hope that I am not alone in feeling that there is, at present, a fundamental disjunction in world affairs, centring on the extraordinary disproportion that has arisen in the last few years between the sources of East/West tension on the one hand, and all the war talk and the nuclear neurosis on the other. The tensions are real, and result largely from real Soviet actions. But they are containable with firmness and imagination.

At present, the East/West atmosphere is overheated. The public sense that we have reached a position where it would be difficult for either side to climb down in the face of some relatively minor incident. People are in favour of defence: but not of trials of strength, tests of nerve, or gladiatorial gestures.

Nuclear war is remote in the extreme. But it is the job of governments to make it unthinkable. We are playing the Soviet game if we act or speak in ways which create alarm or despondency, where coolness and determination are needed.

Once the fundamental sense of proportion has gone, other disproportions arise. Because of undeniable failures in the management of the relationship with Moscow, Washington is attracting a disproportionate amount of censure from otherwise sensible people, who sometimes go so far as to equate the two superpowers.

And—to come full circle—all this leads to a third massive disproportion: and this is between the difficulties faced by NATO, and the drastic cures sometimes proposed which would nearly always be far worse than the disease.

I believe—and I certainly hope—that 1984 will see the restoration of some balance in all three areas. A greater sense of political and historical perspective would be reassuring, not only for public opinion; it would help to solve the problems of NATO itself.

The Illusion of Options

Atlanticist orthodoxy was recently summarised broadly as follows: the Russians are a political and military threat to Europe; morality and prudence suggest that the US should lead in its defence; and that the US should therefore try to deter, and if necessary defeat, any Soviet attack. On that basis—and for many other reasons—I remain unashamedly orthodox.

I am not against new thinking—stagnation and complacency would be the worst thing of all for the Alliance. But here, as elsewhere, I am against what I call the illusion of options.

A neutral Europe would be morally, as well as militarily indefensible. I doubt, moreover, whether Europe has a realistic option of self-defence, except in assocation with the United States. Nor do I believe that isolationism is a real option for America: leaving aside the whole of history, culture, and common sense, let us mention only one, rather sordid, contemporary commercial reason: nearly 50 per cent of American direct investment is now in Europe—and a lot, incidentally, in Britain.

Along with these false strategic options, we have invented false policy options too. To my mind, the most remarkable recent example was over Poland. Three years ago, you will recall, the

Alliance was about to founder on what was widely seen at the time as an unbridgeable, transatlantic split over the Polish crisis. It is worth looking back now at the editorials on both sides of the Atlantic. If it was not clear to everyone then, it should be obvious now, that there was never any serious choice about the way to react to events in Poland. The option of intervention never existed. The option of doing nothing did not exist either. What the Alliance did—a mixture of economic and political sanctions—was all it could do. As it happens, it did it rather well, give or take a bit of surface friction.

This is not to suggest that there is nothing to be done. There is, of course, much to be done within the Alliance itself. Take, for example, the question of the need to strengthen conventional forces. When General Rodgers and Monsignor Bruce Kent agree, there must be something in it.

But new orthodoxes should be exposed to healthy criticism, just as the old ones they displaced. I see the need for improvements, and adjustments; but I do not see any panacea. Not only would any serious build up in conventional forces be hideously expensive; it would also make war theoretically more tolerable. For both reasons, it might be more difficult to keep public support for such a policy; even more difficult than for the present deterrence mixture.

These simple factors will, I hope, be considered alongside the more notional and abstract aspects of the problem. Again it is a matter of keeping strategy and politics in line.

The Absence of Assessments

But the heart of the matter lies elsewhere. If half the effort and imagination that is invested in strategic studies were devoted instead to agreeing a sober and considered political assessment of Soviet intentions, NATO itself would be more secure; these strategies themselves would be easier to define; they would enjoy more public understanding and support; and the East/West relationship would be more stable and secure as a result.

Let us be absolutely honest with ourselves. This assessment will be affected not only by Soviet actions, but to some extent, by our own current perceptions and preoccupations. The Soviet Union will look rather more threatening during a recession than in periods of relative prosperity. In periods of economic difficulty, military options will appear to narrow. These are marginal factors when compared with the reality of the challenge from

Moscow. Angola, Ethiopia, Afghanistan and Central America are what really matter. But there will be no lack of people to dramatise on the margin, and in such circumstances, a spiral of self-doubt, uncertainty and compensatory assertiveness is easily engendered.

At such periods, the tendency to look at the Soviet Union from different angles increases. Some claim that the Soviet military build-up and undeniable expansionist tendencies reflect an inherently aggressive intent. Others suggest that the Soviet tendency to over-insurance is largely a result of insecurity. The scope for false debates—as for false options—is infinite.

Surely countries are not dissimilar to people. 'Surely one must admit that the same elements and characteristics that appear in the state must exist in every one of us. Where else could they have come from?' That was not me: that was Plato.

Surely it is a truism of individual psychology that insecurity and aggressive behaviour are two sides of the same coin. I do not understand why the Soviet Union cannot be simultaneously inherently insecure; and inherently aggressive.

But it follows that if we are to come to a well-based and mature Alliance consensus on Soviet intentions, we need to see the Russians as people—in the factual, not the sentimental sense—and to meet and talk to them. New leaders also need new assessments.

I am not being romantic about the value of personal diplomacy. I am simply saying that the lack of contact with Soviet reality can lead to dangerously volatile views of the Russians. We are now seeing a horribly predictable reaction to some of the more extreme transatlantic voices which have dominated the debate in recent years. We are moving into a new, apologetic phase. Revisionism always revises too much. Before, nobody bothered much to look at anything through Soviet eyes. Now, some are straining over backwards to get the Soviet angle of vision on everything. The question is being asked—is there a Soviet threat at all? But we do not need these dramatic reappraisals. The Soviet threat is like Dr Johnson's famous stone: it is just there. And if you do not believe it, ask a Czech to kick a Russian and see what happens.

Revisionists come and go—they were there in the late 1940s too—and after the Vietnam war. Sometimes they are well-intentioned, and well-informed people. But they tend to forget that the purpose of knowing more about the Russians is to defend our interests—not theirs.

Unstable assessments lead to inconsistent policies. They make waves in the Alliance, in public opinion and East/West relations themselves. They are a recipe for insecurity.

We need to keep a stern and steady eye on Soviet precepts and practice. Looking back over Soviet behaviour since the war, it is easy to detect fluctuations, and delineate phases in Soviet policies. But the overwhelming impression is one of a certain relentless continuity. There is sufficient evidence of ruthlessness, whether against internal dissent, or what are seen as external threats, to justify a permanent degree of western apprehension. There is equal evidence of Soviet mischief-making and expansionism in the third world to justify a similar mistrust there—whether or not these activities are interpreted as the legitimate search for areas of influence of a great power; or as bridgeheads in a communist crusade.

The roots of Soviet behaviour are at home. Here the inherent difficulty of reading and interpreting developments is obvious. They are not made any easier by estrangement. But again, the impression is one of continuity. There is something familiar about the plight of Soviet agriculture; of the steady decline in growth rates and productivity; of the disputes between centralisers and decentralisers; and of the burden of the military incubus.

I believe that the Soviet Union is on the downward slope of history. But it is a long slope, and a big country. I suspect that the continuity, and the threat will be with us for some time. We are talking about a country which seems to manage without visible leadership for months on end, and goes on functioning on automatic pilot, as it were. Imagine what the strength of inertia at the other end of Soviet society must be like.

Pre-emptive Policies

Yet our assessments and our policies must not be too static: they must be forward looking too. We should be ready not only to neutralise Soviet threats wherever they arise, but for pre-emptive political action as well. Whilst alert for the unexpected, we should not overlook the obvious.

There is a lot of talk in the manuals about crisis control. But the political context for successful crisis control must surely be built up over long periods. In eastern Europe, for example, it is not too soon to start now.

Eastern Europe is a sullen mass of discontent. It is dangerous for our own security, and of little practical help to the peoples of these countries to take the attitude 'the worse, the better'.

Imagine the atmosphere in central Europe if a quarter of what has happened in Poland happens in East Germany in ten years time. Think in particular of the atmosphere in Berlin itself.

Are we simply to keep up our guard, and wait and see? In my view, several forms of pre-emptive action are possible, against a background of secure defences. The first is to continue to assert the legitimate cultural, economic and political rights of fellow European states in the East, and our own right to have normal dealings with them. Secondly, the West should make it clear privately, as well as publicly, to the Russians that this attitude is not a calculated threat to the security of the Soviet state. And thirdly—and this too is a long term policy—we should evolve imaginative economic measures to encourage prosperity, stability and a greater measure of independence in these countries. The Marshall Plan was offered to the Russians in far more difficult circumstances than today. Times have changed. But the basic philosophy of the Marshall approach in my view remains valid.

There is a time for sanctions; but there is a time for more positive policies too. I note that Lech Walesa recently called for the abandoning of Western sanctions against Poland. I hope the West will not want to be more catholic than the Polish popes.

The Tyranny of Numbers

Another aspect of public anxiety is over-reliance on the strategy of technology, and the tyranny of numbers. The old adage that there is 'safety in numbers' comes to mind: but it does not mean as much when we are talking of missiles rather than men. The man in the street might be forgiven for thinking that there is more safety in balanced deterrence based on mutual knowledge. Numbers frighten when they are not understood, and when even the experts argue. Pure science and ideological vehemence is a particularly dangerous mixture.

Obviously numbers matter: no-one is advocating unreason, emotionalism or sentimentality in our attitude to defence—except, of course, CND. But we shall not secure a consensus around mathematical abstractions or obscure technical formulae.

The communiqué of the NATO ministerial meeting last December spoke of our determination to maintain 'adequate' military strength. In nuclear terms 'adequate' is a word we should use more often if we mean by it, not exact equivalence in every field, but an overall, reliable sufficiency.

Over-reliance on numbers can de-stabilise public opinion in many ways. It is bad enough when the numbers are big and abstract; it is even worse when they turn out to be wrong. The CIA has just revised downwards its estimate of Soviet military spending in the latter part of the 1970s. Instead of growing at about 4 per cent, the rate was apparently more like 2 per cent—roughly the same as overall Soviet economic growth.

There is plenty of small print to balance the picture for the expert, and NATO does not function on the CIA's figures. But the example is a warning against over-reliance on figures alone. They are liable to arouse less anxiety and uncertainty if they are placed in a stable political context.

Western governments—including our own—rightly contend that weapons themselves do not cause war. It follows that we ought to pay at least as much attention to the politics as the weapons.

In a period of recession the link between defence and civilian spending is also closer to the forefront of the public mind: yet another reason for getting the numbers right, and making it clear that they are only part of the problem. Analysts may claim that they are only 1 per cent out on their estimate of Soviet military spending. But a layman might think that 1 per cent on, for example, the total American defence budget of $3 trillion is a handy sum of money. More sophisticated observers may also speculate on the impact on interest rates, and western growth potential, of vacillating assessments of defence expenditure and their impact on budget deficits.

In Britain, we shall certainly have to keep a close eye on our defence spending, relative to other priorities. Amongst many statistics on the subject, one that caught my fancy in particular was the ratio of our defence spending share to the prosperity index share. By this yardstick, Britain's effort is almost double that of most of our partners. So, in Alliance terms, it is difficult to argue that we are not pulling our weight.

I hope that none of this sounds too gloomy. I do not underestimate what has been achieved over the last few years, particularly in the cruise crisis. NATO has been through a sort of catharsis and held together under considerable strain. Europe has taken the full brunt of Moscow's propaganda pressures and blandishments without succumbing. The Russians have suffered a major diplomatic setback.

But we must also learn from the experience of these difficult years. We could have done many things better. We have modernised our nuclear weapons. It is time to modernise our view of the East/West relationship too.

As the American presidential elections approach, we find ourselves living with the consequences of the failure to play the diplomatic card as energetically as the defence card. This puts Moscow in a strong position over the resumption of arms control talks. Moscow has no election this year.

But it raises another danger for the Alliance in 1984. The gadarene shuffle back to Moscow is already under way. But it is important to return to the dialogue in good order. Stockholm will be our first test. There must be no undignified scramble for the middle ground, or competition in developing a privileged dialogue. We urgently need an internal Alliance dialogue first. Otherwise the excesses of indiscriminate bilateral diplomacy with Moscow will breed more suspicions within the Alliance and complicate its negotiating stance. The imminence of an American election, a French presidency of the community and the intermittencies of the Soviet leadership will be further complications. They will also inspire the Russians to drive a wedge amongst Alliance governments, now that they have failed to drive a wedge between governments and peoples.

Conclusion

It is customary to finish a speech on NATO on a heartening note. I see no reason to depart from that custom. The Alliance, particularly over the last few years, resembles one of those Russian dolls that wobble about, but never actually fall over.

But wobbling itself is a distracting activity. It is also unnecessary: the threat from Moscow does not wax and wane with that speed. Wobbling disorientates one's friends. God knows what it does to the adversary. Above all, we should remember that western strength is an amalgam of economic, social and political muscle. It does not depend alone—as the Russians do—on pure military force, or on the purity of its military doctrines.

Earlier I was sceptical about the prospects for a European defence community. But imagine for a moment that this was to come about. Like all military powers, the first thing it would do would be to seek allies. What more natural ally than the United States of America? What more sensible name for such an Alliance than the North Atlantic Treaty Organisation? Which is a way of saying that, if NATO did not exist, it would have to be invented.

Perspectives of the World Scene: Prospects for American Power and Influence

HON EDWARD J. STREATOR

Minister, United States Embassy

The articles in this series originated in lectures on The Year Ahead given at the RUSI from January to March 1984

AFTER more than three years of the Reagan Administration, the building blocks of US policy and of the economic and military foundations are firmly in place. Do not be misled by the partisanship of this election year: we are in fact on the way to re-establishing the fundamental domestic consensus which supported American foreign and defence policy in the two decades following World War II. I want to discuss the evidence of that consensus, about its consequences for US policy, and about the need for a similar process of consensus building — or perhaps I should say consensus re-building — in the Alliance.

A NEW AMERICAN CONSENSUS

What is the evidence of a new American consensus? Some is obvious. President Reagan was elected by an extraordinary majority. He was provided in 1980 with a Republican Senate, the first since 1952. American power was a key issue in that campaign. When the election was over, it was clear the President had been given a mandate to reverse a dangerous decline in US military capabilities and in our political confidence. Since then, the President, true to his word, has done just that. He has also made extraordinary demands on the American people at a time of some economic hardship. Nonetheless, the President's popular support, based on poll results, has increased. It has been a very long while since a President, at this stage in his first Administration, has been able to maintain the high level of popular support we see today. This support persists despite concerns about American policy in Lebanon and Central America: it is expressed, for example, in poll results showing a majority of Americans feel 'more secure internationally' now than when the President took office. On the economic front, moreover, the US recovery is proceeding apace. Growth was 6.1 per cent in 1983, while inflation for the year was 4.3 per cent. The outlook is for growth of 4.5 per cent in 1984, and continued growth beyond.

Obviously, if these trends continue, the President will be a very strong contender for re-election — a prospect further enhanced by his handling of the Grenada rescue mission, the shooting down of the Korean airliner and his overtures to the Soviet Union to which Andropov responded encouragingly.

If you want more evidence of broad and deep support of Reagan policies, look at the profound changes in the American political debate. Seven years ago, Jimmy Carter campaigned on a platform calling for a 5 per cent real reduction in defence spending. Now, no serious candidate from any major party calls for cuts. The only question is how much defence spending should increase. The debate has changed in other ways. That is not the only example of change: do you think, for example, that a new American President — no matter what his party — would or could be any less concerned than Ronald Reagan with subversion in Central America; of Soviet expansion in South-West Asia; or the threat posed by burgeoning Soviet missile inventories; or Southern Africa? Do you think any new President would want to be seen to be doing less about these problems? No President could afford it. Indeed, opposition politicians in the United States seem to have recognised what many Europeans have missed: that the present Administration's policies are as strongly supported by the American people as the policies of any President in recent times, and the fact that the US once again is projecting its authority in situations outside the NATO area should be good news in the wake of the inward turning years after Vietnam and Watergate.

The consensus favouring a determined defence and a tougher foreign policy has opened up new possibilities. Look what it has done, for example, for Alliance defences. This Administration came to office needing to tackle two defence tasks at once: improving readiness and modernising the weapons inventory. Both are expensive. We plan to spend 1.8 trillion dollars on defence over the next five years, but consider the results already. Readiness and sustainability are up, with marked improvements in areas like training. For example, plane crews now average 20 hours a month flight time versus 13 hours as recently as 1978. Reserve stocks are in better shape: the Falklands conflict brought home once again how equipment and ammunition expenditure rates have multiplied in modern warfare — and we are taking steps to meet this challenge to our own forces. Frankly, we are doing better than most Europeans on this front. Weapons production also is up. You know about the MX missile, the B-1B bomber and nuclear carrier construction programmes. Other programmes will increase the number of F–15s, F–14s, Bradley Fighting Vehicles, M–1 tanks and other key weapon systems. These are large and expensive programmes. In the vital category of medium tanks, for example, we plan to increase stocks by 40 per cent by 1988, and there will be 50 more C–5s to bring those tanks to Europe as needed.

It shows what you can do when the people are behind you. Of course, our forces are only adequate if they meet the threat. And the threat is growing. Since 1975, the Soviets have produced 54,000 tanks and other armoured vehicles. The allies together have built about 11,000. They have churned out 6,000 tactical combat aircraft vs. 3,000 for the West — they have built 61 attack submarines vs. 27. And the new sophistication of Soviet weaponry is frightening.

So there is no reason for complacency — especially with our costs escalating. But the American response has been realistic and firm. We are on the way back.

American Influence

I have described the outlook for American power. I want to speculate as well on American influence. We are spending a lot of money on defence; but will it mean a more effective foreign policy? Here again, the forming American consensus gives grounds for optimism. It actually has provided the Administration more room to conduct foreign policy with consistency, moderation and resolve. These are, I submit, the hallmarks of the Reagan approach.

First, consistency. Europeans, from De Tocqueville to Schmidt, have seen American 'self-contradictory behaviour' as the most conspicuous failing of American policy. Even as Europe quarrels over the future of its community, even as the politics of

Europe are strained by stresses over nuclear deployments, our best friends on this side of the water complain about America's uncertain trumpet, about the alleged shifts in policy which they say confuse allies and adversaries alike.

There have been changes in American foreign policy over the last decade; we have been groping — all of us — to come to terms with a world in which the relative military power and economic weight of the United States has diminished, while the demands on us have increased. But I submit the changes have been variations on a constant theme. If you do not agree, compare our record of consistency with Europe's: six years ago, allies adopted a Long Term Defence Programme. American spending has grown every year since then, always by more than 3 per cent and sometimes by much more. Britain also has made substantial increases. Elsewhere, real increases in defence spending had begun to melt early in this decade. What we see instead are real increases in the number of theories explaining why we do not need real increases in defence.

Or consider the nuclear issue. In 1979 the NATO allies decided on a relatively modest deployment of Cruise and Pershing missiles. The aim was to counter the Soviet SS–20 threat, and to reassert the commitment of American nuclear forces to European security. In 1983, some of the same Europeans who participated in that decision have joined in denouncing it. Torturing logic, they condemn Cruise and Pershing missiles as militarily useless on the one hand, and as a dangerous contribution to the arms race on the other.

A final example: when I arrived here many years ago, the complaint against my country was lack of leadership, lack of self-confidence, lack of coherent policy. Now the United States is accused of being too assertive, of attempting to dictate policy, of trying to foist our vision of Western security on unwilling allies. No wonder successive Administrations have despaired of modulating policy to satisfy European opinion. How can they fail to notice, for example, that many of those urging us to reverse our policy on Intermediate Nuclear Forces (INF) were denouncing us — not so long ago — for reversing course on the neutron bomb. How could we ever be trusted again, they asked then? And if we heeded them now? How long would it be before the old complaints — inconsistency, lack of leadership, lack of direction — were heard again?

So where does consistency lie? The United States has not wavered from the 1979 twin track decision. The United States has not shirked the obligation in that decision — certainly unique in arms control history — of seeking to negotiate away the very systems we are deploying. The United States has never imagined that, as a nation, it could enjoy the benefits of military alliance in a nuclear age without accepting the risks — including the nuclear risks.

If there has been wavering, it has been elsewhere. Henry Kissinger said on 13 January 1984 that, 'the heart of the problem is that in nearly every country, the consensus on defence and foreign policy has broken down'. That has been a major weakness, pointing up the need to rebuild consensus across the Alliance, as Ronald Reagan is doing in the US.

American Resolve and Moderation

The second quality I mentioned as contributing to national influence was resolve. Here the US record is clear. One need not see Soviet influence in every international crisis to realise that the Soviets are opportunists. Occasionally, as in Afghanistan, they act blatantly. More often, as in Central America and the Caribbean, their methods are less direct. The Reagan Administration pledged from the beginning to oppose aggression and subversion by the Soviets and their surrogates worldwide. It has redeemed that pledge in the Caribbean, in Central America, in South-West Asia, in the Middle East and elsewhere.

This Administration has raised the cost of aggressive policies, while always holding out the possibility of peaceful settlement of real differences. It has made clear that US interests cannot be ignored. At the same time, the Reagan Administration has recognised the importance of seeking to deal sensibly with localised and regional conflict where such conflict impinges on Western interests. We have not, for example, had to paste an East-West confrontational label on the dispute between Britain and Argentina to try to be helpful in restoring peace and friendly relations.

The last of the qualities which I said enhance our national influence is moderation. My Government has been criticised on this score. In the eyes of some, the Reagan Administration courts East/West confrontation. What the record shows — on the contrary — is an extraordinary effort to avoid crises, and to maintain a framework for East/West communication. There have simply been no rash actions by the present American

Administration. Affronts to patience and decency have brought no hip shots in responses.

Two recent examples demonstrate this very clearly. One is the President's handling of the Korean airliner incident. In that case, the President spoke for all Americans in denouncing a barbaric act. But he did not yield to demands for other steps. There was, for example, no interruption of our preparations to join with European nations and the Soviets in the Stockholm Conference on Disarmament in Europe. Indeed, within a few weeks of the KAL tragedy, the President announced his intention to send Secretary Schultz to the opening sessions of that Conference, where the Secretary renewed his dialogue with Gromyko.

The Soviet break-off of arms control negotiations is another example. This President has been accused of having no love for arms control, but note: following the Soviet walk-out, our delegations stayed at the table. There was no escalation of rhetoric from Washington. The only threats came from the other side. The key event of this troubled season was not a hardening of American policy. It was the President's remarkable speech holding out his hope for a better East/West relationship.

This, then, is not a record of confrontation. It is a record of realism and serious endeavour to deal seriously with real differences. It is also a record of moderation, but based on hard-headed recognition that nations cannot bargain from weakness.

The Importance of NATO

In conclusion, I will mention another and final piece of the puzzle. So far, I have discussed the United States as if it stood alone in world affairs. In fact, of course, it has been nearly 50 years since Americans have been able to reckon their security in isolation. We are members of an Alliance. We must measure our strength in terms of Alliance strength — our influence in terms of Alliance influence — and our vulnerabilities in terms of Alliance vulnerabilities. Do the benefits of Alliance outweigh the vulnerabilities? Are we stronger because of NATO?

The President thinks so, and his Administration has been as strongly pro-NATO as any in memory. But some in my country disagree. They argue that our soldiers in Europe are in danger, burdened by increasingly stringent political constraints on training, operational planning and weapons. These commentators point out that the West's industrial advantage has been squandered because of the failure of standardisation, inadequate forward planning and stagnant or falling European expenditures on defence. And some say that Europe is intellectually bankrupt on defence, incapable of contributing usefully to Alliance strategy and content to react for the most part negatively to US initiatives. They conclude that the remedy for the United States is disengagement from Europe, making the oceans our first line of defence.

That is not going to happen. Disengagement is not part of the emerging American consensus. But the critics have a point. There is a tendency in Europe to shelter in the lee of US policy. One of my colleagues, pondering the history of the dual track decision, has suggested that next time we ask our European allies first to get together without us and decide what sort of nuclear deterrence they require. He predicts that the outcome of such a meeting would be the resumption of the 30 Years War. This is unfair; but let us face it, tempers are strained and the psychological mood in some quarters is ugly.

NATO can only survive as a partnership, to which all sides contribute materially and intellectually. An Alliance in which the United States proposes and the allies dispose — in which other members can agree only in criticising US initiatives — in which some accept the benefits of NATO but cavil over the costs and reject the risks — will not long endure.

I began by discussing a new US consensus. I will close with a plea for a new consensus within NATO. It has been 35 years since NATO's founding — a long time in politics. The last several years have seen us engaged in necessary programmes of force improvement. Our attention has been diverted to the mechanics of defence, perhaps to the neglect of the larger purposes the Alliance serves. We need, I submit, to look again at the broader picture and decide what it is we want the Alliance to do. Most of all, Europeans will have to decide where their priorities lie — whether for Europe the benefits of Alliance still outweigh the risks.

Asking the question honestly should conjure up a vision of what the world would be like for each of us in isolation. It would remind us that reasons for collective defence are stronger now than ever. Most of all, it would be an exercise in consensus rebuilding. Because — without doubt — the answer now will be the same as it was 30 years ago.

Samuel Goldwyn said, 'I never make predictions especially about the future.' Let me nonetheless risk a final prediction: with a new European consensus to match the consensus emerging in the United States, the Alliance will still be hard to beat.

Perspectives of the World Scene: Perceptions of Soviet Power and Influence

HELMUT SONNENFELDT

Guest Scholar, The Brookings Institution, Washington, DC. Mr Sonnenfeldt served in the US Government from 1952–77 in a variety of appointments. These included Head of the Office of Research and Analysis for the USSR and Eastern Europe in the Department of State, membership of the National Security Council dealing with US-European and East-West relations, and then Counsellor to the Department of State.

The articles in this series originated in lectures on The Year Ahead given at the RUSI from January to March 1984.

MY SUBJECT, as you are aware, is perceptions of Soviet power and influence. That, as you will recognise very quickly, is a rather vague subject. Concepts like power and influence, however precisely they might be defined, have many intangible elements. I hope therefore you will be tolerant of my imprecisions and impressionistic judgments. Moreover, the notion of perceptions has become a fashionable way to describe any problem or inconsistency — one simply says: "that's my perception and somebody else may have a different perception". Nothing is what it really is; it is only a perception. Thus that part of my topic, too, lends itself to a certain amount of vagueness.

Let me nonetheless make, however vague and impressionistic, some comments about Soviet power and Soviet influence as I see them. Inevitably, I must cast my vision backward a bit because I think the present circumstances and any prognostication for the future are bound to be influenced by one's view of the past. In the early period after the Bolshevik Revolution, the power and influence of Russia as it came to be the Soviet Union were due far less to physical strength than to its reputation, for better or worse, as a revolutionary power. For some, what had happened in Leningrad, Moscow and then Russia as a whole between 1917 and the early 1920s was the wave of the future. Someone — the Webbs reputedly — said they had seen the future and it worked.

This was the inspiration for similar movements in other countries, mostly Western, European, in the post World War I era. Obviously, for the same reason, to some, what had happened in Russia was the source of subversion and political upheaval and was seen as a threat rather than an inspiration and a hope. Yet it was basically a weak country in a military sense, although huge and clearly capable of absorbing enormous physical hardship as it had demonstrated during the war.

The view of Bolshevik Russia as a source of revolution and a guidepost to the reorganisation of society, whether one saw it as a hope or a source of subversion, was exaggerated. It was neither as much of a model for a better life nor as serious a source of subversion as many people in those days thought. Indeed, the Soviets themselves, even when Lenin was still alive and certainly afterwards, with all their ebullience at having won what they chose to think of as a revolution, soon felt encircled by the outside world. And well they should have, since they were challenging the status quo and represented themselves as prophets of a new order in the desolate circumstances of the post World War I scene. But as time went on, their power, weight and strength did not become such that Hitler, even allowing for his irrationality, could not feel capable by 1940–41 of making a run at destroying the Soviet Union. And there were not a few in the West, and not all that distant from this building, who thought that he might just do so; or that at the very least both Germany and Russia would exhaust each other to the benefit of the rest of the world.

Post World War II

The failure of the Hitlerian adventure — the Russian-Soviet capacity to dip deeply into some physical as well as non-physical resources, and the coincidence that others were also fighting Hitlerian Germany, did turn the Soviet Union into a victor power at the end of World War II after enormous exertions and sacrifices and suffering. Although severely damaged, and set back in the programme of forced industrialisation which Stalin had initiated in the 1930s, Soviet Russia emerged as the most powerful land power in Eurasia after World War II. It sought in both the *de jure* and the *de facto* peace arrangements after World War II, to buttress its security through zones of control and influence around the periphery, as well as the maintenance of massive military power. The Soviets early in the post-war period and perhaps even during the war, unlike the United States which was the other power that had the real option, decided not to demobilise and dismantle its military establishment but to maintain it.

In the process of surrounding itself with a satellite empire and other zones of influence or control and in the process of maintaining a massive military establishment, Stalin sowed the seeds of many later difficulties, not least in Eastern Europe and with China. And, of course, the policies of seeking from the outcome of World War II the maximum feasible security guarantees beyond the border of Soviet Russia provoked Western reactions. Above all, they helped to bring about a fundamental change in the traditional American aloofness from international affairs or at least a change from the episodic American involvement in international affairs, and produced American involvement in Europe and the indefinite presence of American military power on the Eurasian land mass.

The Soviets in this period retained some of the aura of a revolutionary and progressive power. But perhaps more important, and in many ways more unfortunate, was that in the West there tended to be widespread acceptance of the Stalinist myth, of the irreversibility of "revolutions". If it had been properly understood in the West that what had taken place in Russia was not so much a revolution as a coup, and what had happened in Eastern Europe were basically a series of forcible take-overs of governments by communist groups and Soviet controlled security forces, perhaps this sense of irreversibility would not have ingrained itself as much on the Western mentality as it seemed to have in that period. This sense amounted to a substantial bonus to the physical power that the Soviet Union represented in the post-World War II era. The idea of irreversibility, incidentally, was not shared by the enunciator of the policy of containment, George Kennan. In those days, he spoke, as some Reaganites do today, about the fundamental instability of the Soviet system and the presence within it of the seeds of its own destruction, especially if its expansionary propensity could be contained.

Stalin's Caution

Stalin, for his part, seeking to consolidate the gains from World War II, was in fact cautious about excessive expansion. One of his main disagreements with Tito concerned precisely that issue and this was not properly perceived — to use the word in the title of this talk — in the West at the time. But Stalin disguised his caution. It was difficult to recognise it because he was interested in frightening or even terrorising the outside world. He wanted to see firmly fixed the notion of irreversibility, of historical inevitability. It was both a shield and a sword for the Soviet Union in attempting to preserve and promote its own interests.

Stalin apparently saw few, if any, opportunities for expansion in the decolonialisation process that began in the aftermath of World War II. He considered very little in that process as worth expending Soviet substance on. Indeed, he and his ideological acolytes questioned whether what was happening in the European empires was in fact genuine decolonisation. Thus, at the end of the Stalin era, Soviet Russia was a major continental power on the Eurasian land mass. It was widely accepted as a great world power. It sat in the UN Security Council with a veto and in the United Nation itself with three seats. Few people questioned that they were one of the great post-war actors and should be so regarded.

Stalin had concentrated much of his effort on rebuilding and consolidation, though in a context of increasingly Byzantine and debilitating power struggles and manoeuvring for his succession. It is difficult, at least for me, to discern what in fact was Stalin's own concept of a future world order or whether he had one. Of course, it involved power for the Soviet Union. But this was the man who had invented the notion of socialism in one country, partly out of preference and partly out of necessity. I find it far from clear how or even whether, despite the irreversibility myth, he envisaged a world populated by socialist powers on the Soviet model. He could not conceive of any socialist powers on any other model. That indeed was part of the problem. More likely, his vision of the world was one of struggle as his vision of the Soviet Union itself was one of struggle, of suspicion, of police power and of constant concern about security in the personal sense, a vision of struggle for the survival of the regime and of the Soviet Union. With this obsession Stalin probably never got around to having an operationally significant concept of a world order dominated by the Soviet Union and emulating it. In that sense, it may be said that containment worked, although in the West this judgment was far from clear and unchallenged. We did after all have the Korean War and certainly not a passive Soviet Union.

We will probably never know what Stalin's own expectations and plans might have been with respect to regions beyond those where the Red Army had come to rest or where other arrangements, subversive or otherwise, had been made for the installation of Soviet power. But in the post-Stalin period a significant element, in terms of Soviet power and influence has been that the Soviets broke out of the continental mould. Militarily, they did so by acquiring weapons and military implements with a reach beyond the Eurasian land mass, aircraft and then missiles, and, of course, a navy which gradually in the 1950s and 1960s became 'blue water'.

Challenging America

Moreover, Soviet military programmes in the 1950s, 1960s and thereafter were designed to begin and then to accelerate a process of undermining what had become the Western concept of defence for Europe, that is, the reliance on American strategic and nuclear power to offset the advantages of continental — Eurasian continental — Russia *vis-à-vis* the West European peninsula. As the Soviets came to challenge American strategic power and mobility, they challenged the very concept, which the West in its wisdom and with the constraints under which it operated had come to decide was the safest and best way of protecting Western Europe. That is a problem which clearly remains with us. The Western defence concept is in question because of what the Soviets have done and are doing on their side militarily.

Politically, the Soviets broke out of the continental mould by adjusting their views of decolonisation and finding and exploiting opportunities to expand their role, influence and, selectively, their presence in regions more remote from Russia. Their methods were to support the grievances of groups of peoples around the world, particularly against the metropolitan powers but also among each other, to supply them with arms, and to provide a certain political backing, as well as some economic support. Psychologically and ideologically, as they broke out of the Stalin mould and continental limits, the Soviets of Khrushchev's day seemed genuinely to believe that they could be a model for the emerging countries, with their theories and experience of struggle, industrialisation, modernisation and social and political organisation, Soviet leaders thought they had an answer, that would be appealing in the "Third World". They adjusted doctrinal formulations to meet these aspirations and pretensions and what they thought were the aspirations among peoples in the former colonial regions and in still colonial regions emerging as part of the international arena of independent powers.

Thus the assertion of Soviet power and interests began to become global in character. The revolutionary mystique seemed to have a second wind in this period. Americans may have taken this Soviet plunge into the world to the fringes of and beyond Eurasia more seriously than others. Certainly in the Kennedy administration it was considered to be the biggest challenge of the day. Indeed, the Kennedy administration made perhaps the most extensive US commitments, "Fight any foe, support any friend", in the context of the new Soviet expansionism, although the Kennedy administration was in fact schizophrenic in its approach to the Soviets. (The ambivalence was manifested in the famous speech at American University by John F. Kennedy in 1963. The first half was about Soviet expansion and its dangers, the second half dealt with how the United States must deal with the Soviet Union in order to cope with the common danger of nuclear conflict.)

Still, the Europeans seemed to be less impressed with Soviet global involvement. They were preoccupied with their own affairs and, I suppose, they had seen empires come and go and were not quite as struck by the Soviet imperial plunge as the Americans. Curiously enough, too, in the Third World, if I may use that bad shorthand term, by and large, people were also less impressed by Soviet involvement in their affairs. Of course, they wanted what help they could get from the Soviets. Sometimes that was considerable in the political and military realms, and, for individual countries, quite substantial in economic terms. But most of them did not consider themselves particularly vulnerable or enticed by the appeals of Soviet communism. In fact, most of them turned out not to be very susceptible to the appeals of Soviet communism. There was a variety of reasons for this, having to do with both the inherent character of Soviet communism and the skills, talents and temperaments of the practitioners of Soviet communism.

But, interestingly, while the Americans took the Soviet push seriously and the Europeans and Third World countries did less so, the Chinese took it very seriously; they indeed set about, starting in the late 1950s, to challenge the implications of Soviet policy in the Third World by contesting Soviet hegemony in the entire communist world. This in turn served to undermine the Soviet notion, whatever its precise content, that philosophically at least it was possible to envisage a harmonious world of diverse communists.

Stalin had had no such notions. But once he was gone there were Russians, Khrushchev among then, who did. The Chinese severely challenged that notion under the impact of the Soviet imperial impulse, which asserted itself in the 1950s. Along with this, the East Europeans repeatedly demonstrated what I have in the past referred to as the unnatural character of the Soviet empire as a base for a global order shaped by Soviet example. Again and again we have seen that it is not and cannot be such a base, as long as the Soviets insist on organising affairs in Eastern Europe as they do.

In the 1970s, the US, for reasons involving American over-extension, domestic dissention and many other factors, sought a *modus vivendi* with the Soviet Union based on containment of Soviet military expansion but also on acceptance of a global Soviet role, albeit one characterised by mutual restraint and caution. The United States, in this period, expected other international actors — Europeans, Chinese, Japanese and others — to play a role in maintaining global balance by participating in the containment of Soviet expansionism. But, of course, it was seen as a balance in which the Soviets were bound to be a major actor.

The nature of Soviet power is such that if military instruments are constrained, that power is likely to contract. The other elements of power simply are less competitive for the Soviet Union. Thus, with the uncertainties in the US and European self-preoccupations, the Soviets did in fact use, in the latter part of the 1970s, various forms of military power, sometimes via proxies, to manoeuvre for geopolitical gains. Some of those were impressive.

It may be said retrospectively, that the period from 1970 to about 1977, under Brezhnev, was something like the golden age of Bolshevik Russia. Its interests and ambitions fared reasonably well, for the reasons I have indicated, in the world at large. There was a certain stability within the Soviet Union; stagnation was not yet obvious. There seemed to be a general acquiescence in regime policies, at least among wide circles of the populations. The elites were reaping the rewards of being elites. Perhaps one of Brezhnev's greater achievements was that, under him the average age of the Politbureau became higher than the average age of the Soviet population, which it had not been in the past.

Soviet foreign activism in the 1970s did in due course produce a reaction in the United States, during the last part of the Carter administration and then in the Reagan administration. First, to readjust the military balance by correcting deficiencies in strategic forces, in long-range intervention forces and in the European nuclear and conventional balance. Second, particularly in the Reagan administration, a more robust, though still quite cautious, policy to reverse Soviet global expansion. Third, and most important from the standpoint of the Reagan administration, an effort through non-inflationary economic growth to make it possible for the United States to maintain its defence obligations. The question of whether the Reagan administration is succeeding is one of the issues being debated in the American election campaign and in the international community in general.

The Western Alliance

There are now some serious questions about the future character of the Western Alliance and the ability of the West to reach and maintain common approaches about how to cope with Soviet power in the future. In my view, there is greater fluidity in the European area than for many years, not in the sense of the fears of the 1940s — that is, of Soviet takeovers and Communist Party subversion on behalf of the Soviet Union — but there have developed new attractions between East and West in Europe, particularly between the two parts of Germany.

There are serious and, I think, more than tactical and procedural differences between the United States and the West Europeans, allowing for differences within each, over the matter of East-West economic relations. This is important because for the Soviets, Western Europe represents something of an economic arsenal, important to support the economies of the East Europeans and to help the Soviets avoid basic shifts in their own economic and political priorities.

I may note here that differences between Americans and Europeans on economic relations with the East are to some extent encouraged by the possibility that the Europeans will fall behind in the area of high technology, and will find that the best customers for both their efficient (or even not so efficient) traditional industries are in the East. Meanwhile, there are signs that the Soviets themselves are over-extended in their Third World ambitions. It is not clear at the moment how much they can and will invest to promote these ambitions, and to exploit fluctuating American fortunes in the Third World.

In a sense then, Soviet power and influence are on a plateau, a high plateau no doubt, but seemingly stalled. How then to describe Soviet objectives, as you asked me to do, at the conclusion?

Soviet Objectives

It is a good question. The Soviets may be asking themselves, too. It is always said that interests are permanent and that the Soviets know their interests perhaps better than others. That may be true, but, interests and objectives are not identical.

Broadly speaking, an overwhelming current Soviet objective must be to address the domestic issues of stagnation, apathy, inefficiency, generational change, demographic change. All of them pose more questions than answers, It is a partial list, but I would guess that any Politbureau and Secretariat — the 28 or 30 people that make up the top group in the Soviet Union — must somehow have those issues on their agenda. Second, to keep control of Eastern Europe; again an objective that hides within it a bundle of complexities, choices, dilemmas and trade-offs. Thirdly, as already indicated, to enlist Western Europe for economic support and to prevent it from being or becoming in the future an arena that applies significant military contraints on the Soviet Union. Fourth, since they are involved there now, to keep an acceptable regime in Afghanistan at tolerable cost; in that and other ways as well to preserve options for Soviet policy in post-Khomeini Iran. Fifth, to modulate the conflict with China. But above all, to build an infrastructure in the Soviet East as a long term barrier against China. And, in that context, to prevent a US-China-Japan alliance. (Europeans, as well as Japanese, should ask themselves to what degree they want to be partners in the Soviet effort to industrialise Siberia, largely as a bulwark against an emerging China and as a means of supporting the Soviet military presence in the Far East and in Central Asia which is now extraordinarily expensive because of the long line of communications). Sixth, to avoid over-exposure in remote regions while seeking whatever influence they can maintain and obtain there. Seventh, a *modus vivendi* with the United States, if possible by inhibiting American military programmes. Notwithstanding the present ugly tone and Soviet sulking, I believe in fact it is a Soviet objective to seek a *modus vivendi*. I do not mean by that a "Peace of Westphalia". I mean a distant *modus vivendi* in which the Soviet Union feels that it will be left alone to pursue its own vast agenda.

Finally, and possibly contradicting many of the above points, to preserve the party elite monopoly and to contain and, where possible, to exclude intrusions from the outside world that undermine that monopoly. That may not be altogether feasible if the Soviets really wish to rely on the Western industrialised world to make up the gap in their investment and to support their ambitions with respect to the industrialisation of Siberia.

These goals may strike you as being stated in a rather conservative fashion. My stress on consolidation and on avoiding over-exposure is not intended to suggest passivity. The Soviets will undoubtedly resist encroachments. But their priority will be on building power over the long haul. I do not see them having now or in the foreseeable future a grand vision of how to organise a congenial world. They will still see themselves basically in a hostile and uncongenial world with at least as many dangers as opportunities.

Such attitudes may be best suited to the temperament of the people who run the Soviet Union. They no doubt could lash out if they felt excessively challenged, if some opportunity beckoned or if they felt that they were not properly treated as a great power. That is always a danger. But so is the danger that the West, and others, will squander their own assets and that the Soviets, despite the enormous flaws in their power, would by sheer tenacity and staying power become the world's single greatest power. I think this too is unlikely. But if there is a Soviet vision nowadays it may well be that somehow they will out-last all others and somehow emerge in such a way that they can say that they are reasonably secure. But I do not think the Soviets see that as around the corner, if indeed they see such glowing prospects at all.

Part II — Regional Strategic Review

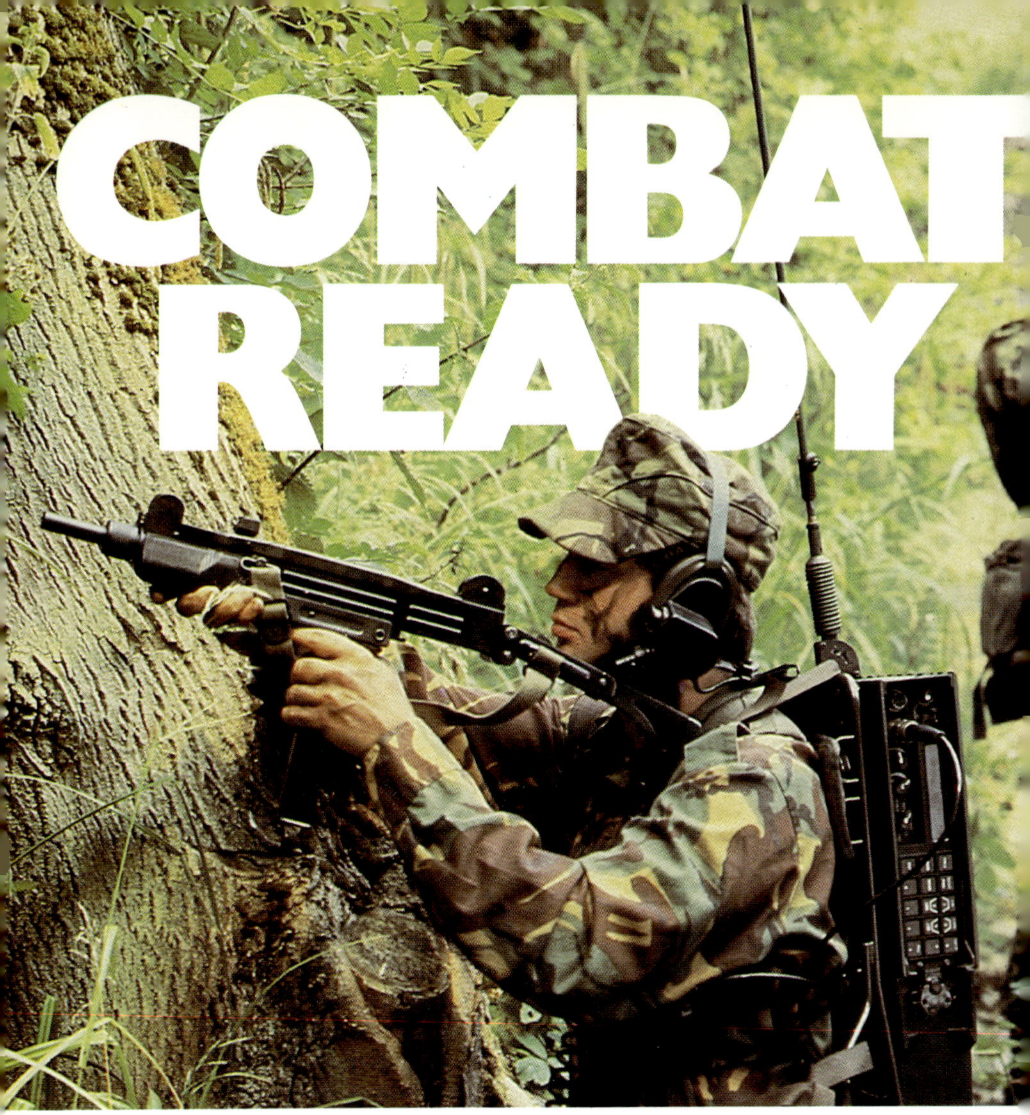

Easy to operate in extreme conditions and rugged enough to keep on working in the harshest environments, Plessey tactical radios are designed, built and tested to be as tough as the fighting men who use them. Combat ready. Plessey tactical radio.

From simple manpacks to sophisticated vehicle installations and advanced ECM/ECCM systems, all are fully proven in active service. And to meet the growing EW threat –both today and in the future–Plessey is now introducing a new single-channel tactical radio system. It's called System 4000 and provides a range of HF/VHF transceivers and applique units designed to meet the total tactical communications needs of an army.

At the forefront of world electronics Plessey can offer procurement and logistic advantages that are hard to match.

Talk to Plessey about your future needs now.

Plessey Military Communications Limited, Vicarage Lane, Ilford, Essex, United Kingdom IG1 4AQ. Telephone: London (01) 478 3040. Telex: 897971.

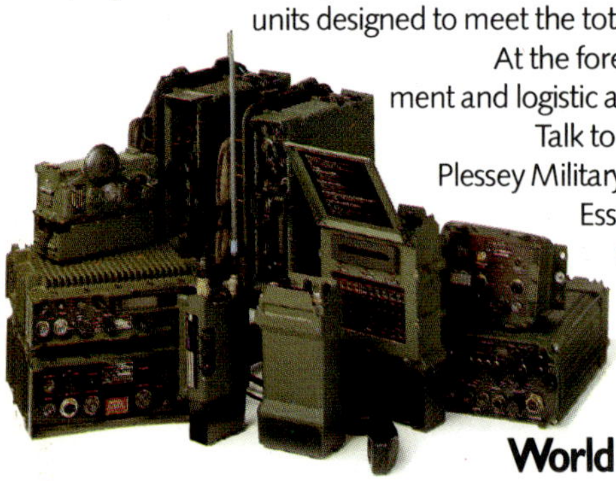

PLESSEY

World leadership in military communications

How Neutral is the Irish Republic?

SIR JOHN BIGGS-DAVISON

Sir John Biggs-Davison is Member of Parliament for Epping Forest. He is Vice-Chairman of the Conservative Parliamentary Foreign and Commonwealth Affairs Committee and Chairman of the Conservative Parliamentary Northen Ireland Committee. He is author, with George Chowdharay-Best, of The Cross of St Patrick, a history of Catholic Unionism, to be published by Kensal Press.

THE Republic of Ireland is commonly counted among the neutrals. But its attitude to the superpowers and their alliances is more complicated than that. Dublin has never adopted a formal position of permanent neutrality like that of Switzerland and of Austria which is based upon the Swiss model. True enough, ultra-republicans and leftist militants have postulated the permanence of the Republic's abstention from any military alliance. But this is seen by countrymen at least as distinguished as one more Irish myth.

Before the independence of Southern Ireland, it was an abiding truism among separatists that England's danger was Ireland's opportunity. Conversely, Ireland was regarded on the British side of the Irish Sea as an island from which Britain could be invaded. 'Had I gone to Ireland instead of Egypt', said Napoleon Bonaparte, 'the Empire was at an end'. His General Dumouriez said in 1808:

> The fate of the British Empire depends on that of Ireland. That island is open to invasion in more than thirty deep bays on all its coasts.

In seeking to exploit Irish grievances and dominate Ireland in order to strike at England, imperial Spain, revolutionary France and the France of Napoleon were following examples that go back to mediaeval times. The Kaiser armed both Irish Nationalists and Ulster Loyalists. Berlin's calculation was that if Britain were embroiled in civil war, its influence upon the affairs of the continent could be nullified. Elements in revolutionary Ireland accepted the patronage of Imperial Germany and then of the new Soviet government. The Bolsheviks, like Napoleon, considered Ireland and Egypt as two chinks in the armour of the British Empire.

Strategic Union

In 1800, Pitt the Younger brought about the parliamentary union of Ireland with Great Britain (there was before then one Crown but two parliaments) to frustrate Napoleonic ambitions. In two Battles of the Atlantic in two world wars German U-boats, first of the Kaiser and then of Hitler, would have starved Britain out, had she not had the use of Irish ports and bases, limited in the 1939–45 conflict (since Eire was neutral) to those in Northern Ireland, which remained an integral part of the United Kingdom. 'The occupation of Ireland', said Hitler on 3 December 1941, 'might lead to the end of the war'. As a young Royal Marine subaltern, the present writer was embarked for a possible British forestalling operation in Ireland.

When the treaty which made most of Ireland an independent member of the British Commonwealth on the lines of Canada was being painfully negotiated, Winston Churchill, then Colonial Secretary in the Lloyd George coalition government, became intimate with the brilliant guerrilla leader, Michael Collins. In the first volume of his World War II memoirs, Churchill recalls how during those negotiations he

> brought Admiral Beatty to the Colonial Office to explain to Michael Collins the importance of bringing supplies into Britain. Collins was immediately convinced. 'Of course you must have the ports', he said. 'They are necessary for your life'.

Apart from installations in Ulster, Admiralty rights and properties were retained under the Treaty at Berehaven, Queenstown (Cobh) and Lough Swilly. British care and maintenance parties looked after the harbour defences. Such limitations on the independence of the Irish Free State were justified by, for example, the judge and moderate Nationalist, Sir James O'Connor, in his *History of Ireland 1798–1924*. His book was published in 1925 before the Statute of Westminster legally formulated in 1931 the principle contained in the report of the Balfour Committee of the 1926 Imperial Conference of the equal status under the Crown of the United Kingdom and the Dominions. At that conference Kevin O'Higgins, representing the Free State, proposed, according to Leo Amery's record of a last talk shortly before O'Higgins's assassination,

> a more intimate economic and military cooperation between the United Kingdom and Eire than existed within the Wider Commonwealth . . .

This would

> be the natural consequence of our geographical position and past history.

According to his biographer, Terence de Vere White, O'Higgins forecast that

> Some day Anglo-Irish relations will be represented by a Dual Monarchy — two quite independent Kingdoms, and, perhaps, a Defence Treaty.

In his book, Sir James O'Connor went so far as to say:

> The two countries have been a political unit for seven centuries. The Union was a bargain, of sorts. . . . An Ireland held by hostile forces would probably ensure British Surrender. All the countries that have ever been at war with Great Britain have been fully aware of this fact — Spain, France and Germany. Sinn Feiners admit it. Their paper *Nationality*[1] refers to Ireland as 'the key of the Atlantic'; 'Ireland lies across the sea routes of England'; Ireland has 'the key of the ocean in her hands'. Admiral Mahan, of the US Navy, said: 'The ambition of the Irish separatists, if realized, would be even more threatening to the national life of Great Britain than the secession of the South was to the American Union'.

Sir James then made comparison with the Monroe doctrine, United States control of the Panama Canal and its 'suzerainty over Cuba'. Britain was entitled to refuse Ireland 'unfettered self-determination . . . Abraham Lincoln would not have wasted a second thought on the subject'.

De Valera himself had used the analogy of the United States and Cuba when he contended in 1920 that Britain could safeguard herself without infringing Ireland's claim to independence.

> Why doesn't Britain do with Ireland as the United States did with Cuba? Why doesn't Britain declare a Monroe doctrine for the two neighbouring islands?

Since Cuba was virtually an American protectorate, an Ireland so situated could hardly be rated a permanent neutral in the terms conceived by, for example, Sir Roger Casement, who, writing in the *Irish Review* of July 1913, on 'Ireland, Germany and the next war', called for 'a neutralised, independent European state under international guarantee'. However, article V of the draft Treaty 'A' which the Irish plenipotentiaries were to put to the British Government in 1921, read thus:

> Ireland accepts and the British Commonwealth guarantees the perpetual neutrality of Ireland and the integrity and inviolability of Irish territory; and both in its own interest and in friendly regard to the strategic interest of the British Commonwealth binds itself to enter into no compact, and to take no action, nor permit any action to be taken, inconsistent with the obligation of preserving its own neutrality and inviolability and to repel with force any attempt to violate its territory or to use its territorial waters for warlike purposes.

Southern Recognition of the Border

The Irish Treaty and the Tripartite Agreement of 1925, concluded between Dublin, London and the Northern Ireland Government after the abortive Boundary Commission and solemnly deposited with the League of Nations, recognised the right of the North to separate self-determination and its status within the United Kingdom. But the ending of partition was dominant in the policy of Eamon de Valera who came to power after the general election of 1932. In 1934, a scheme was put to London which demonstrates how little is new in the options propounded in the report of the New Ireland Forum. De Valera proposed a sovereign and federal Irish Commonwealth, the Northern Irish and Irish Free State Parliaments continuing within their own territories. Reciprocal citizenship between Ireland and Britain would follow as also preferential trade agreements and a defensive and military alliance 'recognising the strategic unity of these islands'. The proviso, however, was that Irish forces would occupy all ports.

De Valera would before long gain the ports; but he ended his long political career without making progress towards a United Ireland. Indeed by breaching the Treaty, chipping away the Crown and removing the symbols of imperial connexion, he antagonised the Northern majority. He also involved his country in economic war with Britain. When 'peace' was made in 1938 Neville Chamberlain, who gave up much else that year, gave up the ports. The Dominions Secretary, Malcolm MacDonald, said that most of Chamberlain's Cabinet colleagues believed that:

> the very importance of those ports in the event of war threw the balance of argument, paradoxically, on the side of our voluntarily resigning our Treaty rights to occupy them.

The Chiefs of Staff held that, if necessary, French and Ulster bases would afford sufficient protection for the North Atlantic trade. Churchill thought otherwise. Alone, with the Ulster Unionist MPs, he voted against this grand gesture of placation. He warned the House of Commons on 5 May that if war came it would

> be no use saying, 'Then we will retake the ports'. You will have no right to do so. To violate Irish neutrality should it be declared at the moment of a great war may put you out of court in the opinion of the world, and may vitiate the cause by which you may be involved in war. If ever we have to fight again, we shall be fighting in the name of law, of respect for the rights of small countries . . .

The writer cannot, however, but recall the misgivings he felt on those very grounds when in 1940 he took part with his RM battalion in the occupation of Iceland! Professor Nicholas Mansergh[2] believes that Churchill's bitterness (which Cabinet colleagues restrained) 'hardened Irish resolve to hold the ports'.

De Valera gave no undertaking that the Royal Navy could use the ports, although he requested British advice on their defence. But he did show 'a certain consideration for Britain'. Information was exchanged on coast-watching and weather forecasting; high-level secret talks were held and military manoeuvres too, of a kind. On the other hand, negotiations with Britain which would have resulted in more active involvement broke down; and it was lucky for Eire that, unlike the 15 other European states which had been neutral when war broke out, she emerged from the war with her neutrality unshaken. Her armed forces were stronger, but as ill-equipped, as ever.

Neutral but Warlike

Despite Southern Irish neutrality in World War II, individual Irishmen were free to join HM Forces. Many did so; and in October 1941, in part prompted by his cousin Sir Shane Leslie, Winston Churchill mooted with the Service Departments the possibility of forming an Irish Brigade or Division within the British Army. Despite objections, an 'Irish Brigade' was formed from battalions of the Royal Inniskillings, the Royal Irish Fusiliers and the London Irish Rifles. Some of the troops came from Northern Ireland; not all were of Irish blood. Yet figures collected in 1942 showed that in the whole of the British Army 23,549 men were born in Eire compared to 28,287 in Northern Ireland. By 1944, Eire's share had increased to nearly 28,000. Much larger figures of up to 300,000 were published in the press. Their authenticity was disputed (for example by St. John Ervine in his magisterial biography of Graigavon). General Gough found that 165,000 in the Armed Forces gave Irish Addresses for their next of kin. Amongst these must have been many who had migrated to Great Britain before the war. 38,554 men from the Twenty-Six Counties were officially listed as volunteering in Belfast.

Conscription was not imposed in Northern Ireland. But Eire citizens resident in Great Britain were liable to call-up if they had been on the mainland for two years; they were given the option of returning to Eire within a fortnight if they received their papers. In 1944, the War Office estimated that there were upwards of 5,000 deserters from the British Army in Eire.

Patrick Keatinge, in his fascinating and well-named study *A Singular Stance* (Institute of Public Administration, Dublin, 1984), identifies three stages in the development of Irish neutrality. The first, from 1922 to 1939, was, he considers, marked by failure to transform a political idea into policy. The second, during World War II, is distinguished by the development of such a policy; the third arose from an experience of European integration after 1961.

In 1945, the position was not at first promising for Irish neutrality. Eire was not initially admitted into the United Nations, which was the victorious alliance transformed into a world organisation; and when in 1949 the United States representative in Dublin broached the possibility of adherence to the North Atlantic Treaty, the official reply was that this could only happen if Dublin were enabled to apply on behalf of a United Ireland. This implies that Irish neutrality was not absolute; indeed, Conor Cruise O'Brien has argued that if Fine Gael had been able to constitute a single-party Government, Eire would have joined NATO. Moreover, in March 1951, the stormy Seán MacBride, then Irish Minister for External Affairs, stated in an interview with President Truman that Partition was the only obstacle to Irish membership of the organisation and that there was the possibility of a bilateral defence pact with the United States. In 1950, MacBride had declared that there is 'no nation in the World with whom we have closer links'. In 1954, however, de Valera was opposed to this idea. Keatinge concludes that up to the time of Eire's admission to the United Nations in 1955, there was no 'coherent doctrine' of neutrality.

Eire played a formative part in the evolution of the modern Commonwealth of equals. It set store by its membership of the old League of Nations with its purpose of collective security. It prizes its place in the United Nations. Irish troops have participated worthily and suffered fatal casualities in several peace-keeping operations.

Not that UN membership wrought immediate change of policy. The Republic's Minister for External Affairs, Liam Cosgrave, proclaimed Eire's intention to 'avoid becoming associated with particular blocs or groups so far as possible', but also spoke of the preservation of 'Christian civilisation' and thus of 'those powers principally responsible for the defence of the free world in their resistance to the spread of Communist power and influence'.

Cosgrave's *Fianna Fáil* successor was Frank Aiken. He had fought for the Republic against the Treaty and the Free State and now became the author of a more neutralist policy. Aiken backed India's proposal to discuss the admission of Communist China to the UN. Nevertheless the Republic did not join, or rather was not invited to join, the Non-Aligned Movement when it was formed in 1961, despite support by Jawaharlal Nehru. Instead, Ireland became associated with the European Economic Community, from which other European neutrals, Austria, Sweden and Switzerland, were excluded or self-excluded.

In 1959 Seán Lemass became *Taioseach* at the head of a *Fianna Fáil* Government. Like Cosgrave he made neutrality the consequence of Partition. Ireland could not ally herself formally with a state seen to be in 'illegal' occupation of territory claimed under de Valera's 1937 constitution. Nevertheless, if Western civilisation were threatened in any conflict there would be no doubt where the 'interests and sympathies' at least of the Republic would lie. Lemass moreover told *The Scotsman* (February 1961) that Ireland could, in his view, contribute more effectively to the support of free democratic principles outside NATO than within it.

European Dimensions

Irish policy had to reckon with the inherent contradiction between applying to join the EEC and remaining neutral. So

Lemass put a gloss upon his country's doctrine. Thus in March 1962, he questioned in the Dáil the logic of the proposition that membership of NATO necessarily implied recognition of British Sovereignty over Northern Ireland. In an interview with the *New York Times* (18 July 1962), he asserted that Ireland might have to yield 'even the technical label of neutrality. We are prepared to go into this integrated Europe without any reservation . . . in the field of foreign policy and defence'.

In 1963, President de Gaulle said '*non*' to British membership of the EEC. The door was effectively barred until the General's resignation in 1969. There was no possibility of the Irish Republic joining the Communities while the United Kingdom was outside. The two national economies were interdependent and the two currencies were closely aligned.

In 1972 the Republic held a referendum on whether to adhere to the Rome Treaty. Those in favour, who included both the two larger parties, argued that, on the one hand, there was no foreseeable threat to Irish neutrality and, on the other, that neutrality was in any event conditional on circumstances. The *Taoiseach,* Jack Lynch, declared firmly (16 and 23 July 1969) that Ireland had no traditional policy of neutrality like Sweden, Switzerland and Austria, and, having become a member, would 'naturally be interested in the defence of the territories embraced by the Communities. There is no question of neutrality there'. The electorate gave Europe a decisive endorsement.

The Treaties are economic not political or military. However, Cosgrave said in 1967 that defence was 'at the forefront of the thinking behind the drafting of the Rome treaty'. The member states of the Communities engaged in European political cooperation; but the nearest they came to intervention in the defence field was their adoption of a unanimous nine-member stance in the European Security Conference which led to the Helsinki final act of 1975. There were clear defence implications to the Tindemans Report on European Union; and although in 1978 the Irish Minister for Foreign Affairs, Patrick Hillery, now President of Ireland, said that the Republic would not join NATO,

> if it ever gets to the point, some time in the future, that the EEC was being attacked, we would have to play our role and carry out our obligations and responsibilities.

In May 1978, the Republic took exception to the British Commissioner, Christopher Tugendhat's, proposal, in line with that of the German Foreign Minister, Dietrich Genscher, for defence to be included, for economic as well as political reasons, in the European Community Ministers' foreign policy discussions. Closer cooperation in defence procurement was necessary if Europeans were to catch up with the United States arms industry, particularly those concerned with high technology.

Serious difficulties also sprang from the meeting in December 1980 between the *Taoiseach,* Charles Haughey, and the British Prime Minister, Margaret Thatcher. This had aroused speculation that the Republic would be making concessions on defence in return for British withdrawal from Northern Ireland. Haughey, in a debate in the *Dáil* (11 March 1981) acknowledged, as had *Fine Gael,* that full political union of the EEC states would mean the end of Irish neutrality. He also accepted that if Ireland were re-unified, defence arrangements for the whole island would have to be reviewed.

FALKLANDS FACTOR

But in the spring of 1982, the whole issue of Irish neutrality was thrown into bitter debate by the Falklands war. Haughey, at the end of a *Fianna Fáil* minority administration, took a high line of Irish neutrality which he presented as more of a permanent principle than had either of the two major Irish political parties for two decades past. But by the end of the year, a *Fine Gael* – Labour coalition was returned to power, and, according to Trevor Salmon of the University of St Andrews (*Round Table,* April 1984), the Republic's attitude to the Falklands should '*not* be seen as confirmation of Irish neutrality', but merely as an example of 'Irish wariness of overt links with military questions'.

On 5 April 1983, the *Taoiseach,* Garret FitzGerald, reaffirmed the Republic's position in an interview published in the *Irish Times.* The Republic had a 'sense of common involvement with people in other countries in Western Europe who seek to preserve our system of government' but this did not mean that 'we have any role to play . . . in the matter of defence'. In July 1983, the Minister for Foreign Affairs, Peter Barry, told *Dáil Éireann* that the policy of 'military neutrality' might actually help to preserve the peace since if the Republic were inside NATO it would make little difference to the strength of the Alliance whereas outside it the Republic could play a 'modest but constructive role as a neutral country'.

When addressing *Seanad Eireann* in February 1984, the Minister pronounced against seeking observer status with the Non-Aligned Movement. That would not help to promote Ireland's aims.

Whereas the two major parties have spoken much of 'military neutrality', the Irish Labour Party has consistently advocated what Keatinge has termed 'fundamental neutrality'. Whatever the nuances, the Irish Republic spends less on defence than do most other neutral countries; for Dublin is well aware that for Britain and her allies the integrity of the entire British Isles is a vital interest. One may hark back to 1925 when the Executive Council (Cabinet) of the Irish Free State argued that its army should be:

> so organised, trained and equipped as to render it capable, should the necessity arise, of full and complete coordination with the British Government in the defence of the *Saorstat* [Free State] territory whether against actual hostilities or against violation of neutrality on the part of a common enemy.

When it came to 'actual hostilities', de Valera pursued a policy of neutrality that sometimes favoured Britain and her allies. But only the bases in Northern Ireland were at their disposal. As Churchill said on 6 May 1943:

> Only one great chance of entry remained open because loyal Ulster gave us the full use of the Northern Ireland ports and waters, and thus ensured the free working of the Clyde and Mersey.

General Eisenhower echoed this praise when he visited Belfast in August 1945.

When Eire was in limbo between Dominion and Republic it was assumed or at least strongly hoped that Britain's war would be that of the Commonwealth as a whole. On 16 September 1939, Anthony Eden, then Secretary of State for the Dominions, analysed a dilemma for Chamberlain's War Cabinet:–

> On the constitutional side the question of any formal recognition by this country of the neutrality of Eire presents a serious difficulty. We do not want formally to recognise Eire as a neutral while Eire remains a member of the British Commonwealth. To do this would be to surrender the hitherto accepted constitutional theory of the indivisibility of the Crown. Equally we do not want to take the line that Eire is no longer a member of the British Commonwealth. This would involve the rejection of the policy followed with the assent of the other Dominions since the establishment of the new Constitution

of Eire in 1937 and would moreover have serious repercussions in many directions, e.g. the status under United Kingdom law of individual Irishmen.

When war came Britain was beholden to many gallant 'individual Irishmen'.

Ulster Essential

Since the war, the Crown can no longer be considered as indivisible. As long desired by de Valera, republican status has been reconciled with Commonwealth membership. The Commonwealth is not any more a military alliance, although several of its member states belong to various defence pacts. Yet, when Eire was declared a Republic outside the Commonwealth, while retaining by agreement most of the advantages of membership, a Cabinet paper published for the Labour Government in 1948 noted that with Eire ceasing to owe any allegiance to the Crown, Northern Ireland became a matter of first-class strategic importance. The paper said:

> So far as can be foreseen, it will never be to Great Britain's advantage that Northern Ireland should become part of a territory outside His Majesty's jurisdiction. Indeed, it seems unlikely that Great Britain would ever be able to agree to this even if the people of Northern Ireland desired (it).

A far cry from the more recent and more grudging formula that Northern Ireland would remain part of the United Kingdom until its people decided otherwise!

From Churchill's time on, successive British governments and successive American administrations have sought or speculated upon an ending of partition in return for the entry of a united Ireland into a Western alliance. Nationalists now saw 'England's danger' as 'Ireland's opportunity' for reunification. A memorandum which Enoch Powell could quote in support of his allegations of Foreign Office designs upon the Union is that of the former Commonwealth Relations Office in 1951:

> Historically, Ireland, which has never been able to protect herself against invasion, has been, as she is today, a political base for attack on the United Kingdom.... Failing some firm and satisfactory assurance as to the attitude in war of a United Ireland, of which the present Republic was a major part, there are strong strategic arguments for the retention of the friendly bastion of the Six Counties.

Those 'Six Counties' form an integral part of the United Kingdom by the free will of nearly every Protestant in the province and nearly every second Catholic. Which is just as well for the security of the north-east Atlantic and the airspace of our country. According to a recent poll, 84 per cent of the people of the Republic favour continued neutrality and the New Ireland Forum was silent on a matter of the deepest concern to the vast majority in the North.

And yet . . . the last to fall in the British liberation of the Falklands was a young Irishman from the Republic.

Notes

[1] 8 December 1917.

[2] *Survey of British Commonwealth Affairs: Problems of Wartime Cooperation and Post-War Change, 1939–1952.*

Bibliography

The Formulation of Irish Foreign Policy
By Patrick Keatinge
Institute of Public Administration, 1984

A Singular Stance: Irish Neutrality in the 1980s
By Patrick Keatinge
Institute of Public Administration, 1984

Irish Foreign Policy
Address by Dr G. Fitzgerald TD
Dail, 9 May 1973

Irish Foreign Policy
Address by Dr Garret Fitzgerald TD
Fletcher School of Law and Diplomacy,
Medford, Mass. USA, 1 October 1973

Independent Ireland
By Ronan Fanning
Helicon Ltd, Dublin, 1983

Ulster Six British Counties
By Sir John Biggs-Davison MP
Salisbury Group, 1982

In Time of War
By Robert Fisk
Andre Deutsch, 1983

Republicans and Imperialists:
Anglo-Irish Relations in the 1930s
By Deirdre McMahon
Yale University Press, 1984

De Valera and the Irish Question 1917–1973
By John Bowman
Oxford University Press, 1982

Ireland in the War Years
By Joseph T. Carroll
David and Charles, 1975

Irish Neutrality and the USA 1939–47
By T. Ryle Dwyer
Gill and Macmillan, 1977

The South Eastern Flank: Political Dilemmas and Strategic Considerations

PROFESSOR JAMES BROWN
Department of Political Science, Southern Methodist University, Texas

THE SOUTHERN Flank of NATO offers a wide range of perspectives, more than any other NATO region. It is isolated from central Europe and is geographically fragmented. The principal focus of orientation for the NATO forces in this region is maintaining freedom of transit in the Mediterranean. Naval power, therefore, plays a dominant role in defence planning and force projection for the region.

Recently, Admiral William J. Crowe, former NATO commander of Allied Forces Southern Europe, lamented that NATO is still based on the outdated assumption that war would begin in Central Europe rather than the Persian Gulf or the Middle East. Admiral Crowe called this strategy "shaky".[1]

Moreover, this region's strategic importance has been dramatically increased by events in the area. Turkey is the only Alliance nation in the Middle East and it sits on the flank of any Soviet thrust into Iran or the Persian Gulf. Straddling the Straits of Bosphorus and the Dardanelles, it virtually controls the Soviet Union's only means of egress into the Mediterranean, while Greece monitors Soviet use of the Aegean Sea and contributes to the naval readiness of the Adriatic Sea. Geostrategically, both Greece and Turkey lie athwart the direct avenues of Soviet expansionism into the Arab world and Africa.

Geographically, the Southern Flank is unique and complex as compared with the Central Front. First, there is the profound difference in how forces are arrayed and power is projected. The terrain is rugged, the area sparsely populated and off-road mobility is difficult. Employment of heavy vehicles is, at best, difficult. In the Central Front there exists a framework of substantial stability between NATO and the Warsaw Pact, stability which includes geography, as well as political and military considerations.[2] Combat would take place in an environment characterised by dense population, urbanisation, a highly developed logistics network, with significant networks of road and rail facilities. This clearly structures the reactions of the parties involved and thereby limits the type of actions that can be taken. In the southern region the boundaries between the two alliances are less distinct. It is the Mediterranean which serves as the common denominator for East-West presence in the region.[3] In the Central Front the two superpowers and their allies have assigned basically analogous missions to their forces. But in the Southern Flank both the United States and the Soviet Union have interests that transcend their respective alliances. Relations with the United States are more important to Greece and Turkey than their NATO commitment. In fact, both countries tend to evaluate their national security concerns from a nationalistic perspective, thus detaching them from the "Atlantic" context. Greece today views the Warsaw Pact as being a lesser threat than Turkey, its neighbouring NATO ally.[4] Such interpretations colour both nations' views toward the United States and NATO, and directly effect how crises will be met in this region and perhaps the Middle East and Persian Gulf.

Both superpowers have major client states in this region. These complex relationships could lead to circumstances wherein the superpowers confront each other exclusively in defence of these interests or those of their client states.

There are, however, three common denominators shared by all. First, the Mediterranean Sea washes their shores and is seen as a vital thoroughfare. Second, the presence of the United States' Sixth Fleet and the Soviet Union's Fifth Escadra conditions events. Last, the politico-economic conditions of Greece and Turkey, as well as the other nations in the region, in most cases, reveal signs of more or less marked instability, leading to expectations that changes might occur and thereby significantly alter the existing *status quo*.

The Military Balance

From the standpoint of security, geographic characteristics of the Southern Flank make sea power a critical component for reinforcement and resupply of ground forces. This circumstance, of course, underlines the need for effective sea control; otherwise, coherent defence of the Southern Flank is difficult, if not impractical.

For many years, the US Sixth Fleet operated virtually unhindered in the Mediterranean. In the late 1960s and 1970s, however, the Soviet Fifth Escadra greatly expanded its presence, which in turn has facilitated promotion of Soviet diplomatic objectives in the region. From a coastal navy with a principal mission of displaying the flag, the Soviet Navy today has developed significant sea-denial capabilities.[5] In short, the Soviet naval build-up has produced an uneasy balance in the Mediterranean in the sense that the United States and NATO no longer exercise undisputed control of the area. On the other hand, the Soviet Union is not in a position to deny the West the maritime routes in the Mediterranean or in the Middle East. Control or denial of the sealanes by the United States or the Soviet Union ultimately hinges on land-based air power. Lacking effective sea-launched air power to inflict major damage on the Sixth Fleet, the Soviets could do so by land-based air power.[6] Launching Backfire (TU–26) and Blinder (TU–22) bombers from bases in the Crimea makes the Sixth Fleet, as well as the entire Mediterranean basin, vulnerable.[7] In addition, Libya possesses a force of Soviet-built aircraft which far exceeds that country's reasonable defence needs and which have the potential to affect the entire region.[8] If the Soviet Union deployed a mixed force of Backfire bombers, MiG fighters, and Sukhoi fighter-bombers on Libyan airfields, it would considerably shift the balance of power away from the United States Sixth Fleet and NATO. There is a consensus in intelligence estimates indicating that Colonel Muammar Quadaffi would grant the Soviet Union the use of these facilities in an East-West confrontation.

This underlines the importance of land-based tactical aircraft stationed in Europe, and in particular, in Greece and Turkey.[9] Most of the deployable aircraft in Greece and Turkey are at least 20 years old, but the current assumption is that the United States and the Soviet Union could, if necessary, provide newer and more effective aircraft, (for example, F–15 and F–16, MiG–25, 27 and SU–25) if necessary. The upgrading of the Greek and Turkish air forces with new fighters, either F–16s or F–18s, would greatly enhance their air capabilities.[10] Presently, Turkey is negotiating with Egypt for the purchase of 35 F–5E (Phantoms). This is an interesting exercise in bazaar bargaining since Saudi Arabia is underwriting the Turkish purchase. With this acquisition the Turkish Air Force will retire F–100s, a Korean War-vintage aircraft.

At present, the Warsaw Pact far exceeds the NATO forces in total number of tactical aircraft, while the Alliance still has an edge in equipment as well as in fighting capabilities.[11] NATO is not only bringing into service new fighter aircraft, Tornado for example, but it has augmented its aircraft with newer avionics and advanced laser-guided and precision-guided munitions. It has also enhanced its overall capabilities with the deployment of early warning and control capabilities (AWACS, E–2CS, and Nimrods). These systems can be positioned to the Southern Flank if the situation warrants. Without the protection provided by tactical aircraft, however, the Sixth Fleet is vulnerable.

A further complicating factor is the expansion and modernisation of Soviet and Warsaw Pact land forces in the Southern Flank area. Current estimates are that the Warsaw Pact nations have deployed some 35 divisions on the Greco-Turkish border in contrast to NATO forces numbering some 32 divisions, mainly infantry units. Most of the Warsaw Pact divisions are mechanised, and armoured, and possess a favourable tank ratio of about three-to-one. They are on terrain suitable for armoured offensive operations and could easily be reinforced by at least two airborne/air mobile divisions. The task of the Greek and Turkish forces is rendered difficult defensively by the narrowness of the area between the borders (Thrace) and the Aegean Sea (30–50 miles in width), although it is likely that in any general war the bulk of the Bulgarian forces would be directed eastward toward the Dardannelles and Istanbul. In the east, Turkey has a 380 mile land frontier with the Soviet Union. The terrain is mountainous and rugged and favourable for defensive operations. Turkey's Third Army at Ezurum faces some 15 motorised infantry divisions classified as catagory 3.[12] Both Greek and Turkish forces are lacking anti-tank weapons, radar and armoured attack helicopters, and many of their weapon systems, especially the Turkish ones, require updating, being in some cases vintage World War II.[13] In addition, both are lacking command, control and communications systems (C^3) for more effective battlefield control. Massive modernisation programmes are in effect but economic constraints are taking their toll.

The Soviets have deployed Intermediate-Range Ballistic Missiles (IRBMs) including the 3–MIRV SS–20s, in the northwest Crimea and northern fringes of the Transcaucasian

Federation. Presumably, some of these missiles would be targeted on NATO's Southern Flank.[14] In response, the United States, with NATO approval, will soon place medium-range Pershing-II and Cruise missiles in Western Europe. Neither system will be extended to Greece or Turkey.[15]

If Greece was neutralised, Turkey would be isolated from the nearest friendly land border by 800 miles of rugged and unfriendly terrain.[16] A Warsaw Pact thrust from Bulgaria could then assail the Bosphorus and Dardanelles without fear of a flank attack. Communications between the western and eastern Mediterranean and NATO would be complicated. If, on the other hand, Turkey was attacked or decided to remain neutral, Greece's eastern flank would be exposed to Soviet naval and air attacks and Warsaw Pact forces could attempt to reach the Aegean through Thrace, unhindered from the east. The Soviets would still have the arduous task of paralysing military bases on the Greek islands and simultaneously keeping a wary eye on the Sixth Fleet.

The Political Variables

Despite shifts in the military balance on NATO's Southern Flank, military power may be irrelevant in resolving the problems facing the region. The Soviet Union, for the most part, has been opportunistic, responding and reacting to problems it did not create and has not resolved. The problems stem from political, economic and social changes in Greece and Turkey and in the international environment of the past two decades, which directly affect their relations with the United States and NATO. Foreign policy in Greece and Turkey is but an extension and reflection of domestic bickering and alignments. It revolves around the Greek-Turkish conflict and its numerous political, economic and military strands.

The cohesion of NATO is minimally discussed. Each party has some legitimate grounds for dissatisfaction with NATO members, particularly with the United States. A closer examination of the respective politics of each nation will shed additional light on the overall problems facing the Southern Flank.

Greece

The election of the charismatic Andreas Papandreou and PASOK (Panhellenic Socialist Union) in 1981[17] reflects a shift towards the left and some disillusion with the Western Alliance and the United States. Papandreou's campaign centered on the slogan *allaghi* (change) — change across all sectors of society. According to PASOK's ideology, Greece is an economically under-developed state, and is politically, economically and militarily dependent on the West. The previous post-World War II conservative governments pursued, according to Papandreou, a "mono-dimensional" policy of dependence that led to a series of concessions, policy ambivalence and sacrifice of sovereign rights vital to Greek interests.[18] During the campaign, Papandreou called for fundamental innovation in the domestic and foreign policy areas. His was the party that was going to change everything, but which in effect has changed very little.

On the domestic side, PASOK's promise of change is most evident in a broad range of liberalising social legislation,[19] but economic measures have been somewhat less far-reaching than expected. Papandreou's pledge of nationalisation has been translated into a vague policy aimed at greater worker participation in decision making.[20] Inflation is still high (about 20 per cent), and stagnating production, falling investments, export and invisible earnings in decline, unemployment on the rise and a weakening of consumer demand, do not portend well for Greece's economic prosperity. The projected increase for 1983 in the GNP was estimated at a low of 2.0 per cent.[21] The recessionary policies introduced by Papandreou have not as yet taken hold.[22] These domestic factors have imposed a strain on the government resulting in a more militant foreign policy. Papandreou's militant stance feeds his anti-Americanism and propensity toward non-alignment, which he sees as the proper affiliation for Greece. Prior to his electoral victory, he called for Greece's withdrawal from NATO, a reappraisal of Greek membership in the European Economic Community (EEC), and a tougher position on the issues that confront Greece and Turkey (Cyprus and the Aegean Sea).

Accession to the seat of government has had a tempering affect on Papandreou's action: the rhetoric has been strident, but devoid of action. He has stated that Greece "does not want to take unilateral measures and pull any surprises and is prepared to discuss relations with NATO and the United States in the belief that mutually acceptable solutions to differences can be found."[23] He reasons that any withdrawal from NATO or the closing of US military facilities will only result in a tilt toward Turkey by the United States and NATO.

Papandreou, in a letter to President Reagan on 4 February 1983, declared that preserving "... the balance of power in the Aegean" is a basic condition for achieving a Defence and Economic Cooperation Agreement (DECA).[24] In fact, he has stated that "... the threat we perceive and feel comes from one of our allies, Turkey. We do not feel ourselves threatened from the north".[25] This explicitly meant that the unwritten practice established by the US Congress in the mid-1970s of a 7–10 ratio, Greek to Turkish military aid, must be continued.

As a result of his pragmatism, Greece and the United States initialed a new defence and economic cooperation agreement which ensures the continued presence of American military bases in Greece for at least five years.[26] Athens also received a vague commitment from the United States permitting Greece to halt any use of the bases that would threaten Greek relations with friendly countries in the Middle East. Greece may further curtail activities of the bases in the event of a national emergency. Maintaining the 7–10 ratio, Greece will receive $500 million (m) in military aid; Turkey's share will be $755 m. For Greece the agreement is a watershed. For the United States it relieves a major irritant in US-Greek relations and removes a serious obstacle to resolving the other political and military issues confronting the Southern Flank.

One critical constraint on Papandreou is the Greek armed forces. They are staunchly nationalistic, very pro-Western, and they share the commonly-held perception that both the United States and NATO favour Turkey. The perpetuation of such laden nationalistic issues as the 7–10 ratio, the conclusion of a favourable DECA agreement, Cyprus and the Aegean Sea, benefit Papandreou and permit him to continue conducting his foreign policy largely without interference from the military, which has a historical proclivity toward intervention.[27]

Papandreou's ultimate vision continues to be the dissolution of all cold-war military alliances, including NATO and the Warsaw Pact. Recently, he advocated the establishment of a nuclear free zone for the Balkans.[28] Today, there are approximately 16 bases on Greek soil that contain US nuclear weapons. NATO is viewed as an extension of American cold-war policy which, Papandreou would argue, has been responsible for subverting Greek sovereignty and national interests, failing to guarantee Greece's frontiers against Turkish threat, the 1967 military dictatorship and the 1974 Cyprus conflict.

Recent polls indicate that strong opposition exists to Greek membership in NATO and that Greeks hold unfavourable opinions about the United States, more so than the Soviet Union.[29] The polls suggest that a majority want Greece to "completely get out of NATO" (53 per cent), want US bases to go (70 per cent), and consider the presence of US forces on Greek soil a source of additional danger to their security (52 per cent).[30]

A partial explanation of the deleterious relations with the United States is attributable to two basic causes. The first was the US policy toward Greece under the Junta (1967–1974). Many Greeks today contend that the United States has frequently meddled in the politics of their country,[31] and that it is somehow responsible for the installation of the Junta government. In fact, the Junta went out of its way to encourage the allegation of complicity, thus assuming the mantle of legitimacy. Although no concrete evidence to support these claims exists, it was true that initially the United States did not denounce the regime. The tedium of rationalisation and false hopes employed by American policy-makers to justify their attitudes toward the Junta disappointed not only ousted parliamentarians, but led to the deterioration of public attitude toward the United States.

The short-term gains for the United States were rewarding. American bases in Greece remained available during the June 1967 war and the September 1970 crises in Jordan. The Nixon Administration was successful in negotiating home porting privileges for the Sixth Fleet in the Piraeus region. George Papadopoulos, the initial Junta strongman, not only displayed his loyalty to NATO, but also held secret meetings with Turkey over the knotty Cyprus issue, and even attempted to bring "the renegade" Archbishop Makarios into line.[32] Failing that, Athens then orchestrated a series of aborted attempts against the Archbishop's life, in the belief that the United States wanted Cyprus as part of NATO and hoped to remove Makarios' dangerous influence by supporting *Enosis* (Union) with Greece.[33] This led to the ill-fated *coup d'état,* initiated by the then Junta strongman, D. Ioannides, to overthrow the legitimate Cyprus government of Makarios. This event, of course, was the second cause for deteriorating relations with the United States. Inevitably, the stability of relations between Greece and the United States impacts on NATO and directly on Turkey as well.

Turkey

With the advent of a multi-party system in the 1950s, Turkey has experienced intermittent, and at times, severe political instability. Twice in recent history (1960 and 1971), the Turkish armed forces have intervened in the political arena. Despite these interventions, Turkey made considerable headway during this time towards establishing democratic institutions. Two major personalities and their followers dominated the political scene: Bülent Ecevit's Republican People's Party, and Süleyman Demirel's Justice Party. Both Demirel and Ecevit harbour deep personal antagonism towards one another that compounded basic differences between the major political parties. These differences made it impossible for either party to govern.[34] Consequently, minor parliamentary groups exercised disproportionate influence and, what was worse, caused deadlocks and ensuing paralysis in the legislative process.[35]

This instability was aggravated by a rapidly growing, yet deficit-ridden, economy and social disruption caused by industrial growth. The resulting flow of people from the rural to urban areas produced the *geçekondus* (shanty towns) which were the spawning grounds for terrorism that gripped Turkey during this period.[36] Uncertainty on Turkey's borders, due to the 1979 invasion of Afghanistan by the Soviet Union, and the demise of Shah Pahlevi in Iran further exacerbated conditions. The combination of domestic social tensions and insecurity on the borders was apparently too much for the Turkish military to bear. For a third time, in September 1980, they intervened. A National Security Council, headed by Chief of Staff General Kenan Evren, assumed authority. This *coup d'état* was not unexpected.[37] The reluctance of the military to undertake this *coup* lies in the fact that their two previous attempts were not completely successful, although constitutional government was restored quickly.

Since the military takeover, inflation has receded to about 25 per cent from an all time high of over 100 per cent in 1980. The Turkish economy grew by 4.2 per cent in 1982, and is projected to reach the 7 per cent level in 1984.[38] Terrorism has been dramatically reduced. Martial law authorities have been "even-handed" in prosecuting terrorists, whereas even-handedness was a commodity unfamiliar to the previous civilian governments.

Within a year, the National Security Council had taken steps to reinstitute democracy. As a first step, a Consultative Assembly of 160 members was established in 1981 and mandated to draft a new constitution, with the primary intention of strengthening the office of President, and strengthening a two-party system. The latter was in order to break the parliamentary impasse which gave minority parties disproportionate strength in forming coalition governments. The constitution, containing 176 articles[39], was ratified by popular referendum in November 1982, and this same referendum elected General Evren as President of the Republic for a seven year term.[40] On 24 April 1983, the National Security Council approved the law governing the activities of political parties. The political arena was immediately invaded by dozens of aspirants (most of whom were newcomers to politics) trying to form new parties.[41]

The revival of political parties introduces uncertainties into Turkey's political life. There are bound to be some tremors permeating the political system during the next several months until relationships between the military, the new parties, and the ousted politicians become clear. Uneasiness may prevail if it appears that political power is likely to slip into unwelcome hands or if terrorist activities resume as a result of politics. There is no doubt that the military government's goals reach beyond establishing law and order; they seek a long-term transformation of Turkey into a more stable democracy by reshaping public institutions.

The parliamentary elections that took place in November 1983, have moved Turkey toward the restoration of civilian rule. The Turkish parliament resumed its activities with an entirely new membership and a new form. The centre-right Motherland Party, led by Prime Minister Turgut Ozal, commands a comfortable majority with 212 of the parliamentary seats. This and the other two parties (National Democratic Party — 71 seats, and the Populist Party — 117 seats) represented in Parliament were established in August 1983, with the consent of the National Security Council. Former political leaders and their parties were barred from politics. With the election of the Ozal government, the National Security Council transformed itself into the Presidential Advisory Council. Its purpose is to advise President Evren on major international and domestic issues, but in practical terms it not only serves as a liaison between the Turkish armed forces and the civilian regime, but more importantly, as a guardian so that the pre-1980 political, economic, and social excesses should not again prevail.

General Evren and the National Security Council were quick to emphasise, after their intervention in 1980, that Turkey would remain an active member of NATO and continue close relations with the United States. In addition, Turkey's concerns focus on its proximity to the Soviet Union and the instability of its Middle East neighbours.

The Cyprus conflict of 1964 marked the turning point in Turkey's foreign and national security policies.[42] This was not merely because of frustrations when Turkey was prevented from pursuing a national policy about Cyprus. More important was the realisation that subtle changes were taking place in the interaction between the United States and the Soviet Union that were bound to affect security relationships between the United States, NATO and Turkey. The Johnson letter directly contributed to this feeling.[43] This forced Turkey to re-examine its view of the security afforded by NATO. No longer did it appear to provide firm, all-embracing and early automatic collective security. Although NATO continued to be the basis of Turkey's security policy, it remained for the 1974 Cyprus crisis to precipitate the most serious damage to the relations between Turkey, the United States, Greece and NATO, and to benefit the Soviet Union.

Greek-NATO-US-Turkish Imbroglio

As on previous occasions when the Cyprus issue flared, the overriding United States concern was not the rights or wrongs on either side or the fate of the two communities on the island, but rather the best way to limit the potential damage to NATO and to the American strategic interests in the Mediterranean. Thus the United States sought to defuse the situation and, above all, to prevent a war between Greece and Turkey that would be disastrous for all concerned. While the American intervention in 1963–64 had succeeded in averting a confrontation between these two NATO allies, it did nothing to further a permanent solution of the Cyprus problem.

In July 1974, acting on orders from Athens, Greek military forces, backed by the Cyprus national guard, attempted to overthrow the government of Archbishop Makarios.[44] This time Ankara invoked its right of intervention without waiting for reaction from Washington. Most important it aroused the resentment of both allies, each of which felt that the United States had betrayed it in supporting the other. The immediate impact was felt by NATO with Greece's withdrawal from the military wing. Six years would lapse before Greece would return to the integrated military command structure.

Turkey's response was less immediate, but in the long run may prove more injurious. The most serious cause of friction between Ankara and Washington (resulting from the Cyprus crisis) was the arms embargo imposed by the United States Congress in 1975, and ultimately rescinded in 1978.[45] This action, regarded by most Turks as an insult to a loyal ally, aroused widespread Turkish indignation.[46] The lifting of the embargo and the 1980 United States-Turkish Defence Agreement improved relations, but Turkish pride and national sensibilities had been offended, and these have traditionally been potent political forces in Turkey. Recently, Minister of Defence Haluk Bayulken warned the United States that "[a]n embargo against Turkey will be perilous for Turkish-US relations". The " . . . Turkish people will not tolerate another test of pressure like the arms embargo".[47] In particular, faith in the United States as a dependable ally has been burdened with an extra psychological dimension, and will in the future manifest itself in "unanticipated ways in how Ankara proceeds in its relations with the United States and NATO".[48]

The lifting of the embargo strengthened Papandreou's hand domestically. Papandreou, the first Greek Prime Minister to visit Cyprus, has been emphatic in rejecting any solution imposed by force, and refuses to de-internationalise the problem or to allow NATO to serve as a mediator.[49]

The Cyprus imbroglio has festered for years. It culminated on 15 November 1983, when the leader of the Turkish minority, Rauf Denktash, declared the Turkish Republic of Northern Cyprus an independent state. The Turkish Cypriots, with less than 20 per cent of the population, control about 30 per cent of Cyprus with the assistance of some 17,000 Turkish forces. This move by Denktash is fraught with dangers. The emergence of the Turkish Cypriot state changes the political and military map of the area. It will increase tensions between East and West and it will complicate life in NATO and the Balkans. Furthermore, it perpetuates the conflict between Greece and Turkey, even more than previously. Also, it violates the United Nations resolution on maintaining the territorial integrity and sovereignty of Cyprus and undermines the recent efforts of UN Secretary General Javier Perez de Cuellar to work out a settlement between the Greek and Turkish communities. Lastly, a permanent split will greatly complicate the United States' relations with both Athens and Ankara. It might lead again to pressure in Congress to embargo arms to Turkey, as in 1974.

This declaratory step by Denktash should not be regarded as irreversible. There is a ray of hope. In proclaiming a Turkish Cypriot state Denktash also renewed his commitment to negotiate for a single "federated state" composed of both Greek and Turkish Cypriots. This has been his goal in negotiations for years. So it is not necessary to take what has been done as a *fait accompli*. An optimistic view is that Denktash has staked out a new hard position in the difficult negotiations that must follow. Perhaps there is room for creative rather than condemnatory diplomacy.

In addition to Cyprus, two other issues complicate relations between these allies. The first issue concerns the right to explore for minerals, primarily oil, beneath the Aegean Sea. Under international law, nations have a right to explore for mineral wealth on their continental shelf, but the Greek Islands (Chios, Kos, Lesbos, Samos, etc.) and the Turkish mainland share the same shelf. Based on the 1958 Geneva Convention concerning the Continental Shelf, Greece maintains that these and other islands have their own continental shelf. Turkey contends that these islands have special characteristics that require a special solution. Further clouding the issue are the limits of the territorial waters surrounding these islands and the militarisation and fortification of them and others (for example, Rhodes). This quandary is viewed by Turkey as provocative and in general appears to be a violation of the 1923 Treaty of Lausanne.[50] This latter problem led Turkey to create the Army of the Aegean.[51] By way of retort, Greece has strengthened the High Military Command of the Interior and Islands (ASDEN) and created "D" Corps with headquarters in Xanthi (60 miles from the Turkish border) to offset the mobilisation and deployment of troops on the Maritsa River. In general, however, Turkey currently does not consider Greece a potential threat.

The second issue concerns the control of air space over the Aegean. This was partially resolved in February 1980, when civil aviation flights over this area were resumed. The question of the two countries' military flights into the area still remains deadlocked, awaiting settlement within the framework of NATO.[52] The linkage between the bilateral, Aegean issues and the Cyprus questions remain unclear, since progress on one would presumably create an environment of greater trust for moving forward on the other. To date, however, neither Greece nor Turkey has attempted a bold initiative to break the impasse.[53] Time is waning! Papandreou is perhaps one of the very few Greek politicians today who can negotiate with Ankara and arrive at some resolution of these knotty problems. Such a meeting would be reminiscent of the E.Venizelos-K.Atatürk Summit in 1930 when these two leaders reconciled their outstanding differences.[54]

Casting about Seeking Supporters

Greece and Turkey's preoccupation with each other, their differences with the United States, and their disappointment in Western Europe's level of assistance, caused each to cast about in the international arena for supporters.

The Soviet connection

The issues that divide the Alliance in the Southern Flank benefit the Soviet Union. Greece today views the Soviet Union and the Warsaw Pact as less threatening than its ally, Turkey. Turkey's view of the Soviet Union and the threat it poses is coloured not only by its extensive geographic exposure, but by historical relations with its northern neighbour. Neither country presently fears a Soviet attack. Instead, both have responded favourably to Soviet overtures for improved relations by exchanging high level diplomatic visits. More importantly, both nations have consummated major trade agreements with the Soviets.

In the case of Turkey, no significant change in policy has taken place since the arrival of the Evren government. Today, the Soviet Union is one of Turkey's major trading partners, and as such, Turkey receives more aid than most Third World nations. It compares quite favourably with aid currently given to Turkey by Western nations. Specifically, in 1982 a new trade pact was signed which stipulated a 33 per cent increase in commerce: the Soviets pledged to provide oil, fertiliser, timber and electricity in exchange for Turkish textiles and food-stuffs. This agreement was considered a setback for the United States' effort to limit Western economic ties with the Soviet Union because of the Polish dilemma.[55]

Soviet intentions are for a neutral Turkey; but an independent Turkish foreign policy which stays loyal to contractual ties with the West, and undertakes a step-by-step restoration of confidence between the two, is to be encouraged.[56] Being adjacent to Turkey gives the Soviet Union a natural advantage and conditions the USSR to think of Turkey as part of its defensive perimeter. A politically neutral or friendly Turkey can relieve Soviet vulnerability from the south, even if it cannot totally eliminate concern.[57]

One can interpret Greece's relations with the Soviet Union in the last two years as part of an effort to diversify Greek foreign policy. Papandreou has described Greece's foreign policy " . . . as an independent and multi-directional policy. This means they are striving for friendly relations and the development of cooperation with all countries, irrespective of their bloc membership."[58]

Specifically, relations with the Soviet Union have been improving steadily during the last five years. By 1979, Greece was importing a large amount of oil and began increasing contacts in the fields of shipping, tourism, sports, and commerce. In the same year, an agreement was signed to provide Soviet commercial and auxiliary combat ships with repairs at the Neorion Shipbuilding Company on the Island of Syros. Although this development raised some consternation in Washington and NATO circles, Greek officials view Soviet naval deployment in the Mediterranean as part of US-Soviet strategic rivalry in the Middle East and Africa and not a direct threat to Greece's security.[59]

Beginning in 1982, coinciding with the beginning of discussions for the renewal of the DECA agreement with the United States, the Soviet press began more favourable coverage of Greece. This culminated in February 1983 with the visit of Soviet Prime Minister Nikolay Tikhonov to Athens, where he was given the "red carpet treatment".[60] This visit resulted in a series of long-term agreements in economic, industrial, scientific and technical fields.[61]

The agreement does not represent any significant new level of cooperation, but the visit by Tikhonov aroused interest in the United States and NATO because it was the first by a Soviet Prime Minister and gave rise to on-going concern about Papandreou's foreign policy. It cannot be assumed, however, that Greece today is moving toward a position where greater Soviet influence could be imposed on Greek policies. These relations have brought no fundamental changes in the USSR's position: they have not supported the issue of Cyprus or the question of air space and seabed jurisdiction in the Aegean Sea, except rhetorically.

Both Greece and Turkey have intensified their relations with their Balkan neighbours at all levels — in trade, tourism, industry and economics. Indeed, they seem to be competitors in these fields. Relations with Bulgaria have been normalised as long as the borders remain quiet and the Soviet Union stations no troops there.[62] Relations with Albania are correct. If the Albanians invite the Soviets to return to the naval base at Vlorë (their "window" to the Mediterranean until May 1961) and if a crisis in Yugoslavia brings pro-Soviet leadership to power, neither Greece nor Turkey can afford to take a relaxed attitude toward Soviet naval activities in the Mediterranean. A Soviet foothold in the Adriatic would outflank and isolate Greece and Turkey and could make communications between NATO and the Southern Flank more difficult. Equally, if Greece were lost to NATO, the movement of war material by sea to Turkey and Italy in wartime would be severely disrupted.

In summary, Greece's major objective in the Balkans has not been to secure allies against Turkey but rather to relieve its borders from tensions in case of an attack from Turkey.[63] Turkey senses vulnerability (especially from Bulgaria), which ensures that top priority will be given to the security of that region. It is the Warsaw Pact that weighs on Turkish priorities and plans, and not the individual Balkan members.

The Middle East

Both Greece and Turkey recognise the economic and political significance of the Middle East and have in the last five years exerted their efforts toward expanding relations in that region.

Turkey's intent is to be accepted as a friend of the Arabs, and on closer look, is coming to terms with its historical past.[64] In addition, these political developments took place at a time when Turkey's economy was in dangerous straits. Its dependency on Arab oil, which amounts to about 80 per cent of its consumption, was clearly a vital variable in its *rapprochement* with the Islamic world.[65] As relations improved with certain key Arab countries (for example, South Arabia, Iraq, Kuwait),[66] Turkey began to be more assertive in Western forums about a special knowledge of and access to the Middle East. These shifts represent economic self-interest for Turkey, acknowledgment of certain cultural realities among the Turkish masses (among whom Islamic practices are gaining in importance), and an awareness of a special contribution it can make to European states, who are also dependent on Persian Gulf oil.[67]

Saudi Arabia, in particular, assists Turkey economically and militarily for the sake of regional stability. This is a necessity in light of Iran and the impact that a fundamentalist Islamic state has on the entire region. In addition, the Iran-Iraq war further contributes to the instability of the region.[68] It is interesting to note that Turkey's relations with Iran are intriguing, not only because that country is a direct antithesis, under its present leadership, of Kemalist secularism, but also because Turkey has had to quietly combat efforts by the Tehran government to export its Islamic revolution. Iran is leaning heavily on Turkey for the export of cereals and products and possibly for political mediation.[69] In fact, Turkey is the only nation in the area on good terms with both Iran and Iraq.[70]

Ankara's relations with Syria, its neighbour to the south, are correct but distant. Sources of discord are present. The Turkish province of Hatay (Alexandretta) is claimed by Syria from time to time. In addition, Syria's radical secular regime has supplied and supported Turkish rebels,[71] especially the Armenians, who have undertaken terrorist attacks on Turkish diplomats throughout the world. Furthering this estrangement is Syria's close relations with the Soviet Union.[72]

The Libyan connection that developed after the 1975 United States arms embargo is an important source of financial assistance for Turkey: an energy source at concessionary prices, millions of dollars in grants, and employment of some 100,000 Turkish construction workers. Recently, problems have begun to surface in their relations, as Libya's financial position is faltering due to oil prices.[73] Turkey will not forget that Libya came to her assistance during the Cyprus dispute, at which time Libya transferred to the Turkish Air Force five F-5s, including spare parts. More recently, Libyan Air Force officers are being trained by Turkey.[74]

What is the price tag for Turkey's connection with the Arab world? In the past few years Arab nations have indicated that Turkey's NATO connection need not be an impediment to closer ties. The declaration of its special relationships to the Middle East is also relevant for Turkey's position with regard to possible NATO responsibilities beyond the NATO arena. Some Turkish diplomats have indicated that Turkey in the past was too acquiescent and did not adequately protect its own special needs and interests. Below the surface lies some scepticism and a loss of confidence in the United States because of the embargo episode. Turkey's reluctance publicly to embrace the Rapid Deployment Force (RDF) does not mean that Turkey would refuse to assist Saudi Arabia or other Persian Gulf states, if approached. Rather, it means that Turkey has become more explicit about its other regional orientations, and reserves the right to determine when and how Turkish soil will be used. Each case will be judged on its individual merits.

Although Greece has strong historical and economic ties in the Middle East, its focus presently is on the Arab-Israeli conflict and Papandreou's PASOK solidarity with the Palestine Liberation Organisation's (PLO) cause. Party ideology was the basis of the decision five days after the election to invite PLO leader Yasser Arafat to visit Athens. The visit, Arafat's first to an EEC country, took place in December 1981. In the process, the PLO's mission was upgraded to the same level as Israel's. Greece participated actively in the evacuation of the PLO from Beirut in August 1982,[75] and Papandreou has sharply condemned all recent unilateral Israeli actions in Lebanon. Greek support of the PLO has naturally strained relations with Israel, although Athens insists that its support of Israel's right to exist as a state has not been affected.

Libya's Muammar Qaddafi was expected in Athens in April 1982. It is not at all clear why Qaddafi's visit was postponed. Security reasons may have been a factor, or, as was rumoured in Athens, American pressure was telling.

Greece's perspective in the Middle East is symbolic of its new independent foreign policy. Its policies, however, have wider implications concerning how military facilities in Greece will be used by the United States and NATO. For example, will intelligence surveillance missions out of Athens Air Base (Ellinikon) be continued against Libya under this new agreement? Can the RFD or logistical support for such a force be deployed from Greece?

Meeting the Threat

There are few signs of an emerging solution to the problems in the Alliance's Southern Flank. Diversity and adaptation are the major trends of the day and possibly for the indefinite future. They inevitably make for uncertainty as far as political-military commitments are concerned. They result in the eschewing of any long-range institutional arrangements that stability and security usually require. The overall political and social fluidity in the Mediterranean and the Middle East-Persian Gulf has therefore increased further. In particular, the events in the entire Middle East region have put into motion a whole series of developments that are bound to have repercussions outside of the immediate region. They add a new political-military dimension which the Alliance is ill-prepared to handle.

In strategic terms, it is difficult to decouple the Middle East-Persian Gulf region from NATO's Southern Flank. Neither the Western powers nor the Soviet Union presently has established permanent forward bases in this region; thus the logistic constraints on anything more than a presence in the area would be formidable unless greater investments are made. With the exception of the permanent United States base at Diego Garcia, all facilities in the Persian Gulf are temporary and whatever might be stored at them will be under the control of the host government.[76] To this extent, the region is a vacuum, and the military force that settles in place first will have greater tactical advantages. In this context, continued United States access to Greek and Turkish bases and possible access to Egypt, Israel, Oman, Saudi Arabia and Bahrain could be crucial. From a strictly geographical standpoint, the Turkish bases are the best placed strategically.[77] The map, showing the nominal approximate combat radii for American aircraft based in Turkey, east of Incirlik, makes the strategic value of the Turkish bases evident. With the F–111s, strike missions could cover the important sources of attack from the Transcaucasus and Crimea, and could also reach all important sites in the Gulf region.[78] An F–15 fighter F–16, or F–18 (one of the types will ultimately be purchased by Greece and Turkey) might perform both intercept as well as strike missions. For most of the aircraft with shorter combat radii Turkey might provide the only bases in the area from which attacks could be initiated. Eastern Turkey has at least four excellent bases (Mus, Batman, Erzurum and Diyarbakir), which are now being remodelled and their runways expanded in order to serve this purpose. In all, Turkey has some 26 US and NATO bases. Seven are Air Force installations, one is for the Army and the remainder are primarily storage and logistical sites and intelligence bases. Four of these intelligence installations are major operations — Diyarbakir, Sinop, Karamürsel and Belbosi. These installations also have the advant-

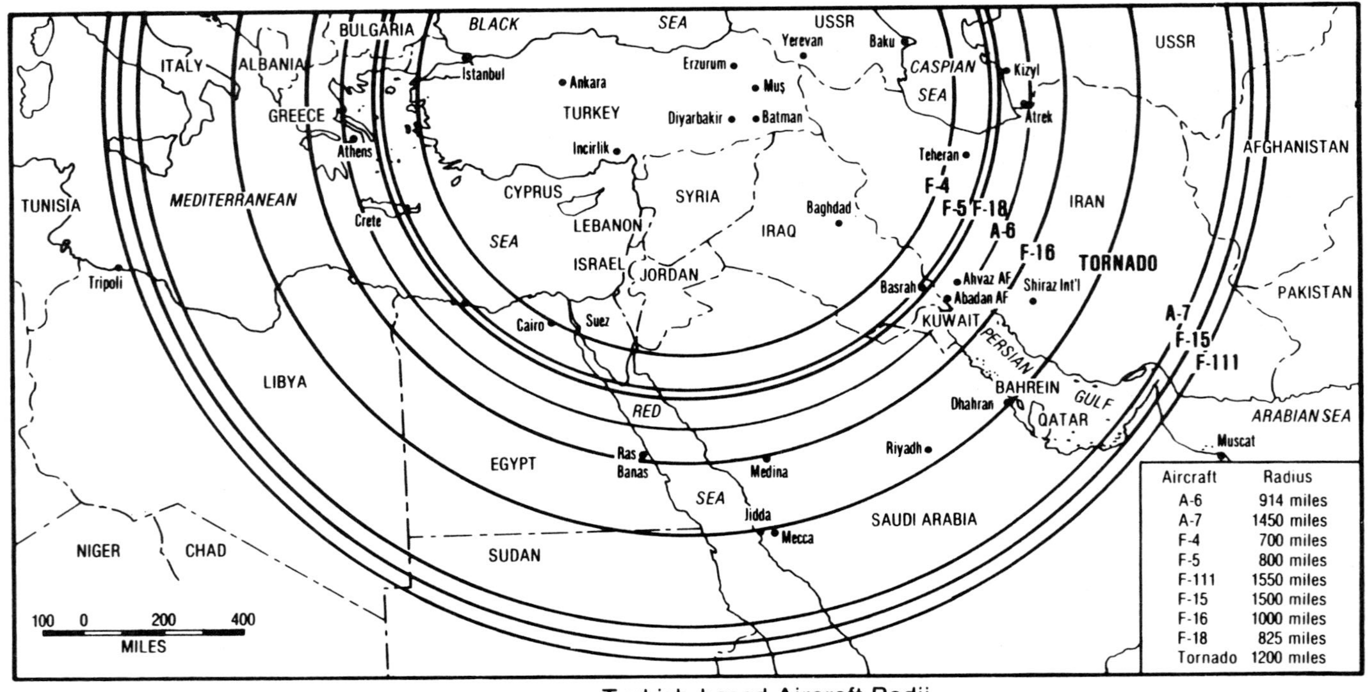

Turkish-based Aircraft Radii

age of being part of the NATO Air Defence Ground Environment stations (NADGE).

The major installations in Greece used by the United States and NATO are: Souda Bay and Iraklion air bases in Crete and Ellinikon Air Base in Athens; Nea Makri naval communications stations near Athens; and another 20 that serve as communications sites and storage units for nuclear weapons. Use of these Greek bases provides, among other things, direct operational and logistical support for the Sixth Fleet, important communications links, reconnaissance information, surveillance of Soviet and other nations' activities (for example, Libya, Syria) in the eastern Mediterranean, support for US and NATO airlift and logistics flights, and ammunition and supply storage sites. Loss of access to these bases would make the task of carrying out their functions much more difficult and complicated.

It is important to note that air and naval facilities in other countries in the Middle East–Persian Gulf would require considerable capital investment to bring them up to standard (see Table 1). Beyond that, most of the Middle East countries are extremely sensitive about a visible US presence (for example, Saudi Arabia, Egypt, Somalia, etc.).[79] The US is usually granted discretionary use rights with respect to facilities and required to consult with the host government on major exercises and deployments. This suggests that the allegiances of the respective countries would play a major role in determining the success or failure of any major military operation in the region. Moreover,

TABLE 1. Rapid Deployment Force Facilities in the Persian Gulf Region

	Air Force	Army	Navy
Bahrain	1		1
Diego Garcia*	1	1	1
Egypt	5	1	2
Kenya	1	1	1
Oman	3		1
Somalia	2		2
Saudi Arabia	2		1

*The US base is in a quite different category from the facilities of the other countries. It is currently the only permanent US base between Manila and Naples. A coral atoll, the island is situated at the virtual centre of the Indian Ocean.

Source: James P. Wootten, *Regional Support Facilities for the Rapid Deployment Force* (Washington: Congressional Research Service), 1982.

most of these nations are in the throes of modernisation, and the maintenance of political and economic stability will be telling in the kind of support they may provide.

On paper, the Soviet Union has great geographical advantages over the West, especially in the context of operations against the Persian Gulf. The Soviet border is only 600 miles from Iranian ports on the Gulf, and Soviet forces in Afghanistan are just 400 miles from the Straits of Hormuz. Their lines of communication are much shorter (and probably entirely overland) than those of US forces. Soviet forces would have to travel only one-seventh as far as US units coming from the United States and they could use both long and short-haul aircraft. However, the US probably has more capable friends and allies in the region who could provide vital support in a crisis or war.

A Soviet attack against Iran would be almost impossible to stop unless there was an early strategic warning and if US forces were already deployed in forward positions and if the Iranians were equipped, trained and ready to fight. Obviously, the farther the scene of conflict from Soviet borders, the more difficult Soviet logistical problems would be, and the easier it would be for the United States and its allies to mount a counter-operation.

The NATO Alliance has yet to face squarely the problem of protecting its own direct interests in the Persian Gulf. Since the 1967 war, NATO members have often been explicit about limiting NATO's interests and responsibilities to the formal treaty area, which stops at the eastern borders of Turkey and at the Tropic of Cancer. In May 1981, NATO, for the first time, officially recognised the need for its members to help facilitate area deployment by other members and to compensate for any gaps in NATO's force structure that might result from such deployments. These suggested areas of cooperation included the Middle East–Persian Gulf. This was further reaffirmed in the NATO ministerial communiqué of June 1983. Specifically, this communiqué recognises that situations may arise which threaten the vital interests of the West, and if it is established that NATO's common interest is involved they will engage in timely consultation. This communiqué assumes the support and assistance of virtually all NATO members.[80] Based on historical experience, however, it may be difficult for the United States to acquire firm approval of the members for RDF operations or to compensate for the diversion of US forces.[81] The communiqué states:

> that member nations, *as they may decide*, have a wide and diverse range of possibilities from which to choose in making useful contributions to promote stability and deterrence in regions outside the treaty area involving vital western interests.[82]

Should NATO redraw its boundaries formally to include the Middle East–Persian Gulf? In strategic terms the answer should, no doubt, be yes. In political terms, however, it is very difficult to imagine this happening without precipitating a major crisis. Too many ambiguities abound within NATO regarding defence priorities to make this a realistic alternative.

Nevertheless, the political considerations do not mean that greater cooperation and agreement within NATO or external threats is not possible. Because of the geographic proximity of Greece and Turkey to the Middle East region, it makes sense to think of them as part of the Soviet Union's southern front, which stretches from the Adriatic to Pakistan.[83] Within this catchment area lie many of the potentially explosive scenarios that may involve NATO and Soviet military power — Yugoslavia, Arab-Israeli conflict, Iran, Afghanistan, etc. It is necessary, therefore, that some formal recognition by NATO's leadership (beyond mere consultation) and individual country initiatives, take place for linking local conflicts and overall Western strategic interests. It would go a long way towards eliminating the artificial boundaries that assume NATO's wartime responsibilities stop at Turkey's eastern border. Anything short of this will still require that the United States continue to take the initiative. There may be no need to redraw NATO's institutional map, but there is a need to accept the fact that this map may be irrelevant in a future war, since it no longer encompasses all of NATO's major assets.[84]

In the complex *milieu* of the 1980s, alarmism regarding the growing Soviet threat is not an effective source of policy. This does not imply that the Soviet threat no longer exists, but the threat today is less immediate and less direct. More important, in the case of Greece and Turkey, neither regards it as the principal source of their insecurity. The need for an assertive and cooperative policy among the allies spills over into the Greco-Turkish imbroglio. This type of assistance would blunt any Soviet attempt to exploit instabilities, both real and latent, on the Southern Flank. Such a policy is even more important in view of the potential for instability elsewhere in southern Europe (Yugoslavia) and the Middle East.

The domestic political scene, particularly in Greece and

Turkey, does not permit imaginative moves by their political leaders in reconciling differences. In fact, both countries are likely to seek greater autonomy in foreign relations, much to the chagrin of the United States and NATO. To attempt the prevention of such a development might alienate them and further weaken their ties with the West. US and NATO leaders should recognise these shifts in policy as concomitant developments resulting in the ever-changing domestic and international environment.

Both Greece and Turkey must be assured that they are valued members of the NATO community, and they must be urged to share goals that include, but extend beyond, the narrow boundaries of national security and regional settings. Only under such conditions will both countries make positive contributions to collective defence, and only under such conditions can the United States and NATO repair the fissures in the Southern Flank and re-establish genuine cooperative relations with both allies.

We may now be at the watershed where NATO objectives in the eastern Mediterranean are better served by affording greater credence to political, rather than military, means. This is especially significant in light of the potentially explosive situation in the Middle East–Persian Gulf. As a result, the eastern Mediterranean now takes on additional importance as one of the most strategically critical sea areas, and any reduction in US or NATO strength shifts the balance of power towards the Soviet Union. The key to a secure Mediterranean rests in a stable and durable Southern Flank.

NOTES

[1] *Los Angeles Times,* 29 April 1982, p. 2B. See also Admiral Crowe's lecture to RUSI in March 1983 *Journal.*

[2] Problems within Eastern European countries, such as the Polish crises, are considered as internal problems of the Warsaw Pact. Overall stability between the two alliances is not affected.

[3] Turkey has a 380 mile land frontier with the Soviet Union. Greece borders the Balkan states of Albania, Bulgaria, and Yugoslavia.

[4] This affects and complicates the command structure of NATO.

[5] The Sixth Fleet usually consists of 1 aircraft carrier, 14 escort vessels, 5 nuclear submarines, and 58 combat aircraft. The Fifth Escadra is composed of 1 helicopter carrier, 8 escort vessels, 8–9 attack submarines with nuclear capabilities. These forces are part of the Black Sea Fleet deployed out of Sevastopol. Soviet land-based aircraft are also part of the Black Sea Fleet. The Soviet Navy, because of its lack of access to port facilities in the Mediterranean, will utilise anchorages. These are primarily found in Greek waters

off the coast of Kithera Island, northern Cyprus, and east and south of the island of Crete.

[6] A Kiev class carrier with 15–20 Forger A-V/STOL aircraft periodically deploys in the Mediterranean. The Forgers have a combat radius of about 200 miles.

[7] The Backfire bomber has a combat radius of 3400 miles, while the Blinder's radius is 1925 miles. Both are air refuelable.

[8] Libya's air force inventory includes Blinder bombers, plus Mirages and MiG–23 and MiG–25 fighters.

[9] The flexibility of the air force in deploying its aircraft makes comparisons difficult.

[10] A decision by both governments should be forthcoming shortly. The final decision may rest on which company provides the best "offset" package. This will provide the purchasing country with a chance to finance and co-produce a good part of the aircraft. These "offsets" often include the production and sale of a country's commercial products.

[11] For example, an F-4 Phantom is a good match for the most advanced aircraft that Bulgaria and Romania possess (MiG–23s).

[12] Category 3 units are about 25 per cent of strength, possibly complete with fighting vehicles (some obsolescence).

[13] Greece's armed forces are far better off regarding modernisation than those of Turkey. Turkey will very shortly begin to upgrade her M–48 tanks with the new 105mm gun and new diesel engines. With these modifications, they will be able to hold their own against Russian armour, except for the T–72.

[14] Nuclear warheads are stockpiled in both Greece and Turkey. Both may expect to suffer Soviet counter strike and pre-emptive measures.

[15] Recently General K. Evren did not rule out the possibility of such systems being deployed in Turkey.

[16] Thanos Veremis, *Greek Security Considerations* (Athens: Papazisses Publishers, 1980), p. 103.

[17] PASOK won by an absolute majority with 48.06 per cent of the vote and 172 out of 300 seats in Parliament. The New Democracy Party received 35.86 per cent of the vote and 115 seats, and the Communist Party of the Exterior 10.92 per cent of the vote for 13 seats.

[18] Van Coufoudakis, "Ideology and Pragmatism in Greek Foreign Policy", *Current History,* December 1982, p. 426.

[19] Changes relating to the separation of church and state, civil marriages, family law, and women's eligibility for education and pensions.

[20] Coufoudakis, op. cit., p. 427. Recent legislation takes away from public sector employees the right to call a strike, except when a majority of the members have voted by secret ballot.

[21] For details see *Greece Quarterly Economic Review, No. 2* (London: The Economist Intelligence Unit, 1983).

[22] The Drachma was devalued by 15.5 per cent and there was a draw-down of the nation's oil reserves to reduce petroleum imports, in order to reduce the deficit.

[23] Coufoudakis, op. cit., pp. 428–429.

[24] *Foreign Broadcast Information Service* (*FBIS*), Vol. VII, February 7, 1983, p. 51.

[25] Ibid., Vol. VII, June 3, 1983, p. 52.

[26] Complete details have not, as yet, been released. But the agreement is understood to include US assistance in helping Greece's infant arms industry.

[27] Attempted *coups d'état* continue to plague the polity of Greece, as recently as six months ago. When Papandreou took office he also became defence minister. He is wary of the military, especially the army. In February 1983, a major reshuffling took place at the senior officers' level. He forced many of the senior ranks to retire so that younger and more sympathetic PASOK officers could be advanced.

[28] *FBIS,* Vol. VII, May 16, 1983, p. 56.
[29] Panayiotes Dimitras, "Greece's New Isolationism?", *Public Opinion Quarterly,* February/ March, 1983, pp. 14–15. A survey of 700 individuals was carried out in the greater Athens area where one third of Greece's population resides.
[30] Ibid.
[31] See Lawrence Wittner, *American Intervention in Greece,* 1943–1949 (New York: Columbia University Press, 1982).
[32] Thanos Veremis, *Greek Security: Issues and Politics* (London: The International Institute of Strategic Studies, *Adelphi Papers*), p. 19.
[33] Ibid.
[34] Six coalition governments have ruled Turkey from early 1970 to 1981.
[35] In the six months prior to the *coups d'état* 136 ballots were cast for office of President, yet no one could be elected because of party feuding and the disproportionate influence of minor parties.
[36] Undermining the legitimacy of the polity were armed uprisings of Kurds and other ethnic and religious minorities. In 1980, 200–250 people a month were being killed between various warring groups. To stem the flow of armed attacks, Ankara recently (with the permission of Iraq) crossed their mutual borders with 20,000 armed troops and gendarmarie (across a 25 mile front) in order to eliminate base camps of the rebels.
[37] *FBIS,* Vol. VII, 2 January, 1980.
[38] *Turkey Quarterly Economic Review, No. 2* (London: The Economist Intelligence Unit, 1983).
[39] In addition, there are 16 provisional articles pertaining to the transitional period of Evren's seven year Presidency.
[40] Ninety-two per cent of votes cast favoured passage of the constitution. These votes cast represented 91 per cent of the electorate.
[41] The new parties will have to secure 10 per cent of the vote. This will be the threshold percentage to secure representation in Parliament.
[42] Duygu Bozoğlu Sezer, "Turkey's Security Policies" (London: International Institute for Strategic Studies, *Adelphi Paper,* 1981), pp. 36–37.
[43] In the mid-1960s, US President Lyndon Johnson sent a letter to Turkish Prime Minister Ismet Inonou suggesting that the United States might not come to Turkey's aid in the event of a Soviet attack. Consequently, Turkey decided against intervening in Cyprus despite what it perceived as a legitimate pretext under the Zurich-London accords of 1960 to intervene on behalf of the island's 18 per cent Turkish minority. Johnson's letter humiliated Turkey and made the Turkish armed forces appear to have been manipulated by the self-interest of the US. For details of President Johnson's letter and President Inonou's reply, see *Middle East Journal,* Summer, 1966, pp. 386–93.
[44] It is estimated that over 10,000 Greek officers and NCOs had come to Cyprus secretly.
[45] For details see *Congressional-Executive Relations and the Turkish Arms Embargo* (Washington: US Government Printing Office, 1981).
[46] Predictably, Turkey responded by temporarily closing 26 US-Turkish bases.
[47] *FBIS,* Vol. VII, 13 May 1983, p. T1.
[48] Interviews conducted in Ankara at the Ministry of Foreign Affairs on 28 May 1981.
[49] The United Nations adopted a resolution on 13 May 1983 calling for the early withdrawal of Turkish troops from the island, the return of refugees to their homes, and a renewed effort by the UN Secretary General to find a solution to the problem. As a result of this resolution bizonal talks have been suspended.
[50] Both Greece and Turkey observe the six-mile limit in territorial waters. If Greece extends the limit to 12 miles, Turkey has given notice that it would be a *casus belli.*
[51] The Army of the Aegean (4th Army) is more on paper than a reality.

[52] The exact command and control arrangements in the Aegean are still in conflict. Greece would like to re-establish the pre-1970 control arrangements. As a result of the new arrangements under the "Roger's Plan" two centres were created: one commanded by a Turkish general in Izmir, and on the Greek side, a headquarters in Larrisa controlled by a Greek officer. This latter headquarters has not, as yet, been established. The Aegean conflict festers daily with accusations from both sides that their territorial air space has been infringed. In March 1983, Greece refused to participate in a NATO exercise when the Island of Lemnos was excluded. This island is strategically located almost at the mouth of the Dardanelles.

[53] A further aggravating issue for Turkey was Greece's admittance into the EEC in 1980. This was a psychological blow for Turkey because of how she views her relations with the West.

[54] In June 1983, at the NATO Ministerial meeting, the Greek and Turkish foreign ministers met and discussed problems of mutual concern. This meeting has now spawned additional ones, beginning in July 1983 between senior foreign ministry officials to discuss tourism and economic problems.

[55] *US Interests in the Eastern Mediterranean: Turkey, Greece and Cyprus. A report prepared for the Subcommittee on Europe and the Middle East of the Committee on Foreign Affairs of the US House of Representatives* (Washington: US Printing Office, June 1983), pp. 24–25.

[56] To date, Moscow has avoided linking economic aid to specific political demands. The 1978 Turkish–Soviet Agreement entitled "Principles of Good-Neighbourly and Friendly Relations" did state that neither nation would allow the use of its territory "... for the commission of aggression or subversive actions against the other state..." Literal interpretation of this clause would prevent the operation of US and NATO surveillance bases along Turkey's northern frontiers.

[57] Sezer, op. cit., p. 34.

[58] *FBIS,* Vol. VII, May 13, 1983, p. S4.

[59] After 1981, Greece did not permit the Soviet auxiliary units of the fleet to be repaired at Neorion. Since Papandreou came to power this action has been rescinded.

[60] A prelude to Tikhonou's visit to Athens was the visit of K. Karamanlis to Moscow in 1979.

[61] For details see *FBIS,* Vol. VII, February 23–25, 1983. This agreement provoked the EEC to ask for clarification because bilateral economic agreements are not in keeping with EEC membership.

[62] Many of the weapons that the terrorists possessed throughout the chaotic anarchistic period of the 1980s originated in Bulgaria. The flow of weapons and terrorists has slowed down in the last year.

[63] Veremis, op. cit., p. 9.

[64] Sezer, op. cit., pp. 36–37.

[65] James Brown, "Turkey's Policy in Flux", *Current History,* January 1983, p. 37.

[66] Turkey's trade links with Egypt and Jordan have been tenuous in the past, but are presently being strengthened.

[67] *US Interests in The Eastern Mediterranean: Turkey, Greece and Cyprus,* op. cit., p. 14.

[68] Both Turkey and Saudi Arabia serve on the Islamic Goodwill Mission, which seeks a resolution of the Iran–Iraq conflict.

[69] An exchange of prisoners took place between Iran and Iraq out of Ankara on 1 May 1983. It was through the auspices of the International Red Crescent.

[70] *US Interests in the Eastern Mediterranean: Turkey, Greece and Cyprus,* op. cit., p. 15.

[71] In March 1973, Foreign Minister Ilter Türkmen visited Damascus and was given assurances that aid and comfort would not be given to terrorist groups.

[72] Turkish military leaders profess no concern over the newly installed Syrian SA-5s with

Soviet crews, which pose a threat to Incirliks' operations and areas where the Sixth Fleet operates in the eastern Mediterranean.

[73] Libya has of late, not been fulfilling her contractual obligations to Turkish contractors and labourers. *FBIS,* Vol. VII, 10 May 1983.

[74] *FBIS,* Vol. VII, 25 August, 1981.

[75] During the seige of West Beirut, Greece accepted 200–300 wounded Palestinian fighters for treatment in Greek hospitals.

[76] James P. Wootten, *Regional Support Facilities for the Rapid Deployment Force* (Washington: Congressional Research Service, 1982), p. 2.

[77] Albert Wohlstetter, *Meeting the Threat in the Persian Gulf* (Marina Del Ray, California: European American Institute for Security Research, 1981), p. 180.

[78] A NATO fighter-bomber (F–111) flying out of Mus could cover the entire Transcaucasian border region without having to refuel, and put NATO planes some 550 miles from Teheran and 700 miles from the mouth of the Persian Gulf. By contrast, the RFD base at Ras Banas, Egypt is at least 1000 miles from the Persian Gulf.

[79] Recent discussions between the United States and Egypt on the Ras Banas base have been stalled. If these negotiations falter the RDF force would lose one of its important staging areas for the Persian Gulf.

[80] Both Greece and Spain reserved a part or all of their government's position on this communiqué.

[81] Both France and Britain have cooperated in providing forces for the Middle East–Persian Gulf. France has a large permanent naval presence in the Indian Ocean (12–20 combat vessels) operating out of Djibouti and Mayotte. The French forces include approximately 6000 ground forces. Britain is less visible in her military presence but has extensive military advisors throughout the Persian Gulf. Also, she conducts naval exercises annually in the region.

[82] Emphasis added by the author.

[83] Geoffrey Kemp, "East–West Strategy in the Middle East–Persian Gulf", in Kenneth A. Myers (ed.), *NATO The Next Thirty Years* (Boulder: Westview Press, 1980), p. 220.

[84] Ibid.

The Cape Route and the Persian Gulf: A Warsaw Pact Perspective

Dr Christopher Coker

Dr Christopher Coker is a Lecturer in International Relations at the London School of Economics and Political Science and is the author of several books and articles on NATO, the Alliance and Africa

The oil crisis of 1973 and the collapse of the Portuguese empire in Southern Africa were both seminal events for NATO's strategic planners. Ever since contingency plans have been given new life as have force configurations which go well beyond mere contingency planning. The Rapid Deployment Force in the Middle East, now renamed Central Command to stress its importance; the discussion of out-of-area operations which finds NATO as usual divided and largely incapable of concerted action, have become familiar points of departure for those who set themselves the task of assessing the strategic threat which the Alliance faces. Out-of-area problems, in fact, have spawned a large body of literature on both sides of the Atlantic.

Less attention, if any, has been given to Warsaw Pact out-of-area interests, none at all to its out-of-area planning. This paper will discuss what those interests encompass in the sphere of shipping, oil and strategic minerals; look at the extent to which the Warsaw Pact as an organisation has intervened outside the European theatre; and enquire whether the Warsaw Pact has an overall strategy.

The Pact, in fact, finds itself in a curious predicament. To address the NATO 'threat' outside Europe is to speak to its own image in a mirror, an image a little altered by a flaw in the glass which throws back a likeness not of what it is, but of what it might become if its dependence on oil and strategic minerals were to increase substantially over the next few years.

The Cape Route and Soviet Bloc Shipping

For those who are so preoccupied by the threat to Western shipping posed by the rapid growth of the Soviet blue water

STRATEGIC MAP OF AFRICA AS SEEN BY THE WARSAW PACT
(Azimuthal Equidistant Projection centred on Cape Town)

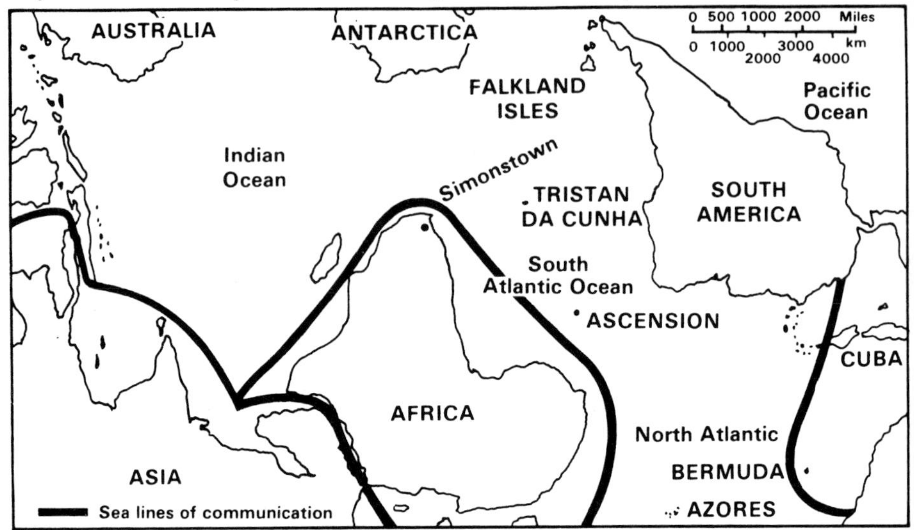

AUSTRALIA
ANTARCTICA
FALKLAND ISLES
0 500 1000 2000 Miles
0 1000 2000 3000 4000 km
Pacific Ocean
Indian Ocean
Simonstown
TRISTAN DA CUNHA
SOUTH AMERICA
South Atlantic Ocean
ASCENSION
CUBA
AFRICA
North Atlantic
BERMUDA
AZORES
ASIA
Sea lines of communication

STRATEGIC MAP OF AFRICA AS SEEN BY NATO

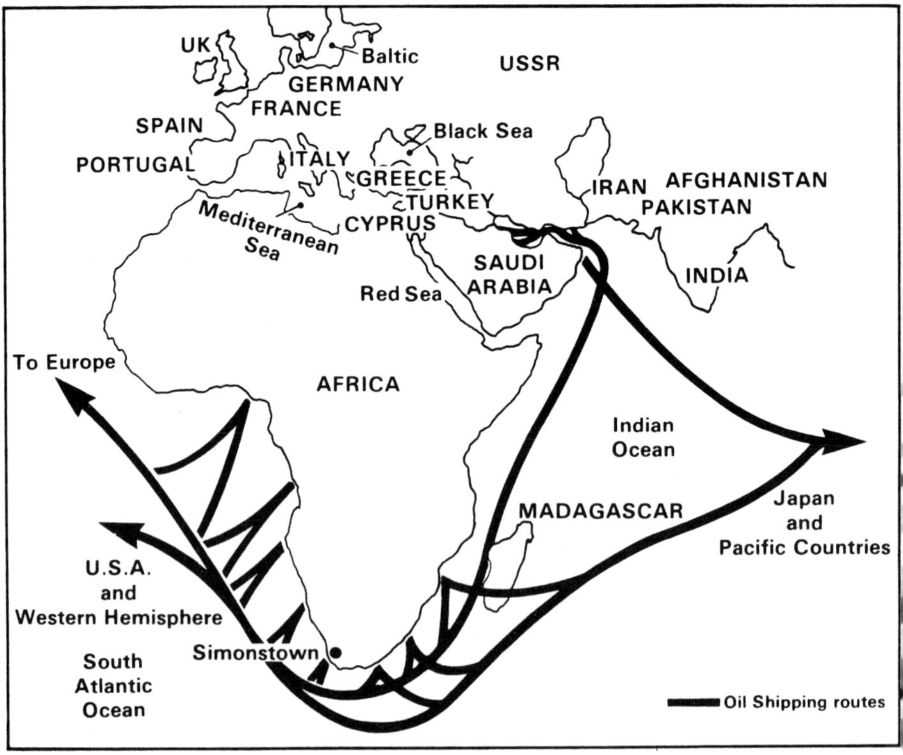

UK
Baltic
USSR
GERMANY
FRANCE
SPAIN
PORTUGAL
ITALY
Black Sea
GREECE
TURKEY
IRAN
AFGHANISTAN
PAKISTAN
Mediterranean Sea
CYPRUS
SAUDI ARABIA
INDIA
Red Sea
To Europe
AFRICA
Indian Ocean
MADAGASCAR
Japan and Pacific Countries
U.S.A. and Western Hemisphere
Simonstown
South Atlantic Ocean
Oil Shipping routes

navy, it is not surprising that so little thought is given to East European interests, or, for that matter, the interests of the Soviet merchant fleet, Morflot, which is now the sixth largest in the world, and which since 1980 has had more dry cargo ships on order than any other.

In its strategic planning, Moscow is in no position totally to disregard the interests of its allies which are so tied to developments south of the Tropic of Cancer that one Soviet writer has questioned whether the strategy of interdiction has a future.[1] Other Soviet writers have laid great stress on the fact that the Cape route carries a substantial percentage of East European shipping which is in constant risk of interdiction by the West. NATO may well fear an armed attack along the Cape route, but the Warsaw Pact faces a threat at the Cape itself — for its members have no doubt on whose side South Africa will be counted were war to break out.[2]

The Soviet Navy has many missions but it is worth remembering that Admiral Gorshkov lists the protection of 'state interests' as its primary role in time of peace. While it is unlikely that the threats to shipping lanes will necessarily determine Soviet policy, they may well influence it. The Soviet Navy's mission may well be one of sea denial rather than sea control, but the distinction is hardly valid in its day to day operations.

It is worth bearing in mind the extent of Soviet bloc shipping activities. In 1977, Morflot carried over 10 per cent of Eastern Europe's East African trade, a percentage which has continued to rise ever since.[3] In 1980, Poland's Best Line was so competitive that at one point it looked as though the East African Shipping Line (EASL) might be forced out of business. In the period 1982–83, that is in only 18 months, Morflot launched no fewer than 31 sailings on the East Africa route.[4]

Off the West African coast, the Soviet Union operates a shipping line jointly with Poland and the GDR. In fact, at any one time 18 per cent of the Soviet merchant fleet is to be found in the waters off Cape Verde.[5] West Africa is also the largest area of activity for Poland's seaborne trade in the Third World, as well as a major transit route for its material and liquid fuel imports.

But it is, of course, the presence of Morflot which is crucial to any understanding of the Soviet Union's own preoccupation with the safety of its shipping and the security of its main trade routes. All in all, Morflot carries 50 per cent of its trade, substantially more cargo from freight owners of non-Russian origin, and earns more foreign currency than any other activity except for the export of oil and arms.[6] Given the scope of these operations, it would be surprising if the Soviet Union were not anxious about the security of its shipping. Its concerns are no less real than our own; indeed, in some respects they may even be greater.

It must always be remembered that its merchant fleet constitutes the third most important element in the international network for the movement of raw materials, complementing its rail and pipeline systems. At present, the Russians are increasing their tanker fleet to supplement or replace their existing vessels with those of the *Marshall Vasilievski* class with a capacity of 65,000 tons. The latter may play an important role in carrying supplies of oil and minerals from the Middle East and Southern Africa.[7] In this light, it is difficult objectively to evaluate who represents the greater threat to the other: NATO or the Warsaw Pact.

Persian Gulf

The shelling of the Romanian cargo ship *Olanesti* in the Shatt-al-Arab four years ago, a few months into the Iraq-Iran war, provided a stark reminder of Eastern Europe's vulnerability in the Middle East, and the extent to which its dependence on OPEC oil has grown from being a marginal to a significant component of its oil imports.

In this respect, no country is more vulnerable than Czechoslovakia which began importing oil from Iran long before the 1973 crisis. After the Soviet Union began to impose energy quotas on its COMECON partners, Iran emerged as a major supplier. Until the fall of the Shah forced a major rethinking, Prague expected to obtain up to a third of all its oil imports from Iran by the end of the 1980s — a much larger percentage than would have been the case for any other COMECON member.[8]

The extent of Czechoslovakia's dependence may not be typical, but the trend is. As the implicit discount given by the Soviet Union for its own oil exports fell in a few years from 60 per cent to 25 per cent of the OPEC price, and as the Russians began to impose strict quotas on the amount of oil they were prepared to sell at a discount, so Eastern Europe was increasingly forced to look to the OPEC producers. They were strongly influenced at the time by the not unreasonable assumption that after the OPEC price rises of 1973–74 world energy prices would, for the most part, remain stable and that energy production in the Gulf would continue at present levels, or beyond. Neither the second round of OPEC price increases in 1979–81, nor the political developments that unseated the Shah and precipitated a war between Eastern Europe's two principal suppliers could have been, or were, foreseen.

The Iranian revolution revealed just how vulnerable the East Europeans were to political instability and political events over which neither they nor the Soviet Union had much control. Before the Shah's fall, Czechoslovakia had expected to import up to 3,600m cubic metres of natural gas a year by 1985, but after 1979, it could no longer count on such deliveries and had to admit that negotiations on other possibilities had ended without concrete result.[9]

Other countries were similarly affected, including Romania, traditionally a net oil exporter, who managed to sign an agreement in 1980 to purchase an extra 60,000 barrels of Iranian crude, an amount which, in addition to its existing purchases merely brought imports back to their 1978 level.[10] But Romania's relations with Iran have an amusing sequel. So anxious was Bucharest to increase Iranian purchases that it sent a Moslem delegation to Teheran in March 1979, the first time a communist country had despatched a religious delegation abroad to obtain economic concessions from another state. The fact that there were fewer than 40,000 members of the Moslem community in Romania made the manoeuvre even more transparent.

Southern African Minerals

For almost 15 years, the Soviet Union has been attempting to gain access to strategic minerals on privileged terms, nowhere more so than in Southern Africa. Neo-mercantilism has been a major theme of Soviet writing[11] and has been amply revealed in the content of Soviet speeches for those who care to analyse them. As early as his economic report to the 23rd CPSU Congress in April 1966, Kosygin talked of the need to use economic power to gain a privileged economic position in the Third World and the need to supplement the old strategy of using it to buy political influence. This policy appears to have been continued under Kosygin's successor, Nikolai Tikhonov, who was responsible for negotiating a major economic and technical agreement with Angola two years ago. The reasons why the Soviet Union should have chosen to espouse neo-mercantilism are quite simple: both the quality and quantity of its own mineral exports have begun to decline substantially in recent years.

The subject is an exhaustive one which I have discussed elsewhere.[12] Two examples are all that space allows here, although both are highly revealing. While the Soviet Union clearly remains quantitatively self-sufficient in chromite, the quality of its own ore has fallen precipitously. In the late 1970s, it was forced on two occasions to turn to African suppliers, buying 2000 tonnes from Zambia and Zaire. In this instance, the East Europeans anticipated the Russians. Purchases of copper from Zambia in 1970 represented the first sustained attempt by COMECON, as an institution, to develop a coherent minerals strategy.[13]

Even more serious than lapses in the quality of Soviet imports, however, is the prospect of imminent shortages. COMECON now faces the threat of a declining share in the world output of several minerals including such vital commodities as copper, bauxite and phosphates. It is also confronted with the prospect, not of short term shortages of the type which have traditionally plagued the western world as a result of cyclical factors — such as unexpected political crises or protracted strikes — but of long term supply shortages arising from a structural deficit with which it is much more difficult to live. COMECON has already suffered from such shortages, most notably of aluminium and coking coal during periods of oversupply in the world market. In some circumstances it may be faced with a sustained regional disequilibrium between supply and demand.[14]

It is hardly surprising, therefore, that its respective members have begun to invest large capital sums in raw material extraction and processing. Of the East European countries, none has been more consistent in the development of Third World reserves than East Germany. By 1979 the GDR had set up 500 complete plants in the Third World which, according to its Secretary for Foreign Trade had created the conditions for a reliable, long term supply of raw materials.[15] In Southern Africa its focus of interest has largely been directed at Mozambique. As the costs of developing and mining its own coal resources have risen by at least 50 per cent, it has naturally become interested in overseas supplies. In 1977, the East Germans took over the management of the Moatize fields which, with 700m tons, are some of the richest in the region.

Unfortunately, the East Germans have found that political developments are as unpredictable in Africa as they are in the

Middle East, and perhaps, more to the point, that the Soviet Union has played only a marginal role in shaping them. Back in 1977, attempts to pump out the Chipanga 7 coal mine in Moatize after the onset of severe flooding were hampered by persistent Rhodesian raids on the railway line which, in turn, stopped the import of diesel fuel for the pumps.[16] Five years later, the East Germans stood by helplessly as attacks by anti-FRELIMO guerrillas brought to an abrupt halt the renovation of the Condo-Derunde railway, causing a bottleneck on the line to the Moatize fields where more than a year's production of coal was stockpiled.[17]

Warsaw Pact Out-of-area Operations

Despite their real economic interests in the Third World, the members of the Warsaw Pact are acutely aware of their weak position. As they look to the Middle East and Southern Africa, they see that their principal ally the Soviet Union has been excluded by the United States from any constructive role in regional security. In the Middle East, the Geneva Conference is merely a memory. The Camp David process has effectively squeezed Moscow out of account. Indeed, Moscow has ceased to be a major factor in the Arab–Israeli dispute since the Fahmi–Gromyko talks seven years ago. It is difficult, therefore, to detect any specific Warsaw Pact initiative in the region. The only constructive role has been played by Romania which tried to keep channels open even to Sadat as in 1981 when Ceausescu's special envoy, Vasile Pungan, briefed the Egyptian government on the Warsaw Pact summit which had just met in Moscow. Even though Bucharest originally accepted the Camp David accords as a step on the road to a 'just and durable Middle East settlement', it is interesting that the actual terms Ceausescu's has advocated for a comprehensive political settlement have in recent years, grown increasingly nearer to those advocated by Moscow: that Israel should withdraw from the occupied territories; that it should accept the creation of an independent Palestinian state and the PLO as the sole representative of the Palestinian people; and that such a settlement must be reached within the framework of an international conference with the mandatory participation of the Soviet Union. It is certainly not in Romania's interests for the regional order in the Middle East to be determined by the NATO powers whose own priorities, in the event of another political or economic crisis, might differ considerably from its own.

Similar considerations appear to apply to the Gulf. During a visit to Kuwait in October 1982, Hungary's Head of State defending the right of the Gulf states 'to maintain their own security to the exclusion of foreign powers', condemned imperialist attempts to place the region and its oilfields under foreign hegemony, a veiled reference to the Rapid Deployment Force and the ever burgeoning American presence.

Nevertheless, despite this unanimity, the Pact has been unable to act decisively in defence of its interests. More often than not, its members have had to strike up their own bilateral deals with the Arab states. In the short term, they have made some headway in narrowing the oil deficit they suffered when Iran and Iraq went to war by exchanging arms for oil. At the beginning of 1981, the Iraqi Minister for Industry and Minerals visited Bucharest to discuss increasing oil supplies in return for spare parts. Romania has also been courted by Iran which, in a surprising move, offered more flexible credit terms for oil purchases in exchange for arms.[18]

In Southern Africa, by comparison, it does seem possible to talk of a Warsaw Pact initiative — in fact, three such initiatives, even if none of them came to very much. And it does seem possible to detect a strategy for the region which has influenced the thinking of its members. It was Richard Löwenthal who argued some years ago that the Soviet Union had begun to move from an old-style anti-imperialism to a new concept, that of counter-imperialism — 'a strategy of fighting imperialism by using the familiar imperialist methods of establishing zones of political and economic influence linked to the Soviet Union by firm ties'.[19] One need not subscribe to Löwenthal's model entirely to accept that the Warsaw Pact has recently pursued a policy designed to counter NATO threats to its Third World allies, whether those threats are more imaginary than real. As the GDR leader Erich Honnecker told a conference in East Berlin in October 1980, the support the East had given to movements of national liberation had 'nothing in common with the export of revolution', but was aimed solely against the export of counter-revolution by the West.[20]

East German attempts to discredit the Anglo-American initiative in Zimbabwe and the Contact Group's efforts in Namibia were intended to counter a NATO-orchestrated 'offensive against the national liberation forces in Africa.' During a tour of Africa the year before, Honnecker had warned the Front Line States against the extension of NATO's field of activity to Africa,[21] a persistent theme of East German diplomacy. East Germany's intervention is interesting because it seems to represent an overall Warsaw Pact strategy which was first formulated in November 1978 during a meeting of its Consultative Committee, when aid to the liberation movements was specifically discussed in the context of aid to the Front Line States. The Pact appears to have guaranteed them against South African intervention, a subject which five years later appears to have been high on the agenda of the meeting at Hradcany Castle where once again there was general condemnation of 'recent acts of aggression committed by the apartheid regime, against the progressive peoples of Southern Africa'.

That the task of defending the FLS fell mostly to the GDR seems clear from the absence of its Defence Minister, General Hoffmann, from an important meeting of the Pact's Military Council in Budapest. His tour of Southern Africa which took place at precisely the same time clearly revealed where the priorities of the organisation really lay. Given the fact that the GDR is second only to the Soviet Union in importance, it seems quite probable that it has assumed responsibility for a military strategy which has the express backing of its Warsaw Pact allies. There appear to have been three occasions on which the GDR acted to defend the FLS, or to press ahead with an initiative at variance with Western aims and objectives. In May 1977, *The Observer* carried a report that the GDR had been allocated the task of destabilising Zaire and thus forcing it to withdraw its support for the FNLA guerrillas who had been harrying the MPLA government for several years.

On behalf of the other Pact members, Berlin apparently agreed to two courses of action: first, to provide the FNLC guerrillas with military equipment including a strike capacity against the Zairean air force so that the movement could mount a lightning thrust against, among other targets, the military base at Kamina; and secondly, to create 45 separate pockets of 'permanent revolution' in Shaba, supported with arms from Angolan bases.[22]

In the course of 1977, a large number of Czech heavy duty military transports were delivered to the FNLC who also received military training from several hundred German experts. It seems that this programme was deliberately kept separate from Cuban support; and that it was clearly understood from the outset that the GDR would not get involved directly even at the cost of military failure.

The second major initiative in which the GDR became involved was a last minute attempt to forestall a settlement in Zimbabwe orchestrated by Britain and the United States. The story first appeared in David Martin's book *The Struggle for Zimbabwe* (1981) and seems to have encompassed a plan to defeat international recognition for the government of Abel Muzorewa which had been brought into existence by a highly controversial internal settlement with Ian Smith. The plan called for the forces of ZANU and ZAPU to declare themselves the legal government of Zimbabwe at a base inside the country, not far from the South African border, under the protection of Mozambique's army. The GDR promised in return massive military aid to prevent either Rhodesia or South Africa from invading Mozambique itself. This rather foolhardy plan was vetoed at the eleventh hour by the FLS themselves who had no particular wish at this juncture to escalate a guerrilla war into a major conventional confrontation between Rhodesia and its immediate neighbours.

Finally, the GDR seems to have played a major role in the Soviet Union's rather transparent attempt in 1982 to meet the joint American–South African call for the withdrawal of Cuban troops from Angola as a *quid pro quo* for a settlement in Namibia by transferring the Cubans to Mozambique and replacing them with East German soldiers. Between October and December, there was a significant increase in East German interest. The East German Defence Minister had official talks with Raoul Castro, his Cuban counterpart. In November, there was a meeting between the East German Defence Minister and the chief of Mozambique's air force. The Angolan Defence Minister paid a five day official visit to the GDR and Cuba. The chief of the East German general staff visited Cuba as well.

All this activity suggests a coordinated initiative: to transfer the duties of the Cuban forces to East Germany, with the possible participation of Bulgaria and Hungary whose Defence Minister also visited Angola in this period to observe the struggle and returned to Budapest with a comprehensive military agreement between the two countries. Only South Africa's uncompromising insistence that it would not tolerate the transfer of Cuban troops elsewhere in Southern Africa brought this initiative to an end.

It is not altogether surprising that given its economic interests in Southern Africa, the Warsaw Pact should have become directly involved since 1978. Recent developments within the Pact itself have pointed to a much greater coordination of effort. In the Brezhnev years, the Political Consultative Committee gained in importance. To facilitate the better coordination of foreign policy, meetings of the Foreign Ministers have been convened regularly since 1969, and in 1976 a Committee of Foreign Ministers was added to the Pact's formal command structure.

Soviet intervention in Angola merely highlighted an issue which had previously been the subject of speculation: the possibility that the East Europeans might be called upon to render some form of military assistance outside Europe. It has been widely rumoured that Soviet leaders twice made such an appeal — in 1969 at the time of the Sino–Soviet border clashes and in 1979 during the Chinese invasion of Vietnam. The need to deter the West and its supposed client South Africa from challenging the new political order in Southern Africa may have constituted a third case which has still to be resolved.

NOTES

[1] Dmitry Volsky 'A strategy without a Future' *New Times,* 3 August 1978.

[2] Dmitry Volsky 'Southern version of NATO' *New Times,* 25 September 1978.

[3] James Ellis 'Expansion of the Soviet Merchant Fleet — Implications for the West' *NATO Review* 3 1979 pp. 22 (ref 4).

[4] *The Challenge of Soviet Shipping* (London: Aims of Industry 1983) p. 9.

[5] Michael Davidchik/Robert Mahoney 'Soviet Civil Fleets in the Third World' in Bradford Dismukes/James McConnel *Soviet Naval Policy in the Third World* (New York: Pergamon 1979).

[6] Robert Athay 'Perspectives on Soviet Merchant Shipping' in Michael McGwire (ed) *Soviet Naval Deployments* (New York: Praeger 1973) p. 101.

[7] David Scrivener 'Merchant Marine in Soviet Naval Strategy' *Marine Policy* 7:2 April 1983 p. 119.

[8] *Rude Pravo,* 12 November 1976.

[9] *Rude Pravo,* 15 August 1979.

[10] *The New York Times,* 23 April 1980.

[11] See in particular V I Kiselyova *Africa: Integration and Problems of Economic Relations* (Moscow: Nauka Publishers 1972) R Ulyanovsky 'The Energy Crisis and the Struggle of the Newly Independent Countries for Economic Equality' *Narody Asii i Afriki* No 8 June 1976 pp. 25–6; and E Tarabin 'The Third World and Imperialism: Something New in the Correlation of Forces' *Mirovaia Ekonomika Mezdunarodnye Otnosheniya* No 2 February 1976.

[12] See the author's forthcoming *NATO, the Warsaw Pact and Africa* to be published by the RUSI, 1985.

[13] Arpad Orosz *Trade of African Developing Countries up to 1970 and Prognosis up to 1980* Studies on Developing Countries No 70 (Budapest: Institute for World Economy 1975) p. 70.

[14] Istvan Dobozi 'Projected Trends of World Raw Material and Energy Markets up to

2000' *Studies on Developing Countries* No 110 (Budapest: Institute for World Economics 1982) p. 20.

[15] *Neues Deutschland,* 28/29 April 1979.

[16] *African Economic Digest* 1:24 October 1980.

[17] *African Economic Digest* 3:36 December 1982.

[18] *Petroleum Economist* No 7 July 1981, p. 311.

[19] Richard Löwenthal *Model or Ally: the Communist Powers and the Developing Countries* (Oxford Univ Press 1977), pp. 359–76.

[20] Opening address at the International Conference of Third World Groups, East Berlin, October 1980.

[21] Cited *Africa Contemporary Record 1979–80* (ed) Colin Legum (London: Rex Collings 1980) p. A167.

[22] *The Observer,* 21 May 1978.

Defence and Security in Europe: A German View

REAR ADMIRAL DR KURT FISCHER

Defence Attache, Embassy of the Federal Republic of Germany, London

DEFENCE planning for the Federal Republic of Germany has always been based on the premise that the goals of her security policy can only be achieved within the framework of the North Atlantic Alliance, that commonality of security interests is a prerequisitc for her safety. Such commonalty of security interests applies as much to the direct East–West confrontation in Europe as it does to the global dimension of security caused by political and ideological antagonism.

No other European country has so many neighbours as Germany. Her situation in the centre of Europe makes her external security dependent upon the balance of power in Europe. In this century such a balance could not be kept without assistance from outside Europe. After two wars, Europe and Germany are divided, both are linked directly to the policies of the two opposing world powers. The peoples of the Western part of Europe aligned themselves by choice; the nations of Eastern Europe were chained to the Soviet Union without a choice. The foundation of the Federal Republic of Germany, assisted by the Western allies and by the own free will of her inhabitants to build a free and democratic society, brought about the decision for an integration into the West. This was made manifest on 5 May 1955 as the Federal Republic of Germany became the fifteenth country to accede to the North Atlantic Treaty. This historic decision linked her fate with that of the community of free democratic peoples.

The development of a state of military equilibrium between NATO and the Warsaw Pact is the most important factor for the security of the Atlantic Alliance. The confrontation of the military forces of the two superpowers in central Europe has created both a stability lacking in other parts of the world and a military build-up in peacetime hitherto unknown in history.

This concentration of forces in Europe is part of the global balance between East and West which, for four decades, has been the basis of security of the West and peace in Europe. It is the objective of the Alliance to stabilise this balance on the lowest possible level of armament. Any one-sided change would threaten this security. This is why, with the relentless arms build-up by the Soviets, it is now necessary to aim for conformable adjustments by increasing defence efforts which go hand in hand with an active arms control policy.

Any attempt to attain a more relaxed relationship with the Soviet Union can only be made on the basis of a stable state of military equilibrium. NATO's aim is not to gain military superiority or to threaten the states of the Warsaw Pact, but the Alliance is designed along defensive lines and confines its military capabilities to the minimum potential needed for defence against any direct threat.

Despite the political and ideological differences existing between the two systems, constructive relations between East and West are important. The last four decades have shown that relations, even treaties, are feasible and make peace more secure. For this the political cohesion and the strategic unity of the Western Alliance are essential prerequisites. This would not only be of benefit to the allied countries within NATO but also to the wider international political scene. Thus, German security continues to be based on the North Atlantic Alliance and the presence of strong allied forces on German soil. Likewise, there can be no substitute for the Alliance in terms of the defence readiness and political will of the Federal Republic of Germany.

The security of Europe is a geographical, economic and military problem for all the nations facing the Soviet Union as a continental power. Geography puts the Soviet Union in a central position opposite the comparably smaller Western part of the European continent. Maintaining the political and military balance in the East–West relationship and restoring it wherever it is endangered must, therefore, always be the Alliance's priority.

Germany's Contribution

Germany's contribution to the defence of the Alliance corresponds to her specific geographic situation along the roughly 1,000 miles of dividing line between NATO and the

Warsaw Pact. The German combat forces are the only ones in the Alliance already assigned to NATO in peacetime. The *Bundeswehr,* with its 36 field army brigades and six home defence brigades, provides 50 per cent of NATO land forces in central Europe, 50 per cent of ground air defence and 30 per cent of all combat aircraft. For the defence of the northern flank at sea, the German navy provides about a third of all the European naval forces available, including 70 per cent of the NATO naval forces in the Baltic and 100 per cent of its naval air forces. The *Bundeswehr* has made considerable efforts to strengthen the conventional combat forces of NATO. In 1982, two additional brigades of the Territorial Army were earmarked for assignment to NATO and another four brigades restructured so that they can cooperate with other NATO forces or be placed under NATO command and control. Additionally, it has been agreed to expand the area of operations of the German navy to the entire northern flank to give NATO commanders more flexibility in the conduct of operations in line with the growing Soviet naval threat from the Kola peninsula.

Moreover, in April 1982, the Federal Government reached an agreement with the United States Government to strengthen NATO conventional forces with a view to support the rapid reinforcements of US troops. According to this Wartime Host Nation Support (WHNS) Agreement, the United States undertakes to reinforce its divisions and air elements stationed in Germany in crisis or war by six divisions and by 30 air squadrons within ten days. The German Government agreed to set up and to maintain a comprehensive support organisation of 1,500 personnel in peacetime which, in a crisis, would be augmented by roughly 90,000 men from the reserve.

The greatest financial contributions to European security are made by the Federal Republic of Germany together with the United States, the United Kingdom and France. The national shares in the total defence expenditure of all NATO nations in 1982 were as follows:

Total Defence Expenditure

United States	66.1	per cent
United Kingdom	8.2	,, ,,
Federal Republic of Germany	7.5	,, ,,
France	7.4	,, ,,
Italy	3.1	,, ,,
Canada	2.1	,, ,,

The remainder was shared by the other NATO countries. The European share of NATO's overall expenditure has risen from 22 to 33 per cent by NATO criteria during the past 25 years. At present, the Federal Republic of Germany pays 29.2 per cent — including expenditure on Berlin — the largest contribution to the European share in the NATO budget.

Conscription in Germany makes an essential contribution to its ability to keep forces of 495,000 men strong in peacetime. Conscription also guarantees that the *Bundeswehr* can be augmented in crisis to 1.3 million men within three days.

From the aspect of defence spending, the Federal Republic of Germany carries a heavy burden to fulfill further NATO tasks — for example in the NATO infrastructure and Airborne Warning and Control System (AWACS). Germany bears by far the largest European share, namely 26.5 per cent, of NATO's common infrastructure programmes. Looking at AWACS, Germany, with her share of 31 per cent, comes second only to the United States. Furthermore, the Federal Republic of Germany provides major portions of NATO's budgets. With 15.5 per cent, she bears the third highest share of the civilian budget of NATO, with 19.4 per cent the fourth highest share in the military budget of NATO.

Allied Forces in Germany

The stationing of forces in peacetime is a main feature of NATO's deterrence strategy. In no other allied country are so many forces stationed as in the Federal Republic of Germany. This ensures that the principle of collective forward defence as a main part of NATO strategy is kept visible. On the other hand, this also puts a heavy burden on the citizens of Germany. Military forces of six allied nations are stationed on German soil:

233,000 from the United States
65,000 from the United Kingdom
50,000 from France
32,000 from Belgium
6,700 from the Netherlands
5,400 from Canada

Altogether, there are 392,000 allied servicemen and 325,000 dependents living in the Federal Republic of Germany. Another 9,500 men from the protective powers are stationed in West Berlin: 3,700 Americans, 3,100 British and 2,700 French.

Furthermore, there is no other Western country in NATO with such a concentration of military installations in a confined space. For military purposes, an area of 402,800 hectares is used, of that 253,000 ha for the *Bundeswehr* and 149,000 ha for the allied forces. Nowhere in the world is air traffic as dense as in the air space above the Federal Republic of Germany. There are four million flights every year of which 580,000 are military — 380,000 carried out by German and 200,000 by allied forces. Of this total 110,000 flights a year are at low-level. Furthermore, there is no other country in the West where more military exercises are conducted in such a confined area as in the Federal Republic of Germany. Every year some 5,000 military exercises are held lasting from three to four days and involving up to 2,000 men. Eighty exercises with more than 2,000 men involved last more than four days. The cost of damage caused by these exercises totals about 240 million DM a year.

To provide and maintain all this, the Federal Budget in 1984 totals 58,95 billion DM on the basis of uniform NATO criteria. That means 3.2 per cent more than last year. The necessity of consolidating the Federal Budget on the one hand and maintaining the combat strength and operational readiness of the German forces on the other has led to a balanced compromise. The Defence Budget's rate of increase goes almost entirely into capital outlay: into research and development, into the replacement of new generations of major weapon systems and into infrastructure, both national and NATO.

No member of the Alliance, other than the Federal Republic of Germany is situated at the spear point of the Warsaw Pact forces. NATO's response to this situation is the military integration and stationing in peacetime of forces from various allied countries on German soil. Today, combat-ready forces of six allied nations are present to make clear to a possible aggressor that any attack upon the Federal Republic of Germany would be tantamount to an attack upon her allies.

Forward Defence

The governing principle of NATO's defence planning, in view of the geostrategic situation in central Europe, is forward defence. This is not a political doctrine but the consequence of the very fact that the West German territory is but a narrow corridor lying across the avenue of attack towards Western Europe: less than 300 km to Rotterdam, just 200 km to the

Rhine at Karlsruhe. This corridor is confronted with the bulk of the most combat-effective ground and air forces of the Warsaw Pact. The Federal Republic of Germany is all the more affected since 25 per cent of the West German population live in a border area only 100 km deep, where also approximately 30 per cent of the industrial production base is located. This fact denies the Federal Republic of Germany any alternative to the concept of forward defence.

The principle of forward defence compels the Warsaw Pact to take comprehensive steps to mobilise and to concentrate additional forces if it intends to launch an attack with any prospects of success. On the other hand, forward defence does not exclude the necessity of flexible defence. Mobility and fire power of NATO's armoured forces along the intra-German border will allow forces to concentrate, to mount local counter-attacks and carry out flanking operations.

It has been proposed that forward defence should be substituted by defence-in-area to make more use of time and area. The advantages of this manner of fighting are seen in weakening an enemy during his advance into West German territory and finally bringing him to a halt in depth. The advocates of this defence-in-area strategy neglect to consider that due to the very specific situation of the Federal Republic of Germany, there is no space available to fight such a delaying action against an aggressor. The densely populated areas near the border-line with their economic infrastructures prohibit such a strategy. Deterrence means to be ready to defend NATO territory by every means so that from the very first moment, an aggressor will have to bear the full brunt of the defence. The situation of the Federal Republic of Germany is not suited to a kind of defence which would give up ground in order to gain time. Therefore, forward defence is the cornerstone of any military strategy. Retaking lost territory calls for strong mechanised forces and air superiority. Defence-in-area would be a strategy in favour of the conduct of war rather than its prevention. This would assist any aggressor from the East, for once he has gained impetus in a major attack, he could rely on the conventional power of his ground and air forces and the defender would not stand the slightest military chance of stopping him.

The capability of successful forward defence is ultimately determined by the available reserves in terms of personnel and material. At present, these reserves are just about adequate. Any further reduction would result in the loss of our defence capability. For the allied forces to be effective in combat, sufficient stocks of conventional ammunition and other reserves such as POL have to be on hand. Only continuous and appropriate efforts in peacetime could build up an adequate stock-pile to provide the fighting forces with everything they need.

Military Balance

The allied forces in central Europe are capable of effective defence against an attack. Due to the Warsaw Pact's superiority which is considerable, as well as its options of attack in central Europe, the capability for conventional defence requires a high standard of training, equipment and armament combined with an operational readiness of both personnel and material. Any assessment of the military balance of forces between NATO and the Warsaw Pact has to take into account, that owing to strategic nuclear parity and the continuing nuclear build-up by the Soviets in all fields, conventional forces are gaining in importance.

Furthermore, one has to bear in mind that the disparity of land forces of both sides has increased in Europe, even though the Western Alliance has been able to gain ground at least in some areas. The former lead of NATO's land forces in combined arms combat has lessened. Structural changes, especially in Soviet land forces, have essentially improved the operational as well as tactical flexibility of the armies of the Warsaw Pact. As air attack forces of both NATO and Warsaw Pact are almost equal in strength but NATO's ground-based air defence is inferior, it facilitates the Warsaw Pact to give its offensive operations air support. Moreover, NATO's lead in quality has decreased since the 1970s. So the numerical superiority of the Warsaw Pact forces has gained in weight.

This shows that the situation of NATO has become more difficult. Due to the Warsaw Pact's conventional superiority, NATO has to rely on nuclear deterrent for the near future. On the other hand, NATO has to strengthen its conventional capabilities to avoid any necessity for the use of nuclear weapons at an early stage and has to reduce its dependence on nuclear escalation. Although the Federal Government is and has been prepared to examine new strategic ideas, it does not believe — keeping in mind what has been stated above — that a strategic revolution is in sight. It has issued some principles which, from a German perspective, are not to be violated:

- The paramount aim of German security policy is the prevention of war — both nuclear and conventional.
- This can be achieved only by credible deterrence.
- Deterrence calls for the discernible ability and preparedness for military defence at every level.
- The population of a country must accept and support a strategy, since deterrence also requires the will of the people to assert themselves.
- One's own strategy must be understood and considered effective by every potential enemy.
- For the Federal Republic of Germany, there can be no national defence and consequently no national military strategy.
- The forces and resources necessary for the conduct of a strategy must be financially feasible and the necessary manpower must be available.
- No less secure zones or zones of differing risk must be allowed to exist in the Alliance or in the Federal Republic of Germany.
- Strategy and arms control efforts must be in consonance.

With these guiding principles on record, the North Atlantic Alliance will be able to serve the free peoples in Europe and North America. It will continue to be adaptable to demands and conditions of the future because the Alliance will continue to exist in the spirit it was founded — ready to defend, ready to negotiate arms control and disarmament and a threat only to an aggressor.

UK Defence Policy: Seeking Better Value for Money

DR K. HARTLEY
Director, Institute for Research in the Social Sciences, York University

DEFENCE is costly. For 1984–85, the UK planned to spend some £17 billion (bn) or about 5.5 per cent of national income on military forces designed to "keep the peace". Moreover, since 1978–79, real defence spending has increased by over 20 per cent during a period of recession and major constraints on public expenditure. The rise reflects the costliness of modern weapons. An Invincible class aircraft carrier costs approximately £300 million (m) (without its aircraft); a nuclear-powered fleet submarine some £200m; a Tornado strike aircraft about £13m per copy; a VC–10 tanker £11.2m and a Challenger Tank £1.7m (unit production costs, 1982 –83 prices). More worryingly, the trend is towards rising real weapons costs. A new strike aircraft is four times as costly as its predecessor, a new missile is 3.5 times as costly and a frigate is three times more expensive. In the 40 years since 1940, the unit cost of a tank has quadrupled whilst that of a fighter aircraft has increased 15 to 25 times (in constant prices and for a given quantity).[1] In addition to being costly to acquire, complex modern weapons can be unreliable and costly to operate and maintain. For instance, US evidence showed that over 40 per cent of F14 and F15 aircraft were not mission capable at any given moment, with breakdowns occurring every 20–30 minutes of flying time and 34–98 maintenance man hours needed per sortie.[2] Not surprisingly, the 1984 UK Defence Statement declared that "the resources which can be devoted to defence are not limitless", but that there is scope for improving efficiency to secure "better value for money".[3] Efficiency is central to economics.

The Imperatives of Defence Economics

Where defence budgets are limited, weapons costs are rising in real terms and HM Forces have numerous competing claims for expenditure, the UK cannot avoid making difficult choices. Economics suggests four related general principles which can be usefully applied to the debate about UK defence policy in the 1980s and 1990s.

(i) *The principle of choice*

Defence is a standard economic problem in that it involves society making complex choices about the allocation of scarce resources which have alternative uses. Decisions are required on the level of defence spending and the allocation of a limited budget between manpower and weapons, between nuclear and conventional forces, between the Army, Navy and RAF, and between different regions of the world. Sacrifices arise with each set of choices. For instance, current defence spending involves a major sacrifice of expenditure on other "things" such as education, health, roads, information technology, foreign holidays, personal computers and videos. Similarly, within the defence budget, the Trident programme will involve the sacrifice of about £9 bn of expenditure on conventional forces (1983–84 prices). In making these choices, society has to decide how highly it values defence compared with the alternatives and it has to express its views on different types of military expenditure (especially nuclear versus conventional forces). These preferences are expressed through the ballot box which, in a General Election, is only a limited indicator of society's views on any specific issues. In this situation, governments and bureaucracies in the form of the Ministry of Defence and the armed forces have considerable opportunities for pursuing their interpretation of the "national interest".

(ii) *The principle of substitution*

Defence output can be provided by alternative combinations of, say, domestic and alliance expenditures, manpower and weapons, nuclear or conventional forces, or army, navy and air forces. For example, Britain might attempt to "free ride" within NATO by relying more on defence provided by its allies. It could rely on US cruise missiles instead of Trident and on American fighter aircraft for UK air defence. Or, the Royal Navy's Trident submarines might replace parts of the British Army, whilst aircraft could replace ships and tanks.

(iii) *The principle of efficiency*

Choices and substitution possibilities cannot be separated from efficiency considerations. Civil servants and military commanders require inducements to economise by substituting cheaper for more expensive inputs. Incentives are needed to consider the possible substitution of, say, foreign for British-built weapons, women for men, civilians for soldiers, reservists for regulars and missiles for aircraft. Similarly, efficiency also requires consideration of the extra costs and additional benefits of different outputs. Is it worth paying, say, an extra 30 per cent on R & D costs to increase the performance of a weapon by 1 per cent? Without incentives, there is every inducement to spend rather than to economise. Indeed, with the present system, there are no rewards for economising and not spending. The RAF is unlikely to economise if all the savings are used to buy more aircraft carriers for the Navy. Nor are the Services as a whole likely to seek economies if it means major budget cuts and job losses next time around and if all the savings accrue to rival Ministries or ultimately to the Treasury! But efforts to assess and improve efficiency have to be related to output. Any bureaucracy can economise by reducing output, particularly by cutting those activities which are likely to increase its chances of obtaining a larger budget in the future. The problems of measuring defence output complicate any government's effects to improve efficiency. Even so, military staffs should be able to inform governments of what different defence budgets are actually buying.

(iv) *The principle of competition*

Rivalry between private companies risking their own funds generates improved efficiency. In contrast, monopoly leads to inefficiency, higher prices, restricted choice and a lack of dynamism. Monopoly is a major feature of the UK's defence effort. HM Forces insist upon providing a complete range of defence activities so as to guarantee "military standards and discipline". They undertake their own recruitment and training, they maintain their equipment and they provide an "across the board" range of supporting activities such as catering, hospitals, military bands and transportation. Inefficiency is likely because the military are monopoly suppliers, protected from public and private sector rivals. Without rivalry, there are no alternative sources of information and no alternative cost yardsticks to measure the efficiency of the military "in-house" units. Similarly, UK weapons markets are often non-competitive, especially for high technology projects. They contain one or a few suppliers, either state — or privately — owned (for example British Aerospace, British Shipbuilders, Rolls Royce). Also, firms have been protected from the entry of new domestic and foreign rivals, with cost-plus contracts providing the financial basis for inefficiency, cost escalation and "gold plating".[4] Thus, a genuine competition for the military's in-house activities and weapons contracts provides a mechanism for seeking lower-cost methods of supplying a given service or weapon, and for questioning whether the existing services and equipment are worthwhile. In this way, competition would allow regular re-contracting. Rivalry would provide the military with accurate information on any extra costs of buying British weapons and of maintaining its in-house activities. How much extra is it willing to pay for these "products"? It must be remembered that with a given defence budget, more spent on UK-built aircraft and on military catering means less to spend on other things, such as missiles for the aircraft, and tanks for the army.

The result of many of these defence choices is reflected in the current UK defence budget (see Table). This budget buys an output which provides protection or some probability of survival in different conflict situations. Ideally, for sensible public choices on military expenditure, society needs to know what the current budget is buying and what might be the effects on protection of spending, say, 10 per cent more or less on defence. Would a 10 per cent cut mean that the UK would be unable to undertake a Falklands type operation? Would a 10 per cent rise buy an extra two days of conventional war in Europe before using nuclear weapons? Answers to such questions are complicated by uncertainty. Modern weapons and force structures can involve planning horizons of up to 40 years (for example, Trident). Assumptions have to be made about the future defence expenditures of the UK, its allies and potential enemies and likely technical progress in weapons. Uncertainty could mean that today's enemies are tomorrow's allies. Defence budgets, weapons and forces have to be sufficiently flexible and adaptable to cope with a variety of unforeseen contingencies and the prospects of technological obsolescence. Budget flexibility is, however, constrained by contractual commitments to manpower and weapons and the costs of re-negotiating existing contracts. Currently, about 50 per cent of planned expenditure on major equipment three years ahead might be regarded as uncommitted, with almost complete flexibility being achieved within ten years. Flexibility is also required because, unlike state education and health programmes, the effectiveness of UK defence expenditure can be reduced by the military spending of its potential enemies! A technological breakthrough can render obsolescent a whole generation of weapons together with the training and skills of military units. The technological arms race has also resulted in rising weapons costs as rival nations have demanded continuous improvements in performance. In real terms, the costs of high technology weapons have been rising at a faster rate than defence budgets. The result has been smaller forces. Between 1978 and 1984, real defence spending rose by 23 per cent and yet the number of front line RAF squadrons declined from 65 to 60. In the circumstances, Britain cannot avoid major defence choices in the 1980s and 1990s. A limited defence budget and rising weapons costs mean that something will have to be sacrificed.

What are the options for UK defence policy? There are four possible solutions, involving various assumptions about the level and composition of defence budgets. First, defence spending could be increased. Second, the UK could accept a reduction in the military effectiveness of its forces. Third, a major commitment could be sacrificed. Fourth, there might be efficiency improvements in the procurements of weapons and defence services. Each of these options will be assessed, the aim being to illustrate the application of the general economic principles outlined above. In actuality, governments are likely to select some mix of these policies. Nonetheless, detailed consideration of each option provides much clearer insights into the nature and implications of defence choices. It will be shown that references to "essential" and "politically impossible to change" should be carefully investigated for their cost consequences and their likely contribution to the protection of UK citizens.

Table UK Defence, 1984–85.

Programme	Expenditure (£m)	Manpower (000s) Services	Civilians	Output (Examples)
1. *Nuclear strategic forces*	384	2.3	3.8	4 Polaris submarines.
2. *Navy general purpose combat forces*	2493	43.3	9.1	96 combat vessels (carriers, destroyers, frigates, submarines).
3. *European theatre ground forces*	2626	101.2	23.2	48 infantry battalions; 19 armoured regiments
BAOR, Berlin	1843	60.3		16 infantry battalions; 13 armoured regiments
Home forces	783	40.9		32 infantry battalions; 6 armoured regiments.
4. *Other Army combat forces*	197	14.9	7.0	8 infantry battalions.
5. *Air Force general purpose forces*	3409	59.6	9.4	31 combat aircraft squadrons (20 in the UK and 11 in W. Germany).
6. *Reserve and Auxiliary formations*	357	2.9	3.6	35 infantry battalions; 5 armoured regiments.
7. *Research and development*	2097	1.3	25.9	53% on aircraft, missiles and electronics.
8. *Training*	1310	66.3	17.4	40% on the army.
9. *Repair facilities in UK*	931	8.0	67.2	3 Royal Dockyards.
10. *Other support functions*	2811	36.1	46.9	Whitehall organisations; Service pensions.
11. *War stocks*	549			
Total UK Defence Budget	17033	335.8	213.6	
US Forces in UK		27.0	25.0	360 aircraft; 160 cruise missiles (by 1988).
UK defence industries				
(a) On UK defence contracts	11072		565.0	British Aerospace, British Shipbuilders, Ferranti, GEC, Plessey,
(b) on defence exports	2600		145.0	Rolls Royce, Royal Ordnance Factories, Westland.

Notes: (i) Expenditure on UK defence contracts consists of equipment, buildings, miscellaneous stores and services. These expenditures are *included* in the total UK defence budget.

(ii) The civilian employment figures for US Forces in UK and for UK defence industries are based on direct and indirect effects (assume a multiplier of 1.8 applied to direct employment).

Source Cmnd 9227 (1984).

Increased Defence Spending

This option involves the inevitable sacrifice of civil goods. Much will depend on society's willingness to pay for protection during peace-time and when the defence budget already exceeds state expenditure on education. However, increased spending might also be required if the UK substituted conventional forces for its strategic nuclear weapons. Critics point out that whether measured in absolute terms, by per capita or by share of national income, the UK already spends more on defence than any of its major European allies. Certainly, UK defence spending absorbs considerable resources. It employs almost 1 million people directly and some 1.7 million if indirect effects are included. Furthermore, annual expenditure on defence R & D exceeds £2,000m, involving a considerable number of scarce scientists and engineers (See Table). Aerospace, electronics, the Royal Ordnance Factories and shipbuilding are defence-intensive industries, whilst the south-east and south-west regions are the major beneficiaries from defence employment. One view claims that the UK's relatively high defence burden has adversely affected its economic performance as reflected in a relatively low growth rate, inflation and balance of payments crises. These adverse effects are believed to result from the diversion of investment, scientists and skilled labour from civil production. However, doubts arise about simple, single explanations for complex economic problems. Why focus on defence as the cause of all our problems: does spending on health, restaurant meals and gambling have similar adverse effects? Moreover, OECD evidence suggests that "the figures, however manipulated, simply do not support any hypothesis of a connection between military expenditure and the worsening economic performance of the Western industrial world".[5]

Nevertheless, no one denies that defence is costly: all economic activity involves sacrifices. The central question is whether the current levels of military spending are worthwhile, particularly in terms of the benefits in the form of protection and security. In this context, defence is similar to insurance. In a perfectly safe world with no risks, insurance might not be required, but in the actual world of uncertainty, danger, risks and hazards, individuals usually insure themselves, their families and their assets. Defence expenditure is an example of the range of insurance policies which individuals and groups use to protect themselves from hazards, dangers and threats to their way of life. But society usually chooses between guns and butter through the voting mechanism with all its limitations as an accurate indicator of collective preferences. Indeed, within the political market place, defence choices will also be influenced by bureaucracies and interest groups (for example, weapons contractors, CND). The Ministry of Defence and HM Forces are monopoly suppliers of information and defence services. In aiming to raise their budgets, they have every incentive to exaggerate the demand for defence and its social benefits and to underestimate the costs of their preferred policies. Emphasis will be placed on the Warsaw Pact's apparent superiority in numbers of aircraft, nuclear weapons, ships, soldiers and tanks, as well as the major domestic jobs and technology benefits which result from military spending. Cost estimates which are too low can persuade a government to buy too much of a project which appears relatively cheap and the resulting cost escalation and time slippages will be financed by non-competitive cost-plus contracts. Cost escalation factors of two or more in real terms and time slippages of 30 per cent are typical during the development of modern weapons. In total, economic models of bureaucracy predict that they will be inefficient in supplying a given output and are likely to overspend so that they are too large.[6] On this basis, proposals for increased defence spending will focus attention on the classic choice between guns and butter. But increased spending alone does not mean good value for money. Anyone can solve problems via more spending regardless of efficiency principles: a point which is also neglected when NATO nations are urged to raise military spending.

Accept a Reduction in Effectiveness

If the defence budget remains unchanged, the UK could accept a general reduction in the effectiveness of its military forces and in its ability to meet its commitments. The result would be less training, smaller stocks of ammunition, fewer new weapons, delays in the introduction of new equipment and hence a greater use of old and obsolescent weapons. This "fudge it" option is attractive to a vote-sensitive government which can always claim to be meeting its defence commitments as reflected in the numbers of aircraft, ships and soldiers located in Britain, West Germany and elsewhere. Of course, numbers are misleading without reference to the productivity or combat effectiveness of weapons and forces (defence output). Nor does it follow that reduced effectiveness is necessarily an efficient solution. It might persuade budget-conscious bureaucracies to consume more "on-the-job" leisure and organisational slack! Also questions have to be asked about the likely efforts of a "fudge it" policy on defence output. How much less protection will be available and does society regard such a reduction as worthwhile?

SACRIFICE A MAJOR COMMITMENT (DRASTIC SURGERY)

This option involves a long-run reappraisal of UK defence policy, the aim being to evaluate critically the costs and benefits (for example, protection) of current commitments and the implications of re-contracting. Currently, the UK's major commitments embrace the independent strategic nuclear deterrent, the defence of the UK homeland, the land and air defence of continental Europe, a major maritime capability in the eastern Atlantic and a world-wide role, including the Falklands. The budget implications of these commitments are shown in the Table. Savings in the region of say, £1,000m–1,500m per annum might require some 50 per cent reduction in either BAOR or in the Navy, or the withdrawal of RAF combat aircraft from Germany. Similarly, cancellation of the Trident programme would provide a one-off saving of about £9 bn over the planned acquisition period which is equivalent to an average saving of some £600m per annum over the 15 years required for the development and delivery of the system (1983–84 prices). Savings from the drastic surgery option need to be assessed in the context of assumptions about the level of defence expenditure. If total military spending in real terms remains unchanged, the savings become available for increased expenditure on the remaining forces. So, cancellation of Trident would mean additional resources for expanding conventional forces, equivalent to an extra 23 nuclear fleet submarines, or another 400 Tornado aircraft, or an additional 2,500 tanks (assuming life cycle costs at twice unit production costs). Alternatively, the savings from drastic surgery might be used to reduce the defence budget, one aim being to bring the UK into line with that of its major European allies. Here, comparability with France would imply a UK defence budget equivalent to some 4 per cent of its GDP which would require cuts exceeding £3,500m from the 1984–85 budget of some £17 bn. The Table shows that cuts of this magnitude are equivalent to the abolition of BAOR or a large part of the Navy and their associated support expenditures.

Predictably, proposals to reduce or abolish BAOR, or the Navy's surface fleet or the RAFs long-range strike units are likely to encounter opposition from established interest groups. The

Army, for example, would obviously fight to maintain its prestige combat units in BAOR and one of its few remaining overseas postings. The Foreign Office would point to our commitments under the Brussels Treaty (until 1992), the implications for NATO and there would be dire warnings of the consequences of withdrawing our troops from the front line. To some commentators, the prospect of asking questions about BAOR (or the Navy, etc.) is immediately condemned as downright irresponsible, as aiding the enemy, the usual assertion being that present force levels on the Central Front must be maintained. Costs are ignored. Once again, choices cannot be avoided: if we go for one thing, something else has to go and the question is what. Rarely is it asked whether there are alternative ways of achieving defence objectives, what are the costs of the alternatives and what are the implications for the protection of UK citizens. For instance, what would be the cost savings and effects on protection if BAOR or the Navy's surface fleet were reduced by say 20 per cent? Here, it is relevant to remember that the UK's actual commitments to NATO are not sacrosanct and inviolate. Currently, substantial numbers of BAOR troops are actually in Northern Ireland whilst a part of the Navy's surface fleet is located in the South Atlantic and hence not immediately available to NATO! There are also opportunities for substituting the RAF Tornado strike force based in Germany for part of BAOR. Or, in the longer term, the EEC might develop a European defence policy with member states specialising on the basis of their comparative advantage in military forces. Or, relatively expensive regular units might be replaced by cheaper volunteer reservists. After all, there are many examples of foreign nations which rely upon substantial reserve formations in the land, sea and air spheres (for example, Israel, Sweden, Switzerland, USA). In this context, the UK's 1984 Defence Statement recognised the cost-effectiveness of volunteer reserves.[7] Nonetheless, there remain considerable opportunities for expanding the reserve forces, particularly in the sea and air spheres, including the recreation of the flying squadrons of the Royal Auxiliary Air Force (for air defence, maritime patrol and transport). In other words, the drastic surgery option clearly focuses on some of the major choices for UK defence policy. It raises searching questions about current commitments and whether the UK is willing to pay for the modern land, sea and air forces required to continue providing an across the board and balanced defence capability.[8]

Improve Efficiency in the Procurement of Weapons and Defence Services

Policy might seek lower cost methods of acquiring weapons and defence services, as well as aiming to raise the productivity of Service and civilian manpower, including civil servants in the Ministry of Defence. This is the conventional interpretation of obtaining better value for money, although the three options discussed above also involve questions of efficiency. Current policy stresses Management Information Systems for Ministries and top management (MINIS), rationalisation of separate Service staffs, privatisation, contracting out and competition as instruments for improving efficiency. It is claimed that MINIS will provide information on the costs and efficiency of all aspects of the Ministry of Defence. However, the cost data results from non-competitive situations which are unlikely to reflect least cost behaviour. A monopoly Ministry provides opportunities for organisational slack, a quiet life, shirking and the pursuit of self interest. The worry is that self-interested and budget-conscious civil servants will use MINIS to rationalise and defend the *status quo*. After all, the employment contracts of civil servants (and military commanders) provide no inducements to seek savings by substituting cheaper for more expensive inputs. Indeed, bureaucrats lack incentives to cooperate in policies aimed at improving efficiency: they bear the costs (they are the losers) and they receive no benefits. And in the last resort, politicians need bureaucrats to implement their policies, so that politicians have only limited incentives to regulate bureaucratic behaviour and efficiency. Within this environment, three policy solutions can be suggested.

First, output targets and efficiency incentives might be introduced into the employment contracts of civil servants and military commanders. Here, there are opportunities to experiment with short-term contracts for civil servants, payment-by-results, and fixed budgets which offer rewards for savings and penalties for over-spending. Second, the established property rights of the Services could be changed. For example, why not introduce formal competitions at regular intervals to allow, say, the Army to compete with the RAF and UK air defence; or the RAF to compete with the Navy for anti-submarine defence? Third, there could be a major extension of privatisation, civilianisation, contracting-out and competition. Current policy is moving in this direction with privatisation involving the Royal

Ordnance Factories, and the contracting-out of aircraft servicing, catering cleaning, equipment repair and warship refitting.[9] But privatisation and contracting-out are not sufficient for efficiency improvements. Rivalry and competitively-determined fixed price contracts are also required. The cost savings from a competitive defence policy are likely to be substantial. Estimated savings of over 30 per cent have followed the introduction of competition, and the contracting-out of MOD cleaning services saved 40 per cent on costs or almost £12m per annum.[10] Savings of this magnitude cannot be ignored in the search for more efficient defence policy. What are the opportunities for using competition to improve efficiency?

A Competitive Policy: The Opportunities and Barriers to Change

A genuine competition will be characterised by four factors. Firstly, the absence of entry barriers, so that UK and foreign firms are allowed to bid for British defence contracts for weapons and for services such as repair, maintenance and cleaning. New entrants with no previous defence experience should be allowed to bid. Secondly, rivalry is required for a *given* weapon (operational requirement) and level of service and for *alternative* performance requirements and levels of service. This requires firms to bid for a given requirement and to indicate what they could offer if their bids were increased or reduced by an extra 10 to 20 per cent. Thirdly, competitively-determined fixed price contracts. Otherwise, prices are meaningless if they can be raised once rivals have been eliminated. With weapons, competition and fixed price contracts can be applied to the total package or at each stage in the development cycle (for example, design, prototypes, production). In the case of risky, high technology weapons, some of the uncertainties can be reduced by purchasing knowledge through relatively cheap demonstrators.[11] With defence services (cleaning, repair, etc.), regular re-contracting is required, with competitions at, say, three to five yearly intervals. Fourthly, the enforcement of penalties for late delivery and poor quality.

Defence is a classic example of protected markets with the Services and the major weapons contractors operating in monopoly situations where rivalry is absent. Such arrangements are likely to be inefficient. Competition can contribute to efficiency improvements and there are extensive opportunities for introducing rivalry into UK defence markets embracing both the in-house units of the armed forces and weapons producers. Why not allow competition for many of the training activities of the forces (for example, drivers, musicians, pilots) and why not permit Dassault, General Dynamics, McDonnell-Douglas and Northrop to compete for RAF contracts? Assume that competition results in typical cost savings of 20 per cent.[12] In the short run, such savings might be available for 30 per cent of the defence budget, resulting in annual savings of some £1,000m. In the long run, if the savings are applied to the total defence budget they indicate an "upper bound" estimate of some £5,000m per annum. Further savings are likely to be available from competition for alternative weapons requirements and levels of service, with different implications for protection. For instance, savings can be obtained by offering subsidies to private firms to incorporate military features into their civil equipment rather than purchasing expensive, specialised and purpose-built military systems (for example, transport aircraft, ships, vehicles; converted oil tankers rather than aircraft carriers).

Proposals for more competition will encounter massive opposition, particularly from the interest groups likely to lose from change. The armed forces will oppose contracting-out, claiming that it will lead to lower quality, and loss of reliability and control. These are testable propositions and the initial experience with contracting-out raises doubts about such criticisms. Moreover, even if the in-house activities of the Services are useful, they are not costless. How much are the forces willing to pay for their in-house units if it means sacrificing other things such as more front line manpower and new weapons?

British defence contractors operating in protected markets and budget-conscious bureaucracies will oppose a competitive procurement policy. A set of myths have arisen which claim that competition will mean undue dependence on the USA, paying monopoly prices for spares, the loss of British jobs and advanced technology, with the UK becoming a nation of "metal bashers" dependent on importing American high technology.[13] The Ministry of Defence has also asserted that there are limits to competition. "We need a strong indigenous defence/industrial base . . . ; and the limited number of British suppliers of certain advanced defence equipment is also a constraint on competition within the United Kingdom".[14]

These arguments raise fundamental questions about the objectives of defence policy. Is it the proper business of the

Ministry of Defence to concern itself with protecting British jobs, technology and the balance of payments, or with protecting UK citizens from armed attack? Which contributes more to the protection of the UK: a strong domestic industrial base or armed forces equipped with modern weapons? References to the "need for a strong domestic industrial base" have to specify the size and appropriate industries (aerospace, electronics, shipbuilding) required for strength, whether the current size exceeds the minimum necessary for strength and whether strength is needed regardless of costs. Certainly a buy-British policy can be costly. For example, the work-sharing arrangement for the UK Phantoms meant that Britain paid an extra 23–43 per cent per copy compared with purchasing off-the-shelf from McAir. Similarly, the UK decided to acquire the British Sting Ray Torpedo at an estimated cost of £920m in 1979 prices, compared with £200m for buying some US Mark 46 torpedoes and modifying existing stocks.[15] Sting Ray was preferred because it was a better weapon: but was it worth an extra £720m? These examples illustrate some of the trade-offs in buying British. For a limited defence budget, a strong domestic industrial base means fewer modern weapons available to the forces and these are usually delivered later. Nor can it be objected that competition is impossible because there are only a few UK suppliers (for example, in aerospace). Monopoly results from a government decision to restrict the market to UK firms. Rival defence contractors exist in high technology areas, particularly in America and Europe. Indeed, the greatest gains from competition are likely in the costly, high technology areas where it is so often claimed that rivalry is impossible and impracticable.

Conclusion

Choice is central to economics and UK defence policy cannot avoid choices. Something will have to go: what goes and what will be the effects on the protection of the UK? Economists seek to estimate "trade-offs" in the form of the sacrifices involved in pursuing one set of policies rather than some alternative. There are no costless solutions. Current UK defence policy recognises that resources are limited and that there is scope for improving efficiency. Nonetheless, there remain extensive opportunities for applying basic economic principles of choice, substitution, efficiency and competition.

NOTES

[1] Barnaby, F (Ed) *Future War* (Michael Joseph, London, 1984) chapter 11.
[2] Ibid, p. 132.
[3] *Statement on the Defence Estimates 1984,* Cmnd 9227-I (HMSO, London, 1984) p. 12.
[4] Hartley, K. and Tisdell, C. *Micro-Economic Policy* (J. Wiley, London, 1981) chapter 14.
[5] Blackaby, F. 'The Military Sector and the Economy', in Ball, N. and Leitenberg, M. (Eds), *The Structure of the Defense Industry* (Croom Helm, London, 1983) p. 8.
[6] Hartley and Tisdell op cit, chapters 3 and 15.
[7] Cmnd 9227-I op cit, p. 29.
[8] Omega Report *Defence Policy* (Adam Smith Institute, London, 1983).
[9] Cmnd 9227-I op cit, pp. 16–18.
[10] Ibid, pp. 16–17.
[11] Hartley, K, *NATO Arms Cooperation: A Study in Economics and Politics* (George Allen & Unwin, London, 1983) pp. 115–120.
[12] Ibid, chapter 3 and Hartley, K, "Why Contract Out?" in *Contracting Out in the Public Sector* (Royal Institute of Public Administration, London, 1984).
[13] Hartley, K. *NATO Arms Cooperation* op cit, pp. 82–87, 115–120.
[14] Cmnd 9227-I op cit, p. 17.
[15] HC 648, Sixteenth Report from the Public Accounts Committee, *Matters Relating to the Ministry of Defence* (HMSO, London, 1980), p. xiv.

Strategic Vulnerability

LIEUTENANT COLONEL SAM POPE

Lieutenant Colonel Samuel Pope OBE RM joined RUSI as a Research Fellow in 1983 on retiring from the Royal Marines. He is at present finishing a study into the Defence of The Vulnerable Society and writes on Intelligence and Security.

THE SOVIET Union soon recognised that the advent of nuclear weapons at the end of World War II brought about what they describe as a 'revolution in military affairs'. There could in future wars be little chance of survival and no outright victory. The Soviets also recognised that it is important not to lose, and that any 'losing' in future would with all probability occur off the battlefield. They came to appreciate that without nuclear parity, wars and conflict could be lost to a technologically superior West, particularly if undeterred by the prospect of escalation to nuclear war. So the Soviets themselves achieved nuclear parity, if not superiority, and hence added a further dimension to the 'revolution in military affairs', a mutual but hardly controlled avoidance of nuclear war.

The subsequent mutual obsession with balanced forces, arms limitation, missile deployment and counter deployment has tended to overshadow less dramatic but more pervasive and by no means unconnected strategic considerations; in particular the great many economic and political pressures and forms of coercion that are now emerging either because of the need to keep the lid on nuclear capabilities or because existing ones now have become potential means of conflict. The modern trend to label every possible phenomenon has given us 'low intensity conflict' for which definitions vary and are unimportant other than to recognise that any conflict requires at least some form of capability and an intent to use it. But international geo-politics also provide other sources of pressure and coercion which are not so easily labelled; sources which if unrecognised and unprepared for might provide immense contemporary danger both for Western democracies and 'Socialist' regimes. Detecting vulnerabilities of likely opponents can be a matter of great concern when seeking ways of exerting pressure, but conversely the highest priority should be given to recognising the roots of one's own strategic vulnerability. The development of the Soviet political and military structure within the Marxist–Leninist prerogative goes a long way to ensuring that this is so, paranoic as it may appear to many in the West. Western democracies on the other hand could be accused of staggering from one crisis to another, and not without a few own goals being scored.

Pressures and Coercion

Are these pressures and coercions that may have strategic significance identifiable, and can Western democracies improve their ability to avoid them? The short correct answer to those two questions could well be: we do not really know, and may be not. Brief reflection on events in the last ten years or so suggests that any improvement is unlikely without changes of both perception and Western posture to influence such events. From the 1973 oil crisis, to the Iranian Revolution of 1978, and then with the crisis surrounding Lebanon and the Gulf since 1982, the West has lurched through a number of upheavals which were apparently unpredictable but with hindsight must surely provide important lessons. Within and sometimes separate to these milestone events are smaller but equally damaging incidents. The bombing of the US Embassy and their Marine base in Lebanon; the multi-bombing of diplomatic and government buildings in Kuwait; the shooting of a policewoman in central London from the safety of an embassy; all tragic and unpredicted events with far reaching consequences, some of which are yet to be properly appreciated. Such horrendous actions now seem endemic to the changing nature of conflict in the nuclear age. They are, one must hope, at the higher end of the scale of pressures and they clearly deserve to be recognised as part of deep rooted strategic conflict. Whether or not they are accorded such significance is not easy to discern.

Pressures can also stem from those more inert circumstances which strongly suggest a potential for coercion short of war. Apart from such rare natural disasters as the 1972 Managua earthquake in Nicaragua which was certainly of no help to the failing Samoza regime, there is a wide range of political, economic and social factors that may contribute to or even on occasions trigger off more serious underlying strategic conflict. Examples might well include major accidents and systems failures (Serviso, Three Mile Island, and the US East Coast blackout); industrial actions such as those of the Tehran taxi drivers prior to the fall of the Shah, the disruption caused by French lorry drivers in February 1984; the actions of the British National Union of Mineworkers shortly afterwards; and extreme political persuasion that purposefully works through media and education against free democracy; these are but some of the sources of pressure, frequently originating from national internal pressures, that may lend themselves to being exploited over quite long periods of time with the aim of what the Soviets would describe as shifting the 'correlation of forces' in one's favour.

In addition the not so inert circumstances of political violence and terrorism have become a widespread source of coercion, as Professor Paul Wilkinson has explained in his article in the 1984 *RUSI/Brassey's Defence Year Book.* Speaking also at a conference at the RUSI, Professor Wilkinson has described the nature of terrorism as one of both the use of violence against the innocent and a psychological and political weapon which, usually in concert with other tactics, is used to overthrow the democratic system and to control the population. Most terrorist groups realise that public support for democratic values and institutions is a major obstacle to their schemes. Hence the democratic process is a key target.

In his 1984 article, Professor Wilkinson has set out a clear indictment of the Soviet Union's connivance in global terrorism. By 1985 realisation may come to the West of the potential of a small sect of fanatical Shi'ite muslims to gravely effect strategic postures by appalling acts of terrorism such as were commonplace in Iran after the 1978 revolution, and as have been seen since in Beirut and Kuwait.

THE REQUIREMENT FOR IMPROVED AWARENESS

Western reaction to such pressures as those described here in brief remains difficult to define. The 1973 oil crisis did indeed prompt the emergence of the International Energy Agency, paying special attention to an emergency allocation scheme, stockpiling requirements and information gathering. There has also been an increased interest in understanding the economic circumstances and potential sources of pressure affecting advanced industrial nations. But the present verdict on the apparent inability of free democracies to predict and avoid exploitation of their many and often deep rooted vulnerabilities must be unfavourable, if not one of outright guilty. On the other hand the Soviet Union, for all its immense economic problems and potential political upheaval, remains remarkably stable. The Soviets are prone to making bold pronouncements on their own security requirements which are often dismissed by Western commentators as mere rhetoric, but ten to 15 years later it becomes abundantly clear that they have achieved their stated objectives, whether these may be to deploy quantities of highly accurate missiles or to build an ocean going Navy. Whatever their ideological pretensions may be for spreading their form of Socialism beyond the present Soviet bloc, there is little reason to doubt that, often by draconian methods, the survival of their system is given the very highest priority. Which brings us back to the second part of the question posed earlier, can Western democracies improve their own ability to avoid or counter those pressures and coercion that may have strategic significance?

In this short article it would be imprudent to do more than to suggest where to start looking. If just one aspect can be examined here, it should perhaps be the very roots of vulnerability, which it is suggested stem from a failure to appreciate one's circumstances. Survival in strategic terms is likely to be as much a matter of awareness as of capability, for to rely heavily on the latter must invite conflict which in the nuclear age is to be avoided where and whenever any escalation might occur. A principal requirement for insuring against exploitation of one's vulnerabilities is, therefore, strategic intelligence capable of providing both analysis of the nature of the main factors involved, and synthesis or judgment for balancing their relevant importance. Such a synthesis requires a perception which may not be easily attained but is essential for true judgment of vulnerability. The temptation is considerable to mistake 'doing' as being of more importance than 'being', a syndrome not unknown in Whitehall, and elsewhere. The concept of entity as opposed to mobility has to be applied if best possible awareness of 'reality' of circumstances is to be achieved. The problem is to organise this 'reality' so as to avoid being surprised by unexpected pressures or coercion.

Much has been written on the avoidance of strategic military surprise, notably from a nuclear first strike, but there is little to guide advanced industrial countries seeking to reduce vulnerability to slower, less obvious pressures and low intensity threats. If the scholarship applied to vulnerability to nuclear and conventional attack is valid, based on copious research and analysis of recent and long past military operations, surely there may be lessons to be learnt which are applicable to conflict short of war. Such low levels of conflict, may not even be discernible, do not encourage the spending of time and scarce resources on developing expensive forms of strategic intelligence such as those essential for prevention or conduct of general war, even though there may be a greater incentive to exploit vulnerability. Nevertheless, there is surely a paramount requirement to make both long term and current assessment of one's own weakness as well as of likely aggressors' capabilities and intentions. How is this to be done?

An Analysis of Vulnerability

The following framework is suggested. There are four factors which seem to create vulnerability and which ought to be applied to the several stages in a government's assessment of threat and subsequent response. It would seem that if they are applied to each stage in turn, much can be learnt of how governments become prone to vulnerability. These then are the four factors that can create vulnerability to strategic surprise not only in terms of general war but also, it is suggested, in conflict well short of it:

- *Informational.* A government only has a limited amount of correct information of its own internal systems and structures as well as on external dependencies and possible aggressors. A great deal of information can be ambiguous and tends to be immersed in irrelevant, erroneous and even misleading data.
- *Cognitive.* Standard human processes of perception and explanation tend to inhibit accurate analysis. The mind has been likened to a newspaper rather than a computer, that seeks news and sometimes distorts it. It tends to suppress supposed irrelevancies and concentrates on improving what is already accepted wisdom.
- *Organisational.* Patterns of organisational behaviour can cripple a state's perceptions or undermine the implementation of effective response.
- *Political.* Receptivity to warning and adequacy of response can be undermined by political conditions and considerations, both domestic and international.

The stages of assessment and response are, of course, concurrent and interactive but with varying time frames. The process is really, or should be, fluid and evolving, almost like a living organism. So analysis by stages risks distortion; nevertheless a clear understanding of these stages is essential, and although there can be variations in their definition, the one given here well suits our purpose:

- *Information Availability.* Vulnerability is related to the amount and kind of information available.
- *Information Collection.* Vulnerability is related to the degree to which information is gathered in a timely fashion.
- *Perception.* Vulnerability is related to the degree to which the gathered information is accurately interpreted and understood.
- *Response.* Vulnerability is related to the degree to which government, having interpreted the information it has gathered, selects an appropriate response.

Bearing in mind the risk of distortion through separate analysis of each stage, this is now attempted in order to see how valid this approach may be.

First Phase: Availability of Information

The simplest explanation for a state's vulnerability would be that it has no warning of impending circumstances. Information may be unavailable at an early stage for three reasons: firstly, secrecy; secondly, time — the information may become available too late to act on it; and thirdly the information may simply not exist.

It is often said, in retrospect, that a government did in fact have enough information available correctly to predict what would happen. However, detecting the unexpected must inevitably be a problem of having too little information. Threat perception is very much a matter of estimates that would not be needed if all the pertinent information was available and unambiguous. One makes estimates when one does not know; missing information often may be protected by secrecy. With key data missing which would provide an unambiguous answer those making the assessment must guess, thereby allowing preconceptions and other sources of misperception to have more effect.

Timing of events may prevent early realisation that a threat is in existence or growing. Other apparently more threatening circumstances will be receiving priority and realisation of the existence of available information may be too late to take account of it. Awareness of anti-nuclear protest groups was extensive in recent years but little thought was apparently given until it was too late to make a timely response in verifying their likely part in, for instance, the proposed deployment of the neutron bomb or of theatre nuclear weapons.

Finally, information may not yet exist. Capabilities of possible aggressors are often available but his intentions to use them may remain undecided until a late hour. A terrorist group may be reported in a country but without any indication as to their target. The long suspected 'sleeper' may be without a target or support until too late to react.

In this first phase informational factors are clearly significant but those cognitive, organisational and political do not begin to have an effect until the second phase. Yet we can already partially explain the vulnerability of governments to being surprised by a turn of events just by referring to the limitations on the data available to them.

Second Phase: Collection of Information

Assuming that enough information on a likely economic or political threat is available, it is possible to increase vulnerability by failing to gather it. Subsequent review of failure or poor response may tend to concentrate on faulty assessment of the information gathered but overlooking data which was missed. The planning of where information may be obtained from and of how to ensure crucial elements are not overlooked is surely an essential requirement, albeit one prone to accident or luck. Knowing where to look is an art well refined by academics, and many investigative journalists, regardless of whether or not subsequent analysis is competent. Governments are not necessarily so adept at refining this art for their real requirements and can have a greater tendency to reaction rather than prediction. Probably a much greater sense of requirements exists in the more specialised world of international banking or commerce. The broader requirements of government and lack of resources do not encourage such a pragmatic approach.

It is here that 'cognitive' factors can improve or distort the gathering of information by ensuring accurate selection or the reverse. Expectation may not be objective enough to retain a balanced policy. Deception, certainly in considering political vulnerabilities, also plays a part where it can confuse search patterns much like a magician misdirects the attention of his audience.

Organisational factors can have an effect through routines being too unresponsive or insensitive to intermittent or occasional availability of information. At the level of national government, bureaucratic demarcations or disputes may cause gaps, as well as duplication leading to conflicting assessment. The provision of too much easily obtained information and insufficient of the difficult but may be crucial is a sure reason for distortion.

Certain political considerations may contribute to a government's vulnerability in this phase by curbing the gathering of data. This may be a more prevalent factor in military operations than in lesser forms of conflict but it surely must occur when investigating political coercion. Indeed the problems of confidentiality and reasons for eliciting information could be more than enough to prevent certain lines being sufficiently researched.

Clearly a government cannot collect all the information available about everything. Choices must be made and they may be wrong ones. So what is of much greater importance is that the information gathered in is properly understood, as this vital process can go a long way to making allowance for what may be missing.

Third Phase: Perception

So, having discussed how vulnerability can occur or be increased because information on threatening circumstances is unavailable or not gathered in, the next possibility is that the information obtained is misread. Again we can group factors that inhibit accurate perception of warning into the same four categories: informational, cognitive, organisational and political.

Information does not come neatly packaged and labelled, usually quite the contrary. There are many ambiguities to be overcome as to reliability of sources, apparent lack of substance, and the significance of the many elements of the total information available. Perception can be severely affected by a mass of irrelevant information which nevertheless has to be first digested, by false information and by apparently important information that is, in fact, concerned with other quite different important matters. A combination of such informational constraints make it difficult to form any initial perception, and equally may inhibit adaptation to real changes of circumstances.

Even if very good information is received, it is still probable that inadequate preparation is made to meet serious change primarily because of the ways people individually and collectively think. A great deal has been written and said on why this may be so. We now attempt to precis analysis of why this might be.[1]

Perception involves selecting categories and evaluation of thoughts by a cognitive process already present in the mind. Data is not received passively but rather is subjected to a vigorous process based on what the mind already 'knows'. This previous knowledge guides the search for information, the selection of specifics for attention, the sorting and labelling, and the making of judgments. This process can take different forms but in its most fundamental one relies on powerful assumptions and beliefs about important aspects of reality, i.e. are people rational, is there an underlying order to things, or are they random in character? Another process relies on 'values' or deeply ingrained subjective preferences as to what one expects of reality.

A far more elaborate process is an interplay of assumptions and values with considerable amounts of past information, often referred to as 'images'. Complex as these may be they can have the effect of greatly simplifying portions of reality. These can be more readily identified and better examined, but in a reflexive, habitual fashion.

Much more consciously designed and slightly nearer to the formal process of the military appreciation are 'hypotheses and theories'. They emerge from an often only dimly perceived network of asumptions, values and images; much more vaguely perceived and less understood than deductions in the formal appreciation, they can become an unconscious and reflex process, but of a more tentative and open nature. Evaluation can be made against alternatives and tools created to make sense out of reality, to be retained or discarded depending on their utility.

Finally, elements of assumptions, values, images and hypotheses or theories formulate into 'strategies and plans' which link objectives to courses of action available. So perception can be translated into action. These strategies and plans are yet more open and tentative, and subject to critical evaluation and revision on the basis of incoming information. However, they can suffer from a deterioration in critical judgment in relation to how well they have become established.

All variations of these processes apply to groups as well as individuals but become subject to various social factors which encourage formulation and maintenance of group 'understanding'. Like individuals, groups develop unique forms and stimuli that reflect an amalgamation of individual minds. However to attempt absorption of all available aspects of the possible permutations of these processes would mean chaos and confusion. So perception has a natural bias to being selective, and a powerful tendency towards balance and consistency. The process attempts to minimise confusion and uncertainty in favour of an orderly, reliable and efficient treatment of the many and varied stimuli. Various possibilities are formed and the bias tends towards those that seemingly fit, rather than the best possible solution, i.e. the mind "makes do" with what seems to work. The eventual emergence of artificial intelligence could greatly simplify and improve on this process.

So how flexible are these processes of the mind and the perceptions they dictate, particularly in the face of contrary evidence? It is generally understood that they are resistant to change, sometimes extremely so, for the following reasons (among others). First prior experience and learning make for comfort and usefulness. It can be extremely costly and disturbing to discard them for other forms of knowledge. Second, the thought process is integral to an individual's or group's self-identity. To alter this process alters that identity, which is not easily or comfortably done, and indeed should only be attempted with care since a stable identity is important to survival in this world. A fact recognised by those who are successful at practising subversion.

Third, since perception involves a process of selection from available stimuli, such sampling will have a tendency towards conformity and will reinforce the perceived efficiency of the process. Fourth, much information is ambiguous, so it becomes adapted to fit existing perceptions and underlying themes of the thought process. Finally, in seeking out stimuli and evaluating them, there is a bias against seeing them as consistent with alternative perceptions. We are biased towards seeing what we expect to see, and against seeing different things differently.

Thus preconceptions or predispositions preset patterns of perception. Portions of this mental equipment can be challenged, revised, or even discarded; under the right circumstances this can even be done quickly and smoothly. But such changes cannot be continuous and are not normal. The norm is that things are relatively static, applied routinely and repetitively.

Willingness to change will vary with individual or group circumstances so generalising about inertia attached to preconceptions would be difficult beyond stating that it is always substantial.

It follows that there is a strong tendency to overlook information that clashes with existing views, to interpret such information in ways that sustain these views, or to reject it. Where indications start to grow views tend to shift to the minimum extent necessary, starting with the most flexible and conscious parts of the mind's processes. As perceptions develop it takes considerably more and better information to lead to their rejection than their retention, even if they originally emerged from quite limited or ambiguous stimuli.

These cognitive factors we have examined may well be the predominant ones affecting strategic vulnerability, but it is by no means the whole story and the complexity of government organisations cannot easily escape scrutiny. Political and military intelligence can be recognised within their own entities, and organisations in one form or another have been seen to take account of both, if not always successfully as was demonstrated at the time of the Argentine invasion of the Falkland Islands in April 1982. How then does one take a longer term assessment of the less definable economic and political sources of pressures and coercion in the latter stages of the 20th century, when scarce intelligence resources and government organisations must increasingly focus on nuclear force priorities? The simple hypothesis to be made at this stage is that, if policy and strategies are out of focus, so will be the subordinate organisation with all its bureaucratic constraints. If in time of acute danger intelligence systems can be faulty, how can assessments of nebulous, ill defined circumstances ensure urgent reaction? Angelo Codevilla, who has served on the US Senate Select Committee on Intelligence, suggests that any system for analysing intelligence can work well if everyone connected with it believes his own life depends on its success.[2] Ideology also may help for totalitarian states but pluralist societies must surely accept greater levels of uncertainty.

If vulnerability to critical pressures is inherent in the nature of modern government organisations, the conclusion of Harold Wilensky may well be correct that "intelligence failures are built into complex organisations".[3] He cites such elements as hierarchy, specialisation, centralisation, the stages of organisational development, tensions between superiors and subordinates, preoccupation with immediate problems and an intolerance for ambiguity as contributing to intelligence failures. It would require a more detailed exploration of government organisations than has probably yet been attempted before such organisational factors can be eradicated as contributors to vulnerability.

The last of the four factors to be applied to the perceptive stage of our framework is the political one. Governments do not seem to have the reflective ability of academic organisations, having evolved or been designed for reflex action. Their learning process is not deeply embedded into their character as their primary aim is to impose rather than to learn. To concentrate investigation on a government's perceptual-cum-analytical process may well produce distortion as this tends to be done within a narrow and self-centred framework directed towards action. There is little time and inclination to learn in the way that an academic observer would be inclined to do so.

If it is really so that perception is more a synthesis of the circumstances surrounding governmental decision rather than an essential preliminary, then vulnerability to increasing danger in whatever form because of misperception can hardly be unexpected. Vulnerability linked to the nature of government ensures repetition of mistakes because the reality of government itself does not change. A striking example of this is the failure of frequently changing democratically elected governments in the West to appreciate properly the true nature of Soviet military power and its many manifestations in circumstances which Western governments perceive as being primarily political. Soviet perceptions of vulnerability may well be more ingrained into their system which appears to place survival, at least of the 'Party', as by far the highest governmental objective.

The possession of power presents a situation where action is less dependent on learning, as knowledge is already gained; others without power have to strive to reach a similar level. Governments can rest on the accumulation and exercise of power so that the need to learn in order to act is correspondingly reduced. Officials with power can brush aside information that does not easily fit their perceptions; they can refuse to learn of the true nature of an impending crisis, can reject warning of aggressors' intentions, can discount evidence of their own unpreparedness, and can concentrate on their own plans to alleviate or avoid potential national disaster.

Decision and action in a government involve struggles over defining a problem, efforts to create some form of workable consensus, and the construction of a policy. Along with this goes the unavoidable matter of timing, as problems can often only be confronted when the time is right politically. So in addition to ambiguous data, problems of perception and organisation, there are strong inhibitions on assimilating information when there are political incentives not to do so. In the worst case governments can often appreciate the nature of advanced warning despite the many constraints against doing so, but they fail to overcome or avoid the additional political factors that ensure disaster.

Fourth Phase: Response to Warning

The final stage in this analysis of vulnerability is to question why insufficient response is made to warnings of future danger. National leaders may well not be oblivious to approaching events and lower level officials are frequently more sensitive to the warning signs than their superiors; but certain precautions that might well have been taken are not. Why is this so?

The first problem to be overcome is the one already discussed of the overall ambiguity of the available information. As resources for response are always inadequate nothing definite can be planned until sufficient, accurate information is to hand. The constraints of deception, secrecy, and general 'noise' created by superfluous information can only inhibit timely response. Second, one must make an accurate assessment of circumstances based on correct assumptions and knowledge. Preconceptions of the capabilities and intentions of possible aggressors together with unfounded confidence that one is invulnerable to such a threat will almost certainly ensure little enthusiasm for any response. In addition preoccupation with other serious threats will only exacerbate this neglect.

Third, it is not difficult to suggest organisational deficiencies that can inhibit realistic response. Indeed it is a widely held assumption that conflict short of war is something governments tend to 'muddle through'. They are better organised to coordinate resources for the distribution of wealth and for the protection of citizens from each other, rather than coping with unusual economic pressures and external subversion. One can probably also cite bureaucratic rivalry and conflicting interests, poor organisation at differing levels and ill defined objectives. In addition, the 'cry-wolf' syndrome dulls any incentive to respond by overworking the organisation for no good cause.

Finally, the political factors surrounding response can be formidable. Panic in the market place and on the Stock Exchange must be avoided, misguided whistle-blowers discouraged, and a calm, confident style of government sustained. Highly sensitive matters concerning public information or economic stability must be finely judged. A public with little awareness of the real circumstances can on occasion escalate a crisis beyond easy redemption, if not beyond control. A government ill-informed and unprepared can exacerbate the situation, making society highly vulnerable to any pressures directed at it.

The problem posed was how to organise one's concept of reality so as to avoid being 'surprised'. Explanation has been given in some detail as to how the problem can be examined in its various stages of information availability and collection, perception of the circumstances, and subsequent response. It has been suggested that although knowledge is power, it can incite a form of arrogance, while lack of knowledge, i.e. ignorance, causes confusion. Both lead to faulty analysis and response. This explanation may well be rejected on the grounds of simplicity but it is suggested that it does at least provide the bricks with which to build a better understanding of the strategic vulnerabilities apparently endemic in the West since the onset of 'the revolution in military affairs'.

Immediate Strategic Requirements

There is no shortage of potential strategic vulnerabilities on which to exercise the pattern of analysis that has been depicted. In the broadest terms they are of a nature economic-cum-political, social-cum-political, or in some cases purely political. In the economic field, there could be a myriad of long term potential vulnerabilities calling for new ways of detection and judgment of their significance. Scandinavian countries have taken a lead in such analysis and reorganisation: Sweden, in particular, has a detailed 'total defence' plan that considers its whole economic defence structure under the headings of systems such as communications, transportation, and power supplies; foreign dependencies such as energy, mineral resources, and food; and structures such as financial markets, government, and crisis management. Other countries may find a different approach to the problem suits their circumstances better.

Prophets of tomorrow's world suggest seven more, all encompassing vulnerabilities: population growth, food distribution, mineral shortages, degradation of environment, nuclear abuse, abuse of science, and greed — this last being the human factor that can manifest itself in apathy and moral blindness. These would seem to cover the broadest range of possibilities, perhaps too nebulous to tackle in the short term, but important as future goals.

There is, however, one area of blindness or misconception afflicting the free democracies of the West in urgent need of better 'reality'. This is the declared intention and methodology of Marxism–Leninism to spread the ideological struggle worldwide, and specifically the Soviet evolution of military doctrine and its subordinate military science to support this intention through the 'armed struggle'. Soviet success in the last 30 years in responding to their doctrinal requirements stemming from awareness of the meaning for the Soviet Union of the 'revolution in military affairs' has been both immense and surprising. It would seem imperative for the West to make very careful and timely assessment of what this really means, and in particular where strategic vulnerability may lurk before any more 'surprises' occur.

Notes

1 Robert Jenis, *Perceptions and Misperception in International Politics* (Princeton: Princeton University Press, 1976) is the principle source from which this precis is drawn.

2 Angelo Codevilla, 'Comparative Histological Experience of Doctrine and Organisation' in Roy Godson, ed., *Intelligence Requirements for the 1980s: Analysis and Estimates* (London, Transaction, 1980).

3 Harold Wilensky, *Organisational Intelligence* (New York, Basic Books, 1967).

Prospects for the Middle East

PHILIP WINDSOR

Philip Windsor is a Reader in the Department of International Relations at the London School of Economics and Political Science

THIS essay is not and cannot be considered prediction specially in terms of such a notoriously unpredictable area as the Middle East. Rather, it is about the way in which the events of the Middle East might or might not be adding up to a certain pattern and the way in which they impinge on some of the other developments in the world. And one obviously calls on the past and not on the future in order to talk about some of these questions.

Nineteen eighty-four is likely to be a crucial year for the Middle East in the particular sense that some of the developments which have hitherto been regarded separately might start coming together and might also in themselves be taking a more ominous or acute turn. And in that sense I would like first to look at some of the *points de répère* then try to see what possible interaction there might be between them. It is conventional in discussing the Middle East to concentrate on certain specific areas. The Middle East itself is a conventional term which covers an area extending from Casablanca to Baghdad, from the Golden Horn to the Horn of Africa. In that sense there are different areas to the Middle East in which developments can proceed separately. There is the area of the Gulf, the area of the Levant and the area of the Maghreb to name only the three most prominent.

Up to now it has been possible to conceive that developments in the Gulf have been kept fairly separate from developments in the Levant. The Israeli/Lebanese/Syrian triangle has obviously been very greatly affected by the revolution in Iran. And it is quite clear that the Iran/Iraq war has had its own impact on alignments inside that triangle. But it is also clear that due to a combination of superpower stand-off and rather skilful diplomacy, particularly on the part of Saudi Arabia, the Iran/Iraq war itself has been relatively well contained. The long, terrible attrition which has been the characteristic of that war has not in fact spilled over into other forms of conflict, as for example between Syria and Jordan. It is also clear that in spite of certain American hopes which were pinned on Saudi mediation after the Israeli/Lebanese disengagement agreement of 15 May 1983, the hope that the Saudis would somehow swing the Syrians behind this, Saudi Arabia cannot deliver very much in terms of American policy in the Levant. It carries a lot of clout in the Gulf and in the counsels of OPEC. But on the other hand, the attempts to bring Syria into some kind of framework of agreement for resolving the impasse in the Lebanon, have not succeeded at all.

So up to now it has generally been possible to speak of different kinds of developments in the Middle East impinging upon each other but not deriving their momentum, not changing their context or their nature from the way they interact. I am going to suggest it is possible in the near future that these events might begin to impinge upon each other, and that might do so because the situation itself is becoming more crucial, and acute, in different forms of conflict, mediation and diplomacy.

The Gulf War

If one takes the Gulf War first, it seems that the long period of a contained war of attrition will probably come to a critical point shortly. Whether Iran can sustain a massive offensive operations for very long is perhaps a different question. But the point is that the effects of a major offensive would change the character of the war. And the reasoning I would adduce goes something like this: up to now Iran has been winning a long war of attrition. In many ways it has already won such a war. The regime of Saddam Hussein in Iraq is in very serious trouble. The ability of the Iraqi forces and of the Iraqi economy to withstand a massive onslaught is perhaps in doubt even though Iraq has been receiving for more than two-and-a-half years subsidies of between one and two billion dollars a month from other Arab states, notably in the Gulf, and even though the Iraqi forces have been stiffened by advisers, technicians and so-called volunteers.

This long war of attrition is certainly being won by Iran. The Iraqi response is to threaten a short war of attrition, that is to say, to cut off Iranian access to the revenues Iran needs for spare parts and the equipment of forces-in-being. The way to do so is not just, or perhaps even not, to attack Kharg Island itself but to make that island inaccessible to the other oil producing or importing countries. So the Iraqi tactics seem, first of all, to be to demonstrate that their air power can penetrate, as indeed it can, the Iranian defences. Last week they flew over 15 cities in Iran to demonstrate the mobility and capacity of their aircraft, to vaunt the Exocets on lease and the various forms of missile purchased from the Soviet Union and to emphasise the damage they can do. It is a good tactic to hit the wrong ships with your Exocets. It does considerable damage to Lloyds' Register but it also makes the vessels of other countries very chary over approaching Kharg Island. Sinking or crippling the ships of neutral countries makes it difficult for Iran to count on selling its oil through its terminals.

The threat therefore is of a quick war of attrition based on Iraqi air power against a long war of attrition based on Iranian land power. In this sense it also seems that the Iranian response within the context of the Iranian regime, is balanced on the edge of a succession problem between pragmatists who in some ways are increasingly taking control, and the mullahs who are nonetheless the fount of legitimacy in Iran. The response in such circumstances might very well be deliberately to escalate the war so as to make life difficult for foreign ships in the Straits of Hormuz. So each country in a sense is going for the oil jugular of the other. Each in a different context and each attempting to achieve different military and strategic ends, but both likely to affect the lift capacity of foreign nations. And in this context the question has certainly been discussed by the United States and by other members of the international energy community whether there should not be a marine convoy of tankers designed to break any attempt by Iran to block the Straits of Hormuz. Some of the oil importing countries have already given their assent in principle to this idea of a marine convoy, and the Japanese, who up to now have been very reluctant to entertain any such notion, are being pressed very hard indeed by the United States to join in such a venture. This might sound rather anodine when one remembers the proposal for an international maritime force during the Arab/Israeli confrontation, particularly that between Egypt and Israel in 1967. It might also be, however, the kind of response which could change the pattern of containment of the Iraq/Iran war and make it far more difficult to control its effects elsewhere. So in this context the Iraq-Iran war might take a crucial turn away from the long and pointless kind of attrition which has been carried on so far, and particularly if the Iranian offensive does succeed in its original ambition.

One further point we should not forget, the Iranian forces are not very far from Mosul, that Mosul is not only the heartland of Iraqi oil production, but over the past 500 years Mosul has been occupied many times by Iranian forces and that the fear of the Iranians in Iraq is very strong; and equally that the history of Iranian occupations of Mosul has been—generally speaking—one of massacre, including even the massacre of Moslems taking refuge in Christian churches in Mosul itself on the last occasion. It is a very significant psychological point in Iraqi terms. And it is possible that if such should happen, the Iraqi escalation would be as drastic as Iraq can possibly afford. So in those terms too the pattern of events is likely to take a different form this year from the somewhat contained pattern which has been characteristic of the past two or three years.

The Lebanon

Obviously, the other area of major consideration lies in the relationship between Israel and the Arabs, but particularly Israel, Syria and Lebanon in the country of Lebanon itself. Now, this is an American election year, and as a rule American election years are bad news for the Middle East. Israel is liable to try to take advantage of it, as in the old days did the British and French contemplating Suez or whatever. Everyone feels that American decision-making capacity is not quite so hot in an election year as it is in the first year, after the President takes office, and before he starts worrying about mid-term elections. In those terms the temptation to take some kind of action might be strong, or else the assumption prevalent, that the United States is not going to be able to carry through on its own commitments. It is fairly clear, that after Mr Rumsfeld's recent conversation in Damascus, the Syrians assume that they are winning. Syria might, of course, be quite wrong in its calculations. There is certainly a tendency in the present administration in Washington to demonstrate that it has more resolution, and is more ready to take risks than some of its critics might be tempted to give it credit for. But the point here is not so much whether the Syrians are wrong, as that of what effect their views are likely to have on their actions. Here I should like not only to place the Syrians in the context of the American presidential year but also discuss the way they see the development of American politics over recent months.

The outer context of the American-Syrian relationship has been one of near hostilities, one in which the threat of force has been liberally applied by both sides: the Syrians threatening to do their best to bring down the Gemayel government in Lebanon and the United States threatening to retaliate against Syrian-sponsored positions there and even possibly against Syrian positions, though only in the Lebanon itself. And they have, of course, used force against the Syrians. At the same time as they have geared up a dangerous and deliberate intensification of the conflict, of the kind which might involve superpowers in direct confrontation, they have in a sense been allies in the national reconciliation talks both inside Lebanon and at Geneva. Allies in the sense that they both recognise the difficulties of managing a violently unstable combination of forces and have been trying to force the Lebanese factions to talk to each other. One could expatiate at length about the nature and intractability of the Lebanese factions. But the Gemayel government and some of the Christians who support it have been under intense American pressure to negotiate with the others. And the Druzes in the Chouf, the Christians under Franjieh in the north and the Shi'ite militia particularly in Amal in the centre have also been under intense pressure to begin some form of negotiation with their internal enemy. Here is a very peculiar geo-political balance in which the two enemies, Syria and the United States, were also in effect allies trying to deal with Lebanese politics in the last months of last year. But what was catastrophic for the balance of this arrangement was the sudden and somewhat unexpected strategic cooperation agreement between Israel and the United States signed during Shamir's visit to Washington and just before President Gemayel visited Washington.

One might recall here that it was widely expected, and with reason, that when Gemayel went to Washington he was going to renegotiate the terms of the Israeli withdrawal agreement which had been drawn up in May. This was to be in a context which would also take account of Syrian interests and of Syria's apparent hopes of helping to form some kind of new and more stable regime in Lebanon itself. That was what he was supposed to be going there to do. And what he came away saying was that he had discussed the implementation of the original agreement with the United States. In those terms, the Israeli/American strategic cooperation agreement changed the whole pattern of what had been happening in the attempts to rescue both the Lebanon itself and to prevent the hostilities among its neighbours from drifting towards major confrontation. That is the context in which this set of developments in Lebanon must be viewed.

The first question that arises is: in that context what will happen now that the international force has been withdrawn? Originally it was meant to provide a certain breathing space in the Lebanon, to keep a relatively recognisable barrier between the contending factions, and to give the political process of national reconciliation a chance. The purpose was ill-defined and perhaps wisely ill-defined. It was nonetheless recognisable. However, the Americans rather blurred this line themselves by signing a strategic cooperation agreement with Israel which involved flying reconnaisance missions over Syrian positions and Syrian-supported positions in Lebanon, reporting their findings to Israel, so that Israel could use the information to score pinpoint hits on the Syrian-supported positions in the Chouf Mountains and in the Beka'a. Inevitably the force became a target for a retaliatory response. It became a hostage not only to the Lebanese situation but to the Israeli/Syrian relationship. The whole purpose and nature of the force had changed in context and thereby in character. In July two pro-Syrian groups, the Maronite Marada group led by Franjiah and the National Syrian Socialist Party led by Inaam, fought for control of the northern Khoura province. The fighting only concluded when Syria moved troops into the region and threatened to intervene directly. On 25 July the last official link between the Lebanese and Israeli Governments ended when an Israeli liaison office outside Beirut was evacuated. At the end of July the last US marines were withdrawn from the city, leaving Moslem militia to guard the embassy.

The next question is whether there is any hope for President Gemayel. By the middle of August clashes between the Druze militia and the Lebanese army revealed serious deficiencies in its training and morale.The Druze and Shi'ite leaders were pressing Gemayel to accept that the security plan (which aimed to disengage rival forces) was linked with major political reforms. Gemayel really feels that he is on the skids. He has attempted to create some form of dialogue with Moslem groupings that his family and their Maronite followers in the Phalange have had nothing to do with for many years, displaying elaborate courtesies in the talks at Geneva; but he has been inexorably sucked into a quagmire. He is forced to rely on the Maronite Phalange and yet has discovered that the concessions he has been compelled to make have turned many of his Christian supporters against him — and not only the Christian enemies of Franjiah's camp. He has gone too far in seeking reconciliation with the Moslems; but he is not strong enough to establish any real new rapport.

Gemayel's position in Lebanon is becoming weaker daily. The internal question of Gemayel's ability to deliver anything at all must now be called very seriously into question. Whether he will physically survive or whether his government will survive politically has become a very acute consideration. And that brings one to the third question, which is whether the Syrians are not now poised for a major political and perhaps military offensive in the Lebanon. The Americans have withdrawn their forces. They watch the internal collapse of the Gemayel regime proceeding almost by the day; and they are conscious, at least for the time being, of the support of their own clients in the Lebanon, particularly the Druzes, and large sections of the Lebanese Shi'ites. They are taking pains to emphasise — and President Assad himself has said so on many occasions — that they do not want a Syrian Lebanon. They do not wish to incorporate Lebanon into Syria to exercise Syrian control in the Lebanon. Now, when politicians, but particularly a politician like Assad, emphasises the moderations of his aims, I think one should be very careful indeed. It seems to me that they are poised for a new political offensive. They are not over-concerned with risks of a military confrontation which this might bring because they are aware not only of Soviet support but of the dangers of superpower confrontation. In particular, the strategic cooperation agreement serves to emphasise such dangers. The Syrians can exploit them. In many ways Assad has learnt an awful lot from Sadat. Syrian preparedness and ability to run risks in a situation which seems to be tilting in Assad's favour, is one which is likely to grow over this year.

The West Bank

These are the questions on this level. Very briefly I wish to raise a last point where I think developments might become acute. They lie in the Israeli West Bank/Jordanian relationship. There was much misplaced euphoria when King Hussein reconvened his parliament and Arafat embraced him. It looked to many as if somehow whole coalitions of interests in the Arab world were coming together and were likely to accept some form of the Reagan peace plan. I would suggest that such moves for reconciliation and Hussein's recall of the Jordanian parliament have nothing whatsoever to do with the plan. Egypt is the only state in the Arab world which has actually stated its desire for a Palestinian state. No other Arab country has even talked about the desirability of a Palestinian state. And every state in the Fertile Crescent is resolutely hostile to one. Apart from Egypt, all concerned are trying to pre-empt the framework of the Reagan peace plan to achieve different kinds of objectives. Hussein, having recalled the parliament and thereby already torn up the Rabat Agreement of 1974, which recognised the PLO as the sole legitimate representative of the Palestine people, is moving to what he sees as the best chance and the last chance of obtaining any reassertion of Jordanian control over the West Bank in the event that other developments ever bring about an Israeli withdrawal. He is, of course, very pessimistic about any such withdrawal. In his view, the Israelis are obviously there to stay. Indications like the Canal which is so frequently discussed, from the Mediterranean to the Dead Sea — the Med Dead Canal — would represent a vast investment and signify permanent intentions. The most that Hussein might be offered by the Israelis under a different government with less ideological commitment to maintaining the land, might be the following message: "You have the heavily populated areas. You deal with the Palestinians. And we will hold on to our settlements, our strategic control and our line of military positions there. So you have the problems of Nabulus and we will keep control of the West Bank." That is about the kind of maximum concession King Hussein can expect. I doubt whether he is at all interested in the Reagan plan. It seems more likely that he is trying to win PLO support on the West Bank which has been almost unanimous in the past for the Arafat PLO and for some form of reversion to Jordan at some stage in the future. Arafat, on the other hand, sees this opportunity as the last chance for staking some new claim to legitimacy inside the PLO, because his support on the West Bank has been very strong. It would enable him to recover from his savage defeats in the Lebanon and also to move towards the establishment of some kind of Palestinian state, again supposing that by some miracle Israel is ever ready to withdraw.

They present, then, a certain coincidence of tactics. But they have very diverse aims. The crucial question arises from the political activities now under way. The act of recalling the parliament, the search for support from the Palestinians has intensified attitudes hitherto scarcely acknowledged. Both King Hussein and his brother, Crown Prince Hassan, have been going round the camps and townships in Jordan and have been deliberately courting Palestinian support from PLO members and supporters themselves for the King's own initiatives. This also means, in fact, that they are splitting the population of the West Bank. The Mayor of Bethlehem, for example, has come out very strongly in favour of the King's new initiative but has already found himself in acrimonious dispute with the Harvard-trained highly intelligent, very strongly PLO orientated editor of *El Faj*, the most influential Arabic journal in Jerusalem. Some PLO supporters have said, in effect: "We would rather trust the Israelis than trust Hussein". Others declare: "We have no choice but to go along with Hussein. Otherwise we are condemning ourselves, as we have condemned ourselves over so many episodes in the past, to live under permanent Israeli rule".

The West Bank population, hitherto united in support of Arafat's Fatah PLO now risks being torn apart by the impact of King Hussein's initiative. It is not at all inconceivable in this year that a kind of Lebanisation of the West Bank will begin to come about, that factions, parties, different ideologies, different attitudes to the future, different attitudes towards which enemy to deal with first, will become a priority in determining relations between various elements of the West Bank population. Many of them are Christians, who tend to become more radical in this situation, much more so than Moslems. The most radical elements in the PLO are Christian. And they might be fighting each other, not only with words, about their attitude to the manoeuvres going on at present.

Conclusions

These three problems have become more acute in 1984 and are harder to contain than in the past, bloody as they have been in any event. I said that I would discuss something about the interactions. It is going to be very much harder to treat these as separate entities either in terms of superpower relationships or in terms of local power relationships. Egypt is moving back into the mainstream Arab politics, into a position where it hopes to be able to channel and change the forms of dispute. Egypt has put itself centrally in the picture at a well-chosen moment. President Mubarak has played very subtly over the past couple of years. But having been slow to move he is starting to move fast. But what can he manage? How much of the relationship between Arafat and Hussein on which his own position in that respect depends, is in turn going to be dependent on the relationship between the PLO elements in the Lebanon and some of those on the West Bank? And on the relationship between the PLO elements in the Lebanon and some of those on the West Bank. How likely are they in turn to provoke Israeli reactions, and what happens if different elements on the West Bank find that they are targets for Israeli repression or if they intend in turn to retaliate upon the Israelis?

The West Bank, I suspect, will be harder for Israel to control than it has been in the past although the Israeli authorities have been brutal on occasion, particularly in the early spring of 1982. More generally, the outer elements of management and the impact of the superpowers on local powers are going to have less effect upon regional reactions, upon the pattern of escalation in the Gulf War, upon the way in which that is managed which will in turn affect Syria's relations with Jordan; and how Syria reacts to American policies in Lebanon will also depend on the prospects of a maritime convoy and on what happens if there's a shooting match when the maritime convoy goes through. I am suggesting a pattern of more unmanageable interaction in the next few months than has been the case in the past rather compartmentalised form of reaction and management.

Part III — Technology

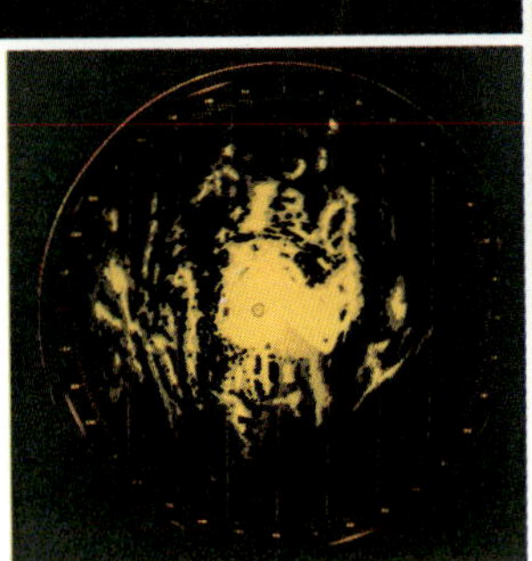

Space: The Military Applications Today and Tomorrow

GROUP CAPTAIN T GARDEN, MA MPhil, RAF

Group Captain Garden is currently Director of Defence Studies for the Royal Air Force. The views expressed in this article are those of the author, and do not necessarily reflect official opinion.

ON 4 OCTOBER 1957, the successful launch into orbit of Sputnik I startled the West, by demonstrating that the Soviet Union had an advanced capability to operate in space. The repercussions for deterrence, and NATO strategy were profound. This was not as a result of concern about future war in space, but because of the potential use of ballistic missiles to threaten the continental United States with nuclear weapons. More than a quarter of a century on, it might have been expected that the military exploitation of space would be both comprehensive and perhaps of over-riding importance. It is of interest to compare the developments of military aviation over a similar period, in the much less rapidly advancing technological period of the early part of this century. In 27 years, aviation advanced from the Wright Brothers first steps into the air, to a worldwide use of air power for offensive, defensive, reconnaissance and transport operations. The use of space has advanced in a much less dramatic way. Military satellites have been developed and deployed, often as a more economical way of carrying out a particular role. On the civil side, manned and unmanned systems have extended scientific knowledge about the earth, the solar system and deep space; but even in this field the level of activity has been patchy. The exploitation of space is undoubtedly an expensive and difficult operation. Is it so expensive and difficult that it will only have marginal strategic importance for the forseeable future, or is it the new strategic high ground as some would suggest? To answer these questions, we need to look at the military applications of space today, and how they may be developed, and also at the proposals and possibilities for novel systems in the future.

Military uses of Space in 1985

Satellites are used extensively by the Soviet Union and the United States for military purposes. They can be launched at short notice for specific missions, or can be placed in medium or long term orbiting positions. With the exception of the Soviet anti-satellite devices, there is no evidence to suggest that any of the satellites currently deployed are armed. Satellites may be used for reconnaissance, communications, navigation, meteorological purposes, geodetic survey and anti-satellite operations.

Reconnaissance satellites

Military reconnaissance satellites can be used for photographic reconnaissance, electronic information gathering, ocean surveillance or for early warning purposes. Around 40 per cent of all military satellites launched are used for photographic reconnaissance. High resolution is obtained by returning the film to earth for processing. Rapid, but less detailed reconnaissance can be achieved by in-flight processing and data transmission to earth. Unclassified estimates of the likely resolution achievable by such systems are of the order of 15–30 cm, which would be more than enough for identifying individual pieces of military equipment deployed. The USA, the USSR and China all operate reconnaissance satellites. France and Japan are developing a capability in this area.

The detection and analysis of electronic signals by satellites can be achieved by adding appropriate sensors to photographic reconnaissance satellites, or specialist vehicles may be used. Little is published about the capabilities of either the American or Soviet electronic surveillance systems. The large area covered by direct line-of-sight gives such satellites a capability to detect signals across the electro-magnetic spectrum, with the appropriate receivers. These can then be relayed by downlink to earth stations.

Another specialist reconnaissance role is that of ocean surveillance. Satellites to detect surface ships and submarines are of interest to both superpowers. Detection can be made by integrating a number of different sensor methods: visual light, electronic radiation and radar.

Finally, reconnaissance satellites are of strategic importance in the early warning role. The use of satellites can extend early warning time to around 30 minutes. The sensors detect an enemy missile almost immediately after launch, through the infra-red radiation of the rocket exhaust.

Reconnaissance satellites operate by detecting a particular part of the electromagnetic spectrum from radio waves, through radar to infra-red and visible light. The frequency band chosen, and the sensor material available, will condition the resolution, and the degradation from atmospheric conditions. Microprocessor developments will enhance the sensor capabilities significantly in the near term. Atmospheric degradation, and ground and sea clutter remain limitations.

Communication satellites

Satellite communications are becoming a vital part of the worldwide civil telecommunications network. The vastly increased line-of-sight range from a space system makes for a much reduced re-broadcasting network. For military uses, satellite communications are allowing very long range control of the battlefield at the lowest level. This may not necessarily be an advantageous development. The Falklands conflict of 1982 demonstrated the importance of satellite communications. Satellites are deployed for command and control of strategic forces, worldwide communications, data relay from other satellites, and for tactical communications. Signals can be carried on frequencies throughout the electromagnetic spectrum, including laser light.

Navigation satellites

Satellite navigation systems have been in operation since 1960. Initially, the principal purpose of the satellites was to act as an in-flight up-date for inertial navigation systems on strategic missiles. More recent developments allow worldwide three-dimensional position fixing for all military applications. The Soviet Union will be deploying GLONASS, and the United States NAVSTAR GPS in the immediate future, to give a universal navigation facility to their forces.

Meteorology

The widescale usage of civilian meteorology satellites has obvious military applications. Current satellites can provide prompt information of weather parameters on a worldwide basis for any military operation. Such information has a bearing on military planning, reconnaissance priorities and navigation of ICBMs.

Geodetic survey

Satellites specifically designed for geodetic survey can provide the essential mapping for the guidance of both ballistic missiles and cruise missiles. The difficulties in realistic testing of missile systems over their wartime orientations has heightened the importance of such survey systems.

Anti-satellite weapons

Both the Soviet Union and the United States have been carrying out research and development on anti-satellite weapon systems. Their approaches have been significantly different. The Soviet Union began testing satellite interceptors in 1967, and has continued a programme since then. The anti-satellite weapon is launched in the same way as a satellite, in order to achieve a close pass to the target. When within range of the target satellite, the anti-satellite interceptor is exploded. While the United States has been conducting research along similar lines, more interest has been generated by its programme to develop an anti-satellite missile which could be launched from an F–15 aircraft at high altitude. Other possible avenues which are being explored include the use of the electro-magnetic pulse (EMP) of an exo-atmospheric nuclear explosion. Particular sensors of reconnaissance systems may also be significantly vulnerable to ground or space-based laser systems.

Current Strategic Importance of Space

Such a review of the developments in the military use of space so far, suggest a relatively restrained use of the new high ground. Those systems deployed are extremely vulnerable to anti-satellite technologies which are either available now, or are soon to be available. The developments have tended to reflect space's ability to provide a better and more cost-effective service in peacetime, rather than a more dependable wartime facility. When considering the strategic importance of space today, the interaction of the vulnerability of the systems against their importance must be examined. There is no doubt that, in the

West, there is a tendency to increasing reliance. This dependence may not be as significant for the Soviet Union. Reconnaissance systems can be complimented by their use of manned aircraft and drones; loss of navigation facilities need not be critical; geodetic survey is essentially a peacetime activity; and meteorological information need not depend on space-based systems. The weak link is the increasing dependence on communication, command and control, and strategic warning through satellite systems. If commanders in peace come to rely on the assured ability to control operations through communication and data transfer via space, they will be offering a vulnerability to be exploited by the opposition. For this reason, research on offensive anti-satellite systems is bound to continue, as must development of defensive measures for irreplaceable systems.

Space and Strategic Defence

If, after 27 years in space, man has not made it another battlefield, it is not for the lack of imagination. During the 1960s, Robert McNamara looked for ways to limit the damage to the American homeland in a future superpower conflict, so as to enhance deterrence. Among the measures considered was the development of anti-ballistic missile (ABM) systems. Yet after significant expenditure, he concluded in 1965 that the enemy could always frustrate any attempt at strategic defence at considerably less cost than the measures taken by the United States. Although we were not privy to the debates which undoubtedly took place in the Soviet Union, it is likely that they also concluded that effective ballistic missile defence (BMD) was likely to founder at that time on financial and technical grounds. Deployment of systems on both sides was likely only to lead to increased deployment of ICBMs.

It was, therefore, in the interests of both the superpowers to prevent wide-scale deployment of ABM systems, and as a result the ABM treaty was negotiated as part of the strategic arms limitations talks in 1972. The SALT 1 ABM Treaty prohibited each country from deploying ABM defensive systems at more than two sites. The 1974 protocol reduced this limit to one site on each side. In the event, the United States has no system deployed, and the Soviet Union has a light ABM ring around Moscow which consists of 32 Galosh missiles.

Ballistic missile defence foundered in the 1960s because the capability which the technology could provide was of dubious effectiveness either in protecting cities or even in a limited aim of protecting missile sites. The cost of deployment would have been very high, given its limited effectiveness, the enemy could counter at much less cost by deploying more ICBMs or more warheads. The effect on the strategic balance, and on stability, was uncertain. In 1983, the debate was re-opened:

> Let me share with you a vision of the future which offers hope. It is, that we embark on a programme to counter the awesome, Soviet missile threat with measures that are defensive . . . What if free people could live secure in the knowledge that their security did not rest upon the threat of instant US retaliation to deter Soviet attack; we could intercept and destroy strategic ballistic missiles before they reached our own soil or that of our allies?
>
> *President Reagan: Speech to the Nation, 23 March 1983*

> Should this conception be converted into reality, this would actually open the floodgates of a runaway race of all types of strategic arms, both offensive and defensive. Such is the real purport of the seamy side, so to say, of Washington's 'defensive conception'.
>
> *General Secretary Andropov:* Pravda, *26 March 1983*

The reason for the re-opening of the debate was the promise of the new BMD technologies. New technologies for space-based systems appeared to be offering the prospect of a real defence against nuclear weapons. But can these new technologies promise a strategy, which enhances stability, and can be afforded, or are we merely seeing history repeating itself? Is the slow development of the military uses of space a reflection of its inherent irrelevance to future conflict? To seek the answer to this question, we can examine the well documented US proposals for a ballistic missile defensive system of the future.

The High Frontier

The main elements of a next generation BMD system are summarised in the High Frontier study. A layered defensive system, which seeks to destroy most hostile ICBMs in their early boost phase, is proposed. Those remaining would be re-attacked during their mid-trajectory phase. Those warheads penetrating the first two layers would be attacked during the terminal phase by ground-based ABM systems. Civil defence measures complement this defensive programme. The study claims that:

> We can deploy in space a purely defensive system of satellites using non-nuclear weapons which will deny any hostile power a rational option for attacking our current and future space vehicles or for delivering a military effective first strike with its strategic ballistic missiles on our country or on the territory of our allies. Such a global ballistic missile defence system is well within our present technological capabilities and can be deployed in space in this decade at less cost than other options that might be available to us to redress the strategic balance.[1]

Not everyone shares this degree of confidence in such a global BMD deployment. In early 1983, President Reagan set up a commission to review the strategic modernisation programme of the United States. Among other topics, the Scowcroft Commission looked at the question of BMD. They found that:

> Applications of current technology offer no real promise of being able to defend the United States against massive nuclear attack in this century. An easier task is to provide ABM defence for fixed hardened targets, such as ICBM silos. However, even this will be a difficult feat if an attacker can use a large number of warheads against each defended target.

To look at these contradictory assessments in more detail, the technological, economic, strategic and arms control implications must all be considered.

ABM Technologies

Since the development of Multiple Independently Targetable Re-entry Vehicles (MIRV) for strategic missile systems, the problem with countering any Intercontinental Ballistic Missile (ICBM) attack has been significantly complicated. Considerable benefit would therefore be gained by an ABM system which destroyed the missile in its early boost phase, before the independent re-entry vehicles (RVs) had separated. Attack during this phase brings two other advantages: boosters are far more visible than RVs for detection, and it is more difficult to provide decoys which look like boosters, than it is to simulate RVs. The major disadvantage is that boost-phase intercept of the ICBMs must take place over enemy territory. This leads to the requirement for a space-based target acquisition and interception system. If the critical boost-phase interception can be achieved from space, then the mid-trajectory interception can also be space-based. The terminal phase of the layered defensive system would be met by ground-based systems defending the expected target area. A successful test of one such US Army ground-based interception system against a single re-entry vehicle was reported in *The Times* of 12 June 1984.

A number of proposals have been made for possible useful lines of research for the space-based systems. These can be divided into approaches based on directed energy techniques, and those dependent on kinetic energy kill mechanisms. The interception problem is formidable, with perhaps 2,000 boosters to be engaged within the first five minutes of their flight. The near instantaneous response of directed energy weapons, either lasers or particle beams, make them an attractive option for this time-urgent task. Laser weapons would kill missiles either by burning through the booster skin, or by producing a shock wave which caused mechanical damage. One calculation of the energy requirement has suggested that a 100 megawatt laser, using a mirror some 4 metres in diameter could cause sufficient damage to a target in approximately one second. If such a hydrogen chloride laser could be deployed in sufficient numbers, it would require 1,000 shuttle flights for energy stores alone. This suggests that for laser-based systems, a nuclear pumped X-ray laser would need to be developed.

Particle beam weapons seek to kill missiles through damage to their electronics. A charged particle beam would suffer from dispersion from unpredictable fluctuations in the earth's magnetic field, and also from ionisation in the earth's atmosphere. A neutral particle beam cannot be accelerated or focused. Any space-based particle beam system would therefore need to accelerate a charged particle beam, focus it and then neutralise it by stripping extra electrons from the atoms. This is a complex process, requiring technology which is currently beyond the state of the art. Consideration of the fuel requirements leads to similar conclusions to the laser, and the likely necessity of a nuclear explosive system for any workable particle beam weapon. One analysis concludes 'all these difficulties point to the conclusion that even though it might be possible to construct an accelerator that would produce a beam of hydrogen atoms intense and energetic enough to cause some damage to the ICBM in its boost phase, a satellite based neutral particle beam ABM system would not be practical'.[2]

Kinetic energy kill systems can either be of the rocket propelled missile type, or the hypervelocity gun system. The High Frontier study sees the deployment of carrier satellites, with conventional missiles as a practical proposition. The total mass of such a system precludes comprehensive deployment. A more promising area for research into kinetic energy kill systems is to be the hypervelocity electro-magnetic rail gun. This system uses a high energy electro-magnetic field to accelerate a hit-to-kill projectile to speeds in the order of 5–25 km per second. Again, the power requirements for such a system are prodigious, and are likely to need nuclear generators.

Whatever system is used to kill the ICBMs, it must be able to cope with a massive simultaneous attack. Target acquisition, tracking and pointing, all give significant technological problems. Numerous counters to each weapon system are already in prospect. The vulnerability of the weapon system itself is a major cause for concern. Already, anti-satellite weapon systems are well advanced, and one analyst has suggested that space-based ABM systems would be particularly vulnerable to space mines. In summary, the outstanding technical problems are the provision of adequate target acquisition, tracking and pointing systems, effective kill mechanisms at attainable energy costs, and protection of the weapon system itself. The Scowcroft Commission concluded that:

> At this time, however, the Commission believes that no ABM technologies appear to combine practicality, survivability, low cost and technical effectiveness sufficiently to justify proceeding beyond the stage of technology development.[3]

Certainly the technology for terminal interception of ballistic missiles has improved since the 1960s. A favoured option for this point defence of US ICBM sites is the Swarmjet. The system uses a launcher with 500 to 1,000 unguided rockets fired simultaneously. Between 5,000 and 10,000 rockets are assessed as giving an 85 per cent probability of intercepting a single re-entry vehicle within the lethal area of the Swarmjet system. Multiplying this requirement across all the possible targets with the more than 7,000 Soviet RVs currently deployed, emphasises the importance of the boost phase interception.

Technology points to the possibility of such a comprehensive layered defensive system, given infinite resources. The question is what can be achieved with finite resources, and whether it is worth doing.

The Economics of BMD

Given the uncertainties of the technologies discussed above, any assessment of the cost of deploying a full layered BMD system must be speculative. The High Frontier study makes a detailed assessment of the costs of deployment. It states that the whole system could be deployed by 1990 for a total cost of $35 billion (bn). However, 'cost data validity for the illustrative High Frontier programs range from hard to very soft'. A comparison with the cost of the UK Trident programme, a much more modest affair, suggests that this may be an order of magnitude under-assessed. The Defensive Technologies Study Team in the United States has already earmarked $11.4 bn merely for research to select appropriate technology paths for ballistic defence through either directed energy weapons or conventional interceptors. The North Atlantic Assembly Scientific and Technical Committee has assessed the cost for a total system in the range of $100–500 bn. For a comparison, the 1983 defence budget for the United States was a total of $240 bn.

Economic considerations are therefore going to play a major part in any decisions on the deployment of a BMD system. Given the economic difficulties that all nations are having in maintaining their force levels, it may be the overriding factor.

Strategic Implications

Even if it is assumed that all the technological problems can be overcome, at a price which is affordable, what are the implications for the security of the West? None of the proponents of BMD, make the claim that it can ever produce a 100 per cent effective defence. The exact per centage of 'leakage' is a matter of some debate. At the upper end of effectiveness, a full deployment would protect adequately against all contingencies except a massive retaliatory counter-city attack. At the lower end of the assessment, the system would merely reduce the vulnerability of the fixed land-based ICBMs from a pre-emptive first strike. Any assessment of the effect of BMD deployment on stability must depend on the prior assessment of effectiveness.

If a high 'leakage' rate, say greater than 10 per cent of incoming missiles, were found to be the likely value, then deployment could not be cost effective. The enemy could always counter more cheaply by increasing his missile numbers. The vulnerability would only be that of land-based systems, and the continuing invulnerability of submarine-launched ballistic missiles would ensure that deterrence continued on the same basis as before.

If the BMD deployment appeared to hold in prospect a real change in the strategic balance, what would the effect be? A simultaneous deployment by both sides of an effective BMD system, might make the possibility of fighting a conventional war both more likely, and more acceptable, in that the risks of unacceptable nuclear destruction of the homeland had been reduced. Should one superpower consider that the other might achieve deployment first, then the prospects for stability could be of concern. The nation losing the race for deployment might feel so threatened, that it needed to take pre-emptive action against the BMD system. Certainly, both sides will feel the need to investigate the technologies, to have the capability to deploy counter-measures, should the other side produce an operational BMD system.

The deployment of only a moderately effective system by either of the superpowers would have significant implications for lesser nuclear powers. In as much as the independent decision centres of Britain and France enhance NATO deterrence, the reduction of the credibility of these systems would have a negative influence on stability. It can be argued that the advantages of acquiring small nuclear weapon capabilities would be reduced to an extent whereby other nations would not wish to proliferate. However, this is by no means necessarily the case, as the pressures on proliferating states come from other lesser powers, who would not be deploying their own BMD systems. Only if the superpowers took on the role of world policeman could their BMD deployments have a positive effect on countering nuclear proliferation.

In summary, because perfect defence is unattainable, nuclear deterrence, through the threat of massive retaliation, should remain effective. Depending on the level of BMD effectiveness, it might be that the prospect of limited war between the superpowers became possible again. In any event both would need to deploy appropriate counter-measures, which could include significant increases in their nuclear systems.

Arms Control Implications

Research and development on ABM systems is permitted by the ABM Treaty. The deployment of anything beyond a single point defence ground-based system would certainly require a renegotiation of the Treaty, and in all probability, termination of it. In the near term, research can continue, but at the stage where field testing of new systems was necessary, the provisions of Article V of the Treaty would have to be broken. At this stage, it would seem unlikely that either side would feel it had much to gain from a new, and less restrictive treaty. It is, of course, possible that the demise of the ABM Treaty would signal the end of the other arms limitation protocols with a view to expanding the offensive capability on both sides.

The Future

The ABM Treaty came out of a mutual realisation that neither superpower could benefit from the deployment of a BMD system in the 1960s. Technology may or may not be able to provide a reasonable degree of protection against ballistic missiles. It does not appear that it will be able to do it cheaply. The strategic implications of deployment of a BMD system are not clear. It may be good politically to be able to assure populations that money is being spent to reduce the risk of their nuclear annihilation, but if this makes war more possible, it is counter-productive. The abrogation of the ABM Treaty could signal another twist in the downward spiral of superpower relations, and thus add to the possibility for conflict. Nevertheless, given that both sides are carrying out research in this area, each must develop appropriate counter-measures against the deployment of a BMD system by the other.

It seems that the train of events is not greatly dissimilar from those in the 1960s. Technology promises some capability, but at a price which may not be affordable. The implications for stability are again ambiguous. The result may then be once again that both sides decide eventually, having conducted sufficient research, that it is in their mutual best interests to abide by the ABM Treaty.

Space offers no easy option; it offers no sanctuary and no automatic control of the earthbound battlefield. Unlike the development of air power, it has not yet shown signs of conferring advantage on the side which can control it. Indeed the history of the military applications of space so far, suggests that it has more pitfalls than advantages. Over reliance on vulnerable space-based systems, which may be available in peacetime, can reduce effectiveness when they are destroyed in the early minutes of any war. Development of future systems will involve financial undertakings, which given finite resources, may threaten far more urgent military needs. Finally, were success to be achievable in space-based defensive systems, it is not clear that the prospect of stability would be enhanced.

Notes

[1] Graham, Daniel O., *The Non-Nuclear Defence of Cities*, Cambridge USA 1983, ABT Books.

[2] Parmentola, J. & Tsipis, K., 'Particle Beam Weapons', *Scientific American*, April 1979, p. 44.

[3] *The Report of the President's Commission on Strategic Forces*, April 1983. (Excerpts from the report were reprinted in *Survival*, July/August 1983, pp. 177–86).

Emerging Technology: Economic and Military Implications for the Alliance

DR FAROOQ HUSSAIN
Dr Hussain is the Alliance Fellow at the RUSI

THE IMPORTANCE of exploiting advances in technology for improving NATO's force posture *vis à vis* the Warsaw Pact is a long established consideration in Alliance politics. The scientific and technological prowess of the United States, Western Europe, and Japan over the Soviet Union and its eastern bloc satellites has been historically perceived as one of the principal means by which western security interests can be protected against an adversary intent on quantitative superiority. Thus inadequacies in the Alliance's force posture have traditionally been framed in a manner that permits superior technology to provide the fix. Technology has been, and largely continues to be seen as the "force multiplier", the means by which smaller forces can deter larger forces by possessing qualitative advantages in performance of weapon systems.

As a result of this view, NATO has never sought to match Warsaw Pact forces tank for tank, aircraft for aircraft, ship for ship. It is important to bear this in mind because the majority of presentations of the relative balance of NATO and Warsaw Pact forces are formulated as a comparison of force ratios of units of military equipment. These static comparisons of total numbers of different types of weapon systems held in the two arsenals do not reflect the relative qualitative advantages that accrue from advanced or superior technology (nor are they supposed to). However, these simplistic comparisons often play a major part in shaping public perceptions of the military balance and help to highlight specific strategic issues of current concern. Paradoxically, while the Alliance has always placed a touching faith in the value of superior technology for redressing differences in overall numbers of systems, no satisfactory or thoroughly sound method of measuring the "force multiplication" effect of superior technology has been established thus far.

Clearly, a large amount of technical and operational analysis is conducted in order to discover the advantages of specific military technologies, but the results of such studies rarely form the basis for major force planning decisions because of the uncertainties associated with the results. These decisions are more significantly influenced by factors of political perception and economic constraints. Thus the kinds of technological opportunities that NATO has sought to exploit during its history have been multi-faceted, they have appeared to address not only problems of relative force balance but also ones associated with the intrinsic political complexity of a democratic alliance.

Technology has been seen not just as a means of meeting numerically superior forces but as method of avoiding very awkward problems of strategy and policy. It is argued here that while this feature of Alliance planning is not necessarily harmful or damaging, it can be. This is because the political, economic, and military circumstances of the Alliance's member nations have changed very significantly during its history, while the search for technological panaceas forms a consistent paradigm of Alliance politics. In the past the resilience of the Alliance was frequently demonstrated by its capacity to recover from significant problems posed by failures in its policy and planning. In recent times this resilience has begun to show the effects of wear and tear, especially in the cases of the neutron bomb and intermediate nuclear force deployment decisions.

As the Alliance moved towards the adoption of its policy of Flexible Response in the mid to late 1960s, the then US Secretary of Defense, Robert S. McNamara, considered that NATO placed undue emphasis upon nuclear weapons. He proposed and attempted to execute significant conventional force improvements while urging a reconsideration of the role US strategic nuclear weapons should play in the future of European security. The result of his efforts, however, was to end in the first significant build-up of short range nuclear systems. It is not the intention here to discuss the reasons behind the concurrent deployment of short range nuclear systems with conventional force improvements but to elaborate some of the arguments that were set out in favour of what were then seen as "tactical" nuclear weapons. It was argued that attempts to match Warsaw Pact conventional force levels on a one for one basis were unrealistic on political and economic grounds for the Alliance's European nations and that very high levels of US forces in Europe faced domestic political opposition. The introduction of short range nuclear weapons was seen as the means by which the Alliance could offset the disparities in the conventional force levels. The short range nuclear weapons were argued as being cost-effective in that they would be a much cheaper way of redressing the weaknesses of NATO's conventional force posture than would be possible if conventional weapon systems were bought. Perhaps most importantly to Europeans, the short range nuclear weapons were seen as a visible American commitment to the nuclear defence of Europe.

Paradoxically, short range nuclear weapons were out of favour with McNamara and his advisers. During the period 1961–67, McNamara sought to convince the Alliance's European members of the efficacy of Flexible Response and to establish the perception of a "firebreak" between nuclear and conventional war. McNamara attempted to encourage the withdrawal of short range nuclear weapons from Europe and place reliance on conventional forces. However, the Alliance's European members were seriously disturbed by this proposal because it appeared to cast doubt on the credibility of the American nuclear shield. Under pressure from the major NATO countries McNamara capitulated and left the continued deployment of short range nuclear weapons in Europe unchanged. Throughout this period, the short range nuclear weapon systems were without well defined tasks or a coherent doctrine for their use and this remains true today. It is unfortunate and reprehensible that those influential in American security policy at this time were unable to control the deployment of these weapons or allow a determined attack on the policy problems they presented, even though they seriously doubted the value of their deployment. As a result an enormous arsenal of short range nuclear weapons emerged in Europe without any credible military purpose.

The Background

Present interests in exploiting what have been called "emerging technologies" to improve NATO's conventional force posture are intimately linked to the problems posed by the deployment of short and intermediate range nuclear weapons in Europe. At this point it is, perhaps, worth describing the major events that put emerging technologies for conventional forces into the spotlight of strategic debate. There are, of course, differences of opinion over the exact interrelationship of these events and the extent to which any one or more of them have been singular in shaping interest in improving the Alliance's conventional force posture through the utilisation of emerging weapons technology. There is no attempt here to provide an historical assessment of these events but rather to present them in approximate chronological order and to develop the major influential themes that they have raised.

In the early part of 1982, a project was formulated to examine the major security issues facing Europe in the future. Composed of academics, senior military personages (predominantly retired), and some analysts of military affairs. This project was the dream child of Caroll Wilson who in the 1950s had led a project to examine the policy and planning problems facing the American nuclear power industry. Sponsored by the American Academy of Arts and Sciences and subsequently financially supported by the Ford Foundation, this project became known as the European Security Study (ESECs). Unrelated to the ESECs study was a separate effort with a more complex background led by senior staff of a major American defence analysis contractor, the BDM Corporation. The BDM Corporation had earlier conducted a major study of Soviet concepts of military operations, particularly with regard to Western Europe, and this work formed the basis for its projected solutions to some critical aspects of NATO's military policy and planning. Lastly, the former US Secretary of Defence, Robert S. McNamara, having left his position as head of the World Bank, turned his interests once again to security matters and began to develop his ideas for reducing European dependence on American nuclear weapons, specifically, through the adoption of a policy of no first use of nuclear weapons.

In autumn 1982, General Bernard Rogers, the Supreme Commander Allied Forces Europe (SACEUR), published an article in the journal *Foreign Affairs* which set his priorities and objectives for NATO's military policy and plans in the coming years. This article constitutes the first public presentation of what has come to be known as the "Rogers Doctrine" although elements of it were given previously by General Rogers in Congressional testimony, and subsequently elaborated in speeches such as the address to the RUSI, London, in October 1982. Though the extent and nature of the interaction should not be over-emphasised, the Rogers Doctrine was developed in concert with the work of the group at BDM, who had visited SACEUR to present their ideas, accompanied on at least one occasion, by representatives of the US legislature with special interests in European security issues. Equally, the efforts of the ESECs Study group had been smiled upon by General Rogers and provided support from senior members of his staff at the Supreme Headquarters Allied Powers Europe (SHAPE).

Many subtle and complicated issues are present in General Roger's exposition of his doctrine, not all of them have been directly elaborated by SACEUR himself. In paraphrasing the central arguments here, no claim is made towards an all-embracing understanding of his position, which no doubt retains some flexibility. However, it is clear that three key issues have played a major role in shaping SACEUR's notions for doctrinal and force posture reform within the Alliance. The first is the transparent anxiety of a very broad base of West European and American public opinion over the direction of existing nuclear weapons policy and plans. Secondly, and perhaps less obvious to the public, is the extent to which any major NATO Commander is aware of the existing and projected constraints (primarily economic), on prospective improvements to NATO's conventional forces in the late 1980s to early 1990s. Lastly, the significant and perplexing changes in the composition, operational doctrine, and level of readiness of Soviet military forces that have been observed in recent years require a carefully considered response, not least in the absence of a consensus of opinion explaining these changes.

The implications of the Rogers Doctrine

With these three concerns in mind it is possible to paraphrase General Rogers's "doctrine" in the following way. There has long been a concern that such short range nuclear systems as are available to SACEUR have very poor direct military utility resulting from the constraints associated with the political decision to initiate the use of nuclear weapons in a future conflict, and from the operational characteristics of the systems themselves: are they to be used early in a potential conflict or not at all? As a consequence, the decision to initiate the use of nuclear weapons is placed upon the shoulders of SACEUR and the relevent National Command Authorities early in a potential conflict because the level of conventional forces does not confidently provide for a situation in which a purely conventional attack could be adequately contained. Thus it is regarded that the threshold at which SACEUR would request and NATO's political authorities (or individual member nations possessing nuclear weapons), would have to consider the release of nuclear weapons in a potential conflict is unacceptably low.

General Rogers has argued that by improving his ability to contain a potential conflict at the conventional level, the threshold at which he would be forced to request nuclear weapons would be raised, thus forcing the Soviet Union, in contemplating aggression against NATO, to be the one to initiate the use of nuclear weapons. The rationale for this view is that both NATO and the Soviet Union would be reluctant to initiate the use of nuclear weapons because of the risks of escalation to theatre-wide and intercontinental nuclear war. As a consequence, it is crucial that the Soviet Union never perceives a level of conventional force superiority over NATO such that they could consider a wholly conventional attack against the Alliance in which they could call the bluff on nuclear first use as delineated in NATO's policy of Flexible Response. In fact, General Rogers has said that he has very little flexibility in response to direct conventional attack, and that the Alliance is actually maintaining a policy of delayed first use of nuclear weapons.

There are two important provisions that must also be considered and which significantly influence the priority and character of the conventional force improvements that NATO might consider. Firstly, Soviet military doctrine and operational concepts increasingly emphasise conventional operations the beginning of any conflict with NATO. They also perceive the chances of victory as being completely lost if NATO has the opportunity to make an early use of its short range nuclear systems. Thus there is a significant incentive for the Soviet Union in planning an attack against NATO to strike pre-emptively at the Alliance's short and intermediate range nuclear systems. The deployment and operational characteristics of the short range nuclear systems held by the Alliance makes them especially vulnerable to such an attack. In the past a Soviet strike against the Alliance's shorter range nuclear systems would have required nuclear weapons, but this is no longer necessary. It is quite conceivable for such an attack to be planned for with the new short range ballistic missiles such as the SS–21,22,23 armed with conventional warheads alone. These systems would also be allocated to other deep rear area targets, but nuclear storage sites and bases are likely to be the highest priority targets. Secondly, throughout its deployment of short range nuclear systems in Europe, NATO has never been able to reconcile the operational characteristics of the systems which require rapid decision making, flexible command and control procedures, and early use to be militarily effective, with a policy that depends heavily on extensive and time consuming political consultation together with the kind of rigidity of command and control and release procedures that it is reasonable to expect for nuclear weapons.

It is at this point that there is a divergence between SACEUR's interests in conventional force improvements as they have been publicly articulated, and those groups (especially the ESECs Study), who perceive the opportunity to raise the nuclear threshold by exploiting emerging technologies for improving NATO's conventional force posture. The principal difference is that SACEUR does not see opportunities in the so-called emerging technologies as a means of withdrawing short range nuclear systems, or for inhibiting their modernisation. Rather, such opportunities as are afforded by the emerging technologies were divided into three main areas of application. These were those that contributed to the forward battle, primarily in anti-armour weapons; those that contributed to the improvement of command and control, intelligence gathering and target acquisition; and those that might make feasible the attack of rear area targets with conventional rather than nuclear warheads. It was this last option that was seized upon by the ESECs Study and others as the principal means of raising the nuclear threshold in Europe.

'Deep Strike' Attacks

The enthusiasm for the idea of obtaining the capability to attack rear area targets (200 kilometres or more beyond the inter-German border) rests wholly with the prospect that such a capability would permit the removal or substantial reduction of NATO's short range nuclear weapons, and raise the threshold at which nuclear weapons might be considered to be used in the event of a conflict between NATO and the Warsaw Pact. In any event, NATO's shorter range nuclear stockpile has been significantly reduced in recent years and could be reduced further. However, SACEUR has never endorsed the view that the shorter range nuclear systems might be totally withdrawn in the event that new conventional technologies provided a means of attacking rear area targets. Nor is there any evidence to suggest that the threshold at which nuclear weapons might be considered for use would necessarily be raised by the introduction of such systems. Apart from serious questions as to the technical feasibility of these systems, there were considerations of cost. In its endorsement of the new technologies for rear area attack, the ESECs study uncritically accepted the data provided by a single source. This data was derived from studies originating at the BDM Corporation which examined Soviet concepts of military operations for central Europe. These BDM studies were undertaken for the United States Department of Defense and the Defense Nuclear Agency and focused specifically on the problems posed by the echelonging of Soviet ground forces. The proposal was that Soviet second echelon forces could be put at risk by attacking them with conventionally armed ballistic missiles such as the Pershing IIs that had formed part of NATO's Intermediate Nuclear Force modernisation programme.

The requirement for "Deep Strikes" at Soviet second echelon forces and other major rear area targets such as air bases, and reception and onward movement facilities (for instance, railway marshalling yards), rests on several assumptions. The first is that in spite of the enormous commitment to forward defence, the Alliance's central region in Germany is more or less indefensible against a major Warsaw Pact conventional attack without requiring a Soviet resort to the use of its own theatre nuclear forces. Consequently, the incentive to initiate the early first use of nuclear weapons rests with NATO. General Rogers himself has argued that this results in a dangerously low threshold at which nuclear weapons use would have to be considered by the Alliance in a future conflict. The risks of initiating nuclear war are so great that the Alliance may be perceived in peacetime as to be extremely reluctant to authorise the first use of nuclear weapons in the event of an attack by Warsaw Pact conventional forces. In effect, the Alliance's policy of initiating the first use of nuclear weapons if conventional defence proved inadequate was considered to be implausible.

SACEUR's remedy for this situation was to improve NATO's conventional forces by a margin that allowed for a successful initial defence at the inter-German border. To add to the Alliance's arsenal conventional weapon systems that allowed attacks to be considered against second echelon targets that would arrive to overwhelm NATO's forward defences, and to maintain sufficient nuclear capability to deter Soviet use of its own nuclear forces. Thus if the Soviet Union were to plan an attack against NATO in the central region of Europe, they could not conceive of any success without initiating the use of their own nuclear weapons first. This they would not do for the risk of escalation which would place the Soviet Union vulnerable to nuclear attack.

Jeffrey Record, in examining the "Deep Strike" proposals in the November 1983 issue of the *Armed Forces Journal* wrote: "Deep Strike is disturbing for a number of reasons, not the least of which is the remarkable lack of serious inquiry attending its promotion and endorsement by key officials and legislators. The strategy's fundamental premises have been accepted as fact by all but a few skeptics; its potentially troublesome military and political implications have been more or less ignored; and practically no one has sought to place Deep Strike in historical context, perhaps because it fares so poorly there compared to how its enthusiasts claim it will fare on tomorrow's battlefield."

Several factors were at play in formulation of the Deep Strike concept and which gave it a glittering appeal. The first was that the proposal formulated the Alliance's problems in terms which allowed concerns over unsatisfactory nuclear policy and inadequate conventional defence to be resolved by the simple expedient of the purchase of new technology, permitting the accomplishment of a mission that was stated to be previously only achievable with the use of nuclear weapons. This technology not only allowed NATO to exploit a fatal flaw in the Soviet concept of operations for a major attack against Western Europe it was also available at bargain basement prices. All the relevent technologies had passed "demonstration tests" and were just awaiting a policy decision for procurement. The tremendous early effort placed by Senator Sam Nunn and then Representative Robin Beard (now NATO Assistant Secretary-General for defence collaboration), and General Bernard Rogers, for a broad European endorsement of this idea was at first quite successful, especially through groups such as ESECs who published a widely reported study recommending the Deep Strike proposals.

Thus the "emerging technologies" for conventional weapon systems as they have been labeled, were intimately associated with the Deep Strike concept of operations, though they would later be bandied about as equally relevant to more mundane applications in conventional force improvement requirements. It should also be noted that the Deep Strike concept and what has become known as the "Rogers Doctrine" has evolved in a convoluted manner from a number of other studies, notably AirLand Battle, and the SHAPE Follow-On-Force-Attack (FOFA) study. These are well described by Boyd Sutton, *et. al.*

in the March/April 1984 issue of *Survival*. An important aspect of the SHAPE FOFA study is that it considered the use of NATO aircraft for a number of Deep Strike roles, including offensive counter-air operations against air bases. The study suggested that the Alliance did not possess enough aircraft for the scope of the targetting associated with the variety of FOFA missions that had been identified and that very large attrition of aircraft were associated with the high sortie rates and depth of penetration required for FOFA missions. It is also not very frequently appreciated that the effect on the Forward Line of Own Troops (FLOT) of FOFA missions was not particularly convincing unless very significant attrition was inflicted on Soviet follow-on forces. It was hard to reconcile the cost of effecting this attrition through FOFA as compared with improving identified deficiencies in NATO's forward deployed ground forces.

It was reasonable to assume in the circumstances (one would suppose), that if alternate means of attacking the FOFA target sets could be found, that were not likely to place such demands on the Alliance's air power, and could be afforded, then this would be the ideal solution. Hence, the proposal for conventionally armed ballistic and/or cruise missiles. But the validity of this proposal rests on central assumptions concerning the military utility of attacking rear area targets in the absence of the capacity adequately to defend forward, the ability to provide the required technology within the limitations of anticipated budgets, and lastly but most importantly, that the political costs associated with the implementation of the new concept and weapons are within the constraints imposed by a democratic alliance. It is to these issues that we may now turn to examine in more detail.

The Cost

The Alliance's policy of forward defence is known to possess a number of weaknesses of which the unfavourable ratio of in-place forces and equipment is the most familiar and commonly cited. Although NATO has never sought to match the Warsaw Pact weapon for weapon, man to man, this has not been the source of complaint about the adequacy of NATO's conventional deterrent. Rather concern is frequently expressed in terms of developments that adversely effect the NATO/Warsaw Pact force ratio.

During the past decade Warsaw Pact force levels have been maintained and the quality of its weapons improved. By comparison NATO until recently, has not introduced significant new equipment, and rarely has equipment been replaced on a one-for-one basis. Thus the adequacy of NATO's conventional forces has been affected not so much by the total numbers of systems possessed by each side, but by the scope and pace of the qualitative improvement of Soviet and some Warsaw Pact forces.

Thus even from the perspective of SACEUR in 1983, the imbalance of conventional forces could have been corrected by relatively small increases in defence expenditure. However, these increases (four rather than three per cent of GNP) proved impossible to obtain.

The task of finding a politically persuasive means of securing increases in defence expenditure required to improve NATO's conventional forces needed a renewed effort, and more politically glamorous packaging. Here the idea of Deep Strike offered "for just a few dollars more" a means by which NATO could buy its way out of trouble. But the manner in which the Deep Strike concept was developed, and its emphasis on attacking moving targets (second echelon forces), was found suspect on two grounds. Firstly, a number of specialists expressed dismay at the priority given to second echelon targets. They argued that the evidence for supposing that rear area attacks were a worthwhile consideration in order to influence the battle at the front was very slim. Notably, Trevor Dupuy writing in the August 1982 issue of *Armed Forces Journal*, described the concept of second echelon attack as a "Red Herring".

Equally perplexing, was the contention that such attacks were technically feasible with the application of emerging technologies. These technologies covered sensors for target acquisition, high speed processing of information for command and control, robust communications, precision guided delivery systems, and smart munitions. Steven Canby pointed out that although some of the sensor technology had accomplished demonstration testing, it had not approached the stage whereby the critical components of the overall system could be put together and the concept validated. He further argued that the prospects for successful technical development of the command, control, communications and intelligence required for Deep Strike were remote, and were in any event likely to be very much more expensive than at first advertised.

Only one type of rear area target proved technically feasible to attack with the proposed conventionally armed ballistic, or cruise missiles — namely fixed area targets such as air bases. These targets have historically been designated for attack by aircraft (currently F-111s and B-52s) with either conventional or nuclear weapons. However, not only are the anticipated attrition rates very high for aircraft on such missions, the conventional munitions available for runway destruction have poor effectiveness. These combined factors require that NATO aircraft be provided with stand-off delivery systems such as cruise missiles with effective conventional warheads for runway destruction. To some extent aircraft might also be able to threaten some second echelon slow-moving targets when armed with cruise missiles, providing that the intelligence, target acquisition and command and control can prove up to the task (which they are currently are unable to do particularly effectively). SHAPE currently proposed to utilise B-52s armed with cruise missiles for this purpose.

Conventionally armed ballistic missiles pose political, economic, and technical problems that would appear to be insurmountable. The technical considerations are associated in a large part with the C^3I required for a ballistic missile wing (whether conventional or nuclear armed). Command decisions to launch "waves" of missiles against targets (particularly if they are moving) must be taken within minutes of receipt of the target acquisition information. Against air bases strikes need to be made prior to an extensive dispersal of aircraft, which would significantly increase the number of targets to be attacked. Strikes against air bases are likely to have to be undertaken earlier rather than later in a conflict.

The political issues concern both Soviet and West European domestic perceptions of the deployment of conventionally armed Pershing IIs. From a Soviet perspective it is bound to be difficult to differentiate conventional from nuclear Pershings. The effect of this perception on the threshold at which nuclear release might be authorised is most likely to be adverse. Some proportion of West European opinion might consider the deployment of conventional Pershing as the indicator of a policy which was inclined towards a "non-nuclear warfighting" capability, dislocating Western Europe from the American nuclear deterrent, and the reaction of a peace movement presently lying in the doldrums is hard to predict, but would likely be problematic for many NATO nations including the Federal Republic of Germany.

Future Prospects

If the Deep Strike options have been temporarily resolved around the "emerged" technology of cruise missiles, what prospects remain for the C^3I and smart munitions? For C^3I at least, very substantial problems of technical feasibility and cost will remain. However, these can only be expected to slow the journey towards real-time target acquisition, data management and weapon system allocation to target. Although the claims for C^3I technologies have been exaggerated by some, the quest for advanced C^3I itself has widespread military support. Smart munitions by comparison have a more haphazard future for they have proved very susceptible to failure under "actual" rather than perfect test conditions. Apart from the remarkable inability to work in weather conditions that are usual in Europe, the vulnerability of the sensors to simple countermeasures is essentially unmeasured. This last problem will perhaps be the least easily overcome.

One aspect of West European reticence over Deep Strike and the emerging technologies was that all the weapons technologies associated with the Deep Strike proposal were of American origin. It was sometimes argued that the Deep Strike concept was more of an expedient for Western Europe to "buy American" weapon systems than an essential element of Alliance conventional force improvement. On the positive side, Deep Strike and emerging technologies focused West European attention towards collaboration in the development and procurement of conventional weapon systems. This initiative was brought into high profile by Secretary of State for Defence, Michael Heseltine, and has attracted considerable attention.

It is too early to establish what level of contribution emerging technologies may make in any future move towards improving NATO's conventional force posture. There are certainly a very wide range of opportunities, but many of these are of long standing and the contribution of advanced technology towards their solution is not certain. Aspects such as mobilisation and readiness and sustainability of forces do not require advanced technological solutions but political commitment.

In the longer term, the debate over Deep Strike and emerging technologies may prove a cautionary tale. It has long been recognised by weapons technologists that NATO cannot afford to depend too heavily on technological superiority alone. For the advantages that accrue from this have proved less and less durable through NATO's history. At the same time the costs of the weapon systems themselves (especially when recalling the relative improvement in performance compared with their predecessors and the threat), has been rather unrewarding. One consequence has been an increasing dependence on the "force multiplier effect" which is not a tangible quantity, rather a semi-quantifiable perception. It may prove exceedingly dangerous to continue to place heavy emphasis on force multiplication effects perceived to be available from advanced technology against an adversary whose observable behaviour so prefers tangible quantity.

Weapon Development 1984: Sea

G R VILLAR

Captain Roger Villar was formerly Captain of HMS Excellent *and Commodore (Intelligence). He was Naval Adviser to British Aerospace Dynamics Group for several years before starting his own naval consultancy business. His book,* Merchant Ships at War: The Falklands Experience, *was published recently.*

THIS SECTION is not intended as a complete review of naval weapons but rather to list current development trends and their purposes in outline so that the reader has a broad idea of where developments are leading. Those who need more detail on specific weapons should refer to one or other of the specialist publications which cover them in considerable detail. The main areas covered here are anti-submarine, anti-air and anti-surface vessel warfare, mine warfare and naval aviation.

ANTI-SUBMARINE WARFARE

Without question, anti-submarine warfare poses the most difficult problems of any for deep water navies. Submarines are immensely difficult to detect and becoming more so. At the same time, their weapons are getting more and more sophisticated and effective. And while conventionally propelled submarines may have some limitations on speed and endurance, these are totally overcome by the nuclear propelled submarine which is unquestionably the most effective sea going weapon system available today. Little wonder, therefore, that immense sums are spent on anti-submarine warfare, nor that there is continuing research into the widest possible fields of technology.

Detection

The prime method of detecting submarines was initially by active sonars. These, however, have distinct limitations in performance because of the difficulties of transmitting sounds through the sea where temperature gradients of all types interfere with its direct path. Ingenious means have been found of overcoming some of these. The first shipborne active sonars, which operated close to the surface, were supplemented by variable depth sonars able to be lowered to some 200 feet depth to get below at least some of the temperature layers which interfered with sound transmission. Lower frequency transducers were developed since these frequencies pass through water better than the original high frequencies. These call for large sonar arrays; so too, does the need for higher powers to extend the range of detection. Schemes such as 'bottom bounce' and 'convergence zone' have been developed whereby a sound beam will initially be bent down, and then up, by the temperature gradients in the ocean, or else be reflected up from the seabed, to emerge some 20 or so miles away where it can detect a submarine. These also require large transducers. In Britain, the destroyer HMS *Matapan* was converted experimentally to carry such a sonar where the transducers ran virtually the full length of her hull on either side. Even at that, they were reckoned to be of about half the size of the transducers which were really needed. Active sonars in submarines have a particular advantage over those in surface ships in that submarines can vary their depth at will to obtain the optimum for sonar detection. However, they do not like using active sonars since it can give away their own position to an enemy.

It was therefore with some relief, just over a decade ago, that designers were able to take advantage of modern signal processing developments to design passive sonars. These rely on detecting the noises which a submarine radiates from its propellors, from the water flowing past its hull, and from the sounds of its machinery. Such sounds emanate over a wide frequency band ranging from very low frequencies of a few Hertz up to much higher. Largely because the sound path is one way, as opposed to the two-way of an active sonar — but also because some is low frequency — these sounds can be detected very much further off. Detection ranges of several hundred kilometres are possible provided the water conditions are right and a submarine is making sufficient noise.

These sounds are not all that easy to detect since they can be lost amongst a background of noises from surface ships, fish, tide flows and the general reverberations and noise which abound in the sea. Large capacity computers and comprehensive signal processing are essential, as are very sensitive detection arrays. It is common practice for surface ships with passive sonars to tow an array of hydrophones which will be half a mile or more in length and which is positioned at the optimum depth for long range detection depending on the sea conditions of the day.

Such arrays are fitted in an increasing number of submarines and surface ships. Good design minimises the towing ships' own noise in the water, and also that of the water flowing over the array, so that high towing speeds of 20 knots or so are possible. It still remains, however, that the slower the towing speed, the less the self-noise which is generated and the better the detection range. Thus ships fitted with these arrays may use 'sprint and drift' techniques, drifting while they listen for targets and then rushing ahead to start another drift. Other ships, such as the American T–AGOS, which are specifically designed to use the SURTASS towed array, are no more than slow moving ocean going tugs. Submarines have an added advantage in using such arrays in that they may vary their depth more readily and achieve the optimum detection range for the particular sea conditions.

These arrays have been at sea in submarines for some years, and are now beginning to be widely fitted in surface ships in the American fleet and increasingly in the British fleet. They are not, despite the excellent results which they can achieve, the full answer to the anti-submarine problem which they were once thought to be. Firstly, they do not distinguish between the side on which a noise may be heard. The towing vessel has to alter course, a somewhat slow and tedious process with so much astern, to determine the proper bearing. Nor are bearings highly accurate, being much better on the beam than on fine angles forward and aft. Secondly, it is not possible to obtain an accurate range although, at short distances, it may be possible to obtain some estimate by measuring the time difference in the receipt of sounds received over different paths, such as the direct path and that reflected from the seabed at known depth. Thus the towed array is a warning system rather than a system which will achieve a precise target location to enable an attack to be carried out. An active sonar is needed as well. Thirdly, experience shows that operators need pretty continuous and realistic training. Ships will need to spend considerable periods at sea, even in peacetime, merely to keep their operators efficient. No simulator capable of giving the same practice is thought yet to be practicable.

Despite all that, however, the towed array is a marked step forward in submarine detection. Unfortunately, the Soviet Union has realised the potential of this and taken countermeasures by quietening its submarines. Conventionally propelled submarines have always been relatively quiet and this has been improved by extensive work on their hull forms to reduce water flow noise, as well as on their propellor designs. Nuclear submarines have suffered from machinery noise. Very extensive work has been done in Western navies to reduce this but, not until recently, in the Soviet fleet. Modern Soviet nuclear submarines are markedly quieter than their predecessors and it is believed that these improvements are also being applied to existing nuclear submarines. The long term future of the passive towed array is therefore not as bright as it was thought to be only a decade ago, and there is thus the beginning of a step back to active sonars, although the solutions available are little better than those outlined above. New helicopter-borne sonars may have some promise but this has yet to be revealed fully.

One other important improvement needs mentioning. With such difficulty in finding any one method of detecting submarines which is truly efficient, there can be great merit in combining the information from many detection systems to give an overall picture. This has been shown to result in a marked improvement in the information available as compared with, say, a single ship relying on its own shipborne detection systems alone. With modern satellite communications it is possible to transmit information from many sources to a single shore-based computer, combine all this into one, and retransmit the result back to ships at sea in almost real time. Ships will still be dependent on their own detection systems for their final attack, but, up to that point, can obtain great benefit from a comprehensive system of this nature.

There are other methods of detection which are well worth mentioning. First is the helicopter. Nearly every frigate or destroyer now carries its own anti-submarine helicopter and some navies have specialised helicopter carriers. The standard detection system is the sonobuoy with passive sonobuoys, achieving detection ranges of a few miles and retransmitting their information back to their parent helicopter. The helicopter may, as in the British fleet, have its own computer for processing this information. Alternatively it may, as in the American fleet, retransmit this information back to its parent ship for processing by shipborne computer. A pattern of, say, three such passive sonobuoys will enclose a target and sometimes give a sufficiently accurate position for an attack. Alternatively, active directional sonobuoys may be carried as well. The smaller helicopters, such as the Wasp and the Lynx, do not generally carry sonobuoys because of limitations of space and weight. Instead they may have dunking sonars operating at high frequency with relatively short range to achieve detection ranges of a few miles only. Although far from ideal for detecting submarines, these can operate in barriers ahead of a fleet and in similar formations, to provide a good chance of detecting a submarine which is endeavouring to come too close.

Second are aircraft, generally shore-based, such as the British Nimrod. These operate broadly in a similar fashion to helicopters using sonobuoys with their own on-board computer. Both aircraft and helicopters also normally carry their own anti-submarine torpedoes so that they do not have to call up any other units to make an attack.

A third method is to use airborne Magnetic Anomaly Detection (MAD) equipment. This is designed to detect the anomalies in the earth's local magnetic field caused by the presence of a submarine. The maximum detection range is of the order of 1000 feet and aircraft and helicopters so fitted will therefore fly as low as possible.

Lastly, SOSUS (Sound Surveillance Under the Sea) should be mentioned. Since the early 1950s, America has been installing huge fixed hydrophone arrays on the edge of its continental shelf to cover the Atlantic Ocean. Although not publicly revealed, they have undoubtedly spread this to some areas of the Pacific also. The hydrophones are connected to the shore by cable and, being situated at some depth, can obtain very long range detections of submarines making a reasonable noise. In the past this has been true of nuclear submarines travelling at some eight knots or more but must now be somewhat suspect for the reasons given earlier. SOSUS has been remarkably effective in the past. Russia has not been able to emulate it because of its more restricted access to the open oceans. The Soviet Union is, however, known to have laid large buoys carrying passive hydrophone arrays and may have something akin to SOSUS in its own home waters.

Weapons

The original weapon for use against submarines was the depth charge, but it suffered from the great disadvantage of taking a finite time to drop to depth during which a submarine could evade. This became increasingly important as submarine diving depths increased. Moreover, surface ships lost contact on their active sonars as they came in close to their targets and these passed beneath the sonar beam. Development therefore led to the ahead-throwing mortar in surface ships capable of firing a pattern of charges about 1000 metres ahead while still in sonar contact. Nevertheless, the difficulty still remained that these took a finite time to drop to depth.

Development, therefore, led to the anti-submarine homing torpedo. These may be air or ship launched and are generally of $12\frac{3}{4}$ inches diameter with both passive and active acoustic homing. Submarines carry a larger 21 inch heavyweight torpedo, such as the American Mark 48 or the new British Spearfish, which is also acoustically guided to a considerable range of ten miles or more.

Torpedoes are now the urgent attack weapon used by ships when sudden contacts are made and are far quicker in operation than any other means. They can be carried by helicopters to make them into autonomous units with their own weapons and detection equipments. Equally maritime patrol aircraft carry torpedoes. Lastly torpedoes may also be fitted in shipborne guided missile systems, such as the British Ikara, with a range of some 20 miles, or the American Asroc. Such systems are now gradually being phased out in favour of the shipborne helicopter.

The alternative to torpedoes is the depth charge. As already commented on, these have fairly considerable inaccuracies. It is possible to overcome some of these with a nuclear depth charge although the politics of using these in anything short of all out nuclear war have yet to be solved.

Summary

Anti-submarine warfare is an expensive and difficult business. Although the modern torpedo is quite exceptionally efficient and lethal, it is complex and costly. It is detection above all which is the most difficult business and which calls for a combination of many different devices on many different types of platform. Each may be able to contribute some part of the story; none will give it all.

Naval Aviation

Organic naval air power has proved its worth over many decades as an essential for any navy which has to operate outside the reach of shore-based air cover. Even operating within such reach, the speed with which aircraft can react when they form an integral part of the fleet, as opposed to having to come out from shore, gives a marked advantage. The concepts of organic naval air power vary widely from nation to nation and often depend on the available money. Organic air power may be highly effective but it is also highly expensive.

Fixed wing aviation

Fixed wing aircraft are required both for the defence of one's own forces and for the classic projection of power. In the latter role in particular, aircraft can operate many hundreds of miles away from their parent ships to give them a reach and power which they could not otherwise attain. Moreover, they are effective not only against enemy shipping, but also against the land in, for example, amphibious operations.

The full development of such fixed wing aircraft is an enormously expensive business and only seen in the American fleet. Here it is typified by the 91,400 ton *Nimitz* which incorporates air defence by Hawkeye airborne early warning aircraft and Mach 2+ Tomcat F-14 fighters; A-6 and A-7 squadrons for long range strike; the more general purpose F-18 which is taking over from the F-4 Phantom; and the S3A Viking anti-submarine patrol aircraft. The cost of that one ship, together with her embarked aircraft and weapons, probably equates to the whole of Britain's annual budget for the Royal Navy. America is the only exponent of this system although Russia is building a large aircraft carrier. France also is hoping to build two smaller nuclear powered aircraft carriers though with less than the full sophistication of the *Nimitz* and her aircraft.

Conventional aircraft carriers of this type are otherwise dying throughout the world. Some old carriers remain, largely of World War II vintage with old aircraft. Although modernised, like the Brazilian *Minas Gerais*, they will come to the end of their lives shortly and it is increasingly doubtful whether money will be found to replace them. In these other non-superpower nations, the alternative concept of the V/STOL Sea Harrier is beginning to take effect.

Sea Harrier, because of its short take off run and vertical landing, can operate from a far smaller deck than existing conventional fixed wing aircraft. Its operation is flexible since, for example, the parent ship does not have to turn into the wind for flying operations. With a speed which just reaches sonic in a shallow dive, it in no way matches the sophisticated Tomcat F–14. But it can be highly effective at short range and, particularly against a lesser enemy than the Soviets, can have a marked superiority. Its performance and superiority were clearly demonstrated in the Falkland Islands campaign both in strike and air defence. As well as Britain, both India and Spain operate Harriers from aircraft carriers as an economical means of providing air power at less than the full level of the American *Nimitz*.

Soviet Russia also operates VTOL aircraft from its four Kiev class carriers. They are not so effective as the Sea Harrier since they are not capable of short take off but only vertical. The big difference here is that the short take off run of the Harrier gives the added advantage of aerodynamic lift from the wings, allowing a much larger payload to be carried. As mentioned above, Russia is building its first large carrier and it is probable that this will have a new fixed wing aircraft instead of the present VTOL.

Rotary wing aviation

Helicopters have come into their own and are becoming more and more widespread. Thus, in the Royal Navy, every ship of frigate size and above, with only one exception, carries its own helicopter. Though generally thought of as anti-submarine weapon systems, they have the widest of other uses including anti-surface vessel strike, minesweeping, amphibious operations, replenishment at sea, surveillance, over-the-horizon targetting for missiles and general communications.

In general, the British fleet makes the most widespread use of helicopters. The initial ship-fit was the 5,500 lb Wasp, intended primarily as an anti-submarine helicopter operating from small frigates. It carried two homing torpedoes and a Magnetic Anomaly Detector (MAD) and was intended to operate largely under the control of its parent ship to attack contacts detected by shipborne sonars. It has been superceded by the 10,500 lb Anglo-French Lynx. This has its own radar, MAD equipment and torpedoes, and, in some foreign versions, will carry a dunking sonar. Some consideration has been given to fitting it with sonobuoys but it is too small to carry the modern heavier type. In the anti-surface vessel role, it can be fitted with the Sea Skua missile.

Because of the limitations of the Lynx, in being both too small to carry sonobuoys and to have great endurance, the tendency is now towards larger helicopters. These can operate autonomously with sonobuoys, dunking sonar and torpedoes. The current example is the 21,000 lb Sea King. It will be superceded in due course by the still larger, circa 28,000 lb Anglo-Italian EH-101, which has just entered full development. Sea King can operate autonomously for some four hours using its sonobuoys and its own on-board computer to process their information, or with dunking sonar, well out of range of its parent ship. EH-101 will operate similarly for longer periods with an increased payload of four torpedoes instead of two to give it a re-attack capability. Both these helicopters are, however, intended primarily for anti-submarine work and will not have an anti-surface vessel strike role.

Because there will never be enough helicopters in frigates and destroyers, alternative platforms are available in Royal Fleet Auxiliaries which may, in some cases, carry up to four Sea Kings. Future replenishment ships may carry a similar number. In addition one merchant ship has been converted to the RFA *Reliant* and also carries anti-submarine helicopters.

The great advantage which such larger helicopters bring is their ability to operate autonomously in search of submarines and in the subsequent attack. With their own on-board computers, they can process their sonobuoy information without reference to their parent ship. Moreover, since they operate passively, enemy submarines are unaware of their presence while searching.

American fleet practice is a little different. They tend to use only the larger helicopters rather than those such as the Lynx. Nor do they have their own sophisticated on-board computers, and must remain within radio range of their parent ship so that sonobuoy information can be transmitted for processing by the ship's computer. They do not use shipborne helicopters for anti-surface vessel strike and prefer to rely on the fixed wing aircraft in their carriers. They do, however, use helicopters very much more widely for replenishment at sea, for amphibious operations, and for minesweeping where they tow noise makers and magnetic sweeps. A helicopter borne mine hunting sonar is also being developed.

Russia does not use its helicopters greatly for anti-submarine work and neither are they so widely fitted throughout the fleet.

Many other nations use helicopters, generally for anti-submarine work as their prime role.

Summary

No one could say that naval aviation is dead, even though the day of the aircraft carrier is passing in many countries. It is more widely used than ever before. The emphasis has perhaps changed with the increasing cost, but the helicopter is finding more and more uses, while the V/STOL Harrier is a proven and economical answer for many who need fixed wing aviation.

Mine Warfare

Mine warfare embraces both mining and mine countermeasures. Until the mid-1970s mining was neglected by the West though the Soviets had been actively developing their capability. Following renewed interest in the USA, Britain has begun a new mine development programme. More attention has, however, been paid in the West to mine countermeasures than to mines. Since the Korean War, Western mine countermeasures have improved markedly to attempt to counter the ever increasing threat of modern Soviet mines.

Although mining has been neglected, it is the most cost-effective of all methods of fighting. World War II statistics are eloquent: the British laid some 76,000 mines offensively. Overall, one in 40 was effective and, in some areas, this rose to one in five. In addition to that direct effect, their presence denied large areas of sea, generally in international waters, to the enemy and complicated his operations. In addition, mines were, and still are, cheap when compared with other weapons.

Minelaying may be either offensive/defensive or protective. Defensive mining is generally intended to deny areas of sea often in international waters, to an enemy. Quite often mined areas will be declared openly although the swept channels through the minefields, which are necessary for one's own ships to pass safely, will be kept highly secret. The mere belief that mines are present, even if they are not, will keep an enemy out of the declared area if he does not call the bluff. Such minefields range from shallow water ground mines laid close to ports to confine entry to a single swept channel; somewhat deeper water mines suitable for laying out to the edge of the continental shelf in up to 200 metres depth in order, for example, to deny the north-west and south-west approaches to the United Kingdom to enemy submarines; to even deeper water mines such as the American Captor which may be laid, for example, in choke points such as the Greenland-Iceland-UK (GRIUK) gap to prevent Soviet submarines sailing into the Atlantic. There are also controlled minefields, such as in the Baltic Straits, actuated by cable leading to the shore.

These mines can be laid relatively simply from a wide variety of platforms. Generally, however, it is necessary to know their position quite accurately. Thus surface ships are favoured as minelayers rather than submarines or aircraft. One major problem is the political will to allow laying to commence, and the time taken to lay a large number, and these may prevent defensive minefields being fully effective in the opening stages of a war.

Offensive mines, as their name implies, are designed to seek out an enemy in his own waters. Aircraft or submarines are the normal and most successful method of laying although, submarines can also be used. Surface ships are likely to be too vulnerable close to an enemy's homeland to be capable of being used. Comparatively light ground mines, operating in relatively shallow water up to perhaps 60 feet or so depth, are the easiest to lay.

Mine countermeasures is not a simple business. Considerable improvements in techniques have been made and these are continuing. Many types of mine have to be moored to the seabed and float clear of it. Even modern deep water mines will often be moored. They can be swept relatively simply by towing a wire sweep, generally between two ships, so that the mooring wires are cut and allow the mine to float to the surface where it can be disposed of. Such sweeps can operate down to a few feet off the sea bottom and are relatively easily installed on board commercial trawlers as well as warships. If mines capable of burying themselves in the seabed are developed, then they go beyond the range of simple wire sweeps. However, none are as yet known to be in existence in deep water.

Ground mines are currently laid in relatively shallow water and can be actuated either acoustically, magnetically, by the pressure wave of a ship passing over them, or by a combination of all three methods. Acoustic mines are swept by towing a suitable noise maker. Magnetic mines are countered by towing a sweep wire in which a heavy current is pulsed rhythmically to create a fluctuating magnetic field.

Pressure mines cannot be so swept and have to be found and destroyed individually. This can only be achieved by specialised mine hunters which search for mines by sonar. Once they are found, a diver or a remotely operated vehicle is sent down to lay a countermining charge. Today's mine hunters have hull-borne sonars which limits their depth of search to about 80 feet. New developments include sonars which can be lowered to cover greater depths. The main problems lie firstly in the cost of such specialised mine hunters with the British 700 ton Hunt class being quoted at some £30 million each. Secondly, in the time taken to find mines and then dispose of them which takes, on average, some 20 minutes for each contact. Although mine hunting sonars are being improved continually, some of the contacts will also not be mines but the other objects which litter the seabed.

The technical means for dealing with mines thus exist or are being developed and improved. The threat is still enormous. Since mines can now be laid in much deeper waters than ever, the areas which they may cover are increased greatly. It needs, therefore, a tremendous effort to clear swept channels and to continue to keep them clear. Though wire sweeping gear is relatively cheap, and may deal with very many types of mine, mine hunters are expensive. A majority of nations have insufficient mine countermeasures vessels to deal with the threat effectively. Technically, the means exist to counter a majority of the known types of mine. Practically, these means are in such short supply because of the quantities and costs needed, that the mining threat becomes very dangerous indeed.

Anti-Surface Vessel Warfare

Quite clearly missiles have revolutionised anti-ship warfare. Although the early missiles were no more than small subsonic aircraft, modern developments are towards small, high speed missiles attacking in quantity. Being offensive weapons, they have a clear advantage over the defensive. Inevitably they will be able to outwit the defences, however comprehensive and sophisticated the latter may be.

Western developments

In the West, initial emphasis was given to sea-skimming missiles which posed particular problems for the defence.

Primarily this was in the difficulty of detecting them in time for the defences to be effective, since they could appear low over the radar horizon with their first possible sighting being at no more than 15 to 20 kilometres. Even a high subsonic speed missile, appearing first at that range, will have no more than 30 seconds or so to go before impact with its target. Moreover, it has to be seen on radar against a confusing background of sea clutter which makes it most difficult to detect. Development in the West has concentrated on such types of missile, generally arriving in succession, to endeavour to overwhelm and saturate the defences. The 70 kilometre Exocet MM40, 90 kilometre Harpoon, and 200 kilometre Otomat, are the most widely used. Similar types of missile also appear in submarine launched versions capable of being fired while submerged. A number of helicopter-borne missiles also exist, ranging from the horizon range British Sea Skua, used on the small Lynx shipborne helicopter, up to much larger types. In some cases, notably the recent British air launched Sea Eagle missile, it is possible for missiles fired from the same platform to be programmed to arrive at the target simultaneously rather than in succession, and from different directions.

One other type of missile can also be particularly effective although it is not widely available throughout the West. This is the anti-radar missile, designed to home on to the target's radar with a steep terminal dive. These missiles may be very small and hard to detect, since they do not require any propellant motor, at least for the terminal stages. Nor do they need large warheads. When the Americans accidentally launched a Shrike missile at one of their own destroyers off Vietnam, its 66 kilogramme warhead destroyed so much of its target's vulnerable radar aerials and other exposed equipment, and caused such fragment damage, that the ship was disabled completely. She was credited with less than half of her normal fighting capability and had to return to harbour for repairs. It gave a solid lesson in the potential vulnerability of modern ships which have a vast quantity of their sensor equipment, on which they depend in order to be able to fight, necessarily exposed and vulnerable.

The only long range missile in the West is the American Tomahawk, capable of 675 kilometres. This also is subsonic and, so far as is known, missiles will arrive at their target singly and not in a coordinated or stream attack.

Soviet Developments

The Soviet approach has been very different and much more comprehensive. They have not hitherto placed great emphasis on sea-skimming missiles although there are some recent reports that they may now be doing so. Instead they have concentrated on either shallow diving terminal trajectories or very steep descents. They now look for very high speed with some missiles flying as fast as Mach 4. Even their submarine launched version is sonic rather than subsonic. As opposed to the conventional warheads used exclusively in the West, they also use a mixture of conventional and nuclear warheads.

Perhaps above all, many of their missiles are large with considerable ranges. At the bottom end of the scale they have the submarine launched SS–N–7 capable of 60 kilometres range at Mach 0.9 which equates broadly with the American Harpoon. In the air they have the 450 kilometre Mach 4 AS4 missile launched from the supersonic Backfire aircraft. At the upper end, they have the huge 13,000 ton Oscar submarine fitted with some 24 launching tubes for the SS–N–13 — a 500 kilometre range missile so designed that all 24 can arrive at their single target simultaneously from different directions. Given that they also can be fired from submerged conditions, the threat to any warship is massive. Many of these may use either radar or infra-red homing or a combination of both. In addition they also use anti-radar missiles.

Long range targetting

Anti-ship missiles with over-the-horizon range can only be used satisfactorily if both the position and identity of the target are well known before firing. It may be possible, at the shorter over-the-horizon ranges, to rely on such information being transmitted by a consort or an aircraft in close contact with the enemy. In general, however, it depends on full ocean surveillance which can only be achieved effectively by satellites. Both United States and Russia are interested in this. The Soviets have been practising missile firings at sea since the early 1970s, using satellite target information. Such information is not necessarily accurate, and it will usually have to be combined with some form of intelligent missile homing system, which enables it to search for and identify its target before the final attack stage, perhaps by recognising its electro-magnetic transmissions from radar.

Summary

There are many other methods of attack against surface ships. Some can be remarkably effective as became apparent in the 1982 Falkland Islands campaign. Ships did nevertheless survive them remarkably well. The full Soviet missile threat could, however, be overwhelming; nor has the West anything to compare with it.

Anti-Air Warfare

Air defence is a relatively simple problem compared with anti-submarine warfare. Nevertheless, there are certain difficulties. Superficially it is simpler because of the greater ease with which targets can be detected by radar rather than by sonar. In fact, these targets may be exceedingly small, designed to appear on radar as even smaller, be of extremely high speed up to three or four times the speed of sound, and come in coordinated mass attacks to overwhelm the defences. Electronic warfare greatly magnifies these problems.

Thus, as with anti-submarine warfare, many defensive systems must be used in combination since none will, by itself, give a satisfactory answer. That is achieved by overlapping defensive layers ranging from supersonic fighter aircraft at the outer extremes to short range guns and decoys at the inner edge. The number of layers used varies from nation to nation as also do the types of weapon and their performance. The available money is the principal deciding factor. America tends to have the greatest number of sophisticated overlapping layers. Soviet practice is substantially different from American only in the absence of long range fighter aircraft. There are reports, however, that the USSR is rectifying that with the construction of its first large nuclear powered aircraft carrier. Smaller nations may perhaps only be able to afford one defensive layer, and then generally the cheapest. Equally they often face a lesser threat.

Fighter defence

Typically the American Mach 2.4 carrier-borne Tomcat fighter aircraft is armed with 60 mile range Phoenix missiles capable of engaging up to six targets at the same time. It requires long range airborne early warning which is provided by Hawkeye aircraft. It is an expensive and costly system and there is a limit to its effectiveness because of the difficulties of getting sufficient warning of an enemy aircraft approach even with airborne early warning. Probably something like 200 miles is the maximum intercept range possible and equates to the range at which Soviet aircraft can launch their anti-ship missiles. As Soviet missiles are developed further and reach to longer range, so will it be necessary to upgrade the performance of the F–14 Tomcat and its weapon system.

An alternative of much lesser performance is the shorter range Sea Harrier, armed with limited range Sidewinder missiles. This is extremely effective at relatively short range but not at long range even though now associated, in the British fleet, with helicopter-borne early warning radars.

Area defence missile systems

Such systems reach out to some 50 to 100 kilometres depending on their type. The last remaining varieties are the British Sea Dart and the American Standard missiles now being fitted with the Aegis system. Sea Dart has a distinctly limited capacity against small high altitude missiles though effective against large missiles and aircraft. It is also limited in its performance in many of its installations through the use of an old surveillance radar. Aegis is a much more comprehensive high performance system. The heart is the AN/SPY–1A phased array radar built into a ship's superstructure and weighing some 60 tons. This has been fitted into the 9055 ton Ticonderoga class of destroyer costing something over £500 million each. It is a highly capable system able to engage a number of targets simultaneously. Its limitations come, perhaps, in the relatively slow speed of the Standard missile of about Mach 2.5 and the fact that no shipborne radar, however powerful, can detect low flying targets at long range when they are below the radar horizon. There are thus gaps in the coverage of the system and possible limitations in its performance against high speed small missile targets.

The Soviet approach has been to develop the very high speed Mach 5, shorter range, SA–N–6 and SA–N–7 missile systems. Such high missile speed minimises the time of flight and therefore the radar warning which is needed. Clearly these are highly effective systems both against aircraft and missiles.

Nevertheless they will suffer, as will all other systems, from a finite level of capability in which they can be saturated by a mass coordinated attack.

Point defence missile systems

Shorter range point defence missile systems are necessarily smaller and cheaper than the longer range area defence systems. Perhaps the most significant factor is in the reduced radar performance which they require. There are still considerable problems. A system such as the British Seawolf, with a maximum intercept range in the order of 5 kilometres, needs to obtain warning of a supersonic sea-skimming attacker at something like 15 kilometres range. That is roughly the limit of the radar horizon as seen by a typical destroyer or frigate. Moreover detection, even at that range, demands a powerful and sophisticated radar if it is to distinguish between an exceedingly small missile at low elevation and a background of sea clutter. The problems can be reduced using a very fast defensive missile with the minimum time of flight so that less radar warning is needed. As yet, however, only Soviet missiles have such very high speed.

There are few point defence missile systems in service in the Western world. The most effective is the British Sea Wolf which is designed to deal with both attacking missiles and aircraft. It is however at sea only in the British fleet and in small numbers. The other most widely fitted system is the Sea Sparrow, available in both American and NATO versions, and adapted into the Italian Aspide/Albatros system. This has a missile of relatively old basic design and cannot be termed an effective defence against modern missile attack. For the longer term, Sea Wolf is being improved and fitted much more widely in the British fleet. There appears to be no other serious contender other than perhaps the air-to-air AMRAAM which the manufacturers are proposing for adaptation to a naval shipborne missile system.

Short range gun systems

Medium calibre guns ranging from 76mm to 5 inch calibre are fitted in many ships. Generally, they are aimed by modern digital fire control systems of exceedingly high accuracy. They are effective against aircraft targets as well as surface targets and for shore bombardment. Their performance against missiles is more suspect for a wide variety of reasons. Primarily this is because missiles are tougher targets than aircraft. It is not easy to achieve direct hits, and near misses, which only damage a missile's control systems or structure to disturb its line of flight, must be achieved at a considerable distance if the missile is not to carry on under its own inertia and still hit the target. In both cases the accuracies required, though theoretically possible, are difficult to achieve in an all purpose system capable of many other roles.

It is easier, for the specific case of defence against missiles, to use smaller very high rate of fire guns. These can be put under tight radar control and be designed to hit a missile's warhead at comparatively short range where the aiming accuracies called for are somewhat less than for the greater range of a larger medium calibre gun. Such short range also enormously simplifies the surveillance radar problems. A number of convincing demonstrations have been carried out and the gun systems available include the American Vulcan/Phalanx, the Swiss Seaguard, the British Sea Dragon, Spanish Meroka, Italian Dardo, and Dutch Goalkeeper. Russia also has its own version. In general terms, it is thought that a calibre of at least 30mm is needed with a high kinetic energy solid shell made of depleted uranium or tungsten. Rates of fire are in the order of 4000 rounds per minute achieved by using a number of barrels in combination.

The doubts about such systems lie only partly in the complexity demanded by using very high rates of fire and having actually to hit a small fast missile low down near to the sea. There have been doubts as to whether even direct hits would explode an attacking missile warhead, particularly with the more modern designs of warhead explosive. These appear to have been overcome although there has been no official word. Clearly, too, there is an understandable reluctance to rely on destroying an attacker at such very short range. These systems are nevertheless being adopted widely as giving a significant, but not total, solution at an acceptable cost.

Electronic warfare

Electronic warfare is more fully covered elsewhere. Great emphasis is now being paid to effective anti-missile defence with decoy systems. Such systems may fire a mixture of chaff and infra-red decoys, either overhead, or else all round a ship. In the former case, known as the seduction mode, an attacking missile will acquire both its target ship and the decoy simultaneously.

Provided there is sufficient relative wind, the two will drift slowly apart and the missile will aim for the mean point between the two. Thus it will miss its real target. In the latter case, known as the distraction mode, decoys either confuse an enemy's surveillance picture so that he fires at the wrong target, or they give a missile more than one target to think of and it will attack the wrong one.

These systems are relatively cheap, certainly when compared with guns and missiles, but they are not easy to use since the timing of firing is critical to success. They require sophisticated surveillance radars and a data handling system. Because ship's radar echoing areas and infra-red signatures may be large, there may be problems in building decoys to simulate the large ships from destroyer size upwards. Finally, modern missile homing systems may be able to distinguish between the clear cut response from a ship's superstructure and the somewhat more blurred return from a cloud of chaff.

Summary

Every type of defensive system has its shortcomings, no matter what its cost and sophistication. Adequate surveillance is a prime problem throughout, although the problems are less with the shorter range systems. The Soviet move to relatively short range anti-missile missile systems using very high speed missiles, in combination with shorter range anti-missile guns systems, is a logical and sensible answer. Even that, however, only goes part way to the overall solution needed. Something such as the Laser Damage Weapon, or Particle Beam, with the speed of light and virtually zero time of flight, is needed to provide a true answer.

All the foregoing categories concern conventional warfare at sea. If the enemy uses nuclear warheads, these could create sufficient over pressure to damage and sink their targets at up to 15 kilometres distant. There is little possibility of dealing with these without the speed of light weapon, and perhaps not even then.

Trends in Maritime Warfare: The Influence and Power of the Super Navies: America and Russia

G R VILLAR

Captain Roger Villar was formerly Captain of HMS Excellent *and Commodore (Intelligence). He was Naval Adviser to British Aerospace Dynamics Group for several years before starting his own naval consultancy business. His book,* Merchant Ships at War: the Falklands Experience, *was published recently.*

SEVENTY years ago, Britain was the dominant world power. Its dominions and empire covered one third of the world's surface. It had a mighty fleet to maintain the *Pax Britannica.* Germany challenged that power in war and lost. Today, the United States of America has immense power and Russia is challenging America. Both countries have built up their sea power to almost unprecedented levels. There are many parallels between the way they use it today compared with Britain and Germany in 1914. But there are also deep and fundamental differences and these affect many nations.

TODAY'S SCENE — DIRECTION AND PURPOSE

Navies are needed for two basic reasons. Firstly, for defence of the homeland; and secondly as instruments of foreign policy. In the latter role in particular, they have a world-wide mobility which is denied to armies and air forces. Many nations cannot afford to develop navies for anything more than defence of their homelands with perhaps some minimal strength to extend their power to neighbouring waters. The two superpowers, however, have an abundant strength which enables them to influence events almost anywhere in the world. To a great extent they operate overseas without any competition from others. The shape of their fleets is, in large part, governed by their overseas interests. Both have totally different foreign policies and purposes, and therefore radically different fleets.

It is interesting to look at these foreign policies, and how fleets have grown to serve them, rather than to study the more conventional use of fleets for home defence or within NATO. The possibilities of all-out war at sea have receded with the nuclear deterrent. Overseas interests and lower level conflicts are becoming more dominant in a world where many nations are becoming more dependent on each other economically for their standards and way of life.

Russia

Soviet foreign policy, without question, calls for an extension of its power world-wide. It is only in the past 20 years or so that Russia has developed its fleet to support its interests in this fashion. Until America showed Russia the value of sea power during the 1962 Cuban crisis, it had developed a fleet only for the defence of its homeland, primarily in the Norwegian Sea area. Russia placed much emphasis on ships and submarines and a naval air arm, equipped with anti-ship missiles designed to attack, initially, the Allied surface fleet and its aircraft carriers operating relatively close to its own home waters. That era immediately after World War II, therefore, saw the development of large numbers of missile-armed fast-attack craft for defence of its inshore waters, and of long range missiles fired from a wide variety of platforms for use further off-shore.

Gradually, that developed to include anti-submarine work with ships such as the two helicopter carriers, *Moskva* and *Leningrad.* It is still arguable whether their development was inspired by the need to protect Russia's own ballistic missile firing submarines or to deal with those of the Allies. They were, however, accompanied by nuclear attack submarines, such as the Victor class, specifically designed to attack other submarines. Those same submarines also extended Soviet power to the North Atlantic to form an immense threat, in war, to NATO's shipping — reinforcing and resupplying its armies in Europe.

Home defence, and the NATO supply lines in the Atlantic, still form a major reason for the development of the Soviet fleet. It also maintains a permanent and large Mediterranean squadron relatively close to home. Increasingly, however, it is also spreading world wide to challenge American power. Soon after the Cuban crisis, ships began to visit such far flung spots as the Indian Ocean on a regular basis. New types of ships and submarines began to appear to support these more distant deployments. The first of four 40,000 ton Kiev class aircraft carriers commissioned in 1975; a specialised fleet support train came with the introduction of the first of six 24,450 ton Boris Chilikin support ships in 1971, followed by the 40,000 ton Berezina in 1977; nuclear submarine development continued at an unprecedented speed in large numbers; and an amphibious assault force began to appear with the first of two 13,000 ton Ivan Rogov dock landing ships commissioned in 1978. Foreign visits were extended with support for Cuba; two or three ships at Luanda in Angola; a permanent squadron in the Indian Ocean which made frequent use of anchorages in the southern Red Sea; and, to the east, an increasing presence at Cam Ranh Bay in Vietnam and the beginnings of a presence reported in Kampuchea. The Pacific fleet was also strengthened.

A general pattern of operations began to emerge. The Soviets did not operate in large task groups but rather with a maximum of two or three ships in company. The objective to their overseas visits appeared to be to influence nations by showing a presence and a power which was sufficient without being overwhelming. It was more in the nature of relatively low level gunboat diplomacy than a massive strength. Only in one case when Soviet ships bombarded the Eritrean rebels are their ships known to have used force in direct pursuit of the national policy. Nevertheless, its presence assisted the Soviets in their foreign policy negotiations as they tried to establish themselves in such places as the Cape Verde Islands and Somalia as much as in Cuba and Angola.

The growing strength of the Soviet fleet overseas began to be of concern to many nations. It started to challenge American power which had hitherto been thought to be supreme and friendly, and it inhibited the freedom of use to which America could put its own seapower since the US always had to think of what the Soviet reaction might be to apparently aggressive actions which might be against Soviet interests. Thus, the American action in the 1962 Cuban crisis when Soviet merchant ships were stopped from bringing in arms might now be much more difficult to repeat. It is at least arguable that America could not have supported Britain more positively during the 1982 Falklands campaign, had America wished to do so, because of the possibility of Soviet retaliatory action in support of the Argentines.

More recent developments have emphasised this trend to overseas power and influence. The 28,000 ton battlecruiser *Kirov* is, without question a superb and powerful surface warship, with an immense capacity for offensive action as well as for effective defence. It is accompanied by many smaller types of ship with highly effective armaments such as the 7,000 ton destroyer *Sovremenny*. The nuclear attack submarine force now includes the 42 knot deep diving Alpha class. The first of the 14,000 ton Oscar class submarines, armed with 24 500 kilometre anti-ship missiles, appeared in 1980. Soviet naval air power now overflies the southern Atlantic, though as yet not in strength. The ships still operate in relatively small groups and in much the same fashion as before. But their presence and visible power is of growing concern. Nor, perhaps, with the slow and steady approach which the Soviets make to any expansion of their foreign presence are large Task Groups needed. Very gradually, and little by little, they are spreading in larger numbers to Cam Ranh Bay, to the southern Atlantic, and still in the Indian Ocean.

Behind it all lies the same original emphasis on defence of the homeland and attack of NATO's shipping in the North Atlantic with a majority of the Soviet fleet maintained in northern waters. The ballistic missile force has been expanded to include the 30,000 ton Typhoon class submarines, the largest submarine ever built with the first being launched in 1980 and the second two years later.

This fleet is immense and powerful. Its armament is of the most modern type with an expenditure on Research and Development which has outstripped even America for many years. The *Kirov* battlecruiser, and the Typhoon, Oscar, and Alpha class submarines are unmatched anywhere in the West. The briefest look at their armament shows that they are designed with an offensive purpose to bring power to bear rather than to defend. They are to be strengthened in the future by the first 60,000 ton nuclear powered aircraft carrier.

America

The purpose of American sea power is much more difficult to analyse. The United States of America sees the Soviet Union as a potential major opponent from which America must be protected, and the US must therefore ensure that its substantial forces are thoroughly up-to-date. The experience of two World Wars also showed the US that events elsewhere, and particularly in Europe, could spill over and affect America, however much it wished to remain aloof. Because of these events, the United States was a founder member of NATO and has remained its most fundamental and powerful member. Immediately after the last World War, America also made a mutual Defence Treaty with Japan and joined with Australia and New Zealand in the defence of the southern Pacific.

But while the Soviet threat still remains paramount, the experience of past World Wars is growing more remote. A new generation has grown up which remembers instead Vietnam and the grievous losses which they suffered in fighting to support others far overseas to no apparent good effect. In other areas, they see Europe increasingly divided and giving less to the common defence than they do themselves. Japan is continually expanding its peacetime economy while spending less than 1 per cent of its Gross National Product on defence.

Necessarily the US ask whether they should continue to defend the west if it cannot do more to defend itself. America has no overseas empire as did Britain in 1914, nor is it heavily dependent on foreign trade for its survival. American dependence on trade is, in fact, steadily increasing but, as yet, extends to comparatively few rare minerals which can be, and are, stockpiled against an emergency. Oil is perhaps a more pressing matter but America is rapidly changing its dependence on supplies from far afield to others closer to home. Already, dependence on supplies from the Arabian Gulf amounts to less than 5 percent of US total useage and it has refused imports of Libyan oil for some years.

America's peacetime economy is, however, huge, diverse and widespread. Its defence is still a very different matter from Britain's one time defence of the empire. The first purpose of American sea power must and can only be to defend American interests. That means defending the US economy and way of life as a first priority. Although the economy is increasingly interwoven with that of others, the US will not necessarily act in the interests of other states when defending it, and indeed could go in quite different directions. The United States can, and probably will, increasingly go its own way.

Moreover the US has problems on its own doorstep in Central America. The Pacific, too, looms larger in American eyes than in those of Europeans. There is thus talk of supporting other nations much less than in the past and of reducing America's contribution to NATO while it increases that in the Pacific and elsewhere. America is still driven by the need to show that it is a superpower and must combat the spread of Soviet influence. It also has a fundamental belief that all peoples should have the right to decide their own futures for themselves, but they must begin to help themselves a little more.

None of those add up to any clear cut policy like the Soviet single-minded purpose of expansion. These factors drive America in quite different directions from Britain's need 70 years ago to protect the empire. America's interests today are increasingly its own and not those of the peoples whom it is believed to be defending. The two may be very different.

America's power to intervene is still overwhelming. A fleet which is building-up to 15 huge aircraft carriers is unmatched anywhere. The amphibious force which goes with it, based on 185,000 personnel of the US Marine Corps, is equally unmatched. There is no doubt that America could bring its power to bear effectively wherever it wished, whatever the Soviets did, if it felt the need. The question must be whether America would feel it worth the risk and in its own interests as much as whether it would risk even a minimal Soviet presence being the starting factor to escalating war to a more serious nuclear level.

In short, American sea power is mighty and appears dominant. It necessarily acts in America's interests and there can be less than a firm guarantee that these will coincide with those of others, even when apparently they are on the same side. Nor can there be any guarantee that it would risk using it were the Soviets also to be present, since to do so could escalate the war.

The Opposing Technologies

Since these two navies have developed for different purposes, they necessarily have different shapes and types of ship and submarine. Sometimes the differences are radical; sometimes less marked. It is noteworthy, however, how the Soviets have developed gradually from the initial defence of their homeland and still favour the basic weapon and ship types which were needed for that purpose. America has built on its experience of World War II to rely on aircraft carriers and amphibious forces with the later addition of the nuclear submarine. Each therefore has an element of tradition rather than logic in its shape. The principal types of ship used by each are as follows:–

Russia

Surface ships. The latest in a long line of continuous development is the 28,000 ton battlecruiser *Kirov* armed with 500 kilometre anti-ship missiles which can undoubtedly be fired on the basis of satellite information of the target. The modern 7800 ton destroyer *Sovremenny* is armed with 220 kilometre anti-ship missiles as well as twin 130mm guns. Although these are but the latest in a long line of developments, among many others, they show clearly the offensive power which is being built into some modern Soviet units. Both these classes are also defended by extremely effective surface-to-air missile systems with capabilities against both missiles and aircraft.

There are also four 43,000 ton Kiev class carriers with a mixture of helicopters and Yak-36 VTOL aircraft as well as long range anti-ship missiles. These do not compare with carriers in service in the American fleet. Nor are the fixed wing aircraft effective and they do not compare, for example, with the British Sea Harrier let alone the far more sophisticated fixed wing aircraft used by the American fleet. Nevertheless, they are the Soviet's first essay into the use of organic naval air power, and the first 60,000 ton aircraft carrier with conventional fixed wing aircraft is already being built.

Amphibious forces. These are centred around the 12,000 strong naval infantry which is intended as the sharp spearhead of an amphibious attack which would be followed-up by less highly specialised troops. Although undoubtedly an effective force, it is limited in its overseas capability by being supported by no more than two large 13,000 ton Ivan Rogov class dock landing ships although there are many of smaller classes.

Submarines. The most recent development is the 14,000 ton Oscar class with twenty-four 500 kilometre anti-ship missiles which can be fired from submerged. The missiles themselves are believed to be programmable so that all can arrive at the target together to saturate the defences. Earlier submarines, such as the Echo and Juliett classes, also have long range anti-ship missiles though of less sophistication.

Modern attack submarine development is exemplified by the 3800 ton Alpha class, with six in service. These are capable of 42+ knots and of diving to 2000 feet, and perhaps to 3000 feet. They are armed for the SS–N–15 45 kilometre nuclear headed anti-submarine missile. It appears that their prime purpose is to deal with other submarines. In addition, there is the more conventional, but nuclear propelled, 6000 ton Victor III class which has been steadily developed from the earlier Victor I which first entered service in 1968.

Naval Air. The most formidable recent development is the Backfire bomber capable of Mach 2+. It has a radius of action of 2950 nautical miles carrying two long range Mach 3+ AS-4 anti-ship missiles. Probably because of the lack of overseas bases, it has not been seen operating other than from bases in Russia itself.

America

Surface ships. The whole design of the surface fleet centres on 13 aircraft carriers with a planned increase to fifteen. These are typified by the 81,600 ton *Nimitz* with 90+ aircraft of all types. Constant development updates the aircraft with, for example, the current fighter being the Mach 2+ F-14 Tomcat armed with anti-aircraft missiles capable of engaging six targets at a time at a range of 60 miles. The prime other types are the 7810 ton Spruance destroyers designed for anti-submarine work and the 9600 ton Ticonderoga class cruisers for anti-aircraft defence.

Amphibious forces. These are centred on the 185,000 strong US Marine Corps and a strong force of major amphibious ships capable of taking them anywhere in the world at short notice. The US Marine Corps is virtually self-contained in terms of equipment with, for example, their own tanks and Harrier aircraft. It is an extremely powerful force with units stationed permanently in the Indian Ocean and others cruising off potential trouble spots as the need arises.

Submarines. The modern attack submarine is the 6900 ton Los Angeles class which broadly equates to the Soviet Victor III. It is very quiet and designed for anti-submarine work though also armed with the anti-ship Harpoon missile. Tomahawk Cruise missiles are to be fitted.

Naval Air. Although there are many naval air bases, such as in the Philippines and Okinawa, a majority of the naval air strength is organic with the aircraft carriers.

Summary

There are major differences not only in the material structure of both fleets, but in the purposes for which they are used. Both navies operate primarily in their own national self-interest. The one projects power through the aircraft carrier and major amphibious forces. It aims to preserve the *status quo* and the national economy. The other favours the submarine and the missile and is firmly aggressive and expansionist, albeit it takes a relatively long term view. It would indeed be interesting in the extreme to see the outcome of a major fight between the two. At present there is little doubt that the Americans would win, but give the Soviets a little time to build more of their Kirovs, Sovremennys, Alphas and Oscars, and perhaps the outcome might be different. Certainly they represent the most formidable sea going threat which the world has ever seen. Nor is their power designed to be anything other than offensive.

Moreover, the Soviets already outnumber the Americans. They have listed in *Jane's Fighting Ships* 143 submarines (and a further 150 conventional submarines) as well as 307 major surface warships of the types discussed above, to compare with 98 submarines and 203 major surface warships in the American fleet. The figures are not entirely representative since the Soviets tend to keep their ships in service later in their lives than do the Americans. Nevertheless, they point the way strongly in which sea power is moving.

The Rest of the World

Fortunately, an all-out conflict between the two super-powers seems increasingly unlikely. The dangers of escalating to nuclear war are seen to be too real and each superpower watches the other with extreme care. But at a lower level their actions have a major impact on the many smaller nations which are also interested in peace and growth. There are a whole host of potential trouble spots today — Grenada, Central America, Southern Africa, the Arabian Gulf, Lebanon, Greece and Turkey arguing over Cyprus, the Falkland Islands, Vietnam and Kampuchea, increasing piracy world wide, and others too. Each holds the seeds of war.

The British Navy is the next largest in the world after those of the two superpowers. It lists in the same categories of ship as already mentioned, 27 submarines and 65 major surface warships and is a relatively minor force despite Britain's world-wide interest. Britains position mirrors that of many other smaller nations. There has been a tremendous growth in world seaborne trade since 1914 when Britain first fought for the defence of the empire. At that time, the world's merchant fleets of steam and motor driven vessels, totalled 45 million tons gross. By the end of 1983, that figure had grown to 423 million tons gross. This phenomenal growth has come in part from the development of the Third World. More and more nations are intertwined in an invisible network of trade where each is increasingly dependent on the other. None of these nations is able to defend its trade itself or its sources of supply; outside support is essential. That support can only come from one or other of the superpowers.

Yet the difficulties of America intervening on their behalf have already been mentioned at some length. If America's own economy is involved, it may wish to intervene though that will not necessarily be in the direct interests of the smaller nations unless these interests happen to coincide. Otherwise, America may well not have the interest or the wish to help. Even if America does, then it may find itself inhibited by Soviet actions and the dangers of escalation. It is, instead, the Soviets who are moving forward slowly and relentlessly, little by little but with few serious interruptions. Where they lose in one area, they generally gain more in another. Where the Soviets do not endanger the peace, it is one of several local trouble spots where interruptions could upset the smooth flow of trade on which the free world depends.

Thus were the flow of oil from the Arabian Gulf to be stopped, Japan would suffer severely since some 68 per cent of her oil comes from that area. With no Japanese forces in the region, only America could come to its help. Should America do so? With so little of its oil coming from there, America's prime interest lies in protecting its economic investment in Saudi Arabia rather than in any other, single factor. If there is no solid reason for the US to intervene however, and it does not do so, the Japanese economy would suffer severely. Because the free world is so intertwined in trade, so too, will their economies suffer as a result of Japanese difficulties. All the lessons of the past are that such events spill over to affect many other nations. America must, in the end, be drawn in.

Conclusion

Though American seapower is increasingly being used in American own self-interest and it is, rightly, becoming disillusioned with the less heroic efforts of its Allies, only America has the power to keep the peace. American interests in doing so are quite different from those which prompted Britain in the days of the empire. But whatever the short term beliefs, in the long term the United States is inescapably tied with the developing and civilised world. Ultimately the United States has no option but to help it.

Weapon Development 1984: Land

CHRIS BELLAMY

The author served as an artillery officer and has an MA in War Studies. He has written widely on defence matters, particularly the Soviet Union, and he is an incorporated linguist.

14.7.1941. 1515 hrs. Fire blow struck on fascist echelons at Orsha rail junction. Results excellent. *Solid sea of fire.*

Military Log of Captain I A Flërov, Red Army Artillery, first *katyusha* battery commander.[1]

Multiple Rocket Launchers and the NATO Multiple Launch Rocket System (MLRS).

THUS the multi-barrelled rocket launcher made its spectacular battlefield debut. Both Soviet and German armies favoured this simple and yet devastating weapon in the bitter battles which followed. During the war, Soviet industry provided the Red Army with over 10,000 multi-barrelled rocket launchers, or 'guards mortars' as they were known, and 12–14 million (m) rockets for them. Over 40 years later, the US Army has completed its first test firing of a system of this type, albeit vastly more powerful and accurate, in September 1983.[2] This is the Vought Multiple Launch Rocket System (MLRS). The British Army expects to receive its first launchers direct from the US in 1985. The adoption of MLRS by two nations which have traditionally shown little interest in such systems is the most exciting and significant development in land weaponry of the mid 1980s. The West Germans, French and Italians, who have multiple rocket systems already, will also receive MLRS, in German *MARS* (*Mittleren Artillerieraketensystem*).

Soviet interest in multi-barrelled rocket launchers has not diminished since the Great Patriotic War. Because there is no recoil to deal with, the launcher can be on an ordinary truck, thus facilitating the combination of high firepower and mobility which the Soviets seek. The Soviets have introduced three new systems recently; a truck mounted system for use by airborne troops with 12 122 mm barrels and a range of 20.5 km; a weapon for possible use at regimental level with 36 122 mm barrels and the same range, and the heavy rocket launcher BM–27 (from

Russian *boyevaya mashina*: war machine). The existence of the latter was first discerned in 1977. The BM–27's 220 mm barrels are arranged as one bank of four on two banks of six, giving good stability from an engineering viewpoint. The chassis is the ZIL–135 also used for the old FROG surface-to-surface missile (SSM). There is probably a shield which can be lowered over the back wheels and possibly also one for the cab, to protect them against the rocket exhaust. BM–27 is estimated to have a range of 35–40 km. In many ways it is comparable to the NATO MLRS, or rather the other way round, as the BM–27 antedates MLRS by at least six years.

Having experienced the effects of Soviet rocket artillery between 1941 and 1945, and having deployed the *Nebelwerfer* then, it is understandable that the Germans have been NATO's most fervent advocates of multiple rocket launchers. In addition, the Germans' very natural desire to keep the nuclear threshold high has led to a search for alternative ways of denying areas to the enemy. This is the *Raumverteidigung* (area defence) concept. The Light Artillery Rocket System (LARS) has been in service for some time and will continue until replaced or supplemented by MLRS from 1987. LARS fires 36 110 mm rockets, arranged in two boxes of 18. The rockets, made by Dynamit–Nobel, can have high explosive, smoke, incendiary, anti-vehicle or anti-armour minelets. A warhead has been developed which will carry either eight AT–1 Pandora anti-vehicle minelets or from three to five Medusa anti-armour minelets. The rockets have a maximum range of 14 km. It was at one time planned to introduce an improved rocket with a range of 20 km, but in view of the decision to proceed with MLRS this was discontinued. LARS can therefore saturate a distant area with mines very quickly, creating an instant obstacle, and the Germans MLRS will have the same ability.

The main reason why the British and Americans have eschewed multiple rocket launchers in the past is the difficulty of supplying ammunition. However, changes in the threat and the nature of the modern battlefield have forced them to revise their views. The same factors have also affected the Soviets' views. Soviet, US and West German forces are all almost exclusively mechanised, and both Western and Warsaw Pact artillery is becoming increasingly self-propelled. This means that the time available to engage, hit and destroy the opposition is reduced while the amount of ammunition needed to have any effect is correspondingly increased. Both the Soviets and the West have drawn the same conclusion; it is necessary to put down more rounds on the target in less time. Soviet Army studies have indicated that one way to do this is to make the battalion (*divizion*) the usual unit of artillery fire, but NATO, which is outnumbered 4 to 1 in artillery pieces, has had to look for other options. The doctrine of Follow-on Forces Attack (FOFA) and the need to hit OMGs before they can rupture NATO forward defences necessitate striking deeply. However, the manned aircraft is rapidly ceasing to be cost effective as a platform for delivering conventional weapons. Once main axes are identified, it is essential to channel, halt and delay advancing Soviet forces. If nuclear weapons are not to be used, some sort of powerful area weapon is needed. All these factors predicate a long range weapon able to deliver a dense concentration of powerful munitions in minimal time — like MLRS. Another problem is locating targets accurately beyond visual observation range. Target information will have to come from enemy electronic emissions and radio or radar direction finding. Such information may not be accurate enough for conventional artillery, but it could be for MLRS with its area coverage.

MLRS has its genesis in the European plan for a joint British–German–Italian rocket system, the RS–80, and in the American General Support Rocket System (GSRS). In 1977 the Americans agreed to increase the calibre of the rockets from the original 210 mm to 227 mm, in order to accommodate the German AT–2 anti-tank mine. On 14 July 1979, the USA, FRG, Great Britain and France concluded a Memorandum of Understanding which established the joint MLRS project and allocated shares of the development work. Italy acceded to the agreement on 29 July 1982.[3]

MLRS has 12 rocket tubes, in two groups of six, mounted on a tracked self-propelled loader-launcher vehicle (SPLL), from FMC's M2/3 family. The three seater cabin for the driver, commander and layer is pressurised with NBC ventilation systems. The vehicle has an inertial navigation system, enabling it to be used independently of a conventional artillery command post. Target coordinates are given to the launcher by the FOO or other artillery commander, and these are punched into the computer which enables the launcher to fire between one and one and a half minutes after arriving in position. The digital display is in five languages. All this technological sophistication is designed to make it easy to train and operate the MLRS, an important consideration, especially if reserves are to be used. For this reason, Vought call it 'the soldier's system'. Of course, the layer can also feed fire control data in manually.

It is remarkable that five countries on both sides of the Atlantic have managed to agree on the system, although some Germans would have preferred to see a different German version on a lighter and cheaper wheeled vehicle. This might also have had better export prospects, but was not adopted.

The US Army is the only army which has carried out MLRS trials at the time of writing. The first MLRS battery was ready for operation at Fort Riley, Kansas, in March 1983 and in autumn of that year, the first test firing on European soil took place on the Grafenwöhr range in southern Germany. In all, the US Army plan to acquire 339 SPLLs with 400,000 M–77 bomblet warheads. The British Army has ordered four SPLLs and 108 rockets from Vought, and the Bundeswehr two launchers. Britain and Germany are both due to receive their MLRS in 1985, for preliminary troop trials. There is some concern among other European partners that Great Britain might obtain some of its other launchers and missiles direct from the USA. The Bundeswehr plans to introduce MLRS between 1987 and 1994.

Preliminary tenders indicated that it would be economically feasible to build MLRS in Europe. The shares of production will be apportioned according to the size of nations' orders, which at the time of writing gives FRG 60 per cent, Great Britain 20 per cent, France 16 per cent and Italy 4 per cent, although the final shares could be different. The main contractor is the FRG's *MLRS–Europaische Produktions–Gesellschaft* (MLRS–EPG). Within MLRS–EPG the leading firm is RTG (*Raketen-Technik Gesellschaft*), which is also the main contractor for development of the AT–2 warhead. The British Contractor is Hunting Engineering, the French contractor, Aerospatiale and the Italian contractor, BPD. Vought is pooled with MLRS–EPG and its partners in the MLRS International Consortium (MIC). MIC expects export orders of a similar order to those placed by the US or European countries. It is planned that 60 per cent of these orders will be met by US industry and 40 by European.

Artillerymen stress that the weapon is the shell or the rocket warhead, and that the gun or rocket is the delivery systems. Great attention has therefore been made to making the warheads of the MLRS rockets as effective as possible. At the time of writing. It is planned to procure the following types of munition:

	USA	FRG	GB	France	Italy
SPLLs	339	200	105	55	20
practice rockets	27,500	16,000	12,500	3,000	1,420
M-77 (bomblet)	400,000	65,000	82,500	32,000	5,400
AT-2 (anti-vehicle/anti-tank)	—	20,000	—	—	600

It will be noted that on present plans only the FRG and, to a very limited extent, Italy, are to procure the AT-2 anti-tank mine rocket. The USA and Great Britain have declared that they have no interest, but it is always possible that their plans may change in the future.

M-77 bomblet rocket (MLRS phase 1)

According to the 14 July 1979 agreement, the USA will pay for the development of the bomblet warhead at an estimated cost of US $340 m. Great Britain and France would contribute US $15 m. The bomblets, which are similar to the M-42 bomblets in conventional artillery shells, are designed for use against unprotected or lightly protected targets, such as enemy towed artillery, air defence assets, C^2 and supply installations and enemy infantry. The warhead weighs 159 kg and contains 644 bomblets each with shaped charge and fragment effect. The rocket has a range of about 32 km. A launcher firing all twelve rockets could thus put 7,728 bomblets in the target area. The time of flight out to maximum range is 50 seconds. The dispersal pattern of the bomblets depends on the height at which they are ejected. One or two launchers might therefore be sufficient to neutralise an enemy artillery battery or command headquarters.

AT-2 anti-tank mine rocket (MLRS phase 2)

The main contractor, RTG, began development of the AT-2 in November 1980. A number of rockets have been fired in tests at White Sands in New Mexico. The AT-2 mine rocket is specifically designed to defeat enemy armour in the forward area of his deployment and to block enemy breakthroughs rapidly. It has a range of about 40 km. Each warhead contains 28 miles. At just over a kilometre over the target the outer aerodynamic casing separates and seven mine distribution units (*Minenverteil-enheiten*), six of which have been carried in the cylindrical part of the rocket and one in the nose-cone, are forced outwards. Seven seconds later four AT–2 mines are ejected from each distribution unit and fall to the ground retarded by parachute.

A launcher therefore disposes of 336 AT–2 mines, and can cover an area about 1000 metres by 400. It is envisaged that one mine would be placed for every half metre of front, which would require five or six launchers to sow a dense thousand metre wide strip.

Terminally guided sub-munition rocket (MLRS phase 3)

The Memorandum of Understanding for the development phase of the terminally guided sub-munition rocket was signed by the end of 1983. Each rocket would contain five or six sub-munitions, and should have a maximum range of about 45 km. It is designed to engage armoured targets which, because their thickest armour is at the front, will be most vulnerable to top attack. Obviously, these must be engaged as far away from the forward line of defence (FLOT or German VRV) as possible. This will help implement the NATO doctrine of follow-on forces attack, by wearing down the second echelon. In fact, the best solution proved to be a sub-munition with a gliding trajectory and a millimetre wave seeker. If certain technical difficulties concerning environmental factors can be overcome, a passive infra-red seeker might also be a possibility although there are particular problems with the low cloud base often encountered in Europe.

The AT–2 anti-tank mine

The AT–2 mine is already in use with LARS. A LARS launcher can fire a total of 180 mines; MLRS will be able to fire 336. It is also used in the West German *Minenwurfsystem* (MiWS-mine launcher system). The MiWS, which is being issued to the Bundeswehr at the time of writing, can dispense 600 AT–2 mines in 10 minutes, ejecting them either side of its M113 APC chassis. The mine is 103.5 mm (four inches) in diameter and is 165 mm (six and a half inches) high. The shaped charge will penetrate 140 mm (five and a half inches) of armour and will blow tracks off vehicles. It is important to stress that 'mobility kills', that is, just rendering a vehicle temporarily immobile, are sufficient to slow or temporarily halt an enemy advance, giving the defender that all-important asset: time. Having landed by parachute, the mine is brought into its operating position by 12 erectors which swing down from the mine body. The mine has six pre-selectable life times. At the end of this time the mine blows itself up, if it has not been detonated already. This is extremely important as our own troops may wish to traverse the ground. The mine is camouflaged and contains devices to protect it against manual and electronic clearing.

The first simultaneous firing of six AT–2 mine carrying rockets took place on 14 July 1983. Besides testing the warhead, the trial also aimed to acquire data on the missile and mine flight paths, to improve the fire control system program and thus accuracy of fire. Each of the six warheads contained six exercise mines and 22 dummies, all painted in bright colours to facilitate locating them in the targets area, except for some olive green ones which proved very difficult to see even on sandy terrain. The tests included running over the exercise mines with tanks to test the release mechanism.

MLRS at war

As noted above, MLRS could be invaluable in inflicting delay on a Soviet attack; '. . . time is the most precious of all', as Suvorov said.[4] One or two MLRS batteries should be able to close a choke point such as either end of a bridge (a useful alternative to a reserve demolition), a narrow defile, a route across a marsh, and so on. The enemy would either have to clear the minefield (very time consuming), bypass it (time consuming, possibly difficult and certainly forcing him to change his plan unexpectedly), or drive through the minefield (expensive and very bad for morale). A delay of even half an hour could provide an exhausted defender with valuable recovery time.

Another use for MLRS, particularly firing the M–77, might be to put an instant minefield down before a threatened platoon or company position. The instant minefield would cause enough casualties among attacking troops to compensate for the defender's inability to engage them while under the crushing Soviet artillery preparation. It would also present the attacker with a totally unexpected obstacle, which junior Soviet commanders would be ill-equipped to deal with.

SOVIET INTEREST IN REMOTELY DELIVERED MINES AND SUBMUNITION PROJECTILES

The Russians have always kept a keen eye on Western military technological developments and the developments described above are no exception. The Soviets realise the threat that Remotely Delivered Mines (RDMs) pose to, in particular, the successful insertion of an OMG. For example, in January 1984 an article on sub-munition projectiles which the Russians call, rather charmingly, *kassetnye snaryady*-'cassette shells', appeared in the popular magazine *Tękhnika i vooruzheniye* (*Technology and Armament*).[5] Capitalist countries, it said, and in particular the USA, were increasingly introducing 'cassette shells' for artillery guns and Multiple Launch Rocket Systems. The latter are referred to as *Reaktivnye sistemy zalpogo ognya* (RSZO), literally 'Rocket volley fire systems'. This is interesting as the Soviets have been leaders in the MRL field for nearly 45 years and have always called them *boyevaya mashina.* For NATO's systems, as opposed to their own, they prefer to use a direct translation of the NATO term. The article illustrated the 105 mm M 413 shell, the 155 mm M 692, the 203 mm. M 404, the 155 mm M 483 A1, and various individual sub-munitions. It mentioned the MLRS with its two types of sub-munition rocket and devoted special attention to the AT–1 and AT–2 anti-tank mines. The following month another article on sub-munition war-heads (*boyevye chasti-BCh*) for rockets appeared.[6] This was couched in terms which suggest that the Soviets are investigating sub-munition warheads for their own use, although using examples 'from the foreign press'. Such warheads, it said, achieved a more equable distribution of explosive over the target area, and were suitable for the destruction of personnel, tanks, APCs and anti-aircraft sites, and for remote mining. It devoted particular attention to the Lance sub-munition warhead.

A sub-munition or improved conventional warhead would be very suitable for the SS–21 *tochka* missile being deployed in Europe. Instant minefields would be very useful in, for example, sealing the flanks of an OMG penetration, preventing counter-attack by manoeuvre forces in the same way that smoke would screen it from fire. However, Soviet requirements are somewhat different from those of NATO, and at the moment the Soviets seem more interested in fuel air explosives as improved conventional munitions. These are ideal area weapons in the absence of nuclear use. Interest in these is likely to increase as the Soviets develop the all-conventional option further.

Extended Range Artillery

Another important development of the early to mid 1980s has been the appearance of extended range artillery systems. Artillery is one area where the Soviets have been consistently ahead of the West: the only system to compare with the formidable 1950s vintage Soviet 130 mm M–46 gun, with its 27–30 km range was the lumbering 175 mm howitzer. With the 2S5 152 mm gun (range 35–40 km) the Soviets remain in the lead with conventional artillery systems. With the need to strike deeply into the enemy's follow-on echelons, and the increasing vulnerability and expense of manned aircraft, more emphasis needs to be placed on conventional artillery systems as well as MLRS. Rocket assisted projectiles were used by the Syrians in the 1973 Middle East war, fired from Soviet M–46 guns. Development of rocket assisted projectiles, which may extend the range of conventional guns by 50 to 100 per cent, continues in the West. The US Divisional Support Weapons System (DSWS) aims to produce a 155 mm howitzer able to fire rocket or rocket-ramjet propelled projectiles known collectively as the Advanced Indirect Fire System (AIFS). These would have a maximum range of about 70 km. However, AIFS is designed primarily as an anti-armour weapon, as only the engagement of high value targets would justify the high cost of rocket assisted shells, and the DSWS, if it ever sees the light of day, will not do so until the 1990s.

In the interim, and for use against softer targets, an elegantly simple solution to the problem of increasing artillery's range has emerged in the shape of Extended Range Sub-Calibre (ERSC) and Full Bore (ERFB) ammunition. The former is a shell which is tapered all the way from the driving band at the back, instead of having a cylindrical centre section, and is thinner than the bore of the gun. This is obviously more aerodynamic; to impart spin to the shell and prevent it wobbling about in the barrel there are two collar-like sabots, one of which mounts the driving band, both of which discard in flight. An ERSC round fired from a 155 mm M–109 howitzer had a range of over 22 km, as opposed to the howitzer's normal range of 14.6 km; a 50 per cent improvement. However, it is obviously wasteful to have a projectile so much thinner than the barrel and because of their shape ERSC rounds are unsuitable for conventional high-explosive (HE) shells.

Another variant of the same principle is the ERFB projectile. This retains the same tapered shape of the ERSC, but is a full

155 mm in diameter at the base. Instead of discarding sabots, the driving band is fixed and the shell is held steady in the barrel by blister like protrusions further up, which are slanted to suit the twist of the rifling. Such shells fired from the Anglo-German-Italian FH–70 155 mm howitzer have increased its range by about 8 km.

The most interesting ERFB development concerns so-called 'base-bleed' technology which was invented in Sweden. This consists of a container attached to the base of the shell, which is filled with a combustible material which burns to generate fuel rich and oxygen deficient gases. This material does not provide extra thrust. What it does do is to increase the pressure in the base area of the shell, reducing the base drag action by 80 per cent. Three types of drag act on a shell in flight: body drag, caused by rotation and friction; wave drag, caused by the shape of the shell's forebody, and base drag, which results from the partial vacuum formed at the base of the shell in flight, pulling it back. ERSB and ERFB projectiles aim to reduce wave drag; base bleed reduces base drag, allowing the shell to decelerate more slowly and thus travel further. As it only acts on base drag, the effect of base bleed is obviously greatest on projectiles where base drag is a high proportion of the total. Base bleed can increase the range of a shell by 13 to 30 per cent compared with non-base bleed ERFB, and correspondingly more of an increase over conventional ammunition. Unlike the rocket assisted projectile, it provides a solution which is simple and relatively cheap. The rights to base bleed are held by IIP, which is a subsidiary of the Belgian firm PRB. The idea obviously has enormous potential.

Base bleed has been applied to the GHN–45 (Gun Howitzer Noricum with a barrel length of 45 calibres) produced by Voest Alpine in Austria. This howitzer fires standard NATO 155 mm ammunition, and can fire a non base-bleed ERFB shell to a range of 30 km. Under the same conditions, it will fire a base-bleed ERFB shell to 39 km, making it comparable with the best Soviet systems. In the Middle East, it was able to attain ranges of 32 km and 43 km with ERFB and ERFB base-bleed shells respectively, without appreciable loss of accuracy.

The above developments are enabling conventional artillery to stretch its range. Rocket assisted projectiles will enable it to stretch further, but they are expensive and lack the qualities which have traditionally been artillery's greatest asset; simplicity and cheapness, and suitability for putting down a large number of projectiles. It may well be that the intermediate improvements; ERFB and ERFB base bleed, represent the ultimate that gun artillery systems can attain without involving other technologies. It seems that there is a limit to what gun artillery can do, and that, as the Russian rocket pioneer Konstantinov observed in the last century, the problem of throwing a very large projectile with a very high velocity can only be solved using the projectile power which can be obtained from rockets.[7]

Large Tactical Missiles and Rockets

Another system whose potential is being exploited in the extension of the land battlefield is the large tactical rocket (unguided) or missile (guided). The early 1980s have seen the deployment of the Soviet SS–21 missile (NATO designation) to Soviet units in East Germany and Czechoslovakia. The SS–21, known to Russian soldiers as *tochka*; 'curtains', was thought to have a maximum range of 120 km but the latest estimates suggest 100 km. The SS–21 is reported to be extremely accurate (the other meaning of *tochka* is 'point'), so it might have some sort of guidance system. It is mounted on a 6 × 6 amphibious transporter-erector-launcher (TEL), based on the chassis of the SA–8 Gecko anti-aircraft missile, but remodelled at the top. There are probably two longitudinal doors which fold to the side to enable the rocket/missile to be elevated into the launching position.[8] The TEL is fully amphibious, being propelled in the water by two jets. The SS–21 is progressively replacing the Frog 7 (range 70 km) as the large divisional tactical rocket system. The SS–21 is believed to be very similar to the American Lance in appearance and characteristics. Like Lance, it can fire a nuclear and (probably) improved conventional warhead. The Soviets are also introducing new missiles at Army and Front level; the SS–23, maximum range 500 km to replace the Scud and the SS–22, maximum range 885 km, to replace the Scaleboard. Virtually nothing is known about these new longer range ground forces missiles.

The Soviets have traditionally relied on surface-to-surface missiles to perform tasks which the West has tended to give to manned aircraft. However, the increased cost and vulnerability of such aircraft, and the head for a NATO ground forces commander to have under his command a system which can strike at follow on forces very quickly has led the United States to develop the Joint Tactical Missile system (JTACM) as the solution to long range interdiction. This is designed to engage targets at ranges of between 50 km (the maximum limit for conventional and improved artillery and MLRS systems), and about 300 km. Airfields would be one obvious target. Making a missile which will travel that far is not a problem; the problem is one which has bedevilled surface to surface artillery since the last century.

Target Acquisition

The mid-19th century military technological revolution produced artillery which could fire further than the human eye could see, or beyond the horizon determined by the contours of the ground. As a result a fundamental change took place; the separation of targeting from the system for delivering the munition. Artillery forward observers were separated from the guns, and signalled target data and corrections to them by flags, telephone and, later, radio.[9] The present and future battlefield is characterised by essentially the same separation of functions, but on a larger scale. It is necessary to 'see' deep behind the enemy's forward echelons. More emphasis is being placed on aircraft unmanned drones and space satellites for surveillance and target acquisition, while surface-to-surface artillery, rockets and missiles must become more important for munitions delivery.

In both world wars, target acquisition was the artilleryman's greatest problem. Distant targets, especially enemy artillery, could only be located by sound ranging or aerial photography. Both of these took time and were not 100 per cent accurate. If a future war is characterised by great mobility and high tempos of operations, as many believe it will be, these methods will not be suitable. What is the point of the Soviets having systems like the 2S5 and BM–27 with maximum ranges of 35–40 km, when they would have great difficulty in identifying targets at that range? Firstly, of course, nobody likes having to use a system at maximum range as its accuracy decreases considerably as the outer limit is approached. Secondly, it is obviously not possible to put every weapon on the Forward Line of Own Troops (FLOT), or anywhere near it. In order to stand any chance of survival, heavy weapons have to be dispersed in breadth and depth. The Soviets might well want to deploy these weapons up to 15 km behind the FLOT and either side of the target, hit targets up to 10 km beyond the FLOT, and have 10 km to spare.

Satellites will clearly play a very significant part in targeting land ordnance in future, and the outcome of the war on land will depend very much on what happens in space as well as in the air. The United States certainly expect the bulk of their intelligence of enemy positions and force movements to come from satellite and airborne surveillance. Great emphasis is being placed on the new Joint Stand Off Target and Reconnaissance System (JSTARS). This is now being developed from technology incorporated in the USAF's *Pave Mover*, which is part of the *Assault Breaker* development programme. Technology is also being derived from the US Army's Battlefield Data System (BDS) and Stand Off Target Acquisition System (SOTAS). SOTAS is crucial to the deployment of the new longer range artillery, MLRS and any future tactical missile system. It detects and tracts the movement, build up and withdrawal of enemy forces beyond the limit of a forward observer's vision. It can operate at night and in adverse weather, giving a moving picture of moving targets in 'real-time'. The information is provided with sufficient accuracy to allow target engagement with artillery, aircraft and other long range weapons. Acquisition is carried out by an airborne element, in a Black Hawk helicopter, while the processing takes place in a vehicle on the ground.[10] Another important part of the patchwork of target acquisition is the high flying Lockheed TR-1 equipped with the Precision Locating/Strike System (PLSS), which would locate radar emitters for subsequent attack.

At the time of writing, NATO armies are placing much emphasis on unmanned drones or Remotely Piloted Vehicles (RPVs) for target acquisition, such as the US Army operated Lockheed Aquila. Another area which will also receive further attention is that of Unattended Ground Sensors (UGS). MLRS could in fact deliver UGS out to its maximum range, in order to cover areas inadequately covered by other means. UGS may be infra-red, acoustic, seismic or magnetic. They are cheap and, most important, disposable. The information provided may be crude, but should be enough to enable drones to be despatched to obtain more precise data. Current drones lack the ability to report back in real time, but this should be remedied when the Phoenix RPV comes into service. Phoenix can conduct surveillance out to 40 or 50 km from the FLOT, by day or night. At shorter ranges, Phoenix can remain in the air for two to three hours and pass target information back to long range artillery instantly. Until Phoenix is in service, NATO forces will have to rely heavily on analysis of enemy electronic emissions and stay behind OPs to acquire targets in the enemy depth.

The Soviets would employ very similar solutions to similar problems. They, too, would place great reliance on satellites and locating NATO radio and radar emissions. Their sound ranging is very good and quick, but it may not be quick enough if the battle takes the form they expect it to. They would also rely on Special Purpose Forces (SPF), 'sleepers', placed before the start of war, and long range reconnaissance patrols.

Main Battle Tanks (MBTs)

Compared with the above qualitative developments in long range indirect fire systems, there has been little change in the tank field in the early 1980s. The widespread introduction of Anti-Tank Guided Missiles (ATGM) did, it is true, lead some to question the viability of the tank, but although ATGMs have affected the way tanks are deployed, and led to the development of special armours, the tank remains the most versatile and robust land weapons system. With the exception of the turretless Swedish S tank and the Israeli Merkava with its turret at the back, tanks in the mid 1980s retain essentially the same layout as those of 60 years ago. Future tanks, however, may be rather different. At the time of writing France, the FRG, UK, Sweden and the USA are all evaluating new tank concepts for the 1990s. These may lead to the disappearance of the familiar turret. Whereas it has proved possible for NATO nations to cooperate in the artillery and MLRS field, and even to build highly complex aircraft such as the Tornado on a collaborative basis, efforts to cooperate in tank design and production have come to naught. FRG has tried to work with the UK and the USA on new tanks, for example, but these attempts have all failed because of cost, timescale and differing pilosophies and requirements. In the future, however, tank development may follow artillery and aircraft down the international road.

The most exciting and original developments have probably taken place in Sweden. The turretless S tank (the Strv 103B) was produced between 1966 and 1971. This is being upgraded at the time of writing, with Bofors Ordnance as the prime contractor. Besides a new automatic gearbox, engine, radiator, generator, silencer and controls, the S tank is getting a laser rangefinder and possibly a computer. A new MBT which could enter service in 1995 is also under study. This is being developed by NB

Utveckling, and would probably be armed with an externally mounted 120 mm gun, like that on Utveckling's UDES XX20 articulated tank destroyer. Prototypes of the latter have been tested in range firing.

Other tank development has been evolutionary. This is particularly marked where Soviet tanks are concerned. The T-64 and T-72 (known Soviet designations) have been extensively modified, and this has given rise to speculation that there are new Soviet tanks. For example, one of the most respected authorities on Soviet tanks, Steven J Zaloga, has suggested that a considerably improved version of the T-72, shown in *Tekhnika i Vooruzhniye* in September, 1980, is called the 'T-74'.[11] That might be, but NATO practice is to refer to such unidentified variants as Soviet Medium Tank (SMT) followed by the year and order in which they were seen, until the Soviet 'T-' designation is formally known. There are at least two such mutations of the T-72 (the original T-72 first entered production in 1971). These are known to NATO as SMT M 1980/1, which has been exported to other Warsaw Pact countries, and SMT M 1981/3, which at the time of writing is in Soviet service only. There is also at least one considerably improved version of the T-64, SMT M 1981/1. The T-72 is believed to have some sort of improved armour, possibly with ceramic inserts in the cast turret armour and ceramic backing to the hull armour. This armour is not comparable with the British Chobham armour and need not result in the slab sided turret shape associated with the new western special armours. There have also been references in some sources to the 'T-80', but these probably refer to the modified T-72s. T-80 would be a Soviet designation referring to a distinctively new tank. No such tank has been seen at the time of writing. If it were it should be referred to simply as 'next Soviet Tank', until its Soviet designation were established. Although the Soviets have watched western developments such as the Swedish S tank with interest, it is most unlikely that a 'next Soviet tank' would be a radical departure from traditional designs.

Turning to NATO tanks, the first production model of the FRG's Leopard 2 was handed over in 1979. 1800 Leopard 2s have been ordered 990 being built by Krauss Maffei and 810 by Krupp-MaK. Final deliveries are due in early 1987. Leopard 2s are also being delivered to the Dutch, who first received them in 1981 and will get the last in 1986, and will be delivered to Switzerland. Krauss-Maffei and Krupp-MaK are also to be awarded definition contracts for the Leopard 3, which might enter production in 1996–97. It is expected that this will be a conventional turreted design.

In the USA, the M1 Abrams MBT is being produced at the Lima Army Tank Plant and the Detroit Arsenal Tank Plant. Both of these are operated by the Land Systems Division of General Dynamics. By the end of 1983, 1489 M1s had been delivered to the US Army. The M1 has been tested by Switzerland, which chose the Leopard 2 in preference, and Saudi Arabia, which has a requirement for 200–300 MBTs. In 1982 General Dynamics were also awarded a $13 m contract for the construction of a so-called Tank Test Bed (TTB). This will have an M1 tank chassis with a crew of three and a 120 mm smoothbore gun overhead, fed by an automatic loader, rather like the Swedish UDES XX20. Trial models of the automatic loader may be built by Rheinmetall and the Northern Ordnance Division of FMC Corporation, but no contracts had been awarded by January 1984.

The British Army received its first Challenger MBT in March 1983, and final deliveries are expected during 1985. Royal Ordnance Factory Leeds is under contract to build 243 Challengers. This is sufficient to equip four regiments (battalions) in BAOR, but more could be ordered. Challenger has been demonstrated in the Middle East where, with FRG's refusal to export Leopard 2 to the area, its only real competitor is the American M1. ROF Leeds is also building 274 Khalid MBTs for Jordan and some tanks for Oman. These orders are both modified Chieftains. Another modified Chieftain, the Chieftain 900, has also been developed primarily for the export market.

Following the collapse of the proposed French/FRG MBT, France is developing the *Engin Principal de Combat* (EPC), the first prototype of which is due to be completed in 1987, with production starting two or three years later. The French Army needs between 1200 and 1500 EPCs, which will probably be called AMX-48s. The ammunition will be interchangeable with the 120 mm Rheinmetall gun on the Leopard 2. In 1983 a prototype of the 43 tonne AMX-40 was exhibited, which is designed for the export market. The Israeli Army, which has more recent experience of real tank warfare than any other, has its own Merkava tank, first produced in 1979. 250 Merkava Mark 1s have been built and the Mark 2 is now in production. The Mark 2 probably has improved fire control and armour protection as well as a more powerful engine. The Merkava

Mark 3 is expected to follow the Mark 2 into production later in the decade. A final interesting development is Egypt's plan to bring a domestically built tank into service in 1984 or 1985. Egypt is also obtaining Soviet T–55s from Romania and 439 M60A3s from the USA. The first of the latter have been delivered.

Conclusion

Although tanks introduced in the 1990s may be radically different from traditional designs, the tanks being introduced in the mid and late 1980s will be very similar to their predecessors and they will certainly be employed in very much the same way. Special armour has challenged the once prevalent view that the tank had lost its primacy. The battle between the tank and the ATGM seems evenly balanced, and artillery may be the deciding factor one way or the other. The world's infantries are being re-equipped with small arms firing smaller calibre ammunition. Although this will enable the individual soldier to carry more ammunition, it does not affect the way he will fight; indeed, if there is ever another major conventional land war, infantry will engage the enemy at ranges far less than those at which the British Expeditionary Force engaged the Germans in 1914. However, the main battle will be fought long before the opposed infantry can see each other. The emphasis placed by both NATO and the Warsaw Pact on 'deep attack' has inevitably placed even more emphasis on long range indirect fire weapons; conventional and extended range artillery, MLRS and large tactical rockets and missiles. This is likely to continue. Improved conventional munitions and, later, terminally guided projectiles will enable more and more of the tasks which now have to be performed by direct fire weapons to be done by indirect fire weapons at much greater ranges. Connected with this is an increase in the importance of air and space surveillance systems for target acquisition.

NOTES

[1] AA Sotnikov *Voyenno-istoricheskiy muzey artillerii, inzhenernykh voysk i voysk svyazi. Kratkiy putevoditel'* (Short guide to the military-historical museum of artillery, engineers and signal troops), 6th edition, Leningrad, 1968, p. 181. '. . . *sploshnoye more ognya*'.

[2] Pierre Touzin 'MLRS with USAREUR', *Armed Forces,* March 1984, p. 87.

[3] This and subsequent information on MLRS is mainly based on Ron Sherman 'MLRS: the Soldier's System' *Military Technology* 28 November 1981, pp. 33–40; Wolfgang Flume

'*Artillerieraketensystem MARS/MLRS*' *Wehrtechnik* 11/1983, pp. 18–33; Charles J Dick 'MLRS: Firepower for the 1990s' *RUSI Journal,* December 1983, pp. 17–22.

[4] A V Suvorov '*Nauka Pobezhdat*' (*The Science of Winning*), 1795. Moscow 1980 edition, p. 8.

[5] Colonel L Zabudkin '*Kassetnye snaryady*', *Tekhnika i vooruzheniye* 1/1984, pp. 36–37.

[6] Colonel V Rokhkachev '*Kassetnye boyevye chasti raket*' *T i V* 2/1984. pp. 8–9. It is notable that whereas Zabudkin's article appeared in the section 'In capitalist countries' armies', Rokhkachev's appeared in the 'Problems and perspectives' section, indicating that the Soviets may be more interested in submunition warheads for their own large tactical missiles than for tube artillery shells.

[7] Royal Artillery Institution *Professional Visits of Artillery Officers* 1861–66: 1862 report, p. 23.

[8] See the author's article 'Soviet Artillery and Tactical Rocket Design' *Jane's Defence Review* Vol 4 No 8 1983, p. 787.

[9] See the author's 'The Russian Artillery and the Origins of Indirect Fire' *Army Quarterly,* April and July 1982.

[10] *Jane's Weapons Systems* 1982–83, p. 266.

[11] Steven J Zaloga 'Soviet T–72 Tank' *Jane's Defence Review* Vol 4 No 5 1983, pp. 423–34.

Trends in Land Warfare: The Operational Art of the European Theatre

CHRIS BELLAMY

The author served as an artillery officer and has an MA in War Studies. He has written widely on defence matters, particularly the Soviet Union, and he is an incorporated linguist. He devised and drew the diagrams.

Thus, what is of supreme importance in war is to attack the enemy's strategy.

Sun Tzu, *the Art of War*

FOR CENTURIES, it was sufficient to apply the term 'strategy' to national defence priorities affecting the initial dispositions of forces and the way armies manoeuvred seeking the most favourable circumstances for engagement. 'Tactics' meant the way a battle was fought when two hostile armies actually met. In the 19th century, the advent of massed conscript armies with railways to transport them quickly and a revolution in weapons technology brought about an extension of the battlefield and more extended deployments. Military action was no longer limited to one or two decisive engagements and operations began to take place continuously, over a long period and across a wide front. The first major examples of this are the American Civil, Russo-Japanese and First World Wars. Although the term 'tactics' continued to be applicable to the way commanders fought individual actions, it was hardly suitable to describe the way higher commanders planned operations of long duration and great spatial scope. At the same time, the goals of those operations were purely military and took place within a single theatre of military operations; they were not, in themselves, 'strategic'. Douglas Haig, for example, compared the whole Western Front experience of 1914–18 to a single, very protracted battle, conforming to all the classic phases of a tactical engagement, but on a larger scale. Meanwhile, the advent of wars that were both total and global gave 'strategy' a new and higher significance. It was applicable to the handling of the war as a whole, including political and economic factors, and questions of allied cooperation. A new term was needed to describe the intermediate level which had emerged. 'Grand tactics' had been used and is still used by some today, but the word now generally accepted is 'operational'. The German General Dr Hugo von Freytag - Loringhoven used the word *operativ* to describe this level when referring to World War I experience in 1920 and in the late 1920s, the Soviets first used the term 'operational art' (*operativnoye iskusstvo*) to refer to a third, different level of military art.[1]

Although both Soviets and Germans therefore recognised the existence of a third dimension, the Soviets envisaged this as army and front (army group) level, whereas the Germans thought of it as division and corps. The fact that the Soviets' operational art was conceived on a larger scale than the Germans' is, in the author's view, one key reason why the Red Army eventually out-thought and out-fought the Wehrmacht in the land/air battle, despite the Wehrmacht's unquestionable superiority in tactical handling. The Soviets thought bigger as far as military objectives were concerned, but at the same time they were able to keep these separate from strategic, political and economic questions.

'Operational art' is now a term also accepted by Israeli and American military thinkers. It occurs in the concept of operations FM 100–5 and in the futuristic *Airland Battle 2000.* (See "The AirLand Battle and NATO's New Doctrinal Debate" by Robert A Gessert, *RUSI Journal,* June 1984.) That the Americans should have espoused the third dimension of military art is not surprising, given their global perspective and the fact that a large slice of their military experience has been continental in the same way as that of the Germans and Russians; notably a fight for life between two contiguous powers in 1861–65. The American Civil War provides highly topical examples of swift mobile operations on a large scale, and these are drawn to the attention of modern American commanders in FM 100–5. The British Army does not acknowledge the operational level at the time of writing. The official American definition of this level follows the Russian quite closely:

> The Operational Level of war uses available military resources to attain strategic goals within a theater of war. Most simply it is the theory of larger unit operations. It also involves planning and conducting campaigns. Campaigns are sustained operations designed to defeat an enemy force in a specified space and time with simultaneous and sequential battles. The disposition of forces,

selection of objectives, and actions taken to weaken or to outmanoeuver the enemy all set the terms of the next battle and exploit tactical gains. They are all part of the operational level of war.[2]

The emphasis on manoeuvre is important. Whereas tactics uses manoeuvre to achieve concentrations of fire, operational art is concerned primarily with manoeuvre alone. It therefore requires 'fire power superiority' (*ognevoye prevoskhodstvo*) as a prerequisite of success.

Now, as throughout the last two centuries, the most powerful concentrations of military force anywhere in the world face each other in Europe. The world's most technologically advanced nations are all involved, and within a month of mobilisation they could put into the field in Germany alone, four million men, 10,000 fixed wing aircraft, 25,000 artillery pieces and 40,000 main battle tanks.[3] However interesting and potentially explosive other theatres may be, however challenging the condition in which forces may have to operate, any analysis of trends in land warfare must focus on Europe, and especially on the three great continental powers whose forces are deployed there: Russia and its allies on the one hand, West Germany and the United States on the other.

Future military historians will probably agree that the most important trend in land warfare in the first half of the 1980s was the Soviet military's attempt to develop the ability to launch an attack on NATO at extremely short notice with the aim of winning if possible, using entirely non-nuclear means. In parallel, Western nations, particularly the Federal Republic of Germany (FRG) and the USA, strove to contain and defeat a Warsaw Pact offensive, again without recourse to nuclear weapons. It is tempting to see the latter as a counter to the former, but chronology suggests that in fact the two camps' doctrines developed in parallel (the word 'doctrine' is used here in the Soviet sense of the expected and preferred course of a future war). This article will examine the way Soviet military art has developed in pursuit of this doctrinal requirement, and then the way the West Germans and Americans would endeavour to counter any offensive. Space precludes the treatment of other armies, and in NATO only the Germans and Americans acknowledge the operational level. It is, however, important to note the position of the French Corps able to reinforce southern Germany, thus giving NATO's deployment there operational depth which is lacking in the north.

Soviet Union and other Warsaw Pact countries

The advantages accruing to the Warsaw Pact because it enjoys commonality of equipment are obvious. Far more important, however, is the fact that all those states practise Soviet military art, in accordance with Soviet military doctrine. Control at the operational level is firmly vested in Soviet officers, although this does not prevent the utilisation of the impressive military traditions and qualities of, in particular, the East Germans and Poles within the context of divisions and possibly corps. Henceforward, 'Soviet' should be taken as referring equally to other Warsaw Pact countries.

After about 1970, Soviet military doctrine admitted the possibility that nuclear weapons would not be used initially in a major war, although it still taught that they would probably be used eventually, and that they would remain the decisive factor in any confict. Their existence would dictate the form of a war, even if they were not actually employed. By the end of the decade, the Soviets were planning how they might bring about the collapse of NATO defence on the European mainland and the swift and successful conclusion of a war using conventional and possibly chemical weapons only. The author believes that this was being worked out during 1978, although the factors infuencing such plans had been identified in earlier works including Reznichenko's *Tactics* (1966) and Savkin's *Basic principles of Operational Art and Tactics* (1972). The latter is one of the most significant works of world military thought of the post war period. In 1978, a number of articles were published stressing air-ground cooperation, the formation of air-ground assault groups and mobile groups. Colonel Wojcic of the Polish General Staff Academy wrote of 'ground-air strike teams' (LPZUs), which, because of the unslackening intensity of their fire power, would make it impossible for the enemy to mend his shattered system of defence. The groups were also needed to destroy enemy nuclear assets.[4] Other articles mentioned the activities of forward detachments and raiding groups during the Great Patriotic War, and Colonel Samoylenko commented specifically on the possibility of using similar methods today.[5] The full significance of these debates is only apparent with hindsight. Although Soviet operational art, both theory and practice, continues to evolve, the main trends had become clear by mid-1982, and in September of that year they were first outlined in the West's open military press.[6]

The new Soviet concept of operations is based on the theatre of military operations (*Teatr Voyennykh Deystvii-TVD*), which may also be called the strategic direction (*Strategicheskoye napravleniye*). The Western TVD is believed to comprise Western Europe including the UK and Spain and possibly southern Norway, but excluding Italy. Within the TVD there would be four overlapping 'strategic operations':

- an air operation,
- an anti-air operation,
- a theatre land (ground forces with air support) operation,
- a naval or coastal operation.

Each of these operations would involve the integration of all types of weapons, including artillery, missiles, air and electronic warfare. Broadly, the air operation seeks to degrade enemy air defence and close support aircraft; the anti-air operation to create conditions permitting the movement of ground forces and air transport. Both of these therefore contribute to the success of the theatre land operation. The latter has sometimes been called the Front operation but this is misleading as it limits its scope to a particular higher formation. The land operation in the Western TVD might well comprise three or four Fronts, and the TVD is coming to play a more prominent role in Soviet planning. This article is concerned with the theatre land operation, which also naturally contains a cardinal air dimension. Close air support is given by army aviation, with helicopters at divisional and army level, and fixed-wing aircraft such as the Frogfoot ground attack aircraft, at Army and Front. The new Soviet concept of theatre land operations is therefore just as much an 'Air Land Battle' as the American.

The nature of the theatre land operation is conditioned by the existence of nuclear weapons. In order to prevent their use, the Soviets would aim:

- to destroy or neutralise as many NATO air and nuclear assets as possible,
- to keep attacking forces as dispersed as possible,
- to make a number of penetrations so as to confuse the enemy as to the direction of the main thrust,
- to get their own forces as close as possible to NATO forces and centres of population, so as to discourage the use of nuclear weapons.
- to paralyse NATO's ability to make the political decision to use nuclear weapons.

This requires the Soviets to shift the centre of gravity of operations to NATO's operational depth as quickly as possible. By 'operational depth', we understand the full extent of West Germany. This has meant the resuscitation of the 'deep operation' (*Glubokaya operatsiya*), first mooted in the 1930s and itself based on the earlier theory of consecutive operations. Like all the Soviet operational concepts, the deep operation has a microcosm at tactical level; the deep battle (*Glubokiy boy*).

The Operational Manoeuvre Group (OMG)

This aspect of the new Soviet concept has attracted much attention although it is important to see it as part of the overall picture. The OMG is nothing new; the Soviets acknowledge explicitly that it is based on the GPW forward detachment (*peredovoy otryad*) and mobile group (*podvizhnaya gruppa*), and the activity of cavalry armies in the Russian Civil War. There are also parallels with Imperial Russian practice.[7] The term itself appeared in Polish military press in 1982; *operacyjna grupa manewrowa,* but it is clearly a Soviet idea. It has been suggested that a Soviet Army might launch a division sized OMG and a Front a larger ('corps') OMG. An OMG breakthrough is shown schematically in Figure 1. However, the difficulties of pushing a whole division through a gap in NATO defence and of controlling it in the enemy depth are obvious and great enough. A Front OMG might therefore differ from a divisional one in function rather than in size. An Army's OMG might operate up to 70 kilometres ahead of the main body of the Army (see Figure 2) and a Front OMG–150 kilometres or more ahead. The OMG is not the same as the familiar second echelon, but it may have replaced it in some circumstances for two reasons. In order to ensure that an OMG breaks through, a strong first echelon is needed. If the penetration is carried out successfully, the enemy defence will be thrown off balance and there is no need for a second echelon. Secondly, much NATO thinking in recent years has sought to defeat a Soviet attack by striking with long range weapons at the Soviet second echelon as it is moving up behind the first. The Soviets now know this. If the OMG passes quickly through the first echelon, the NATO forces' 'deep battle' will be conducted against thin air. It must be emphasised, however, that there is no standard organisation for Armies and Fronts; within them there could be any combination of OMG(s), echelons and special reserves.

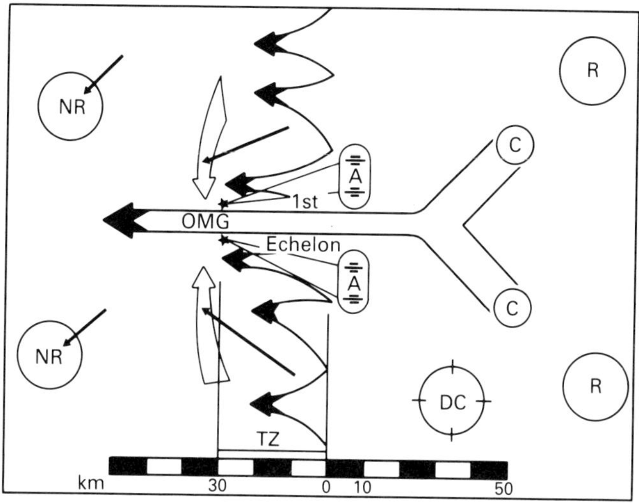

FIGURE 1 Insertion of an Army OMG

A = Artillery and Multiple Rocket Launchers, maximum range ca. 35 km., supporting insertion of OMG.
C = OMG Concentration area
DC = Dummy concentration
NR = NATO reserves
R = Soviet All Arms reserves
TZ = Tactical Zone (25–30 km. wide)
Light arrows = NATO counterattacks
Thin arrows = Air Strikes

An OMG would probably be based on a tank division, but recent literature suggests that it might be augmented with some or all of the following:

- airborne or heliborne assault forces,
- an air element (presumably assault helicopters),
- additional engineer support, especially river crossing and demolition equipment),
- special logistic support including resupply by air,
- additional air defence assets.

There is apparently some debate as to whether the heliborne forces and fighter helicopters should be incorporated in the OMG and move with it, or fly missions from the main

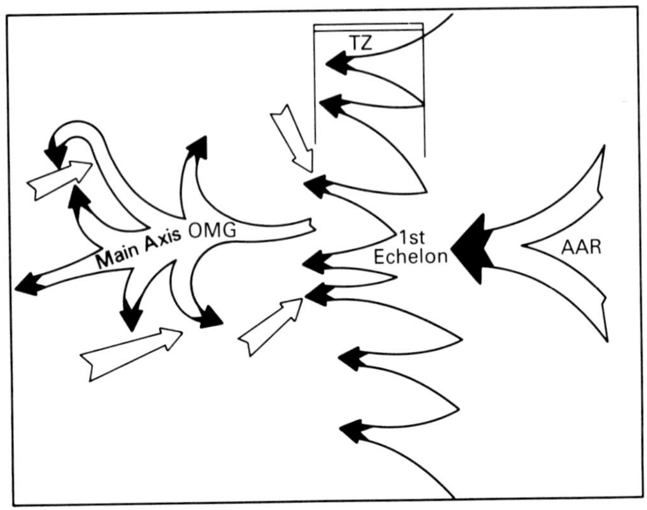

FIGURE 2 Army OMG after insertion

AAR = Soviet All-Arms Reserves

deployment. One obvious compromise would be to start from the main deployment but land in the middle of the OMG and operate from there for as long as possible.

An OMG would be given broad directives but the way these were carried out would be left to the discretion of the commander. The OMG would move fast and far into the enemy depth and might:

- destroy, disrupt or capture enemy nuclear weapons HQs, airfields, Command Control and Communications (C^3), logistic support and the lateral communications needed to move NATO troops to counter a Soviet breakthrough,
- destroy enemy reserves in meeting engagements,
- prevent withdrawal of NATO units,
- pursue withdrawing NATO forces in parallel and destroy them,
- seize NATO rear defensive lines before they can be occupied,
- seize or isolate key political and economic objectives.

The latter might be an objective for the Front OMG(s) (see Figure 3). The appearance of a Soviet OMG deep in the heart of Germany and close to centres of power and industry could

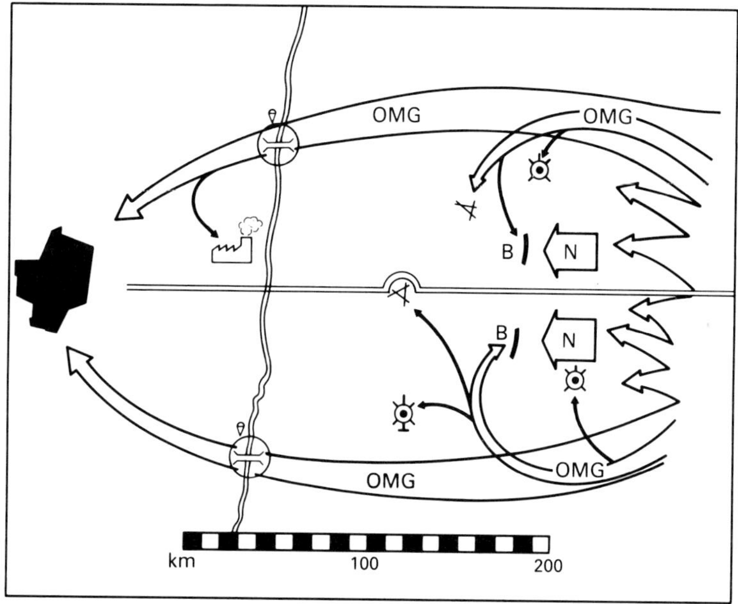

FIGURE 3 Two Front OMGs Converging on a Major Population Centre

Army OMGs move to objectives closer to the Soviet main forces
B = Soviet blocking force (to prevent withdrawal of NATO units)
N = withdrawing NATO forces

Soviet symbol for tactical missile, eg. Lance

Soviet symbol for larger Operational-tactical missile, in this case a Pershing

Soviet symbol for *Front* boundary

Airfield

Industrial centre

Objective captured by airborne force

paralyse political will to resist, and convince some that further resistance was futile. It could fragment parts of the NATO Alliance. 'The moral is to the physical as three is to one.' Strictly speaking, a manoeuvre group launched with this prime aim would be strategic, not operational. A good analogy with this is perhaps Sherman's march through Georgia in 1864.

The most delicate and sensitive phase is obviously the committal of the OMG. Warsaw Pact authorities openly acknowledge that OMGs would be regularly exposed to counter measures and that OMGs and raiding detachments require considerably more in the way of support and protection than forces in the first echelon. In the GPW, an astonishing 70 per cent of Frontal aviation was allocated to the support of mobile groups being inserted, and a modern OMG might attract a similar amount of air and artillery support. Modern Soviet Front artillery (especially the BM–27 and 2S5), has the range to support an OMG during its passage through the main defensive zone and its breakout into the enemy depth while the OMG itself would solve the target acquisition problem. Before being committed, an OMG would probably be held in an assembly area 30–50 kilometres behind the forward Soviet troops. Every possible deception measure would be employed. Given that the OMG would be inserted on the first or second day of hostilities, the deception would not need to be kept up for very long. With the general confusion which would inevitably occur at the outbreak of war, and in view of the massive air operation which would swamp NATO air assets, it is possible that an OMG might not be detected until it was too late to prevent its insertion.

Ground-Air Strike Teams (LPZUs)

The ground-air strike team (*Lądowo-powietrzny zespołuderzeniowy*), also translated, less accurately as the Air Land Assault Group, was first described in the Polish journal *Zołnierz Wolnośći* (*Soldier of Freedom*), in 1978.[7] The article was couched in authoritative terms and the LPZU is clearly an established concept which had been accepted officially by 1981. LPZUs can be deployed by divisions (as reinforced battalions plus the air element), or by armies (reinforced regiments plus air). Although the LPZU is clearly conceived as a tactical unit, an Army subordinated LPZU could just have an operational role. Obviously, the difference between an Army LPZU and an OMG could be very difficult to appreciate in practice. An LPZU might indeed form the forward element of an OMG or an OMG consist of several LPZUs. For these reasons, because tactical units are components of operational formations, and because the LPZU represents the operational level land-air concept on a smaller scale, the LPZU is described here.

Unlike the OMG, the LPZU can be part of the initial assault. If committed during the course of a battle, however, it could act as a 'mini-OMG', breaking through into the interior of the enemy tactical defensive zone (25–30 km wide), or onto the flanks. In that sense it is even more of a descendant of the GPW mobile group or forward detachment than is the OMG. The LPZU acts as a surprise, 'hit and run' force. An Army LPZU might comprise:

Ground Dimension

- 1 motor-rifle or tank regiment (of a division) or independent tank regiment
- 1–2 battalions self-propelled artillery
- support, reconnaissance and anti-aircraft sub-units
- Hind helicopters (transport)

Air Dimension

- 12 Hind helicopters (attack)
- 12 Hip/hook (Heavy lift)
- 12 fighter ground attack sorties per hour (tactical fixed wing air)
- Combat Air Patrol (CAP) Fishbed
- 2 Hip and 6 Hoplite helicopters for C^3.

As with the OMG, it is envisaged that the LPZU would have a corridor blasted for it through an enemy defence. The main targets to be engaged by the fixed wing aircraft supporting the LPZU are: tactical missiles (Lance and Honest John); MLRS, LARS and other artillery plus helicopters on the ground.

Warsaw Pact units are currently experimenting with this concept. The main criticism is that the deployment of the LPZU is too slow, with commanders having more time to plan than they would have in war. There are problems with command and control, including coordination with neighbouring formations on or near boundaries, distinguishing between friend and foe (IFF) when crossing formation boundaries, and coordination of the air assault with the fire of ground artillery.

Integrated Fire Destruction of the Enemy (KOPP)

The term integrated fire destruction of the enemy (KOPP) was, like the OMG, first used in Polish (*Kompleksowe porażenie ogniowe przeciwnika*). In Russian, 'fire destruction' (*ognevoye porazheniye*) is an old term, but the use of *kompleksowy* (combined or composite) is new. Polish porażenie normally has the sense of a stroke or paralysis, and is therefore subtly different from the Russian *porazheniye.* However, in the military sense it must mean the same and 'destruction' is the widely accepted translation, although 'paralysis' might be more apt. It is clear that KOPP is now an officially accepted Warsaw Pact concept. It means crippling the enemy's ability to react and supporting any friendly force from the depths of its own deployment through its commitment to battle to the exploitation of its success. KOPP aims to coordinate the fire effect of all assets to achieve maximum efficiency.

The principle is not new. In the Great Patriotic War, there were many examples of the Soviets employing fire in an integrated way, like the use of long range artillery protected by anti-aircraft guns to smash German advanced airfields. In the absence of nuclear strikes, rapid success for the Soviet ground forces and, in particular, the insertion of OMGs, would have to be accomplished using massive conventional fire power. According to M Zaytsev, the commander of the Group of Soviet Forces Germany (GSFG), up to 50 per cent of the fire power on the modern battlefield would be air delivered. Of the remainder, which would be delivered by ground forces, 80 per cent would be produced by the artillery and rocket troops. Between 1978 and 1983 alone there was a 30 per cent increase in the number of artillery pieces (including multiple rocket launchers) deployed by the Soviets in Europe, and in 1983, the artillery and rocket forces underwent major command changes[8]. This all connected with the reorganisation of front fire support. However, the recent development of the high speed offensive and more flexible tactics have made it very difficult for the artillery to cope with fire support tasks alone. This is because of the difficulty of target acquisition at ranges over 10 kilometres, or at any range once battle is joined, the enormous ammunition requirements required to guarantee effective suppression, and the reduced time available to move and shoot. For this reason, the Soviets are placing more emphasis on direct fire from aircraft, and particularly the armed helicopter. Control of helicopters has been decentralized and Forward Air Controllers (FACs) are being provided more frequently, sometimes down to battalion level. KOPP applies at the operational and tactical levels. One example might be the use of artillery and missiles to neutralise enemy anti-aircraft weapons, while using armed helicopters and fixed wing aircraft to attack enemy artillery positions which are difficult for Soviet artillery to locate and damage. The Soviets are carrying out practical experiments with the concept. One of the major problems is the danger to Soviet helicopters from their own artillery shells. In May 1980, for example, an article by Colonel Dabolin described how it became practice for the Soviet artillery to switch fire to a 'safe' area before helicopters overflew the artillery combat zone, or to limit its fire to targets on the flanks of the helicopters' sectors.[9] This meant that neither artillery nor helicopters could utilise their full potential, and the author suggested a solution using details of trajectories taken from a recent exercise. Another example of KOPP at the tactical level occurs in connexion with the LPZU; the engagement of enemy anti-aircraft weapons by ground forces so as to clear a path for helicopters, and establishing safe corridors through the Soviets' own anti-aircraft defence.

Another change is the addition of a new phase of fire support to the three traditional phases which have characterised artillery and, later, air support since the last century.[10] Fire support now has four phases, of which the first is new:

- *fire protection* (Polish *zabezpieczenie;* the Russian is unknown to the author at the time of writing) of the move from the forming up area to the Soviet forward line of own troops (FLOT),
- *fire preparation* (Russian *podgotovka*) of the attack, commencing 20–30 minutes before the enemy FLOT is reached,
- *fire support* (Russian *podderzhka*), of the attack, as the enemy forward positions are penetrated,
- *fire accompaniment* (Russian *soprovozhdeniye*) of the move into the enemy depth.

The new first phase has been mentioned specifically in the context of amphibious landings and OMGs, but presumably applies to all operations. Its introduction is uncannily timely. The main difference between the 1976 version of the American manual FM 100–5 and the 1982 version was the evolution of the 'deep battle' concept; striking at the Soviets' second echelon forces as they moved up. This idea was discussed in the open military press during 1981.[11] Can it be pure coincidence that the first allusion to 'fire protection' of such forces occurs in an article by the Polish Major Michalak, published in February 1982, and that the new phase was specifically mentioned in an article by the prolific Air Force Colonel Musial, published in May, 1982?[12] Chronology suggests that the American concept evolved in parallel with the Soviet OMG. In obviating the need for a second echelon, the latter might foil the former. However, the new Soviet fire support phase could be a direct response to the American ideas. Of course, it does not take much vision to realise how vulnerable an OMG would be during its concentration and move forward to the FLOT, and since so much could depend on the OMG, it makes sense to give it all possible protection and support. This would include interdiction of enemy assets which might impede the concentration and committal of Soviet 'follow-on' forces, be they OMGs, second echelons or anything else.

The last new concept is the fire strike (*ognevoy udar*). In Russian, as in English, the term 'strike' was used until recently in connection with the use of nuclear weapons. Its application to powerful, paralysing blows by conventional artillery, missiles and air clearly reflects the Soviets' intention to substitute conventional for nuclear fire. When the term was first coined it referred only to a new type of artillery fire support, but in 1980 Marshal Peredel'skiy, the Chief of artillery and rocket troops (replaced in 1983 by Lieutenant General V M Mikhalkin) decreed that there was no need for a new type of fire and that 'fire strike' should apply at the operational level.[13] The definitive comment on fire strike appeared in 1982, in an article by Major General I Vorob'ëv in the Soviet Army newspaper *Red Star.*[14] He referred to 'fire destruction of the enemy', and the increased power and mobility of various means of combat including aircraft. He then mentioned the 'combat potential of artillery and aviation' (fire strike) and of tanks and motor-rifle troops (troop strike). Combat would consist of a series of interrelated blows or strikes. Depending on the time when the blow was struck, a strike might be pre-emptive, meeting or retaliatory and, depending on the way it was delivered — frontal, flanking or combined.

A fire strike is therefore a crushing blow by artillery and air using only conventional armaments delivered as part of an operational plan. KOPP is a concept which applies at the tactical, operational and, indeed, strategic levels (the idea of a single Air or anti-air operation throughout the whole depth of a TVD is a form of KOPP.

Exercise Zapad (West)–81

Zapad–81 was held from 8–12 September 1981. Soviet military leaders described it as a 'milestone' in Soviet military art, suggesting that it marked the end of a period when new operational concepts had been under test. The exercise is constantly cited in military articles and during training. *Zapad-81* did not, apparently, include the simulated employment of nuclear weapons, although the threat of their use was a constant influence on the conduct of operations. 'Mobile groups', airborne, air-mobile and amphibious forces were all employed to project thc centre of gravity of combat as deeply as possible into the enemy rear in order to prevent lateral reinforcement, while the Soviets strove to concentrate their own forces swiftly. It is confirmed that *Zapad-81* also involved air, anti-air and naval operations. In other words, it played out the new Soviet strategic offensive, with its four component 'strategic operations'.

Conclusion

The above is an Outline of the main trends in Soviet thinking about theatre land operations in the early to mid-1980s. In the quest for maximum manoeuvrability and maximum fire power, and the 'deep operation', these reflect earlier Soviet and Imperial Russian ideas, to which new technology and, in particular, the armed helicopter, have added a new dimension. No attempt is made to predict the success or otherwise of operations conducted along these lines. The practical problems of implementing the OMG concept might be insoluble. However, there are precedents for it working and the Soviets are continually experimenting with it in exercises, or at least with the smaller scale LPZU. It is certainly daring and imaginative and must force those who think of the Russians as solid and inflexible to revise their views. Their conception of the 'Air Land Battle' and emphasis on 'integrated fire destruction' are remarkably like the American, but clearly evolved independently.

The Warsaw Pact enjoys commonality of operational thinking, both horizontally, in the sense that all Warsaw Pact countries practise Soviet military art, and vertically, since the same principles apply at all levels. Although Soviet tactics are less flexible than some Soviet officers would wish, their higher formation commanders enjoy great flexibility in, for example, switching their main effort from one axis to another, whereas NATO's have little if any. However, if one generalisation is permitted it is that Russian and Soviet military capabilities have tended to lag behind their impressive military thought. Also, NATO's very diversity could be a source of strength.

THE NATO LAND FORCES TACTICAL DOCTRINE ATP–35 (A)

NATO defines doctrine as 'fundamental principles by which the military forces guide their actions in support of objectives'.[15] Doctrine is authoritative, but requires judgment in application. In setting broad guidelines, what NATO calls doctrine is not dissimilar to Soviet *doktrina.* However, it also lays down principles for the execution of what the Soviets would call military art. The unified NATO doctrine is set out in *Allied Tactical Publication (ATP)–35(A),* covering land operations and associated air support. ATP–35 appeared in 1976, but a substantial review was completed by the beginning of 1983 and the resulting document, ATP–35(A) may be regarded as a completely new publication. ATP–35(A) is, of course, declaredly a 'tactical' doctrine, but it explicitly aims to outline doctrine for combined arms operations at brigade level and above and therefore deals with what the West Germans and Americans call the operational level. The document does not itself acknowledge the existence of the third dimension of war.

A cynic might remark that a doctrine ratified by all NATO's nations must be so bland as to be useless. This author does not agree. ATP–35(A) works on the premise that in the event of an attack, formations of different NATO nations will deploy alongside or pass through one another's area of responsibility or even be grouped in multinational formations.[16] The latter is interesting as it implies that the peacetime deployments of NATO formations are not immutable. The document understands and accepts that the land force doctrine of any nation may go beyond and expand on ATP–35(A). However, this must not lead to a decrease in the ability of their land forces to work effectively together. ATP–35(A) also accepts that national procedures to implement common doctrine may differ markedly. This is not necessarily a problem; ATP–35(A), in addition to providing a common doctrine and vocabulary for land operations, aims to identify areas where more standardization is really needed.

ATP–35(A) regards manoeuvre as a key principle of defence. It is the decisive element at all levels. At the tactical level, defending forces make the best use of the terrain assigned to them in order to concentrate combat power and inflict maximum losses on the enemy.[17] The same would apply at the operational level. ATP–35(A) also stresses that the effectiveness of defence is based primarily on the carefully planned fire of all weapons. The fire of manoeuvre forces, conventional and nuclear artillery, the support of armed helicopters and tactical air forces must be complementary, carefully coordinated and brought to bear with the maximum effect at the right time and place. This is remarkably similar to the Soviet view of KOPP. Most importantly, perhaps, ATP-35(A) insists that whilst the initiative is generally with the attacking force, the defender must not remain passive and wait to react. He must seize and create any opportunity to surprise the enemy and force him to depart from his plans. At every level, the defender must take offensive action to harass the enemy. The defence should therefore be fought with 'imagination, energy and aggressive spirit and with the aim to seize the initiative wherever and whenever possible'.[18] It is recognised that where the majority of the force available is armoured the defence can be conducted with greater flexibility and full use can be made of mobility. In this context, airmobile operations are particularly important. These are defined as operations where combat forces and their equipment move about the battlefield in air vehicles, normally helicopters, under the control of a ground force commander. An airmobile force can attack from any direction, striking objectives in otherwise inaccessible areas, overflying barriers, bypassing enemy positions, and thus achieve surprise. Airmobile forces can permit quick concentration of combat power at key places, and rapid dispersal to reduce vulnerability. They give the commander the ability to reinforce or relieve his forces quickly and over long distances and possibly enabling him to commit a larger part of his force than would otherwise be prudent, relying on a small airmobile reserve. Finally, they enable operations to be conducted independently of a ground line of communications.[19]

Against the common background provided by ATP-35(A), the operational concepts of the major NATO armies can be examined, in order to note where they conform with it and where they could conflict.

The Bundeswehr

Because of its numerical strength, its commitment to defend its homeland and its military tradition, the Bundeswehr must play the major role on NATO's side in any future European land war. The Federal Republic of Germany (FRG) provides 50 per cent of land forces in the Central Region, 50 per cent of ground based air defence and 30 per cent of combat aircraft.

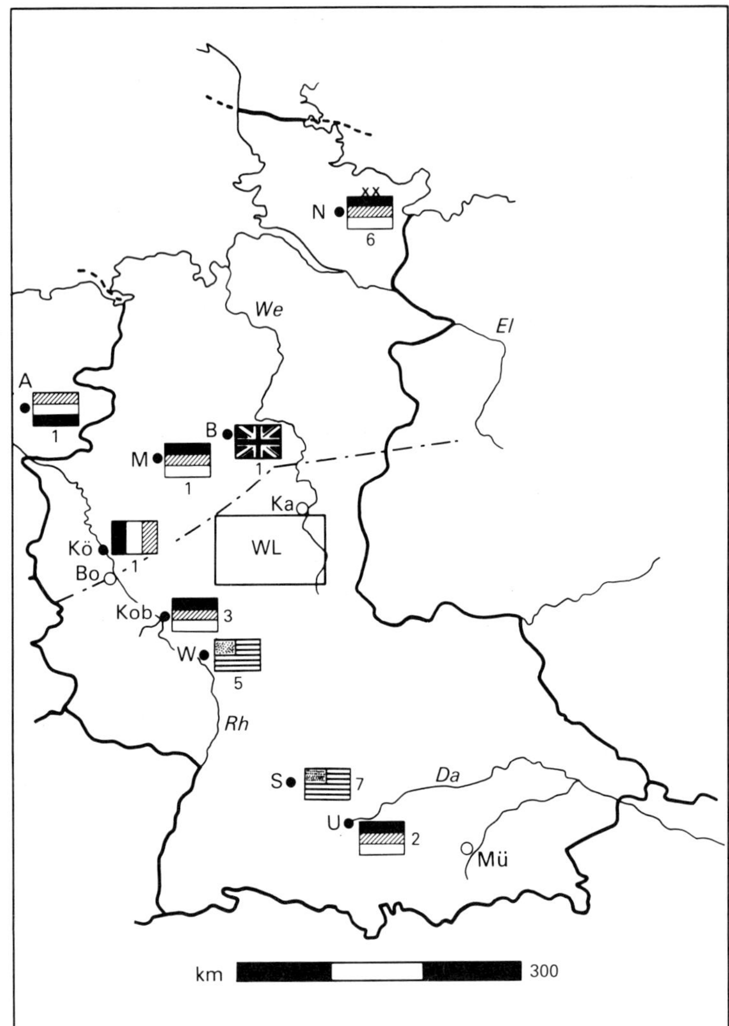

FIGURE 4 NATO Land Forces in West Germany (see opposite)

Because of general conscription, the FRG can afford forces 495,000 strong in peacetime. In a crisis, reservists can be called up to bring the strength to 1.2 million in three days. The reserve comprises about 850,000 men. The Bundeswehr provides three out of the eight full NATO corps deployed in Germany as part of the NATO strategy of forward defence. These are I Corps, based at Munster in peacetime, which has a division detached to Commander Land Forces Jutland, based at Neumunster (see Figure 4), which comes within NATO's northern region (AF-NORTH). Otherwise, I Corps is subordinated to the Northern Army Group (NORTHAG) of NATO's Central Region (AFCENT). The other two corps are in Central Army Group (CENTAG): III Corps based on Koblenz and II Corps in the south, based at Ulm. The Corps contain varying numbers of armoured (*Panzer*) and merchanised infantry (*Panzer-Grenadier*) divisions, except for II Corps which, because of the terrain in southern Germany has a quasi-mountain division (*Gebirgsdivision*) which includes a mountain (*Gebirgs-Jäger*) brigade. There is also an airmobile (*Luftlande*) division, subordinated to III Corps but in fact deployed as three airborne (*Fallschirm-Jäger*) brigades, one to each German corps.

As the 1983 German Defence White Paper argued most convincingly, the FRG has no alternative to the strategy of forward defence (*Vorneverteidigung*). This is defined as 'cohesive defence near the border with the objective of preventing any loss

---

FIGURE 4
NATO Land Forces in West Germany
A = Apeldoorn (1 Dutch Corps)
B = Bielefeld (1 British Corps)
Bo = Bonn
Da = River Danube
El = River Elbe
Ka = Kassel
Kö = Köln (1 Belgian Corps)
Kob = Koblenz (3 West German Corps)
M = Munster (1 West German Corps)
Mü = Münich
N = Neumunster (Detached Division)
Rh = River Rhine
S = Stuttgart (7 US Corps)
U = Ulm (2 West German Corps)
W = Wiesbaden (5 US Corps)
We = River Weser
WL = approximate area of exercise (Wehrhafte Löwen) (see diagrams 6–10)
Dotted line = approximate boundary between NORTHAG and CENTAG

of ground and preventing damage'.[20] Thirty per cent of the population of the FRG live within 100 km of the intra-German border, and this area also contains a quarter of the country's industrial capacity.

The West German concept of land operations is set out in the restricted *Army Regulation (HDv) 100/100*.[21] This is a business-like document which emerged in September 1973. The following description is based on unclassified sources.

In the event of a Warsaw Pact attack, the Bundeswehr's mission would be:

- to stop the attacker near the border and to destroy his shock forces,
- to prevent him from sustaining his attack with fresh forces brought up from the depth of his deployment,
- to recapture any NATO (ie, German) territory he may have taken.

The first two objectives are clearly common to NATO. The recovery of lost ground is laid down as an aim of counter-attack in ATP–35(A), but the Germans place more emphasis on this than other nations for obvious reasons, and it permeates their thinking at operational and tactical levels. The Germans place constant stress on *Beweglichkeit,* which means both 'mobile operations' and 'flexibility of mind'. As noted above, the Germans regard 'operational' as meaning the handling of divisions and corps. A possible corps layout is shown in Figure 5. This corresponds with the standard format for NATO corps set out in ATP–35(A).[22] There are two distinct zones: the delay zone (*Verzögerungszone*) and the main defence zone (*Verteidigungsraum*). The dividing line between them is the Forward Edge of the Battle Area (FEBA), in German *Vorderer Rand der Verteidigung* (*VRV*). This is not the same as the Forward Line of Own Troops (FLOT), as the VRV need not be physically occupied by troops. The corps reserve may consist of an armoured brigade, an airborne brigade, which might also be deployed with the help of the helicopters of the Army Air Corps Regiment, and an anti-tank helicopter regiment. The Germans see their defensive operations essentially as a battle against armour, and concur fully with ATP–35(A) that fully armoured forces offer the greatest flexibility. The only foot infantry is in the *Gebirgs–Jäger* brigade. Anti-tank helicopters are also crucial in the anti-armour battle, and here the Germans also clearly agree with ATP–35(A). They stress that the fire power of helicopters' long range anti-tank weapons, their speed, manoeuvrability and independence of terrain conditions enable them to establish or shift centres of anti-tank resistance very quickly. This is particularly important where wide sectors have to be defended with limited numbers of troops.

A typical armoured division consists of three brigades. The brigade is the main building block of the Bundeswehr. The division in Figure 5 has two armoured brigades and one *Panzer-Grenadier*. One brigade might be deployed forward initially, as a covering or delay force. This would endeavour to delay the enemy for a set period of time, in order to give the rest of the division time to prepare its positions. It would also weaken the enemy's leading elements. Once the covering force has completed its task, it would withdraw through the main defensive area and become the divisional reserve, leaving two brigades forward.

The current brigade structure is the result of re-thinking which began in the early 1970s in connection with the introduction then of a new tactical defensive doctrine. This imposed the requirement to hold ground and to halt the enemy's attack either in front of the *Verteidigungsraum* or in the forward part of it. The new structure was tested in 1976–77, and adopted in the early 1980s as Army Structure (*Heeresstruktur*)–4. Because of the greater power of modern weapons, it was possible to have four smaller battalions, (*Panzer* or *Panzer–Grenadier*) in each brigade instead of three larger ones as previously.

A brigade might be allocated an area up to 15 kilometres wide and 25 deep. Within this area, the commander establishes where the main enemy thrust is to be expected, where obstacles and fire power would be most concentrated. However, the commander must be able to shift the 'point of effort' (*Schwerpunkt*) very quickly if required. The brigade commander must also determine key terrain (*Schlüssel Gelände — SGL*). This has to be retained against all attacks and must be recaptured if lost. Within the Brigade area, individual battalions would be allocated specific areas in which to conduct their own mobile defensive battles. The brigade would, however, have a reserve, probably a tank battalion. This might have three pre-planned tasks:

- to reinforce a forward battalion if an enemy main axis through it had been identified,
- to counter-attack the enemy once his momentum has been lost or if ground has to be recaptured,
- as a counter-penetration force.

The brigade commander also lays down the areas which the artillery is to occupy. These should be sited away from the

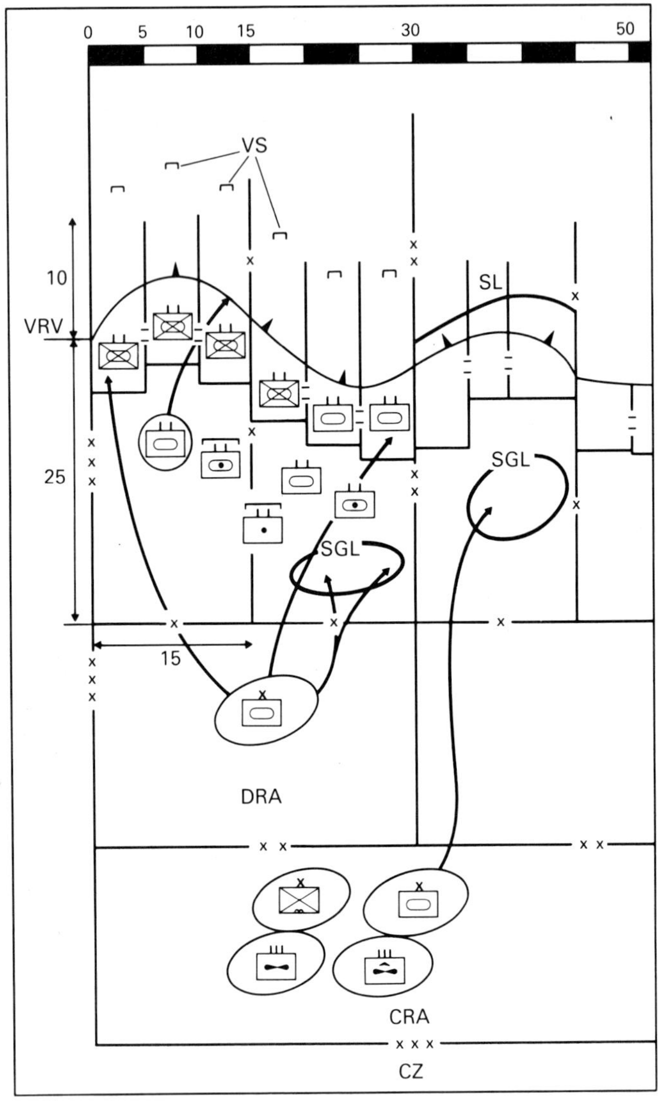

FIGURE 5 Bundeswehr Defence (see opposite)

expected direction of the enemy's main thrust. Rocket artillery plays an important part in the German concept of operations. The Germans obviously wish to keep the nuclear threshold as high as possible in order to preserve their country. Rather than use nuclear weapons, they have the concept of *Raumverteidigung*- 'area defence', which relies on multiple rocket launchers to deliver anti-personnel and anti-tank mines, thus creating an instant obstacle in the same way that a nuclear weapon might, but one which it would be much more difficult for the Soviets to traverse subsequently.

Exercise Wehrhafte Löwen *('Able-bodied Lions'), 16–23 September, 1983*

Much can be learned about the West German concept of operations from this exercise. The aim of the exercise was to enhance the visible presence of NATO, demonstrate NATO forces' ability to cooperate with each other and convince a possible aggressor that they were capable of effectively barring his way west. *Wehrhafte Löwen* constituted an independent part of NATO's 'Autumn Forge' manoeuvres, and involved 48,000 men, 2500 tracked and 13,000 wheeled vehicles and 200 combat aircraft. The exercise was held in the area south of Kassel, which is important as the Fulda Gap would probably be the most attractive route for a Warsaw Pact thrust into CENTAG. The exercise was particularly intended to practise staffs in executing defence preparations, exercising operational command in combat, carrying out defence tasks which in time of tension or war would remain a West German national responsibility. Special emphasis was placed on cooperation between regular army field forces and the Territorial Army (*Territorialheer*), and command of large allied formations.

FIGURE 5
Bundeswehr Defence
VS = *Vorgeschobene Stellungen* (Forward Positions)
VRV = *Vorderer Rand der Verteidigung* (Forward Edge of Defence)
SL = *Sicherungslinie* (Security line)
SGL = *Schlüssel Gelände* (Key Terrain)
DRA = Divisional Rear Area
CRA = Corps rear area
CZ = Communications Zone
Helicopter regiment (transport)

Helicopter regiment (Anti-tank)

FIGURES 6—Phases 1–5. Exercise Wehrhafte Löwen.
Key to the diagrams.
VRV *(Vorderer Rand der Verteidigung)*
Forward Edge of the Defence Area
VZL *(Verzögerungslinie)*
Base line for delaying action
—⊕— Boundary with Liaison Points *(Anschlusspunkt)*
═══ Autobahn
Area where a landing has taken place, either by parachute or by helicopter, or both.
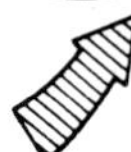
Air Landing Brigade *(Luftlandebrigade)*
Area controlled or defended by skirmishing patrols, *(Operationsraum eines Jagd-Kommandos)*
Area controlled by patrols
Medium transport helicopters of Army Aviation
(dark propeller indicates Army Air)
Medium transport aircraft of the Air Force
(light propeller indicates Air Force)
Initial objectives of III Corps counterattack (phase 5)
Subsequent direction of III Corps counterattack (phase 5)

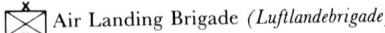

Otherwise, normal NATO military symbols are employed: two lines above a 'box' indicate a battalion, three a regiment, one 'x' a brigade, two 'x's a division, three—a corps. These 'x's also indicate boundaries. Within the 'box' a cross means infantry, an oval armour. A cross and an oval means mechanised infantry. 'Red' forces are shown in a double box.

Figures Phases 1–5 Key, p. 2.
A = Alsfeld
Ba = Baunatel
BH = Bad Hersfeld
Bo = Borken
BR = Borkener Reservoir
D = Dautphetal
F = Frankenberg
G = Gladenbach
H = Homburg
K = Kellerwald
L = Lauterbach
M = Marburg
N = Neustadt
S = Schwalmstadt
SA = Stadtallendorf

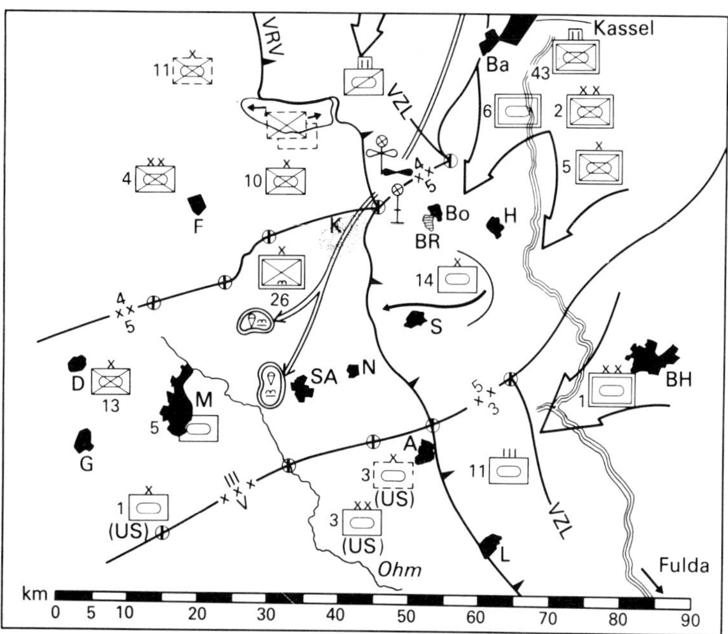

Fig. 6 Phase 1

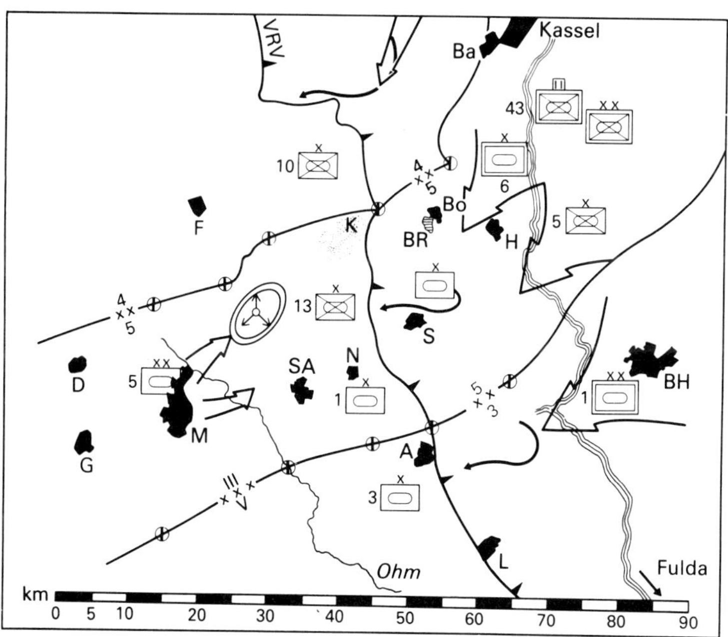

Fig. 6 Phase 2

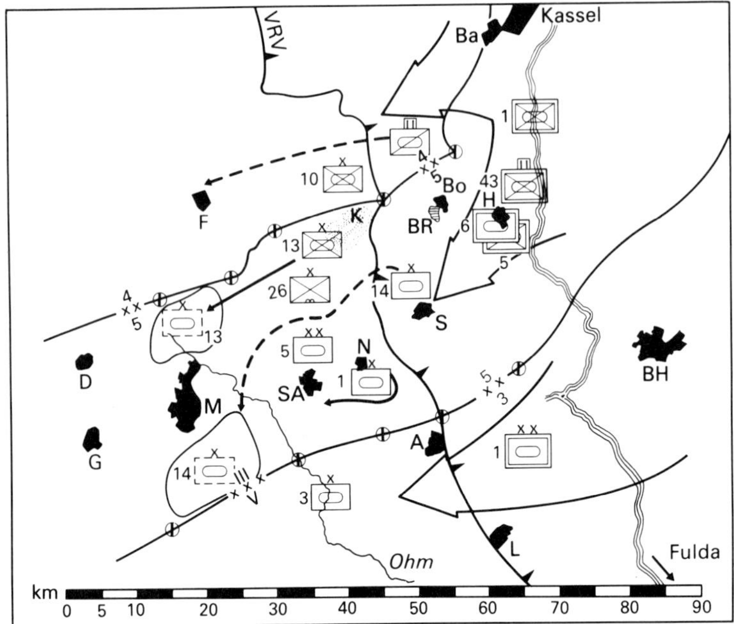

Fig. 6 Phase 3

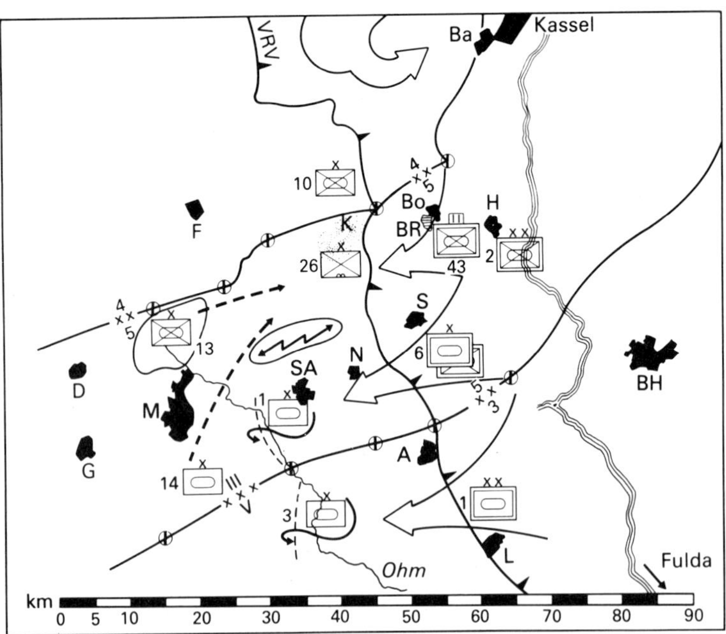

Fig. 6 Phase 4

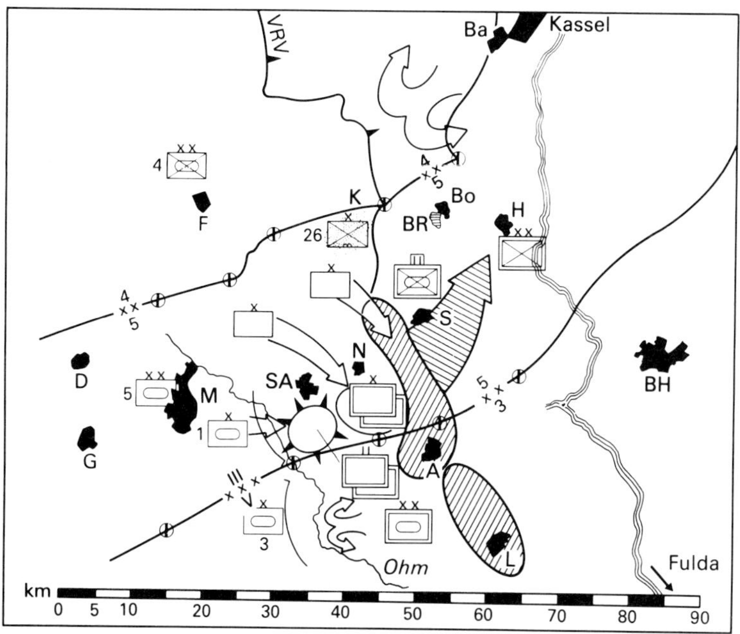

Fig. 6 Phase 5

The main NATO (Blue) force was provided by 5 *Panzer* Division for Diez, together with 1 Brigade of the 3 US Armoured Division and 15 Brigade under US command. 'Blue' also had 26 air landing brigade (*Luftlandebrigade*) later in the exercise. 5 *Panzer* Division was also supported by corps artillery, air and NBC defence assets.

The 'enemy' (red) forces comprised 2 *Panzer-Grenadier* Division from Kassel, 5 *Panzer-Grenadier* Brigade, 6 *Panzer* Brigade, a battle group assembled from elements of 4 *Panzer-Grenadier* Brigade, divisional troops and, initially, 26 *Luftlandebrigade*.

'Interoperability' among the allies was a keynote of the exercise. Thus the German 15 *Panzer* Brigade was placed under US command for the 'Reforger' exercise, whilst 1 Brigade of 3 US Armoured was placed under German command.

Under the pretext of conducting defensive preparations, Redland concentrated its forces on the border with the aim of surprising Blue and making a rapid thrust towards the river Rhine. However, Blue discerned that something was afoot because of its own increased reconnaissance activity. Blueland therefore met Red's attack to the west of the Kassel–Fulda autobahn.

Phase 1: 1800 hrs 18 September — 1200 hrs 19 September

As expected, Red attacked in the night of 18 September with a major air- and heliborne *desant.* In a spectacular drop behind enemy lines, 300 men parachuted into the combat area while their armoured vehicles were landed by CH–53 Sikorsky helicopters. In a second wave Red put down the bulk of 26 *Luftlandebrigade* with its heavy equipment from UH–1–D helicopters. A large part of Blue's 5 *Panzer* Division encountered the Red forces who were consolidating the defence of the areas they had taken. In the border area, 5 Division also carried out a holding battle against 2 *Panzer–Grenadier*, who formed the main body of Red's forces.

Phase 2: 1200 hrs 19 September — 0300 hrs 20 September

The resistance offered by Blue's delaying forces proved stronger than expected and it became clear to Red that they had not achieved full surprise. Nevertheless, Red's air- and heliborne forces managed to gain a foothold behind Blue's FLOT. Red's main forces had as their objective the Borkener reservoir (see map). 5 *Panzer–Grenadier* Brigade attack on the left and 6 Panser Brigade on the right, with 2 Armoured reconnaissance Battalion (*Panzeraufklärungsbataillon*) protecting the right flank. As a result of Blue's stubborn resistance, Red had to switch the axis of its attack to a southerly direction. During the night of 19/20 September, two brigades were therefore committed north of Schwalmstadt. This drive was successful, and it appeared that Red would succeed in its aim of reaching the river Ohm.

Phase 3: 0300 hrs 20 September — 0600 hrs 21 September

Red's 2 *Panzer-Grenadier* Division succeeded in pushing deeply into Blue territory, towards Neustadt — Stadtallendorf. However, the delaying battle conducted by Blue had given their 5 *Panzer–Grenadier* Division time to regroup and the 13 *Panzer–Grenadier* Brigade was relieved by 26 *Luftlandebrigade,* now on the Blue side. Blue's 14 *Panzer* Brigade prepared to counterattack towards the Ohm, but this could only succeed if 26

Luftlandebrigade succeeded in holding vital ground around the Kellerwald and north of Schwalmstadt.

Phase 4: 0600 hrs 21 September — 0430 hrs 22 September

Blue's massive attack in the early hours of 20 September succeeded in its aim of driving deeply into Red's flank. Red's 2 *Panzer-Grenadier* Division had difficulty regrouping in the delaying action, which was to Blue's advantage. Red elements such as those in front of Blue's 1 (US) Brigade were encircled and smashed. The Blue 54 Home Defence Brigade (*Heimatschutzbrigade*) was able to stand its ground against Red.

Phase 5: 0430 hrs 22 September — end of exercise on 23 September

Blue's counterattack was successful. Red's 2 *Panzer-Grenadier* Division had to withdraw to the frontier, although it took a little longer to drive it back than expected.

Lessons

The main lesson emerging from *Wehrhafte Löwen* in the realm of Operational Art concerns the air dimension. This was the first time that III German Corps had committed anti-tank helicopters in close formation in an exercise. The crews of 36 Anti-Tank Helicopter (*Panzerabwehrhubschrauber: PAH*) Regiment demonstrated the manifold capabilities and manoeuvrability of anti-tank helicopters. The combination of high fire power and high speed surprised many foreign observers, and was particularly gratifying to the Bundeswehr who are extremely proud to possess this versatile and potent weapon. Another facet of the air dimension was provided by fixed wing air support. The main tasks of fixed-wing aircraft were battlefield air interdiction, close air support and tactical air reconnaissance. Control of these aircraft by Army Forward Air Controllers (FACs) proved a great success. The Bundeswehr place great stress on the integrated nature of the Air Land battle, as do the Soviets, NATO's common doctrine, and the Americans.

Conclusion

The Bundeswehr is clearly very adept at handling brigades and divisions. *Wehrhafte Löwen* gives cause for comfort in the event of a West German division meeting a Soviet one, or of an individual West German corps meeting a Soviet Army, even if the Soviets tried to exploit boundaries between NATO allies.

However, a Soviet operational commander, on seeing the advance of one of his armies blocked in this way might put another army round the obstacle or pass it through the army which was having difficulties. Some might find cause for concern in the apparently static nature of Bundeswehr defence at the medium and higher levels; divisions and corps seem to be wedded to areas of ground. However, it is clear from *Wehrhafte Löwen* that the Bundeswehr certainly envisages moving whole divisions over considerable distances, and this could be seen as a microcosm of a larger operational (in the Soviet sense) battle. Forward defence and the need to hold West German soil are not incompatible with *Beweglichkeit,* involving the manoeuvre of formations and aggressive counter-attack on a large scale, fully reflecting the 'spirit of the offensive' philosophy of ATP-35(A).

The United States Army

The United States has two corps in Germany, both part of CENTAG (see Figure 4). V Corps is based at Wiesbaden and VII Corps at Stuttgart. It has often been pointed out that the most technologically capable NATO corps — the two American — along with two of the three West German corps, are based in CENTAG where the main Warsaw Pact thrust might not be directed. On the other hand, the shortest route to the Rhine and a major strategic objective, Frankfurt, lies through CENTAG. We should not necessarily assume that NATO's peacetime deployments are immutable, and the Soviets themselves concentrate on the West Germans and Americans as the principal potential opponents on land.[23] For all these reasons, and because of their political influence within the NATO Alliance, the American concept of operations is cardinal.

If war were to break out in Europe in the mid-1980s, the US Army would fight in accordance with the August 1982 version of Field Manual (FM) 100-5. There are many similarities between FM 100-5 and ATP-35(A), although FM 100-5 is a worldwide doctrine. The US Army is quite emphatic that where there is any potential inconsistency regarding doctrine for a European conflict, FM 100-5 would be modified in accordance with the NATO doctrine. The main area of potential disagreement between the US national doctrine and ATP-35(A) concerns 'deep attack'. NATO does have an official doctrine of Follow-On Forces Attack (FOFA). FOFA is classified but apparently envisages attack on enemy second echelon forces (if there are any) with artillery, missiles and air. However, because of the political constraints which would apply in a European war conducted under the constant threat of nuclear use, attack by manoeuvre forces against objectives east of the intra-German border is precluded. FM 100–5 provides for three types of battle:

- thc deep battle (against enemy follow-on forces),
- the close-in battle,
- the battle in one's own rear, against Soviet special purpose forces (*Spetsnaz*), OMGs, etc.

Whereas elsewhere in the world the US might employ manoeuvre forces deep in the enemy rear, thus mirroring Soviet military art, they would not do so where this would conflict with NATO doctrine. Some commentators have twisted the US doctrine to suggest that they would either attack across the intra-German border, or that they would withdraw in order to be able to conduct a deep battle on what was West German territory. This is not the case. The doctrine of deep attack does not imply any lack of faith in forward defence, although the ability to use manoeuvre forces for this purpose may be restricted, at least initially.

FM 100–5 enunciates the 'Air Land Battle' doctrine.[25] This should not be confused with the futuristic study *Air Land Battle 2000*. The semantic similarity has caused confusion not only among outsiders but within the US Army itself. Whereas FM 100–5 deals with contemporary conditions, *Air Land Battle 2000* endeavoured to look up to 20 years ahead. The first version was dated 4 September 1981 and a revised version 10 August 1982. A subsequent study, called *Focus–21* developed the theme of the Air Land battle further, and produced radical recommendations including, for example, the allocation of USAF assets to a corps commander or having an Air Force General command an Army corps. This has now been modified and combined with *Air Land Battle 2000* to produce a new concept of future operations called Army–21. Like *Air Land Battle 2000*, Army–21 aims to provide a framework for the development of equipment. The main problem about attacking follow-on forces is that divisions lack the surveillance equipment to find them, and that whereas corps might be able to see the follow-on echelons, they lack the means to hit them. Too much reliance needs to be placed on non-Army systems, principally those operated by the Air Force. The United States is therefore developing weapons which fit in with the deep attack philosophy, notably the Joint Tactical Missile System

(JTACM). The US Army now regard concepts of operations as driving technological development.

The current Air Land Battle doctrine enunciated in FM 100–5 and the future concept in Army–21 have replaced the former doctrine of 'active defence'. This has been described as a 'manoeuvre' doctrine replacing one of 'attrition'. To talk of 'manoeuvre' and 'attrition' as two opposed alternatives is misleading; there is no necessary confliction between them. Indeed, the deep attack doctrine aims to increase the 'presentation rate' of enemy forces, thus increasing the speed of attrition.

'Alternative' Operational Art

Mention must be made of various 'alternative' schemes for West European defence. There are two main groups. The first comprises a number of proposals for 'mobile' or 'manoeuvre-orientated' defence, as opposed to forward defence.[26] As noted above, the very idea of a clear distinction between the two is flawed. Besides being politically unacceptable, because it presumably necessitates sacrificing large chunks of West Germany, the proposed 'manoeuvre' strategy is only defined in vague generalities which talk about 'rapid and unexpected moves'. These will, we are told, destroy the enemy's mental cohesion and break his spirit and will.[27] The proponents of this strategy are silent about exactly how this is supposed to defeat a Warsaw Pact offensive, how NATO's forces should be deployed initially, what exactly are the vital points which must be excised to render the Warsaw Pact military body inert, and how these points can be reached in time.

The second group of theories rely essentially on those areas of technology where the West is demonstrably superior to the Warsaw Pact. For example, a diagram produced by an organisation called Just Defence in 1983 showed a purported 'non-nuclear, non-provocative defence'. Behind a 4 kilometre wall of mines and pre-laid sensors and a 2 kilometre belt patrolled by motor-cyclists and infantry armed with anti-tank guided missiles, an array of technological novelties waits to destroy the oncoming Warsaw Pact forces, portrayed as tanks and APCs. The threat is presented as inert targets waiting to be picked off like those in the currently popular game of 'space invaders'. The view of the potential enemy is so simplistic as to be laughable, notably because it makes no mention of the powerful Soviet artillery force. Soviet artillery's declared aim is to smash and suppress all these clever and delicate devices by deluging them with a paralysing hail of old-fashioned high explosive and steel. It is this artillery force which, besides obliging NATO to stress manoeuvre within the context of forward defence, has reinforced the emphasis on armour. The main reason why the tank remains the main anti-armour weapon is not that there is anything irreplaceable about its gun, but that it is the only weapons system which has some chance of being able to fight and move under massive suppressive artillery fire.

At the time of writing, the war between Iran and Iraq has been going on for three years, and has assumed World War I dimensions and characteristics. A war in Europe could do the same. There are no easy or purely 'imaginative' ways of winning a war, or even of avoiding defeat. After World War I, there were also those who advocated making brilliant strokes against the enemy's critical nodes, or who thought that new technology could provide the answer. One of the most popular panaceas then was the use of aircraft to deliver poison gas. In the mid-1980s, it is as well to recall the comments of a military historian in 1922:

> There is, in fact, no real assurance that future war will not partake, substantially, of the character of past war, such as that of 1914–1918. And such campaigns, we are asked to believe, should be won by quick, imaginative methods . . . It is a pity one or two soldiers of note have uttered paradoxes suggesting wars are to be won inexpensively . . . That kind of paradox, or persiflage, encourages the superficially clever mind.[28]

Operational Art for NATO

In Soviet eyes, NATO does not have an operational art, and that is its greatest military weakness. Although the United States and West German armies use the term, the Soviets talk of NATO's highest level formations, its corps, as 'tactical' entities. The Army Groups, NORTHAG and CENTAG, are, it is true, equated with Soviet Fronts. But the Supreme Allied Commander Europe (SACEUR) has no operational authority in Soviet eyes. He apparently lacks the power to move VII US Corps from Stuttgart to, say, a blocking position before the Ruhr. It is, of course, possible that plans do exist to manipulate forces according to a larger 'operational' plan in the event of war. This might involve the handling of NATO forces in war not as two separate 'Fronts' (as the Soviets would see them), but as part of a united theatre of military operations. However, such a plan has not been exercised in peace time and Soviet generals would be reluctant to believe that such a plan would work unless it had been exercised. On the other hand, the necessary calculations could be done and such a plan could exist, known only to a very small circle of people. The fact that the West Germans, Americans, British, Belgians and Dutch would all fight their individual corps in a slightly different way need not necessarily matter. Operational art is essentially a matter of manoeuvre, and provided individual corps are competent, the manipulation of great forces over great distances is an intellectual exercise for the operational commander and his immediate staffs at the time. Perhaps this is what Sun Tzu was alluding to when he said:

> These are the strategist's keys to victory. It is not possible to discuss them beforehand.[29]

This article has avoided making specific prescriptions for NATO deployments. However, as part of a theatre operational plan, it would be of great assistance if a ninth NATO corps could be deployed behind the four now in NORTHAG. There has been some discussion that a third US corps could be deployed there. The recent accession of Spain to NATO has provided an opportunity to break with the pattern imposed by the positions which forces reached at the end of the last war. In the author's view, a Spanish corps, or a Spanish division as part of a joint corps, would be a great asset. This should not be taken as implying any lack of confidence in the ability of present forces to hold the border. However, it is only prudent to make some provision to counter an enemy breakthrough on an operational scale, which is, after all, his declared aim. Another Soviet operational movement might be the encirclement of the forward four corps. This would need to be met by a counter-stroke at the same operational level; otherwise, there is a danger that NATO would meet the same fate as the Wehrmacht in 1941–45, engulfed by operations altogether bigger and broader in conception than its own.

Conclusion

There are remarkable similarities between Soviet and American operational art, but it is not clear to what extent the two are interdependent and to what extent the parallels are accidental. For example, it could be argued that even if the

Americans had not evolved the 'deep attack' philosophy, the OMG would have forced them to invent it anyway, as it is necessary to identify OMGs long before they reach the FLOT, in order to prevent them breaking through and destabilising the defence.

NATO has a joint tactical doctrine, but as an alliance it does not recognise the operational level, and it has no operational doctrine. In the author's view, this is a fundamental gap which should be filled. There is no doubt that the Soviets have an expertise at the operational level which transcends the bounds of Western military thought. Soviet military journals are filled with articles which utilise military history as a tool to understand the mechanics of waging war. This may be contrasted with the preoccupation which most Western military journals have with technology and the managerial aspects of defence. It would be ironic and tragic if in a future war a technologically superior West which claims to understand the individual were to be defeated by Warsaw Pact forces possessing superior military skill, greater understanding of the human factor in war, and better leadership at the higher levels. But it would not be the first time in military history that the attributes of the latter had triumphed over those of the former.

My thanks are due to all those who helped, particularly Chris Donnelly and Betty Chojecki of the Soviet Studies Research Centre, RMA Sandhurst, Captain Charles Dick, Captain John Hyden, and to John Romano for translating large amounts of German.

Notes

[1] On Haig; John Terraine, *Douglas Haig, the Educated Soldier,* Hutchinson, London, 1963, p. 481: Colonel Wallace P Franz, 'Grand Tactics' *Military Review* December 1981, pp. 32–60, esp. p. 33. *Sovetskaya Voyennaya Entsiklopediya* (*Soviet Military Encyclopedia*) Vol 6, 1978, pp. 53–60.

[2] General E C Meyer, Chief of Staff, US Army, *FM 100–5 Operations* 20 August, 1982, p. 2–3. A slightly crisper definition is given in *Airland Battle 2000,* 1982 version, pp. 11–12, but unlike *FM 100–5, Airland Battle 2000* is not officially approved.

[3] Elmar Dinter and Paddy Griffith *Not Over by Christmas: NATO's Central Front in World War III,* Antony Bird, Chichester, 1983, p. 6.

[4] Colonel Dr Teofil Wojcic 'Combat vehicles and helicopters on the modern battlefield' *Zołnierz Wolnośći* (*Soldier of Freedom*) (*ZW*) 4 January 1978 and 'In two dimensions: air-ground cooperation' *ZW* 5 January, 1978. USA Translations.

[5] Colonel Ya. Samoylenko *'O reydovykh deystviyakh desantnikov'* ('On raiding actions by *desant* (here, airborne) troops'), in section *Vozdushno-desantnye voyska* (airborne forces) *Voyenny Vestnik (VV)* 4/1978, pp. 43–7.

[6] Christopher Donnelly 'The Soviet Operational Manoeuvre Group: a new Challenge for NATO' *International Defence Review (IDR)* 9/1982, pp. 1177–1186. This article created much interest and Tass immediately denied that the OMG device existed. The subject was further explored in Charles Dick 'Soviet Operational Manoeuvre Groups: A Closer Look' *IDR* 6/1983, pp. 769–776 and Phillip A Petersen and John G Hines 'Military Power in Soviet Strategy against NATO' *RUSI Journal* December 1983, pp. 50–56. The latter contains a detailed and valuable examination of Soviet and Polish sources.

[7] Wojcic 'Combat Vehicles and Helicopters . . . ' The term *Lądowopowietrzny zespoł uderzeniowy* also appears in Captain Lech Konopka '*Problemy lotniczego zabezpieczenia lądowo-powietrznych zespołów uderzeniowych*' ('Problems of aviation support of *LPZUs*') *Przeglad Wojsk Lotniczych i Wojsk Obrony Powietrznej Kraju (PWL i WOPK) (Air Force and Air Defence Force Review)* April(4)/1981, pp. 5–7.

[8] *KOPP* is mentioned explicitely in the OMG context in Colonel Pilot Aleksander Musial '*Dzialanie bojowe lotnictwa na korzyść operacyjnych grup manewrowych*' ('Aviation Combat Operations on behalf of OMGs') *PWL i WOPK*, 7–8/1982 (combined edition), p. 13. Increase in artillery strength; Caspar Weinberger, US Secretary of Defence, *Soviet Military Power,* 1983, p. 22. Colonel General of Tank Troops M Zaytsev *'Organizatsiya PVO — vazhnaya zadacha obshchevoyskogo komandira'* (Organization of Air Defence — a main task of combined arms commanders') *VV* 2/1979, p. 23. Artillery 80%; Lieutenant General I Anashkin *'Za kompleksnoye resheniye problemy'* ('For an all-embracing solution to the problem') *VV* 10/1976, p. 72.

[9] Colonel Ye Dabolin *'Reshaya sovmestnuyu zadachu'* ('Tackling a joint task') *VV* 5/1980, pp, 74–5.

[10] The four new phases are given in Musial *'Rola lotnictwa uderzeniowego w zabezpieczeniu działań desantów morskikh'* ('The role of strike aviation in support of sea assault landings') *PLW i WOPK* 5/1982, pp. 11–12. The Russian artillery envisaged giving fire support in three phases: preparation, support and accompaniment — in the 1880s. Captain J M Grierson RA *The Armed Strength of Russia,* HMSO, London, 1886, p. 488. Now, as then, 'accompaniment' implies not only 'accompanying' the advancing troops with fire, but that the artillery itself may have to move.

[11] General Don A Starry (Commander of US Army Training and Doctrine Command-TRADOC) 'Extending the Battlefield' *Military Review* March, 1981, pp. 32–50.

[12] Major Wojciech Michalak *'Lotnictwo w działaniach rajdowomanewrowych wojsk lądowych'* ('Aviation in raid-manoeuvre operations of the ground forces') *PWL i WOPK* February (2)/1982, pp. 5–9. On p. 8, Michalak divides air operations in support of ground forces into two broad stages: support and protection of their move forward and commitment to battle, and the stage covering their action in the enemy depth. The first phase of the former is 'cover . . . against detection and strikes by enemy air.' Musial's article on support of sea *desants* (see note 10) published in May spelled out the four phases.

[13] Marshal of Artillery G Ye Peredel'skiy *'O role i meste artilleriyskogo diviziona v boyu'* ('On the role and place of the artillery battalion in combat') VV 12/1980, p. 64.

[14] Major General I Vorob'ev *'Oruzhiye i taktiki: komandir i sovremenny boy'* ('Weapons and tactics: the commander and modern combat') *Krasnaya Zvezda* 12 January 1982, p. 2.

[15] NATO Military Agency for Standardization (MAS) *ATP–35(A) Land Force Tactical Doctrine,* 1984 p. C–12.

[16] Ibid., p. 1, para. 1.

[17] Ibid., pp. 3–6, para. 9.

[18] Ibid., pp. 3–7, para. 12.

[19] Ibid., pp. 7–3 and 7–4, para. 8.

[20] Federal Germany Republic, Federal Minister of Defence *White Paper 1983 The Security of the Federal Republic of Germany* Bonn, 20 October 1983, p. 144, para. 268.

[21] HDv 100/100 *Führung im Gefecht*, Command and Control in Battle, September, 1973. This is referred to and cited in John J Mearsheimer 'Maneuver, Mobile Defense and the Central Front' *International Security*, Winter 1981/82 (Vol 6 No 3), pp. 104–122.

[22] *ATP-35(A)*. Diagram 3–1–1 opposite p. 3–18.

[23] See the author's chapter in Philip A Towle, ed. *Estimating Foreign Military Power*, Croom Helm, London, 1982.

[24] See note 2.

[25] Ibid., p. 2–3.

[26] A detailed critique of these views and survey of the literature in Mearesheimer's article, see note 21 above.

[27] Ibid., p. 107, citing William S Lind 'Military Doctrine, Force Structure and the Defense Decision-Making Process', *Air University Review*, XXX No 4 (May–June, 1979), p. 22.

[28] G A B Dewar and Lt Col J H Boraston *Sir Douglas Haig's Command*, London, 1922, Vol 1, p. 167.

[29] Sun Tzu, *The Art of War*, 4th century B.C., translated with introduction by Samuel B Griffith, Oxford University Press, 1982, p. 70.

Weapon Development 1984: Air

M J JACKSON

The author is a correspondent for several foreign defence magazines

IN A YEAR dominated by talk of what NATO describes as 'theatre' and the East as 'operational' missiles, the downing of Korean Air Lines Flight 007 not only indicated the determination of the Soviet Union to defend what it considers are its legitimate security interests but also the limitations of the defence technology of the superpowers.

STRATEGIC THEATRE MISSILES

The loss of KAL 007 may well be related to Soviet work in the development of a new strategic missile system, a field in which the Americans, working in the full glare of publicity, seem to world opinion to be making the running. The first test flight of the MGM-118A Peacekeeper was conducted on 21 June 1983 and a total of 20 development flights are planned by the USAF, although the last four are likely to be conducted after initial deployment which is scheduled for December 1986. The first test flight undoubtedly helped President Reagan secure a $188 billion (bn) appropriation for the Peacekeeper programme including the purchase of 21 production missiles, the programme calling for a total of 100 in Minuteman (LGM-30) silos.

Overshadowed by the MGM-118 is another USAF system (SICM) officially known as the small Intercontinental Ballistic Missile and unofficially as Midgetman, which is beginning to accelerate following recommendations from a panel of senior USAF officers and it was interesting to note that all the candidates for the Democratic presidential nomination have endorsed the concept. Midgetman will be a 13,500 kg missile with a single warhead and it is currently envisaged that several hundred would be purchased and housed in mobile, hardened shelters on Department of Defense land with an option for silo housing. The proposed development plan called for a definition phase lasting a year, a two year pre-fullscale development phase leading to one contractor beginning development from 1986 with first flight in 1988 and initial deployment in 1992. To reduce costs and technological risks, a high degree of competition is envisaged as well as exploiting existing data and programmes; the re-entry vehicle would be the Mk 21 already scheduled for the Peacekeeper, rather than the 100–165 KT MIRV used in Minuteman III or Trident while the guidance system is to be a lighter version of the MGM–118's AIRS (Advanced Inertial Reference System). Contenders for the Midgetman project include Boeing, Martin Marietta, General Dynamics' Convair Division and Bell Textron — all of whom have now received a $5 million (m) concept definition contract for the mobile shelter.

The Soviet Union is known to be developing a similar concept, known in the West as SS–X–25, which the Pentagon describes as a Minuteman-sized system (31,750–34,500 kg), which will be deployed in off-road vehicles in a basing system similar to the one rejected by the United States for M–X. The Pentagon also claims that an MGM–118–size missile (i.e. 86,000 kg) dubbed SS–X–24 is likely to be deployed in silos from 1985. However, it was this medium weight, three-stage, solid-fuel system which was scheduled to be tested the night KAL 007 was shot down, the test being postponed until three days later when it proved a failure, the seventh in ten flights.

The beginning of the year saw the US Navy's Strategic Systems Program Office award Lockheed Missile and Space a $272.3 m contract, which is the first increment of a long term contract, for the manufacture of 30 test Trident II missiles and 52 production rounds. The first test flight is planned for 1987 with deployment in Ohio class SSBNs from 1989. This is the system which has been chosen by the British Government and during early 1984 it was revealed that orders had been placed for 64 launch tubes to fit a fleet of four submarines. Not surprisingly, the cost of the system is steadily escalating, despite cost-cutting measures which reportedly include a decision not to purchase one missile per tube, and it was officially reported to Parliament that the cost of the programme had risen 16 per cent from £7.5 bn to £8.2 bn.

Cruise (ie air-breathing) missiles continue to attract more attention. Deployment of the General Dynamics BGM–109G Tomahawk began in November 1983 while deployment of the air-launched AGM–86B continued with 168 B–52G scheduled to receive it, each carrying 12 missiles. Test flights of the TERCOM system in production missiles began over Canada in early 1984, the missiles remaining attached to the bomber, and were apparently successful but plans to reduce the B-52G force clouded the horizon. Surprisingly, plans for improved models of both missiles did not reach fruition and the key may be in the USAF's request for $98 m into what it described only as 'an advanced strategic missile system'. The USAF is known to be pursuing Stealth technology with the intention of reducing the radar and infra red signatures of Cruise missiles as well as increasing their ECM-ECCM capabilities and it would appear these programmes are achieving some success. General Dynamics' Convair Division, it was revealed on 15 April 1983, were to produce the replacement for the Boeing AGM-86B with a system using a more advanced engine — smaller fuselage and Global Positioning System (GPS) in the guidance, but General Dynamics' hopes of producing a conventionally-tipped Tomahawk, the AGM-109H MRASM (Medium Range Air-to-Surface Missile) were dashed when a US Congressional committee recommended a joint USAF-US Navy design, possibly from Lockheed. The AGM-109H was scheduled to begin flight trials in mid 1984 and enter service late in 1986, being capable of attacking 60 Warsaw Pact major operating bases, as well as 60 dispersed bases, with runway cratering sub-munitions.

The Soviet Union is reported to be developing several Cruise missile designs all with a reported range of 3000 km including an air-launched version, AS-X-15, which may reach squadrons this year and for which new TU-95 Bears, Bear H, are reportedly being built. The ground launched system has the reporting designation SSC-X-4 and has a similar deployment to BGM-109G Tomahawk but is unlikely to be deployed until 1985, while the submarine-launched SS-NX-21 could be deployed with the new Mike class SSGNs this year and possibly with the new Sierras later. A supersonic Cruise missile is reportedly under development but for what purpose it is hard to deduce, although it should be remembered, the Soviet Union has deployed large numbers of Cruise missiles for a variety of tasks since the late 1950s.

The deployment of the Tomahawks in Europe was accompanied by the arrival of the first nine Martin Marietta MGM-31B Pershing II theatre ballistic missiles shortly after the successful completion, on 18 September 1983, of the last of the 18 test flights of which 13 were successful. Pershing II has aroused great fears in the Soviet Union because of its reported precision but, with a range of only 1800 km, it is only a limited threat to the Kremlin's control of the RVSN (*Raketnye Voiska Strategicheskogo Naznacheniya*) most of whose missile fields are not only beyond Pershing II's admitted reach but also beyond the 2500 km range claimed by the Soviet leadership; and it should also be remembered that Russia's submarine-launched missiles pose an identical threat to Washington, and have done so since the early 1960s. There are ways and means of preventing decapitation, such as audio monitoring of communications and a reserve, survivable, launch authority organisation while the organisational, as well as operational, problems of organising a surgical strike and beating the ABM (Anti-Ballistic Missile) warning system are colossal.

In the meantime, the RVSN has continued, despite public pledges, to expand its 'operational' resources for the European direction with 27 bases each deploying nine Pioneer (SS–20) missiles, some with a single 50 KT or 1.5 MT warhead while others have triple 150 KT MIRVs. The Soviet Union, having confirmed what Western experts have known for years about the deployment of nuclear-tipped missiles in eastern Europe, has used the arrival of the new NATO theatre missiles as an excuse to modernise the long range rocket force of the Army, replacing the SS–1 Scud (150–300 km range) and SS–12 Scaleboard (490–900 km) with SS–23 (190–350 km) and SS–22 (540–1000 km).

With more ballistic missiles being deployed in Europe there is a corresponding interest in ballistic missile defence (BMD) where there have been some interesting developments. Strategically both superpowers continue development of missile-based layered systems although test firings of the Low Altitude Defense (LoAD) programme by the United States had mixed fortunes against Minuteman I targets. Nevertheless, full scale development continues both in the United States and the Soviet Union which has conducted a rapid reloading test of its system, Sh 8, with the new C-band ABM–3 phased array radar, with two launches in two hours. On the more exotic level, both superpowers continue to develop lasers and during 1983 an airborne laser destroyed five Sidewinder missiles in a test during the summer.

BMD requires rapid and accurate target acquisition and it was interesting to discover that Raytheon has received a $9.5 m contract from the USAF to evaluate the changes needed to give the Improved Hawk (MIM–23B) and the new MIM–104A Patriot air defence missiles the capability of intercepting Soviet missiles in Europe. Patriot was originally scheduled to have such a capability but financial restrictions meant this was deleted, nevertheless it would seem feasible to modify the system to intercept SS–21, SS–22 and SS–23 although more extensive modifications would be required to intercept SS–20. As Patriot is clearly becoming the backbone of NATO's surface-to-air defences, these potential modifications are of great importance. The I-Hawk is likely to be around for a long time and might be given the capability of intercepting tactical Cruise missiles such as SS–CX–4, and it should be remembered that the old MIM–23A had some ballistic missile interception potential against Frog-type missiles. Several Soviet missile systems are reported to have the ability to intercept ballistic missiles and it has been suggested that the deployment of SA–12s into East Germany, Czechoslovakia and Hungary was not only to improve the overall aid defences of the Warsaw Pact but also to counter Pershing II, the Soviet missile using a phased array radar capable of tracking multiple targets at a maximum range of 100 km at heights from 30m to 30,000m.

Tactical Missiles

If non-nuclear means of attacking heavily defended targets deep in Warsaw Pact territory appear to have received a setback with the collapse of MRASM, work is known to be progressing among NATO partners on a variety of solutions. Companies are known to be studying the technical and financial implications of three systems; a long range stand-off missile, a short range anti-radiation missile and a low cost, powered, off-axis dispenser, with the latter receiving greatest priority. One of the latest contenders might be the Brandt-Dornier Pegase (Pegasus) system currently proposed in three versions; Pegase I — weighing 450 kg and Pegase II — weighing 760 kg which are both free-flying or rocket boost-glide systems or the turbojet powered Pegase III — weighing 760 kg but with a range of 60 km, the payloads including anti-vehicle, anti-armour anti-personnel or anti-runway submunitions, with all three systems capable of launch at high subsonic speed. Pegase I will fly in 1985, Pegase II in 1986 and Pegase III in 1990, with full scale production scheduled for 1988–1989 for Pegase I/II.

Although intelligent weapon systems are gradually making their way forward, one of the most interesting, the Hughes Wasp anti-armour missile, appears to be in doubt despite a successful test firing on 24 April 1983. The USAF has not requested further funding for development apparently because it has doubts about exposing manned aircraft to the more sophisticated defences which are bound to be encountered over the second echelons of Warsaw Pact forces. It now appears to be more willing to give this task to the Joint Tactical Missile System (JTACMS formerly Assault Breaker) and, interestingly enough, Vought have reached an agreement with the Royal Ordnance Factories, Wegmann and Company of West Germany and BPD of Italy to explore the European market for the Improved Lance, or Lance II, a JTACMS contender. The other contender, Martin Marietta, is also reported to be seeking European partners.

The British aerospace industry has had considerable success with missiles, although British Aerospace Dynamics were unsuccessful in their bid to supply Rapier to Spain, which preferred Roland. Yet, Turkey has bought both Rapier and Sea Skua, the helicopter-launched anti-ship missile, while India has bought the Sea Eagle for similar purposes. The creation of BBG (Bodenseewerk-British Aerospace GmbH) to develop and manufacture NATO's Sidewinder replacement, ASRAAM (Advanced Short Range Air-to-Air Missile), saw this programme taking a much delayed step forward and the United States, a major potential buyer, is known to be extremely unhappy about the progress of the programme, which has barely reached the definition stage. The British decision to opt for the national anti-radiation missile, Alarm (Air Launched Anti-Radiation Missile) instead of the Texas Instruments' AGM–88 Harm (High Speed Anti-Radiation Missile) was undoubtedly a political one, aimed at retaining national expertise in a vital and expanding field, although it seems more likely that NATO as a whole will opt for Harm. Although development of Harm is largely complete, and it would have been available when the RAF needed it, it requires specialised on-board systems unlike the autonomous Alarm which promises to be significantly lighter, with corresponding benefits in the amount of ordnance that combat aircraft could carry.

Modernisation of NATO's medium range surface-to-air missile force is an urgent requirement but the cost of such replacement is daunting and members phasing out Nike Hercules and Hawk, which were often supplied at low cost under the Military Assistance Program, are understandably reluctant to commit themselves to a replacement. The United States, however, is adopting imaginative solutions to the problem often with financial benefits to all its partners. In the United Kingdom, it has selected Rapier Blindfire to defend its bases in England and 32 firing units are being bought for operation by three squadrons of the RAF Regiment, the first firing units being handed over at Eglin Air Force Base, Florida on 18 October 1983. A more complex solution for US–West German air defence problems has been produced which not only strengthens base defence but also strengthens the surface-to-air missile belt in central Europe. On 6 December 1983 the two countries signed an agreement involving the purchase of 28 American Patriot fire units each of eight quad launchers with 32 reload rounds and 95 Franco-German Roland fire units each with two launchers and 40 missiles. The Germans will buy outright 14 Patriot fire units (two as trainers) for $1 bn and the Luftwaffe will operate and support 12 US Army systems in West Germany for ten years in addition to the 14 fire units which the US Army will operate. The Americans in turn will buy 27 Roland systems to be operated by the Luftwaffe for ten years which will defend three United States bases, while the West Germans will buy a further 68 Roland systems (eight for training) to protect their own and American bases in Germany, the scheme taking effect between 1985 and 1992. NATO nations which are interested in Patriot include the Netherlands, which wants six or seven fire units and 160 rounds, Belgium (which is considering four fire units and is to scrap its 72 Nikes and return its 36 I–Hawks to Belgium), Denmark and Greece. Italy and Turkey might be considered to have a requirement later but Norway has opted for I–Hawk and the RBS–70, while the United Kingdom appears to be content with the Bloodhound–Rapier mix, although the former is becoming dated. Curiously, the Germans still appear interested in a national, 30 km range surface-to-air missile (FMS–90); while in France, the Defence Ministry is conducting a feasibility study with Thomson CSF and Aerospatiale into a surface-to-air missile for use on land or sea, Sol–Air–90 (SA–90).

This year saw the French air defence industry secure two major air defence contracts in the Middle East. Thomson CSF received a FFr 1200 m contract from Kuwait to modernise the air defence and early warning network by 1986 while a FFr 35 bn contract from Saudi Arabia was awarded to a consortium headed by Thomson includes 12 batteries of 12 Shahine 2 in tracked and sheltered launch platform modes, a new communications network and some coast defence batteries of Matra Otomat Mk 2. To the north, NATO is preparing to modernise the NADGE network along the Mediterranean, with up to 18 E–F band surveillance radars which will be supplemented in Italy by 23 Selenia Spada air defence systems.

Combat Aircraft

Progress on the West's only strategic bomber, the Rockwell B–1B, continued with the first flight of the production version on schedule for December 1984, the company proudly claiming it was $35 m under budget. Such restrictions are unlikely to effect the development of the 'Blackjack' bomber, a 310,000 kg aircraft with 222 kN thrust reportedly capable of an unrefuelled combat radius of 7300 km and apparently intended as a Cruise missile launch platform. Although some Western commentators seem to regard 'Blackjack' as a strategic aircraft, past experience might indicate the Soviet Navy to be the customer and during Soviet exercises in April 1984 the aircraft was reported active, although probably prematurely.

The most important USAF programme decision was the choice of the McDonnell Douglas F–15E Eagle, formerly Enhanced Eagle, for its dual role ground attack tactical aircraft, beating the General Dynamics' contender, the F–16E, formerly F–16XL. The F–15E, of which 392 are required, is an F–15D which has gone through the Multi-Stage Improvement Program (MSIP), receiving a new computer, software and radar, then been modified to accept the LANTIRN bad weather-night attack system as well as conformal fuel tanks and high speed multi-ejection bomb racks. The maximum take-off weight will be 36,741 kg but the aircraft will be capable of carrying 10,880 kg of ordnance and stores. The reported operational performance with conformal tanks, two 2309 litre drop tanks, LANTIRN pod, four AIM–120A AMRAAMs and 12 228 kg bombs would be 1260 km radius in a hi-lo-hi and 897 km in a hi-lo-lo-hi mission. It is planned that the initial F–15Es in the $1.5 bn contract, should be modified on the production line with 'production' beginning in 1986 for delivery in 1988. It is likely that the F–15E would be powered by the Pratt and Whitney F100–PW–220 but no decision has been made at the time of writing. Tests will continue with the F–16E because the 'cranked arrow' wing aircraft has demonstrated high potential for follow-on development, according to General Charles A. Gabriel, the USAF Chief of Staff.

Meanwhile the USAF is already taking steps to develop a replacement for both the F-15 and the F-16 in the Advanced Tactical Fighter (ATF) for which a system programme office has now been created under Colonel Albert C. Piccirillo. The design of the ATF must emphasise efficient supersonic cruise and stealth technology, and the aircraft is likely to incorporate new materials and electronics, advanced radar and vectored thrust — being able to operate from battle-damaged or austere air bases. Study contracts worth an average $705,000 were awarded to Boeing, General Dynamics, Grumman, Lockheed, McDonnell Douglas, Northrop and Rockwell for presentation in the late spring of 1984, while both General Electric and Pratt and Whitney have received a $202 m contract to develop a demonstrator engine. Development of the airframe and engine is scheduled to begin in 1987 with initial deployment in 1993.

The export potential of the ATF may well prove as good as that of the F-15 and F-16. Meanwhile, a crisis was developing at the beginning of the year over the F-X export fighter concept developed under President Carter's Administration. The idea was a laudable attempt to restrict international arms sales by providing the United States Government with less sophisticated, but high performance, combat aircraft which could be offered as alternatives to the F-15, and F-16. Unfortunately, President Carter chose to ignore the fact that nations offered the F-X aircraft, the General Dynamics F-16/79 and the Northrop F-20 Tigershark, would resent being 'fobbed off' with what they could only perceive, rightly or wrongly, as second class aircraft. In January 1984 the dispute erupted when Thailand rejected the F-16/79 and demanded the F-16C, and three months later Singapore reluctantly accepted the offer of eight F-16/79s after its request for F-16As was rejected. It appears, however, that both countries will receive their wishes and that the F-X programme will be quietly interred. In Europe, the F-16A was Turkey's choice with an initial 15 ordered against an ultimate requirement for 160 while Madrid opted to spend $2.6 bn on 72 McDonnell Douglas F/A-18 Hornets in preference to the Panavia Tornado. Interestingly enough, Boeing are proposing a modernised F-4 Phantom with Pratt and Whitney PW-1120 turbojet rated at 92 kN, a Westinghouse APG-66 Pulse Doppler radar, with new avionics and conformal fuel tanks. The company claim a demonstrator could be flying in 1985 and potential customers might include Israel, Spain and Turkey.

In the meantime the RAF has bought 15 F–4Js from the US Navy to replace the squadron of Phantoms sent to Port Stanley. But the backbone of the RAF fighter force will be the Panavia Tornado F.2, of which the first two were officially rolled out on 28 March 1984. The RAF is to buy 165 Tornado F.2s, whose Operational Conversion Unit was to be formed at Coningsby in September, with five squadrons being based at Leuchars and Leeming. The Tornado F.2 is capable of unrefuelled patrols some 700 km from base for more than two hours, its Marconi Avionics Foxhunter radar being capable of track-while-scan on up to 20 aircraft up to 100 km away while its largely missile armament, four Sky Flash and four Sidewinders, permit both snap up and snap down attacks. Five squadrons of Phantoms will be retained to defend the United Kingdom Air Defence Region and both Phantoms and Tornadoes will be supplemented in time of crisis by 72 Hawk T.1A armed with two Sidewinders. The Tornado programme continues to progress satisfactorily with 300 delivered by January 1984 and a sixth batch, consisting of 63 Interdiction Strike (IDS) and 92 Air Defence Version) being ordered during the year. Panavia were awaiting a decision by Greece about purchasing the aircraft and there were signs of Middle East interest, Oman reportedly being interested in eight ADVs. In all, the company could see potential orders for another 100, bringing total orders up to 905, some of which would replace attrition and others might be for a Luftwaffe requirement for an ECR (Electronic Countermeasures and Reconnaissance) aircraft using off-the-shelf equipment from United States sources.

Meanwhile, Europe is seeking a new fighter and on 16 December 1983, France, Germany, Italy, Spain and the United Kingdom signed an outline staff target in Bonn for what was termed the Future European Fighter Aircraft (FEFA), later renamed the European Fighter Aircraft (EFA). The EFA is intended to be a single seat, twin engined air defence fighter, with secondary ground attack role and the five air staffs envisage an agile, STOL aircraft with multi-mode radar and a take-off weight of 12,500 kg, capable of carrying an external load of 4500 kg, maximum speed being more than Mach 1.8 and the combat radius 550 km. Although development will be a joint venture both the United Kingdom and France are bidding for design leadership and are producing technology demonstrators; British Aerospace's EAP (European Aircraft Programme) and Dassault's ACX, the former incorporating experience gained with the Tornado and powered by the RB–199, while the latter will be powered by the Snecma M–88 which began bench tests early in 1984. The EAP was scheduled to be a joint development with the Panavia partners and British Aerospace undoubtedly wished it to be the pre-prototype of the EFA, or ACA as it was once known (Agile Combat Aircraft). But so feverish is the competition and so anxious are the Germans to be seen to remain neutral, that MBB reduced its 15 per cent stake in the aircraft to a nominal 1 per cent leading to some substantial redesign of the rear section which will now incorporate a tornado tail. The Panavia partners and their associates in Turbo-union would undoubtedly prefer to see the expansion of their existing organisations to absorb new partners rather than the creation of a new one, as the French wish, and the success or failure of EFA will depend upon the industrial share-out. It may well be that the French airframe design would be chosen with the Turbo-union engine. When the defence ministers considered initial proposals from industry in June 1984, a European requirement for 800 aircraft was envisaged, of which 600 would be shared equally between France, Germany and the United Kingdom, with prototypes flying in 1990–1991 and the aircraft entering service about 1995.

Israel, too, is seeking to develop a new combat aircraft, the Lavi, and the last major obstacle to its development disappeared when President Reagan permitted Israel to use $330 m of Foreign Military Sale credits for research and development in the United States, as well as $250 m in Israel. The Lavi will be a tactical fighter powered by the Pratt and Whitney 1120 with a maximum take-off weight of 17,000 kg capable of Mach 1.85, operational range being 460 km and the maximum external store load being 10,500 kg. It will feature a new multi-mode Pulse Doppler radar by Elta and an advanced cockpit and the maiden flight is scheduled for late 1985 or early 1986, production beginning in 1991.

In the field of V/STOL, the Indian Naval Air Force ordered another 11 Sea Harrier FRS 51s, while the Fleet Air Arm is to give its small force of Sea Harriers a mid life update with a new multi-mode Pulse Doppler radar to replace Blue Fox, a new radar warning receiver and expanded armament fit, to include four AIM–120A and two ASRAAM on the wing tips, the first modified Sea Harriers appearing in 1988. In the meantime, the first of the McDonnell Douglas AV–8B pre-production aircraft was officially handed over to the United States Marine Corps, with production aircraft scheduled for delivery in 1985 and the RAF receiving its 60 Harrier GR.5s in 1986. The USAF still does not appear to be entirely convinced of the virtues of VSTOL, but it is investigating various concepts and has requested a STOL and manoeuvre technology demonstrator, the objective being to have a supersonic test bed, capable of landing in 457m in all weathers, reflecting the growing belief that USAF aircraft may have to operate on bomb damaged airfields.

One of the most significant events of 1983 was the revelation that the Soviet air force has been substantially reorganised over a two year period. The Air Defence Command (*Voiska Protivo Vozdushnaya Oborona*) was the first to be reorganised into five theatre commands to meet the growing threat from low flying manned bombers and Cruise missiles, fighter strength being halved to 1200 aircraft. But the *Frontovaya Aviatsiya,* or Tactical Aviation, appeared to be unchanged with its units regarded traditionally as flying artillery. The FA has now been restructured for greater integration at theatre level with five air forces replacing the 16 smaller air armies, while five Aviation Armies of the Soviet Union have been created to control long range strike aircraft such as the Su–24 'Fencer' and Tu–16 'Badger', two of these armies having a strategic role with Tu–22M 'Backfires', Tu–22 'Blinders' and Mya–4 'Bisons'. At the same time, the Soviet Union is deploying increasingly sophisticated combat aircraft such as the Su–25 'Frogfoot', Su–27 'Flanker', MiG–29 'Fulcrum', and the MiG–31 'Foxhound', the latter being a development of the MiG–25 — which apparently is to counter the B–1B having an operational radius of 1800 km and an armament of eight AA–9 missiles — and it would appear that the Soviet Union is now following not only the organisational aspects of Western air power but also the design principles.

Helicopters

The end of 1983 saw a resolution of the helicopter *impasse* between France and West Germany with the signing, on 25 November 1983, of an agreement for the development and manufacture of a helicopter for the 1990s. Known to the Germans as PAH–2 (*Panzerabwehrhubschrauber* — Anti-tank Helicopter) and to the French as HAP (*Helicoptere d'Appui Protection*) or HAC–3G (*Helicoptere Anti-Char*) the aircraft will be 5000 kg, powered by two 900 kW MTU–Turbomeca MTM385–R turboshafts. The producers, MBB and Aerospatiale, plan to build 427 aircraft which will be split evenly. The HAP will enter service first, in 1991, serving with the FAR, France's Rapid Deployment Force, armed with a turret-mounted 30mm cannon, Mistral air-to-air missiles and 68 mm rockets, as well as a roof-mounted sensor. The PAH–2 will enter service in 1992 with nose-mounted sensors and eight HOT anti-armour missiles and four air-to-air missiles, while the HAC–3G will enter service in 1995 with a mast mounted sighting system, eight Trinational Third Generation Anti-armour missiles and four Mistrals.

The United States Army, too, is seeking candidates to meet its light helicopter (LHX) requirements beyond the turn of the century, with two versions being considered: LHX–SCAT, a light observation and attack aircraft of which 2900 will be needed to replace the OH–6, OH–58 and AH–1 and LHX–U, another 2000 will be needed to replace the UH–1. A $2.8 bn programme is envisaged beginning in mid 1986 with the aircraft entering service in 1994–1995, all having a single pilot and air-to-air fighting capability. Sikorsky and Boeing Vertol are leading teams to fulfill the ARTI (Advanced Rotorcraft Technology Integration) programme which is the initial phase of LHX and is scheduled to be completed by the end of 1985. One rotary wing aircraft which will not feature in the Army inventory is the Joint Service Tilt Rotor (JVX) project, being developed by Bell and Boeing Vertol based upon the Boeing 301/XV–15. The United States Navy wanted the JVX for transport work, as did the Marine Corps, the USAF wanted it for combat search and rescue while the Army wanted it as an electronic warfare platform with secondary medical evacuation roles. But in the summer of 1983, the Army decided to withdraw from the project because it doubted whether it needed 284 new aircraft for this task, while the USAF is expressing doubts on the grounds that its HH–60D Night Hawks can fulfill the same roles as the JVX. Nevertheless, the Navy and the Marine Corps are determined to press ahead, and Marconi Avionics have mentioned the JVX as a potential platform for their Sky Guardian airborne early warning suite.

The United Kingdom had some success selling 20 Sea King Mk 42Bs to India's Navy as a Sea Eagle platform using MEL Super Searcher radar, while another nine Sea Kings are to be converted to the airborne early warning role using Thorn EMI Electronics Searchwater radar. The successor of the Sea King in both the Royal Navy and the Italian Navy will be the European Helicopter Industries EH–101 for which the United Kingdom and Italy signed a joint funding agreement on 25 January 1984. The £400 m to £500 m programme calls for development to production stage of the 13,000 kg helicopter which will be powered by three of the General Electric CT–7s, rate at 1289 kW, and be capable of carrying a disposable load of 6000 kg. It is likely to feature a Ferranti Blue Kestrel I–J band search radar and the Royal Navy version will feature Marconi Avionics AQS–903 signal processors for sonobuoy sensors while the Italian version will probably have a dunking sonar. Westland Helicopters and Agusta, the partners in EHI, will produce the versions for their respective navies while the Italian company will also produce a utility transport version capable of carrying 24 troops or a Jeep-size vehicle. Surprisingly, the United States Department of Defense directed the United States Navy to consider the EH–101 for the carrier-based anti-submarine helicopter requirement, although the Sikorsky SH–60B Seahawk had been the only contender. The move was probably an attempt to reduce Sikorsky's estimates rather than a serious attempt at standardisation but the chance to bid for the 100 aircraft order was an undoubted boost to EHI morale, although the SH–60 seemed set to beat Westland's Lynx 3 for the Australian frigate order.

Within the Soviet Union new versions of the Mi–8 'Hip' for electronic warfare purposes, were reported and the Pentagon revealed the existence of the Mi–28 'Havoc' attack helicopter estimated to have a speed of 300 kph and a combat radius of 240 km. 'Havoc' is reported to be the Soviet equivalent of the AH–64 Apache and prototypes are currently under test with a view to production early in 1985.

Support Aircraft

The efficiency of air forces is no longer measured merely in terms of numbers of combat aircraft but must be evaluated against the number of support aircraft. The RAF, for example, is substantially expanding its force of dual-purpose transports-tankers with five VC 10K.2s this year, four VC 10K,3s and six Tristar 500s next year — these aircraft gradually replacing the V-bombers, the last Vulcan retiring on 31 March 1984. A possible successor could be the FIMA (Future International Medium Airlifter) being studied by Aerospatiale, British Aerospace, Lockheed and MBB as a replacement for the Hercules and the Transall in the 1990s A Memorandum of Understanding to begin the study was made at the end of 1982 with work to be completed by the end of 1984. At the other end of the scale, Short Brothers have won a $165 m contract to supply 18 Sherpa freighters to the USAF for their European Distribution System Aircraft (EDSA) programme which will involve flying in urgent supplies to United States combat bases in Europe. The contract, which includes an option on a further 48 aircraft, is dubbed C–23A by the USAF, is worth $660 m and within a couple of months, Shorts were announcing small orders for similar aircraft from other, unidentified, air forces.

Heavier airlifters remain the prerogative of the superpowers and the Soviet Union is introducing the An–400 'Condor' with a 73m wing span, powered by four D–18T turbofans, each rated at 223 kN. The 'Condor' is the equivalent of the Lockheed C–5A Galaxy but can reportedly carry 120 tonnes, compared with the Galaxy's 100 tonnes, up to 4600 km. Work is currently underway, upgrading the first C–5A to C–5B standard with roll-out scheduled for July 1985, with a new wing being fitted together with improved avionics. Plans to supplement the C–5 with the McDonnell Douglas C–17 have made little progress with funding still confined to research and development.

Trainers play an important part in air force inventories, not only to produce new aircrew but also, and increasingly, to augment first line strength. Attention is currently being focused on the contest to meet Air Staff Target 412 for a replacement for the Jet Provost. Significantly, this will be a turbo-prop design and four aircraft had been short-listed by the spring of 1984; the Pilatus PC–9, which would be built by British Aerospace, the Embraer Tucano, which would be built by Short Brothers, the NDN–1T Turbo Firecracker and the Australian Aircraft A–20 Wamira. By the early summer of 1984 the Swiss design was undoubtedly the front runner for the 155 aircraft order, with British Aerospace having the prospect of supplying export orders as well as the chance of selling its Hawk 100 and 200 Series aircraft, which were more combat orientated versions of the trainer, and which had reportedly attracted Swiss interest.

Space

President Reagan's announcement that the United States would develop space-based BMD systems using beam weapons by the end of the century, is beginning to shape into a programme whose cost has been estimated at $26 bn by 1989, and this excludes the $9 bn to be spent upon a manned space station in the early 1990s. Initial funding is for $2 bn and the American Defense Secretary, Mr Caspar Weinberger, has pledged that any nuclear umbrella created will be extended to Europe. In the meantime, the United States Navy has created its own Space Command, with headquarters at Dahlgren, Virginia, to control naval space surveillance systems, naval astronautics and part of the naval satellite communications system. It may not last long, for the Joint Chiefs of Staff have recommended that the Navy and USAF Space Commands be merged by 1986 into a four-service joint space command.

The idea of beam weapons has been greeted sceptically by many European scientists but the United States is making progress in this field, with the success being reported on 26 September 1983 of the Airborne Laser Laboratory which engaged and destroyed a low level BQM–34A sub-sonic drone.

The United States is also continuing its ASAT (Anti-Satellite) experiments and on 21 January 1984, an F–15 from Edwards Air Force Base aimed a 1200 kg ASAT rocket at a point in space in the first test firing of the system, the USAF refusing to state the results of the experiments.

Undoubtedly the Soviet Union is conducting similar experiments in its efforts to ensure that it is not left behind in the technological race and there can be little doubt that the objective of the Kremlin, both within and without the atmosphere, is to create qualitative as well as quantitive superiority.

Trends in Air Warfare: Airborne Early Warning

M J JACKSON

The author is a correspondent for several foreign defence magazines

IN THE PAST few years a new NATO command has gradually been gaining strength and during 1984, it was scheduled for a further improvement with the delivery to the RAF of the British Aerospace (BAe) Nimrod AEW.3. The creation of NATO Early Warning Command (NAEW Comd) with headquarters in Maisieres, Belgium, reflects the increasing importance of Airborne Early Warning (AEW) in national and international security, being a modern expression of the centuries-old military principle that the higher you are the further you can see. In modern times, the AEW aircraft not only extends electronic eyesight but also offers the means to counter the risk of surprise attack by low-flying aircraft.

Appropriately, the origins of AEW lie in one particularly devastating surprise air attack, that of the Japanese Navy upon Pearl Harbor in December 1941, and in consequence, the United States Navy has been in the vanguard of AEW development. Aircraft carrier-based task forces were the foundation of the Pacific War strategy because of their power and mobility but the carrier was vulnerable to air attack and a few well-placed bombs could end a campaign, as the Battle of Midway proved so conclusively. Radar reduced this vulnerability by giving some warning to the Combat Information Center (CIC) of approaching aircraft and permitting the CIC to marshal the defences, but the warning time was limited and a coordinated attack could swamp the defences. By 1942, airborne radar was already a proven tool for air interception and anti-submarine warfare. Therefore, it was only natural that the US Navy should consider using aircraft as search radar platforms for air defence purposes, especially as they were being used in radar searches for surface ships using Catalina flying boats.

Project Cadillac was conducted by the Massachusetts Institute of Technology using US Navy funds and was initially aimed at developing a carrier-borne aircraft with a search radar for anti-submarine work, and also to extend the surface vessel's air defence radar cover. Shortly after the project began in 1943, the widely used General Electric AN/APS–20, an E–F band (2–4 GHz) surface search radar was fitted into a ventral dome on a TBM Avenger. A data link was used to transmit raw radar data to warships which would then direct fighter forces, a complex and highly sophisticated arrangement especially with a radar whose performance was degraded by weather and sea state; it was unreliable and had a range of only 80 km in good conditions. The TBM–3W was too late for the war against Japan, forcing the navy to extend sensor range by means of radar picket destroyers which proved vulnerable to air attack, but despite its imperfections it remained in service until 1954. It was usually employed for anti-submarine warfare with the TBM–3S as killer, being surplanted from 1950 by the Grumman AF–2W Guardian (teamed with the AF–2S) which in turn was replaced from 1953 by a version of the Douglas AD Skyraider, nicknamed the 'Guppy'. Developments in detection, processing and weaponry during the early 1950s permitted both search and attack roles to be combined into one airframe, the Grumman S2F Tracker, which began entering service in 1954. The Guppy (AD–3W, AD–4W and AD–5W) gradually concentrated on the AEW role, the latter version, as EA–1E, seeing active service off Vietnam in 1964, but in fact they remained little more than flying radar platforms.

Cadillac I was, essentially, a blind alley but Cadillac II, which began in 1944, proved a freeway to undreamed-of potential. Basically a land-based version of Cadillac I, it had one vital difference, the radar operators were in radio contact with fighters and could direct them towards their target, although it was impossible to give an indication of height. Nevertheless in 1945, 30 Army Air Force B–17Gs were acquired as the PB–1W and crudely modified, some retaining their 0.50 cal machine guns, the 105 km range APS–20B being installed in a ventral radome while extra fuel tanks were added to give a range of 4020 km. Entering service in 1946, they were assigned the defence of naval bases in the United States but their lack of sophistication meant they were little more than stop gaps and within three years a more sophisticated project, based on the Lockheed Constellation, although the production aircraft, the WV–2 Warning Star, used the Super Constellation airframe with the faithful APS–20 in a ventral radome and an AN/APS–45 height-finder radar in a dorsal radome. The WV–2 (later EC–121G) featured communications links with aircraft, ships and shore bases and all five radar operators had electronic access to a central display board. The WV–2 entered service in 1954 joining a version developed by the USAF under the Weapon System 214M Program, the initial RC–121C Constellations being straight conversions of the C–121C transport with 5.4 tonnes of electronic equipment. These formed the basis of the 552nd Airborne Early Warning and Control Wing but were soon replaced by the RC–121D featuring 25 hour endurance. These aircraft were upgraded to EC–121H standard in 1962 with a computer and direct links to NORAD's SAGE (Semi-Automatic Ground Environment).

Six squadrons of RC–121s and five squadrons of WV–2s created the Airborne Early Warning Barriers Pacific and Atlantic providing continuous coverage not only off the United States coast but as far out as Midway Island and Alaska in the west and Iceland in the east; indeed, the last EC–121 sortie was from Keflavik in 1976. The ever increasing threat from ballistic missiles, rather than manned aircraft, reduced the need for the EC–121 while missile-detecting sensors such as Over-the-Horizon (OTH) radars were capable of detecting manned aircraft 1450 km away but not precisely. But while the AEW force was being reduced, events in Indochina meant that any thought of scrapping the concept disappeared.

Following the loss of two F–105s to MiG–17s over North Vietnam, the 552nd AEWC Wing assigned a five aircraft detachment to 2nd Air Division at Tan Son Nhut In South Vietnam, to extend friendly radar coverage. The Big Eye (College Eye from 1 March 1967) Task Force later moved to Thailand and from 1967 was based at Udorn Air Base under 7/13 Air Force. Initially deployed for AEW tasks, it also gave warning of North Vietnamese fighter activity — the EC–121s flying elliptical orbits over the Gulf of Tonkin some 80 km from Haiphong while from May 1966, other aircraft operated over the Plain of Jars in Laos. Like Topsy, the EC–121 role 'growed'; they controlled fighters protecting USAF support aircraft; acted as communications relays for returning strike aircraft and then, gradually, became flying command posts for USAF operations over northern Indochina warning of MiG activity and the launching of surface-to-air missiles. They also provided navigation and vectoring information for emergency flight refuelling and SAR missions, but only three times did they fulfill their traditional role. From April 1965 to August 1973 (when USAF operations officially ended) the EC-121s flew 13,931 sorties, issued 3297 MiG warnings, assisted the destruction of 25 enemy fighter fighters and supported 80 SAR sorties, the task force remaining in the theatre until the following year.

US Naval Activity

US Navy AEW aircraft were also active, for development had continued throughout the 1950s and 1960s. In 1959, the Grumman WF-2 Tracer (later E-1B) entered service with a repackaged APS-20, the AN/APS-82, which proved more reliable and had a 145 km range. More importantly, the 'Willy Fudd' was the first design to integrate radar, communications, displays and navigation systems, yet within five years, it was being replaced by the more advanced Grumman W2F Hawkeye (later E-2) which incorporated the experience of the Naval Tactical Data System (NTDS) programme and could provide naval task forces with detailed data on all air and sea movements within its sensor range as well as automatic target detection. The E-2 also featured a new radar, the General Electric AN/APS-96 with TACCAR pulse compression techniques for high resolution and clutter rejection, the antenna being housed in a 910 kg, 7.3 m diameter, rotating radome (Rotodome) and since the aircraft could fly at 9144 m (compared with 3600 m of Tracer) the equipment not only offered a phenomenal improvement in performance but also a 370 km detection range.

From 1965, the Hawkeye rapidly replaced the E-1 and EA-1 and in Indochina carried out similar duties to the EC-121 but with naval aircraft. Its superior electronics — it could locate an aircraft to within less than two kilometres — meant that by vectoring flight leaders up to 100 strike aircraft could be controlled simultaneously, being guided to their targets by routes which took them around known defensive concentrations. But the APS-96 had only limited overland capability, even with the improved processing provided by the Litton L-304 computer which upgraded the E-2A to the E-2B in the late 1960s. The initial solution was the General Electric AN/APS-120, with OL-93/AP radar detector processor linking the radar to the tracking and intercept computer to provide automatic detection and digital target reports, radar reflection from the tail section and propellors being reduced by the use of glass fibre in the structure. From 1973 the E–2s began to be upgraded to E–2C standard, but from 1977 they were further enhanced with the Advanced Radar Processing Sub-system (ARPS) with better radar performance and a significant improvement in ECCM, the APs–120ARPS later becoming AN/APS–125.

The E–2C is reported to be capable of detecting a fighter at 370 km and a Cruise missile at 185 km while its ESM equipment permits detection at twice these distances and the combination of sensor and processing power is claimed to give the capability of detecting and tracking some 250 targets and up to 40 interceptors or strike aircraft. This potential made it an attractive proposition for overseas customers, the first of whom was Israel (four) followed by Japan (eight), Egypt (four), and Singapore (three) — the folding wings making it possible to house the aircraft in hardened shelters. The Israeli aircraft were able to observe Arab fighters taking-off and in June 1979, vectored ten fighters onto eight MiG–21s which lost six of their number, while the ESM equipment helped detect Syrian SAM acquisition radars in the Beka' a Valley during 1982 with the aid of RPV sorties and were then able to guide aircraft with anti-radiation missiles to the sites. Such incidents have increased demand for AEW aircraft, particularly the Hawkeye, and it featured in extensive trials in France before being rejected in favour of a more advanced system.

AWACS

This had its origins in the early 1960s when the USAF, aware the EC–121 was nearing the end of its useful life, began the Overland Radar Technology Program to develop a long range Pulse Doppler system with good over-land performance, the intention being to use it in a flying command post where the radar operators-controllers were supplemented by an airborne commander and staff. The latter consideration was later removed and flight trials of Airborne Warning And Control System (AWACS) demonstrators led to full scale development from 1973 of the Westinghouse AN/APY–1 E–F Band radar in a Boeing 707–320B airframe with Pratt and Whitney TF–33 turbofans as the Boeing E–3A Sentry. The APY–1 featured a liquid-cooled, slotted, planar-array antenna in a 9.1m diameter rotodome weighing 1540 kg revolving, as in the E–2, at 6rpm with low PRF signals used for long range detection without elevation data beyond 700 km (large aircraft at the same altitude) while high PRF signals were used for height finding, the transmitter being so powerful it has to be switched off when the E–3 is within 4km of a tanker to eliminate the fire risk. Within the aircraft was an IBM CC–1 computer, 11 display consoles (nine situation and two auxiliary) and 13 communications links (HF, VHF, and UHF radios together with data links) for contacting ground command posts, ships, or other aircraft.

The first of 24 aircraft subsequently dubbed 'Core E–3A' Standard was delivered in March 1977, becoming operational with the 552nd AWAC Wing at Tinker Air Force Base Oklahoma, 13 months later and on New Year's Day 1979, it began phasing into NORAD. The E–3A Sentry is a formidable aircraft, cruising at Mach 0.72 at about 8800m with a flight-refuelled endurance of some 22 hours (half this without in-flight refuelling) the APY–1 being capable of detecting a low flying fighter over-the-horizon at 400 km, although the radar horizon is 370 km, while the system can track, automatically, 200 targets. In USAF service it acts as a command and control centre supporting quick reaction deployment and tactical operations by Tactical Air Command units as well as supporting NORAD by acting as an AEW platform as well as a survivable command and control centre for surveillance, identification and tracking of hostile aircraft approaching the continental United States. From 1981, the Block 20 Modification programme began adding six communications links and installing the Joint Tactical Information Distribution System (JTIDS), a high speed, high capacity communications system operating over a single, secure channel and capable of linking up to 98,000 participants. In addition a new, larger capacity, CC–2 computer was added making it possible to track twice as many aircraft as well as providing a basic maritime surveillance capability, the upgraded aircraft becoming E–3Bs. The capability of the E–3 was demonstrated in Europe by the USAF who showed their NATO allies that five could extend radar coverage far beyond the Iron Curtain. This demonstration was a case of preaching to the converted for the Europeans had already recognised the value of the E–3 and wished to create a multinational fleet to supplement the ground radars and control stations of NADGE (NATO Air Defence Ground Environment).

NATO FLEET

The negotiations opened in Washington in 1974 and by January 1976, had crystallised into a $2700 million package, including industrial offset, for a 32 aircraft fleet. By now, however, the Western world was in the middle of the economic recession following the oil crisis and consequently, the discussions became enmeshed in a net of procedural and financial considerations while doubts were also expressed about the over-water capability of the E–3A. The deadlock alarmed the United Kingdom, whose AEW requirement was extremely urgent and had begun a fall-back national solution. With no end to the deadlock in sight, the United Kingdom withdrew from the programme in March 1977, a decision which helped concentrate the remaining partners' minds wonderfully, permitting a rescheduling of the programme to a $2000 m package involving 18 aircraft with Boeing providing the airframe, radar and navigation equipment, while the Europeans provided the remainder to bring the aircraft to E–3B standard, the installation of European equipment being supervised by Dornier while the fleet would be based in West Germany. The new programme was accepted in outline by NATO defence ministers in May 1978 and the detailed purchasing agreement was signed three years later, the United States providing 40 per cent of the cost, West Germany 30 per cent, Canada 10 per cent and the remaining European partners (except the Netherlands and Iceland) between 1 and 5 per cent each. Once agreement was reached, the European AEW force quickly began to take shape with the NATO Airborne Early Warning and Control Programme Management Organisation (NAPMO) to manage the acquisition phase and the creation, in January 1980, of NAEW Comd to control both the E–3 and the British Nimrod AEW.3 aircraft, this gaining full NATO headquarters status ten months later, being co-located with SHAPE headquarters near Casteau, Belgium.

The NATO E–3, which may conveniently, if unofficially, be called NE–3A, are basically 'Core E–3A' Standard with SEL and AEG Telefunken display and communications equipment, their maritime surveillance capability being enhanced significantly (they have another HF radio for maritime operations) an improvement introduced on USAF aircraft from January 1982. The first NE–3A was rolled out on 27 January 1981, handed over to Dornier at Oberfaffenhofen two months later and officially accepted by NATO on 22 January 1982. The aircraft, organised into three squadrons, are officially registered in Luxembourg and crewed by personnel from 11 NATO countries who began training with the 552nd AWAC Wing in July 1980, 370 being trained by the autumn of 1982.

The infrastructure involves a main operation base at Geilenkirchen, West Germany, which was officially turned over to NATO in March 1982 and forward operations bases at Konya, Turkey; Oerland, Norway (strictly a 'forward operation location'); Preveza, Greece; and Trapani, Sicily, this chain of bases beginning activation in October 1983, and completing activation by early 1985. By mid 1985, NAEW Comd's NE–3A component will have 18 aircraft and 2700 personnel.

Operational control of the NAEW Comd force will be in the hands of SACEUR, CINCHAN and SACLANT who will allocate priorities for the assets for the command headquarters to assign aircraft. These will not only carry out surveillance in conjunction with the NATO air defence system and naval forces but will also control both defensive and offensive air operations through the on-board Fighter Allocation and Weapons Controllers, the NE–3As being interfaced with the NADGE radar chain through a $181 m modification programme to the ground stations.

Britain's Experience

The British segment of NAEW Comd had as hesitant an evolution as the NE–3A. During the 1950s, British aircraft carriers had used the AD–4W Skyraider and later the Fairey Gannet AEW.3, both using the APS–20, although the sensor used in the Gannet was constantly refined and completely rebuilt. During the early 1960s, a purpose-built naval AEW system began to evolve but in the middle of the decade, the Government decided the United Kingdom could no longer remain a world power and that defence resources should be concentrated in Europe. With the decision, in 1967, to phase out conventional aircraft carriers from the Royal Navy and make the RAF responsible for fleet air support, the senior service lost its grip on AEW which then became the responsibility of the RAF. They inherited a number of design solutions involving several airframes, including the Comet, as well as a fore and aft scanner solution which was tested in a Comet in 1971.

At the same time, the Soviet air forces began demonstrating their capability to stage conventional air attacks from both the west and east coasts with ever increasing sortie rates over the Atlantic and air exercises clearly demonstrated the limitations of ground-based radars. A land-based AEW aircraft requirement evolved and, as a stop gap, a dozen elderly Shackleton MR.2s were fitted with APS–20(F) radars, removed from Gannets. From 1972, the Shackleton AEW.2s began their patrols but they were noisy, relatively low flying and the APS–20 could not provide height altitude data. In the first flush of European youth, and in a gesture toward standardisation, the government supported the NATO AEW force based on the E–3 but as the negotiations became deadlocked so funding began for a national solution and an exasperated government was able to abandon the NE–3A on 31 March 1977 in favour of a £300 m British system. The Comet airframe with the fore and aft scanner had already been selected, the optimum solution, and during the 1970s work began on an E–F Band Pulse Doppler radar so that within three months of the British Government decision, a trials radar system was flying.

The operational platform was a Comet derivative, the Nimrod MR.1, which became available in some numbers following decisions not to upgrade the whole fleet to MR.2 standards and withdraw a squadron from Malta. The Nimrod AEW.3 fleet strength was scheduled to be 11 aircraft, including upgraded development aircraft, which will be operated by No 8 Squadron at RAF Waddington. It was originally planned to introduce the aircraft into squadron service in 1982 but development problems, apparently with the signal-to-noise ratio of the radar receiver, led to the postponement initially to mid 1983 and later to 1984, with the squadron being scheduled to be at full strength by 1985.

The Nimrod has an endurance of more than ten hours, which can be extended with in-flight refuelling, although this requirement was not in the original design (nor is it found in the NE–3A) being added only in the light of the South Atlantic experience. The Nimrod can operate between 7600 and 12,800m (twice the height of the Shackleton) with 360 degree hemispheric coverage for a minimum of 320 km, unlike the E–3 whose fuselage reportedly creates a 73 km ‘shadow’ below and ahead of the aircraft. The radar will normally operate in medium PRF mode to track low-level aircraft with occasional low PRF sweeps to track shipping movements but while it is optimised for detecting low-level intruders, it is still capable of tracking high altitude aircraft. The 4080M computer processes data from the radar and ESM equipment and displays it on six multi-function displays while external and internal communications are controlled by an automatic management system (AMRICS) which will also be interfaced with JTIDS later.

The Marconi Avionics MSA (Mission System Avionics) which interfaces sensor, processor, displays and communications, is a generation ahead of the E–3s and versions have been offered in French airframes such as the Transall C.160 and Breguet Atlantique to meet the *Armee de l'Air* AEW requirement. However, the French requirement is urgent and after exhaustive tests with the Hawkeye which was rejected, Paris seemed likely at the beginning of 1984 to choose the E–3. The Sentry was also the choice of the Shah of Iran in April 1978, but plans to sell him seven ended with his overthrow; nonetheless, they will still appear in the region. Saudi Arabia is taking delivery of five, ordered in 1981 in a $5 billion (bn) agreement following rejection of the E–2C, but so controversial was the purchase that the aircraft will be 'santised' with the removal of JTIDS and the latest ECCM systems while Americans will be included in the aircrews until 1990. The E–3As will be based at Riyadh then Al-Kharj from 1986 and will operate in support of the Gulf States as well as protecting the vital oil fields.

The enthusiasm for the E–3 reflects not only its technical efficiency but also its diplomatic effectiveness, indeed, the AWACS seems to have replaced the gunboat as a gesture of diplomatic concern. USAF E–3s have been used to monitor the situation during periods of diplomatic tension, their first mission being to observe the border war between the two Yemens three months after becoming operational with NORAD and subsequently they monitored the Soviet occupation of Afghanistan, the Iran-Iraq War and Soviet movements around Poland in 1980 — while the assassinations of the South Korean and Egyptian presidents led to the despatch of E–3s to those countries. So great is the reputation of this sophisticated aircraft that its mere presence in the Sudan in February 1983 was credited with ending Libyan air attacks on border towns, returning in March 1984 following a raid on Omdurman. Future 'diplomatic' operations will no doubt be aided with further enhancements, such as the USAF Block 25 modification programme which will raise ten 'Core E–3As' to E–3C standard with further display consoles and UHF radios as well as Have Quick anti-jamming improvements.

Soviet Developments

The value of AEW has not been lost on the Soviet Union with its chronic air defence problems, indeed the KAL 007 incident clearly demonstrated the weaknesses of the Communist electronics industry which has so far been unable to produce an equivalent to the E-3 or Nimrod, forcing the National Air Defence Command (PVO) to rely on an inadequate chain of ground sensors. Nevertheless, an attempt was made from the early 1960s to overcome the problem using a 'Flat Jack' surveillance radar with 11m diameter rotodome fitted into a Tu-114 airframe. But the Tu-126 'Moss' suffered, technically, not only from inadequate processing but also from a configuration involving two contra-rotating, four-bladed propellors which reflect radar transmissions while the value of AEW was further reduced by Soviet operational procedures which reduced pilot initiative during the interception process to the absolute minimum and must limit the number of interceptors an individual operator can control. The Tu-126 may well have been a disappointment to the PVO for no more than 20 appear to have been purchased in the late 1960s, and by the early 1980s only half were operational. It appears to be used as a gap filler, although its over-land performance is reportedly poor, or as part of a trip-wire force with a small team of fighters over water where it is said to be able to detect quite small aircraft, the normal radar horizon being reported at 300 km.

Because of these limitations, it seems unlikely that reports of a Tu-126 being loaned to the Indian Air Force during the 1971 war with Pakistan are true. The need for AEW in the National Air Defence Command has grown with the deployment of American Cruise missiles and consequently the need to replace the Tu-126 is very great. To create an effective look-down-shoot-down capability, two rotodome solutions are reported to be under development based on the Il-76 and the Il-86 civil aircraft, the latter a similar configuration to the Boeing 707. They will certainly feature more advanced processing for use over land but are unlikely to appear in strength until the latter part of this decade, possibly after the full NAEW Comd has been deployed. The Soviet Union is, therefore, seeking physical as well as electronic counter-measures and has deployed the 250 km slant-range SA-5 'Gammon' surface-to-air missile close to the NATO borders in an effort to 'push back' Western 'eyes', and it may be that the deployment of the same system to Syria may be for a similar purpose. AEW aircraft are vulnerable to such threats because they would usually operate within at least 275 km of a FEBA (Forward Edge of the Battle Area) while over-water aircraft could be especially vulnerable to the underwater-air missiles now under consideration, although maritime communications links would keep them informed of possible submarine locations. In the air they are especially exposed during in-flight refuelling, when they must switch off their radars, for fighters might be able to approach close enough for a missile engagement while the increased use of AEW aircraft indicates the need for an air-to-air anti-radiation missile. Against the latter threat, the Sentry and Nimrod have ECM facilities while their own sensors would play a major role in their survival but as a reserve defence, NATO AEW aircraft have hard points which can be used for Sidewinder-style air-to-air missiles.

Undisputed Value

The value of airborne early warning is now widely accepted and several countries are known to be interested in the concept including Pakistan, Sweden and India which has a requirement for a national AEW system. But there are many factors to consider, not least of which is the expense, both in initial outlay and system life cycle and support, while another vital consideration is the precise operational requirement; flying radar platform, feeding data to ground control, flying command post with communications links to the whole air defence system or something in between. Many potential customers consider the AEW aircraft should be used to enhance their overall defence capability while others are seeking systems which are essentially gap fillers, supplying a need which no ground-based sensor can match. A number of relatively low cost systems have been offered, the simplest being the TCOM Corporation aerostats acting as antenna platforms, linked to ground stations. Airship Industries have proposed their airship as an AEW platform but previous experience of the US Navy with Goodyear ZPS–2Ws and ZFG–3Ws, helium-filled non-rigid airships indicate potential problems. Airships have proved vulnerable to meteorological conditions, have limited altitude and react badly to strong thermal currents over land, while temperature changes led to gas loss. The Lockheed Corporation has offered the APS–125 rotodome system in both the C–130 Hercules and P–3 Orion airframes as a means of reducing cost but the 'tin' tail units and propellors of both aircraft would be likely to create similar problems to that encountered by Tu-126 crews.

Yet, within the last three years a series of practical solutions to the problems of extending AEW coverage have begun to emerge and in the background of all, lies the ghost of Cadillac I. Just as in the first AEW programme, use was made of a maritime surveillance radar so the Royal Navy turned to the same source when the loss of HMS *Sheffield* graphically demonstrated that radar pickets were no substitute for AEW aircraft. Most airborne maritime surveillance radars are designed to provide excellent definition of small objects and in the crash programme, to provide the new generation of aircraft carriers with AEW — the Thorn EMI Searchwater was chosen to fulfill this requirement, a palletised and modified system being installed in a Sea King airframe and despatched south. The new system is not perfect but it achieves results and now all British carriers will embark the Sea King AEW. Similar installations can be made in the Sikorsky CH-53E Super Stallion or Boeing Vertol CH-47 Chinook or any other medium lift helicopter with the result that even navies without aircraft carriers could extend their sea-based sensor range, or alternatively rotary-wing systems could be used as gap fillers over sensitive areas or locations with poor ground-based radar reception. The emergence of multi-mode radars means that even the present generation of light maritime patrol aircraft could be given an AEW capability to meet customer specifications and several manufacturers during 1984 were marketing such systems.

For customers requiring a more sophisticated system, Marconi Avionics during 1984 marketed Skyguardian which could fit almost any airframe. It is based upon the MSA used in the Nimrod but follows a modular concept which can be progressively improved or adapted and is being offered with an assortment of displays, communications and EW equipment to meet almost any customer specification. It does, however, retain the F-Band Pulse Doppler radar with fore and aft scanner but this can fit airframes as different as the Airbus A310-B4 and the Aerospatiale Puma helicopter. Marconi Avionics are prepared to offer the customer the complete range of system options although British Aerospace would prefer the Airbus airframe because it is not only easy to adapt but also would have the best time-on-station, even without in-flight refuelling. Whatever the merits of any particular airframe or sensor, some countries believe their needs cannot be met by aircraft and it is interesting to note that Australia, once regarded as a potential customer for the Hawkeye, is now examining the option of over-the-horizon radar, although this option features poor target resolution and limited fields of view.

The defensive potential of AEW aircraft has been described above but in the future it seems inevitable that such systems will assume a greater offensive role. By observing enemy air activity and Elint monitoring, they can act as a strategic reconnaissance system and possibly provide up-to-date targetting information to out-going sorties while they are actually in the air. Their sensor packages must surely be of value in finding targets for deep strikes with the emerging range of 'smart' and 'brilliant' munitions, indeed they might well take over control of the targetting of surface-to-surface missiles such as Pershing. Certainly, a new form of airborne early warning with direct application to general operations in the European theatre has already been deployed in the shape of the Lockheed TR–1 which began deploying in the United Kingdom during February 1983. Unlike the moving antenna systems used in Hawkeye, Sentry and Nimrod, the AN/UPD–X synthetic aperture radar uses the movement of the aircraft to scan the area on either side of the flight path, the data then being instantly processed into a picture with great ground detail. These provide a visual picture of ground activity deep in Warsaw Pact territory while ESM equipment provides the electronic situation data. Operating at great height, at all times, and in all weathers the TR–1 acts as SACEUR's personal satellite system and could provide early warning of any offensive as well as helping to monitor the progress of such an operation. On a smaller scale, both the United States and British armies are known to be examining airborne, battlefield surveillance radars to provide early warning of Soviet troop movements. The American system SOTAS (Standoff Target Acquisition System) has run into technical difficulties while the British Castor Project is still at the early stages of development, although one of the competitors, Thorn EMI, is known to have tested a synthetic aperture radar in a Canberra airframe.

Not only is AEW likely to be found in a variety of airframes, including V/STOL designs such as the JVX, but it may be encountered with a radically new antennae system. Consideration has been given by several companies to a conformal radar in which electronically-scanned phased array antennas are installed in the wings, fuselage and tail of an aircraft to give 360 degree coverage at a third of the weight of conventional systems. Such a system would demand extremely sophisticated processing but it could be installed in smaller, high performance aircraft with higher survivability, and at one time it was proposed fitting such arrays in helicopter rotor blades.

Finally, some considerations must also be given to space-based AEW systems, indeed one already exists the TRW Block 647 which is in geostationary orbit over the Indian Ocean to carry out infra-red surveillance for the United States ballistic missile warning system. The US Department of Defense is known to be working on a mosaic infra-red sensor for possible deployment in the mid 1990s, to detect not only rockets but also Cruise missiles and manned supersonic bombers, such a system having some use for European defence as a back-up to AEW systems within the atmosphere.

Next year sees the 40th anniversary of the birth of operational AEW, and while it remains an expensive and sophisticated system, it is likely to prove one of the most valuable air defence tools and might be described as literally worth its weight in gold.

Tables

TABLE 1 — PRINCIPAL-TO-SHIP MISSILES

Name	Country	Length (metres)	Launch weight (kg)	Guidance	Range (km)	Speed	Remarks
Exocet MM38	France	5.2	735	Active radar homing Sea-skimmer	45	0.9 Mach	Fitted in RN and many other navies
Exocet MM40	France	5.78	850	Active radar homing Sea-skimmer	70+	0.9 Mach	Tube launched
Otomat	France/Italy	4.81	700	Mid-course update and active radar homing Terminal sea-skimmer	200	0.9 Mach	Fitted in Italian and some other navies. Improved version reported under development named Otomach
Gabriel 1	Israel	3.35	431	Beam riding with semi-active radar homing or optical. Sea-skimmer	20	0.7 Mach	
Gabriel 2	Israel	3.4	522	Probably similar to Gabriel 1	33	0.7 Mach	
Gabriel 3	Israel	3.8	558	Active radar	40	0.7 Mach	
Sea Killer 2	Italy	4.7	300	Beam riding. Sea-skimmer	25	0.8 Mach	Iranian Navy only, but also used as helicopter-to-ship missile
Penguin 1	Norway	3.0	330	Infra-red homing	26	0.7 Mach	
Penguin 2	Norway	3.0	340	Similar to Penguin 1	28	0.7 Mach	
RB O8A	Sweden	5.73	1225	Active radar homing	200?	0.85 Mach	Used for coast defence. Obsolescent
RBS 15	Sweden	4.35	265	Active radar. Sea skimmer	100	0.9 Mach	Under development for Spica class fast attack craft
SS–N–2 A/B/C	USSR	6.4	2315	Active radar or infra-red homing	45 to 80	0.9 Mach	Fitted in *Osa* fast attack craft. *Kashin* and *Kildin* destroyers and *Tarantul* corvettes
SS–N–3	USSR	11.0	4500	Mid-course command update and active radar homing	450+	1.4 Mach	Both surface ships and submarines

TABLE 1 — PRINCIPAL-TO-SHIP MISSILES (*continued*)

Name	Country	Length (metres)	Launch weight (kg)	Guidance	Range (km)	Speed	Remarks
SS–N–9	USSR	9.15	Large	Mid-course command update and active radar homing	110	0.9 Mach	Nanuchka and Sarancha class
SS–N–12	USSR	?	Large	Active radar homing	450	2.5 Mach	Both surface ships and submarines. Successor to SS–N–3
SS–N–14	USSR	7.6	Large	Radio command	55	0.9 Mach	Anti-submarine torpedo carrying missile with probable anti-ship capability
SS–N–19	USSR	?	Large	Probably active radar	500	2 Mach	Fitted in *Kirov* battlecruiser and *Oscar* submarine
SS–N–22	USSR	?	?	?	220	?	New missile in *Sovremenny* and some Tarantul class. An improvement on SS–N–9
Standard ARM	USA	4.57	616	Anti-radar	65	2 Mach	
Harpoon	USA	4.57	668	Active radar homing Sea-skimmer with terminal climb and bunt	90	0.9 Mach	Fitted in USN and many other navies
Tomahawk	USA	6.25	Approx 1100	Active radar homing	450	Subsonic	Over 3000 kms as a cruise missile

TABLE 2 — PRINCIPAL SUBMARINE-TO-SHIP MISSILES

Name	Country	Length (metres)	Launch weight (kg)	Guidance	Range (km)	Speed	Remarks
Exocet SM 39	France	?	?	Probably similar to Exocet MM 40 using active radar homing	?	?	Development of Exocet
SS-N-3	USSR	11.0	4500	Mid-course command update and active radar homing	450	1.5 Mach	Surface launch only
SS-N-7	USSR	6.7	?	Probable active radar homing	55	0.9 Mach	Submerged launch from *Charlie* class submarines
SS-N-9	USSR	9.1	?	Active radar	110	0.9 Mach	Probably in *Papa* class
SS-N-12	USSR	?	Large	Probably similar to SS-N-3	450	2.5 Mach	Surface ships also. Successor to SS-N-3
SS-N-19	USSR	?	Large	Probably active radar	500	2 Mach	Fitted in *Kirov* battlecruiser and *Oscar* submarine
Harpoon	USA	6.40	1069	Active radar homing Sea-skimmer with terminal climb and bunt	110	0.9 Mach	Fitting in USN and RN
SS-N-21	USSR	?	?	?	?	?	Nuclear headed cruise missile

TABLE 3 — PRINCIPAL SUBMARINE-TO-SUBMARINE MISSILES

Name	Country	Length (metres)	Launch weight (kg)	Guidance	Range (km)	Speed	Remarks
SS-N-15	USSR	?	?	?	45	?	Probable nuclear warhead
Subroc	USA	6.40	1786	Inertial pre-programmed	46–55	1 + Mach	Nuclear warhead. Operational 1965 and successor being considered

TABLE 4 — PRINCIPAL SHIP-TO-SUBMARINE MISSILES

Name	Country	Length (metres)	Launch weight (kg)	Guidance	Range (km)	Speed	Remarks
Ikara	Australia	3.45	?	Radio command	24	?	Carries homing torpedo. Modified versions in service in RN and Brazilian navy
Malafon Mk 2	France	5.7	1473	Radio command	15	0.7 Mach	Carries homing torpedo. Obsolete
SUW–N–1	USSR	?	?	Inertial	29	?	Probable nuclear warhead
SS–N–14	USSR	7.6	?	?	55	0.9 Mach	Carries homing torpedo
Asroc	USA	4.7	435	Ballistic	10	?	Carries Mk 46 homing torpedo or nuclear depth bomb

TABLE 5 — PRINCIPAL SURFACE-TO-AIR MISSILES

Name	Country	Length (metres)	Launch weight (kg)	Guidance	Range (km)	Speed	Remarks
Masurca Mk 2	France	8.60	1846	Semi-active radar	45	2.5 Mach	In Colbert. Suffren and Duquesne
Crotale Navale	France	2.90	84	Command to line of sight	18	1.2 Mach approx	
Aspide	Italy	Italian development of the Sea Sparrow missile to fire from the Albatros shipboard system					
SA-N-1 (Goa)	USSR	6.71	?	Radio command	30	1+ Mach	Adaptation of army weapon Obsolescent.
SA-N-2 (Guideline)	USSR	10.58	2268	Radio command	45	1+ Mach	Adaptation of army weapon Non-operational.
SA-N-3 (Goblet)	USSR	6.1	544	Radio command	55	1+ Mach	Adaptation of army weapon
SA-N-4	USSR	3.2	?	Radio command to line of sight	15	2.0 Mach	Widely fitted in USSR navy
SA-N-5	USSR	1.5	14.5	Infra-red	10	1.5 Mach?	Naval adaptation of army SA-7
SA-N-6	USSR	7.0	?	Active radar homing	75+	3.0 Mach	Kirov and Krasina class ships
SA-N-7	USSR	?	?	?	27	3.0 Mach	New system in *Sovremenmy*
SA-N-8	USSR	?	?	?	?	?	Vertical launch short range
Seacat	UK	1.49	62.5	Radio command	6	Subsonic	
Seaslug Mk 2	UK	6.0	1965	Beam riding	45+	2+ Mach	
Sea Dart	UK	4.36	549	Semi-active radar homing	70+	?	
Seawolf	UK	1.98	80	Command to radar line of sight	5+	2+ Mach	
Standard SM-1 (MR)	USA	4.4	590	Semi-active radar homing	20+	2+ Mach	Tartar replacement
Standard SM-1 (ER)	USA	8.0	1318	Semi-active radar homing	55+	2.5+ Mach	Terrier replacement
Standard SM-2 (MR)	USA	?	?	Semi-active radar homing with mid-course command guidance	20+	2? Mach	Designed for Aegis system

TABLE 6 — NATO'S PRINCIPAL TACTICAL NUCLEAR MISSILES

Missile	Numbers deployed in Europe	Range in Miles	Warhead	Remarks
Pershing	90	400	Nuclear or HE	72 deployed by W. Germany. 18 by US. More accurate Pershing II under development with much longer range
Lance	60+	75	Nuclear or HE	36 deployed by US. Remainder by UK, Netherlands, Belgium, W. Germany
Pluton	100	France 75	Nuclear	In service in France

TABLE 7 — WARSAW PACTS PRINCIPAL TACTICAL NUCLEAR MISSILES

Missile	Total numbers	Range in miles	Warhead	Remarks
Frog (various Marks)	600	45	Nuclear or HE	Unguided rocket. Was used by Egypt and Syria in Yom Kippur war
Scud A	200	85	Nuclear or HE	Unguided rocket with radio command for ordering motor cut off
Scud B		170	Nuclear or HE	Inertially guided. There may be more than one type of Scud B
Scaleboard	100?	500	Nuclear	Reputed to carry a 1 MT warhead. Inertially guided

Note. Frog, Scud and Scaleboard are being replaced by new SSM with greater ranges — SS-21, SS-22 and SS-23.

TABLE 8 — MODERN BATTLE TANKS

Model	Country	In service with	Max speed (km/hr)	Max range (km)	Main Armament (mm)	Year Produced
M60 A1	USA	USA Italy Australia Iran Austria Israel	48.3	449	105	1961
M60 A3	USA	USA Israel Saudi Arabia Egypt	48.3	480	105	1978
M48 A2	USA	USA Germany Greece Norway Turkey Spain Jordan Taiwan S. Korea Pakistan	51.5	257	90	1952
M48 A3	USA	USA Israel Vietnam	51.5	464	90	1964
M48 A5	USA	Pakistan S. Korea Greece Iran Turkey Thailand Lebanon	42.2	449	105	1975
XK-1	USA	S. Korea	?	?	105	1983
M1 Abrams	USA	USA	72	450	105	1980
Leopard 1	W. Germany	W. Germany Australia Belgium Canada Denmark Italy Netherlands Norway Turkey	65	580	105	1965
Leopard 2	W. Germany	W. Germany Netherlands Switzerland	72	550	120	1980
Centurion	UK	Egypt Australia Denmark Israel Canada Iraq India	34.6	185	105	1948-60 (Different marks)

TABLE 8 — MODERN BATTLE TANKS *contd.*

Model	Country	In service with	Max speed (km/hr)	Max range (km)	Main Armament (mm)	Year Produced
Centurion *contd.*		Jordan				
		Kuwait				
		Lebanon				
		Netherlands				
		Somalia				
		Switzerland				
		Sweden				
		S. Africa				
Chieftain	UK	UK	48	500	120	1965
		Iran				
		Kuwait				
Chieftain 900	UK	—	72	?	120	1982
Khalid	UK	Jordan	48	500	120	1980
Challenger	UK	UK	60	?	129	1984
Vickers Mk 1	UK	India	53.5	483	105	1963
		Kuwait				
Vijayanta	India	India	53.5	483	105	1965
				Indian Vickers Mk 1 derivative		
Vickers Mk 3	UK	Kenya	50	600	105	1978
		Nigeria				
Vickers Valiant	UK	—	60	600	105/120	1980
AMX 30	France	France	64.4	600	105	1966
		Greece				
		Iraq				
		Lebanon				
		Libya				
		Peru				
		Qatar				
		Saudi Arabia				
		Spain				
		Venezuela				
AMX 32	France	—	65	520	105/120	1981
AMX-40	France	—	?	?	120	1983
OF-40	Italy	UAE	65	600	105	1981
Strv 103B ('S-tank')	Sweden	Sweden	50	390	105	1967
Pz 61	Switzerland	Switzerland	50	300	105	1965
Pz 68	Switzerland	Switzerland	55	300	105	1971
Merkava Mk 1	Israel	Israel	?	?	105	1979
Merkava Mk 2	Israel	Israel	?	?	105	1983
TAM	Argentina	Argentina	75	550	105	1979
		Peru				
T54/55	USSR	USSR	50	620	100	1949
		Poland				
		CSSR				
		E. Germany				
		Cuba				
		Egypt				
		Algeria				
		Finland				

TABLE 8 — MODERN BATTLE TANKS *contd.*

Model	Country	In service with	Max speed (km/hr)	Max range (km)	Main Armament (mm)	Year Produced
T54/55 *contd.*		Syria China Romania India Israel Hungary N. Korea Yugoslavia Morocco Zimbabwe				
T62	USSR	USSR Bulgaria CSSR E. Germany Egypt Poland Romania Syria	48	400	115 (smooth bore)	1961
T64	USSR	USSR Algeria Bulgaria CSSR E. Germany Hungary India Iraq Libya Poland Romania Syria	50 probably	480 (road) 300 (terrain)	initially 115 later 125 (smooth bore)	1967
SMT 1981/1	USSR	USSR	? (T-64 variant)	?	125 (smooth bore)	1981
T-72	USSR	USSR Poland CSSR Syria India	60	480 (road) 300 (terrain)	125 (smooth bore)	1971
SMT 1980/1	USSR	USSR NSWP	? (T-72 variant)	?	125 (smooth bore)	1980
SMT 1981/3	USSR	USSR	? (T-72 variant)	?	125 (smooth bore)	1981
T59	PRC	PRC	50	620	100	late 1950s
T69	PRC	PRC Iraq (?)	50	620	105/106 (smooth bore)	late 1960s

TABLE 9 — WESTERN ANTI-TANK MISSILES

Missile	Country	Description	Max range (m)
Vehicle or Ground Mounted			
Harpon	France	Wire guided using semi-auto IR. Vehicle or helicopter mounted. In service	3,000
SS11 B1	France	Wire guided. Vehicle or helicopter mounted. In service	3,000
SS12	France	Wire guided using semi-auto IR. Vehicle or helicopter mounted. Larger warhead than SS11. In service	6,000
HOT	France, Germany	Wire guided using semi-auto IR. Vehicle or helicopter mounted. In service	4,000
Shillelagh	USA	Gun launched. IR command guidance. Vehicle or helicopter mounted. In service	5,200
TOW	USA	Wire guided using semi-auto IR. Vehicle or helicopter or ground mounted. In service in many countries	3,750
Hellfire	USA	Fire and forget missile. Laser guided. Vehicle, helicopter or ground mounted Under development	?
Swingfire	Britain	Wire guided. Vehicle or ground mounted. In service	4,000
Man portable			
Vigilant	Britain	One man, wire guided, ground launched. In service in many countries	1,375
Bantam	Sweden	One man, wire guided, ground launched. Can be mounted in vehicles or helicopters. In service	2,000
Cobra	Germany	One man, wire guided, launched directly off the ground. In service	2,000
Mamba	Germany	Similar to Cobra but improved performance. In service	2,000
Milan	France, Germany	One or two men, wire guided, using semi-auto IR. Ground tripod or shoulder launched. In service	2,000
Mosquito	Italy	One man, wire guided, ground launched. In service	2,300
Sparviero	Italy	One man, IR guidance. Ground launched. Under development	3,000
Dragon	USA	One man, wire guided, shoulder launched. In service	1,000
RBS-56	Sweden	Two man, wire guided, top attack. Under development	2,000

TABLE 10 — PRINCIPAL TACTICAL GUIDED AIR TO SURFACE WEAPONS

Weapons	Country	Guidance	Range	Remarks
Bullpup	US	Radio Command	11 km	Two versions A and B. A is in use in USN and many NATO nations. B is larger and has a range of 17 km
Maverick	US	TV self guidance	22.5 km	For use against hardpoint targets. In service. IR homer in production. Laser homer under development
Shrike	US	Anti-radiation homing	16 km	For use against ground radars. In service
Standard	US	Anti-radiation homing	25 km +	For use against SAM radars. In service
HARM	US	Anti-radiation homing	18 km	Under development. Homes even if radar switched off
Harpoon	US	Active radar homing	90 km + (?)	Air launched version of ship-to-ship missile. Under development
Walleye	US	TV	12? km	Unpowered glide bomb. In service
Hobos	US	The name given to all unpowered glide bombs guided by TV or by lasers. Many are being developed under the PAVEWAY programme		
TOW	US	Described under Table 9		
Hellfire	US	Described under Table 9		
Sea Skua	Britain	Semi-active radar homing	20? km (?)	For use by helicopters against fast missile boats
Kormoran	Germany	Inertial Nav. Active radar or passive radar homing	37 km	Primarily an anti-ship missile. In production
HOT	France, Germany	Described under Table 9		
Penguin	Norway	IR homing	12–16 km	Air launched version of ship-to-ship missile. Under development
Martel	Britain and France	Two types — anti-radiation homing and TV guidance	30 km +	In service in Britain and France
Sea Eagle	Britain	Active radar guidance	?	Anti-ship missile. Under development
AS12	France	Wire guidance with optical tracking	6 km	In service
AS20	France	Radio command with optical tracking	8 km	In service in many countries
KAM 9	Japan	Wire guidance with optical tracking	4 km	
AS30	France	Radio command with either optical or auto IR tracking	10 km	Missiles can be launched by one aircraft and controlled by another. In service in many countries

TABLE 10 — *continued*

Weapons	Country	Guidance	Range	Remarks
AM39	France	Active radar homing	50–70 km	Air launched version of Exocet ship-to-ship missile. Under development
Marte	Italy	Radio command with radar/ optical tracking	25 km	Air launched version of Sea Killer ship-to-ship missile. Under development
Otomat	Italy	Active radar homing	40 km	Air launched version of ship-to-ship missile
RbO4E	Sweden	Active radar	20 km	In service in Swedish Air Force
RbO5	Sweden	Radio command	9 km?	In service in Swedish Air Force
Kennel (AS-1)	USSR	Beam riding or radio command with active radar or anti-radiation terminal homing	90 km	Probably for use against shipping
Kipper (AS-2)	USSR	Probably radio commanded with active terminal housing	180–210 km	Probably for use against shipping. Carried by Badger
Kangaroo (AS-3)	USSR	Command guidance, probably with terminal radar homing	Estimates vary between 185 and 650 km	Carried by the Bear bomber. Probably now obsolescent
Kitchen (AS-4)	USSR	Probably inertial Nav with terminal radar homing	300 km	Carried by Blinder, Backfire, Bear
Kelt (AS-5)	USSR	Active radar	180 km	Probably for use against shipping. Carried by Badger
Kingfish (AS-6)	USSR	Probably inertial and active terminal homing	200 km	Fitted in the Backfire bomber and Badger
Kerry (AS-7)	USSR	Nav with terminal radar homing	10 km	Fitted in the Su-19 Fencer fighter-bomber
AS 9	USSR	Passive radar seeker	90 km	
AS 15TT	France	Radar tracking, radio altimeter	15 km +	For use by helicopter against AS 15, has radio command guidance with IR or optical tracking
AS 10	USSR	Electro-optical	10–40 km	?

TABLE 11 — AIR-TO-AIR MISSILES

Missile	Country	Homing	Range	Remarks
R530	France	A semi-active radar or IR	18 km	In service in France and other countries
Super 530	France	Semi-active radar	35 km	Higher speed and longer range. Not yet in service
Magic (R550)	France	IR	18 km	A close-combat weapon. In service in France and other countries
Shafrir	Israel	IR	5 km	In service in Israel and perhaps two other countries
Aspide	Italy	Semi-active radar	50–100 km	Coming into service in Italy. Can also be used in the ship-to-air and ground-to-air role
AAM-1	Japan	IR	7 km	In service
Firestreak	Britain	IR	1.2–8 km	In service with RAF and other air forces
Red Top	Britain	IR	12 km	In service with RAF
Sky Flash	Britain	Semi-active radar	50 km	In service with RAF and Swedish Air Force
Falcon	US	Semi-active radar or IR	9–11 km	A number of different versions available
Genie	US	Unguided	9.6 km	Nuclear warhead. In service
Phoenix	US	Semi-active radar with terminal active radar homing	200 km	Mainly used by USN
Sidewinder	US	IR	3–7 km	A number of different versions, now all IR homing, are in service

TABLE 11 — *continued*

Missile	Country	Homing	Range	Remarks
Sparrow	US	Semi-active radar	50 km	In service in USAF, RAF and various NATO air forces
Alkali (AA-1)	USSR	Semi-active radar	6–8 km	Used by tactical air force and Warpac
Anab (AA-3)	USSR	Either a SA radar head or an IR head can be fitted	16 km	Used only by PVO-Strany
Ash (AA-5)	USSR	Either a SA radar or IR can be fitted	30 km	Fitted in Fiddler long-range aircraft. Two versions. Only in PVO-Strany
Atoll (AA-2)	USSR	IR	5–7 km	Similar to the US Sidewinder. Extensive use throughout Warpac
Awl	USSR	Believed that either a SA radar head or an IR head can be fitted	Medium?	Fitted with MiG 23
Acrid (AA-6)	USSR	Either SA radar or IR	22–50 km	Fitted to Foxbat in PVO-Strany
Apex (AA-7)	USSR	Either a SA radar or IR	15–33 km	
Aphid (AA-8)	USSR	IR	7–15 km	Close-combat weapon

Table 12 — Principal Fighter/Interceptors in NATO Europe

Aircraft	Type	Engines	Max. speed	Main air-to-air weapons	Remarks
Lightning	Single-seat fighter	2 × 7,420 kg RR Avon 301 turbojets	Over Mach 2	2 Red Top (or Firestreak) missiles 48 rockets	In service with RAF
Phanton II F4E	Two-seat interceptor tactical interdictor	2 × 8,120 kg GE J79-GE 17 turbojets	Mach 2.4	4 Sparrow III and 4 Sidewinders	In service with RAF and USAF
Starfighter F104G	Single-seat interceptor, tactical strike	1 × 7,165 kg GE J79-GE 11A turbojet	Mach 2.2	Up to 4 Sidewinders	In Service with German, Dutch, Danish, Italian, Belgian Air Forces
Mirage V	Single-seat fighter-bomber	1 × 6,200 SNECMA Atar 9C turbojet	Mach 2.1	2 Sidewinders	In service with Belgian Air Force
Freedom F5	Single-seat lightweight fighter	2 × 1,850 kg GE J85-GE 13 turbojets	Mach 1.4	Up to 4 Sidewinders 2 × 20 mm guns	In service with Dutch Air Force
F15	Single-seat air superiority fighter	2 × 11,340 kg Pratt & Whitney F100-PW-100 afterburning turbo-fans	Mach 2.5 +	Up to 4 Sidewinders 4 Sparrow II	In service with USAF
F16	Single-seat advanced combat fighter	1 × 11,340 kg Pratt & Whitney F100-PW-100 afterburning turbo-fans	Mach 2 +	2 Sidewinders	Coming into service USAF and in the Air Force of Belgium, Denmark. The Netherlands and Norway
Tornado F2	Two seat interceptor	2 × 6,805 kg Turbo Union RB199 turbojet	Mach 2 +	8 Skyflash or Sidewinder	To come into service with RAF
F14	Two seat interceptor	2 × 9,480 Pratt & Whitney TF 30-P412A	Mach 2.4	6 Sparrow, Sidewinder Phoenix	In service with US Navy
Mirage F1	Single seat interceptor	1 × 7,214 Atar 9K50	Mach 2.2	2 R.530, Super 530, Magic Sidewinder	In service with France, Spain Greece
Mirage B III C	Single seat interceptor	1 × 6,000 kg Atar 9 C	Mach 2.2	2 R.530, Sidewinder	In service with France

TABLE 13 — PRINCIPAL TACTICAL SURFACE-TO-AIR MISSILES

Missile	Country	Guidance	Range	Remarks
		LONG AND MEDIUM RANGE		
Nike/Hercules	US	Command	140 km +	Main high-level air defence missile in Europe
Hawk	US	Semi-active radar	35 km	Main medium and low-level air defence missile in Europe
Improved Hawk	US	Semi-active	35 km	Improved data processing and performance against low-level aircraft
Sparrow III	US	Semi-active radar	40 km	Used in other nations systems such as the Italian Spada. Not yet in service
Patriot	US	Command and semi-active radar	Long	Under development to replace Nike and Hawk
Bloodhound II	Britain	Semi-active radar	80 km +	Used by RAF for defence of airfields in Germany and the UK. Also in Switzerland and Singapore
Gainful (SAM6)	USSR	Command	30 km	Used by Egyptians in latest Middle East war. Semi-active radar homing
Ganef (SAM4)	USSR	Command	70 km	In service with Russia
Goa (SAM3)	USSR	Semi-active radar	30 km	In service in Soviet Army and Navy
Guideline (SAM2)	USSR	Command	50 km	Used by Egyptians in latest Middle East war

TABLE 13 — *continued*

Missile	Country	Guidance	Range	Remarks
		CLOSE RANGE		
Crotale	France	Command IR missile gathering	8.5 km	In service in France and as Cactus in S. Africa and as Shahine in Saudi Arabia
Roland II	France, Germany	Command with auto radar aiming	6 km	In service in France, Germany, Brazil, Norway, USA
Indigo	Italy	Beam riding or command. Optical or IR tracking	10 km	In service in Italian Army
Rapier	Britain	Command with optical or radar tracking	5.5 km	In service in British Army. Also sold in Iran, Abu Dhabi, Oman, Australia, Zambia
Spada	Italy	Command, with auto radar homing	100 km	In fixed and mobile forms. In service with Italian Air Force
Tigercat	Britain	Command with optical tracking	4 km	In limited service with overseas air forces
Chaparral	US	IR homing	4 km?	In service in US Army. Uses a modified Sidewinder missile
Redeye	US	IR homing	3 km	Shoulder launched. In service
Stinger	US	IR homing	?	Successor to Redeye. Production begun 1981
Saber	US	Laser-tracking	3 km	Under development

TABLE 13 — *continued*

Missile	Country	Guidance	Range	Remarks
Blowpipe	Britain	Command with optical tracking	3 km?	Shoulder launched but also fitted in vehicles, ships and submarines. In service with the British Army
RBS70	Sweden	Laser beam riding	5 km	Tripod launched
Grail (SAM7)	USSR	IR homing	3.5 km	Used with success by the Egyptians in last Middle East war. Shoulder, ground or vehicle launched
Gecko (SAM8)	USSR	Command	10 km	Vehicle launched. 4 Missiles to each vehicle
Gaskin (SAM9)	USSR	IR homing	6 km	Vehicle launched. 4 Missiles to each vehicle. Larger version of SAM7

Part IV

Defence Literature of the Year

RICHARD TUBB, ALA

A SELECTION of titles in the field of defence studies published during the last 12 months. The works are listed under broad subject headings, bringing together material dealing with specific topics, and in some cases, various aspects of defence in a particular geographical area.

AFGHANISTAN

GALL, SANDY, *Behind Afghan Lines: An Afghan Journal,* (Sidgwick and Jackson, London, 1983), £8.95

HYMAN, ANTHONY, *Afghanistan Under Soviet Domination, 1964–83* (Macmillan, London, 1984), £20.00 (hardback); £7.95 (paperback)

TAPPER, R (Ed), *A Conflict of Tribe and State in Iran and Afghanistan,* (Croom Helm, London, 1983), £19.95

AFRICA

ARLINGHAUS, B E, *Arms for Africa: Military Assistance and Foreign Policy,* (Lexington Books, Lexington, Mass, 1983), £21.45

EBINGER, CHARLES KURTZ, *Foreign Intervention in Civil War: The Politics and Conflict of the Angola Conflict* (Westview Press, Boulder, Colorado, 1983), £21.00

GAVSHON, ARTHUR, *Crisis in Africa: Battleground of East and West,* (Westview Press, Boulder, Colorado, 1983), £26.00

GELDENHUYS, DEON and GUTTERIDGE, WILLIAM, *Instability and Conflict in Southern Africa: South Africa's Role in Regional Security,* (ISC, London, 1983), £3.50

JASTER, R S, *A Regional Security Role for Africa's Front Line States: Experience and Prospects,* (IISS, London, 1983), £2.50. (Adelphi Paper 180)

KITCHEN, H, *US Interest in Africa,* (Praeger, Washington DC, 1983), $6.95

MCCARTHY, MICHAEL, *Dark Continent: Africa as seen by Americans,* (Greenwood Press, Westport, Connecticut/London, 1983), £24.75. (Contributions in Afro-American Studies.)

AIR STRATEGY

BEAVER, PAUL, *Carrier Air Operations Since 1945,* (Arms and Armour Press, London, 1983), £3.95

GUNSTON, BILL and SPICK, MIKE, *Modern Air Combat,* (Salamander, London, 1983), £9.95

ARMS CONTROL AND DISARMAMENT

BARBER, Ed, *Peace Moves: Nuclear Protest in the 1980s,* (Chatto and Windus, London, 1984), £4.95

COLE, PAUL M, and TAYLOR, WILLIAM J, *The Nuclear Freeze Debate: Arms Control Issues for the 1980s,* (Westview Press, Boulder, Colorado, 1984), £14.75

DAHLITZ, JULIE, *Nuclear Arms Control: With Effective International Agreements,* (Allen and Unwin, London, 1984), £15.00 (hardback); £4.95 (paperback)

DYSON, FREEMAN, *Weapons and Hope,* (Harper and Row, New York, 1984), £10.95

RUSSETT, BRUCE, *Prisoners of Insecurity: Nuclear Deterrence, the Arms Race and Arms Control,* (W H Freeman, London, 1983), £12.95 (hardback); £6.50 (paperback)

SIPRI Yearbook 1983, (Taylor and Francis, London, 1983), £26.00

WALLIS, JIM, (Ed), *Peace Makers: Christian Voices from the New Abolitionist Movement.* (Harper and Row, New York, 1983), £3.95

WESTON, BURNS H, (Ed), *Toward Nuclear Disarmament and Global Security: A Search for Alternatives,* (Westview Press, Boulder, Colorado, 1984), £26.00 (hardback); £13.00 (paperback)

AUSTRALIA

ALDRED, JENNIFER and WILKES, JOHN, *Fractured Federation? Australia in the 1980s,* (Allen and Unwin (Australia), 1983), £15.00

PHILLIPS, DENNIS H, *Cold War Two and Australia,* (Allen and Unwin (Australia), 1983), £12.50

BIOGRAPHY

HEIKAL, M, *Autumn of Fury: The Assassination of Sadat,* (Andre Deutsch, London, 1983), £10.95

LINKLATER, MAGNUS and HILTON, ISABEL, *Hitler's Legacy: Klaus Barbie and the Neo Fascists,* (Hodder and Stoughton, London, 1984), £9.95

MEDVEDEV, ZHORES A, *Andropov,* (Blackwell, Oxford, 1983), £7.50

MARSHALL-CORNWALL, GEN. SIR JAMES, *Wars and Rumours of Wars: A Memoir,* (Leo Cooper, London, 1984), £12.95

SOLOVYOV, VLADIMIR, and KLEPIKOVA, ELENA, *Yuri Andropov: A Secret Passage to the Kremlin,* (Robert Hale, London, 1984), £11.50

STEELE, JONATHAN and ABRAHAM, ERIC, *Andropov in Power,* (Martin Robertson, Oxford), 1983, £8.95

THE CARIBBEAN

AMBURSLEY, F and COHEN, R, (Eds), *Crisis in the Caribbean,* (Heinemann, London, 1983), £6.95

CHEMICAL AND BIOLOGICAL WARFARE

EVANS, GRANT, *Yellow Rainmakers: Are the Soviets using Chemical Weapons in South-East Asia?* (Verso Editions, 1983), £15.00 (hardback); £3.95 (paperback)

MILLER, FRANK H and PAXSON, PETER O, *Chemical Defense, Environmental Control Systems Study,* (Society of Automotive Engineers, Warrendale, Penn., 1982), $2.25

CIVIL DEFENCE

KERR, THOMAS J, *Civil Defense in the United States: Bandaid for a Holocaust,* (Westview Press, Boulder, Colorado, 1983), £20.00

NUCLEAR PROTECTION ADVISORY GROUP AND SWISS FEDERAL OFFICE FOR CIVIL DEFENCE, *Makeshift Shelters: Technical Notes on their Construction,* (Octagon, London, 1983), £8.50

OPENSHAW, STAN, (et al), *Doomsday: Britain after Nuclear Attack,* (Basil Blackwell, Oxford, 1983), £15.50 (hardback); £4.95 (paperback)

THIFFAULT, MARK, *Complete Survival Guide,* (Arms and Armour Press, London, 1983), £7.00

COMPUTERS: MILITARY APPLICATIONS

WARD, J W D and TURNER, G N, *Military Data Processing and Microcomputers,* (Brassey's, Oxford, 1982), £13.00 (hardback); £6.50 (paperback)

DEFENCE FORCES: GENERAL

HELLER, MARK A (and others), *The Middle East Military Balance, 1983,* (Westview Press, Boulder, Colorado, 1983), £26.00

INTERNATIONAL INSTITUTE OF STRATEGIC STUDIES, *Military Balance, 1983/84,* (IISS, London, 1983), £7.25

DEFENCE: AIR

GANDER, TERRY, *Encyclopaedia of the Modern Air Force,* (Patrick Stephens, Cambridge, 1984), £18.95

DEFENCE FORCES: ARMY

ASCOLI, DAVID, *A Companion to the British Army, 1660–1983,* (Harrap, London, 1983), £14.50

CARVER, FIELD MARSHAL LORD MICHAEL, *The Seven Ages of the British Army,* (Weidenfeld and Nicolson, London, 1984), £12.95

FARWELL, BYRON, *The Gurkhas,* (Allen Lane, London, 1984), £12.50

GABRIEL, RICHARD, *Fighting Armies, Volumes 1–3,* (All Published by Greenwood Press, Westport, Conn), at £30.95, *Volume 1, Nato and the Warsaw Pact: A Combat Assessment, Volume 2, Antagonists in the Middle East: A Combat Assessment, Volume 3, Non-Aligned, Third World, and Other Ground Forces*

GANDER, T G, *Britain's Armed Forces Today 3: British Army of the Rhine,* (Ian Allan, Shepperton, 1984), £2.95

HACKETT, GEN SIR JOHN, *The Profession of Arms,* (Sidgwick and Jackson, London, 1983), £12.95 (hardback); NEL paperback, £2.50

KEEGAN, JOHN, *World Armies,* (Second Edition), (Macmillan, London, 1983), £45.00

O'NEILL, RICHARD, (Ed), *An Illustrated Guide to the Modern US Army,* (Salamander, London, 1984), £3.95

PITT, BARRIE, *SBS (Special Boat Squadron): The Story of the SBS in the Mediterranean,* (Century, London, 1983), £8.95

SIMPSON, CHARLES M, *Inside the Green Berets: The First Thirty Years,* (Arms and Armour Press, London, 1983), £10.95

DEFENCE FORCES: NAVAL

BEAVER, PAUL, *Britain's Armed Forces Today 2: Fleet Command,* (Ian Allan, Shepperton, 1984), £2.95

BROWN, D K, *A Century of Naval Construction: The History of the Royal Corps of Naval Constructors, 1883–1983,* (Conway Maritime Press, London, 1983), £26.00

DEFENCE MANAGEMENT AND PROCUREMENT

BROGAN, PATRICK and ZARCA, ALBERT, *Deadly Business: The Story of Sam Cummings, the World's Greatest Arms Dealer,* (Michael Joseph, London, 1984), £9.95

DEGRASSE, ROBERT W JNR, *Military Expansion, Economic Decline: The Impact of Military Spending on US Economic Performance,* (Greenwood Press, London, 1983), £21.95 (hardback), £10.50 (paperback)

HOOPER, ROBERT A and HOLLAND, LAUREN H, *The MX Decision: A New Decision in Weapons Procurement Policy?* (Westview Press, Boulder, Colorado, 1984), £17.00

KENNEDY, GAVIN, *Defence Economics,* (Duckworth, London, 1983), £19.50

KRULAK, LT. GEN V H, *Organisation for National Security,* (US Strategic Institute, Washington DC, 1983), £6.50

SHEEHAN, M, *The Arms Race,* (Martin Robertson, Oxford, 1983), £16.50

SORLEY, LEWIS, *Arms Transfers Under Nixon: A Policy Analysis,* (University Press of Kentucky, 1983), £17.60

DEFENCE POLICY

BALL, D, *Targeting for Strategic Deterrence,* (IISS, London, 1983), (Adelphi Paper 185), £2.50

BARNABY, JONATHAN, *Future War,* (Michael Joseph, London, 1983), £9.95

BAYLIS, JOHN, (Ed), *Anglo-American Defence Relations, 1939–1984: The Special Relationship* (Second Edition), (Macmillan, London, 1984) £25.00 (hardback): £7.95 (paperback)

BERTRAM, CHRISTOPH (Ed), *Defence and Consensus: The Domestic*

Aspects of Western Security, (IISS/Macmillan, London, 1984), £20.00

BETTS, RICHARD K, *Surprise Attack: Lessons for Defence Planning,* (Blackwell, Oxford, 1983), £17.50 (hardback), £6.50 (paperback)

BLECHMAN, BARRY M, and LUTTWAK, EDWARD N, *International Security Yearbook, 1983–84* (IISS/Macmillan, London, 1984), £17.50 (hardback), £6.95 (paperback)

CAPITANCHIK, DAVID and EICHENBERG, RICHARD, *Defence and Public Opinion,* (RIIA, London, 1983), £4.95

CHARTERS, D, (and others), *No Substitute for Peace* (Second Edition), (University of New Brunswick, Frederickton, 1983), $2.00

CLOSE, GEN R, *Time for Action,* (Brassey's, Oxford, 1983), £13.50 (hardback); £7.20 (paperback)

DEITCHMAN, SEYMOUR J, *Military Power and the Advance of Technology: General Purpose Military Forces for the 1980s and Beyond,* (Westview Press, Boulder, Colorado, 1983), £24.00 (hardback), £11.00 (paperback)

GRAHAM, D O, *High Frontier: A New National Strategy* (Washington DC, High Frontier, 1982), $15.00

HAFFA, ROBERT P JNR, *The Half War: Planning US Rapid Deployment Forces to Meet a Limited Contingency, 1960–1983,* (Westview Press, Boulder, Colorado, 1983), £21.75

INTERNATIONAL INSTITUTE FOR STRATEGIC STUDIES, *Military Survey, 1983/84,* (IISS, London, 1983), £5.00

KARSTEN, PETER (and others), *Military Threats: A Historical Analysis of the Determinants of Success,* (Greenwood Press, London, 1984), £26.95

ROYAL UNITED INSTITUTE FOR DEFENCE STUDIES, *RUSI and Brassey's Defence Yearbook 1984* (RUSI Brassey's, Oxford, 1984), £25.00 (hardback); £9.90 (flexicover)

RYS, STEVEN L, *US Military Power,* (Arms and Armour Press, London, 1984), £8.95

ELECTRONIC WARFARE

STREETLY, M, *World Electronic Warfare,* (Jane's, London, 1983), £9.95

VAN BRUNT, B, *Applied ECM (Electronic Counter Measures) Volume 2* (Dunn Loring/EW Engineering, 1982), £36.15

FALKLAND ISLANDS

DALYELL, TAM, *One Man's Falklands,* (Cecil Woolf, London, 1983), £5.50 (hardback), £1.95 (paperback)

HOFFMAN, FRITZ L and MINGS, OLGA, *The Sovereignty in Dispute: The Falklands/Malvinas,* (Westview Press, Boulder, Colorado, 1984), £16.00

FROST, MAJ. GEN. JOHN, *2 Para Falklands: The Battalions at War,* (Buchan and Enright, London, 1983), £7.95

KOBURGER, CHARLES W JNR, *Sea Power in the Falklands,* (Praeger, New York, 1983), £14.95

RICE, DESMOND and GAVSHON, ARTHUR, *The Sinking of the Belgrano,* (Secker and Warburg, London, 1984), £9.95

SMITH, JOHN, *74 Days: An Islander's Diary of the Falklands Occupation,* (Century, London, 1984), £10.95

VILLAR, CAPTAIN ROGER, *Merchant Ships at War: The Falklands Experience,* (Conway Maritime, London, 1984), £9.50

WINCHESTER, SIMON, *Prison Diary, Argentina,* (Hogarth Press, London, 1983) £8.95 (hardback), £3.50 (paperback)

HONG KONG

BONAVIA, DAVID, *Hong Kong 1997,* (Columbus Books, Bromley, 1984), £4.95

INSURGENCY AND TERRORISM

HOBSBAWM, PROF E J, *Revolutionaries,* (Quartet Books, London, 1983), £4.95

LAQUEUR, WALTER, *Guerrilla: A Historical and Critical Study,* (Westview Press, Boulder, Colorado, 1983), £22.50

O'SULLIVAN, N, (Ed), *Revolutionary Theory and Political Reality,* (Wheatsheaf, Brighton, 1983), £18.95

STERLING, CLAIRE, *The Time of the Assassins,* (Angus and Robertson (UK), London, 1984), £7.95

WHEATCROFT, ANDREW, *The World Atlas of Revolutions,* (Hamish Hamilton, London, 1983), £12.95 (hardback), £7.95 (paperback)

INTELLIGENCE SERVICES

BARROW, JOHN, *KGB Today: The Hidden Hand,* (Hodder and Stoughton, London, 1984), £9.95

BLOCH, JONATHAN and FITZGERALD, PAT, *British Intelligence and Covert Action: Operations in Africa and the Middle East from 1945 to the Present,* (Junction Books, London, 1983), £5.95

FREEMANTLE, BRIAN, *CIA,* (Michael Joseph, London, 1983), £9.95

GOLITSYN, ANATOLIY, *New Lies For Old,* (Bodley Head, London, 1984) £12.50

SMITH, BRADLEY F, *The Shadow Warriors: OSS and the Origins of the CIA,* (Andre Deutsch, London, 1983), £18.95

STEVENSON, WILLIAM, *Intrepid's Last Case,* (Michael Joseph, London, 1984), £10.95

INTERNATIONAL AFFAIRS

ARBATOV, GEORGI, *Cold War or Détente? The Soviet Viewpoint,* (Zed Books, London, 1983), £16.95 (hardback), £4.95 (paperback)

BERGESEN, A, (Ed), *Crises in the World System,* (Sage Publications, 1983), £19.50 (hardback), £9.75 (paperback)

BOARDMAN, R and KEELEY, J, *Nuclear Exports and World Politics,* (Macmillan, London, 1983), £20.00

BOYD, ANDREW, *Atlas of World Affairs,* (Methuen, London, 1983), £7.95 (hardback), £3.95 (paperback)

CALVERT, PETER, *Revolution and International Politics,* (Frances Pinter, 1984), £15.00

FOREIGN AND COMMONWEALTH OFFICE. *United Nations in 1982.* (HMSO London, HMSO, 1983), £12.50 (paperback)

HARTMAN, TOM and MITCHELL, JOHN, *A World Atlas of Military History, 1945–1984,* (Secker and Warburg, London, 1984), £12.50

HOLBRAAD, CARSTEN, *Middle Powers in International Politics,* (Macmillan, London, 1984), £25.00

HOPPLE, GERALD (and others), *National Security Forecasting and Management,* (Westview Press, Boulder, Colorado, 1983), £18.75

HULETT, LOUISA SUE, *Decade of Détente: Shifting Definitions and Denouements,* (Eurospan, London, 1982), £17.95 (hardback), £7.95 (paperback)

JONSSON, CHRISTER, *Superpowers: Comparing American and Soviet Foreign Policy,* (Frances Pinter, London, 1984), £18.50

KIDRON, MICHAEL and SMITH, DAN, *War Atlas: Armed Conflict, Armed Peace,* (Heinemann, London, 1983), £9.95

KIM, SAMUEL S, *The Quest for a World Order,* (Westview Press,

Boulder, Colorado, 1984), £33.50 (hardback), £14.00 (paperback)

KRASNER, STEPHEN D (Ed), *International Regimes,* (Cornell University Press, 1983), £8.50

McCAULEY, MARTIN, *Origins of the Cold War,* (Longman, London, 1983), £1.95

PAYNE, KEITH B, *Policy and Doctrine,* (Westview Press, Boulder, Colorado, 1983), £14.75

PORTER, B, *Britain, Europe and the World, 1850–1982: Delusions of Grandeur,* (Allen and Unwin, London, 1983), £10.00

STEELE, JONATHAN, *World Power,* (Michael Joseph, London, 1983), £9.95

THAKUR, RAMESH, *Peacekeeping in Vietnam, Canada, India, Poland and the International Commission,* (University of Alberta Press, Edmonton, 1983), $30.00

WETTEREAU, BRUCE, *The Concise Dictionary of World History,* (Robert Hale, London, 1983), £26.95

JAPAN

AKAO, NOBUTOSHI (Ed), *Japan's Economic Security: Resources as a Factor in Foreign Policy,* (Gower/RIIA, Aldershot, 1983), £16.50

CHAPMAN, J W M (and others), *Japan's Quest for Comprehensive Security: Defence, Diplomacy and Dependence,* (Frances Pinter, London, 1983), £16.50

MARITIME STRATEGY

MULLER, DAVID G JNR, *China as a Maritime Power,* (Westview Press, Boulder, Colorado, 1983), £24.00

POTTER, ELMAR B, (Ed), *Sea Power: A Naval History,* (Naval Institute Press, Maryland, 1982), £13.95

RANFT, BRYAN, and TILL, GEOFFREY, *The Sea in Soviet Strategy,* (Macmillan, London, 1983), £25.00

TILL, GEOFFREY, (Ed), *Maritime Strategy and the Nuclear Age,* (Second Edition), (Macmillan, London, 1984), £20.00 (hardback), £7.95 (paperback)

MECHANISED FORCES

FOSS, CHRISTOPHER F, *Jane's Main Battle Tanks* (Jane's, London, 1983), £9.95

FULLER, JOHN FREDERICK CHARLES, *Armoured Warfare: An Anno-*

tated Edition of Lectures on FSR III (Operations Between Mechanised Forces), (Greenwood Press, London, 1983), £24.50

MIDDLE EAST

CLIFTON, TONY and LEROY, CATHERINE, *God Cried,* (Quartet Books, London, 1983), £15.00

COOLEY, J K, *Libya's Sandstorm,* (Sidgwick and Jackson, London, 1983), £12.95

FREEDMAN, ROBERT O, *The Middle East since Camp David,* (Westview Press, Boulder, Colorado, 1984), £20.75 (hardback), £9.75 (paperback)

GILMOUR, DAVID, *Lebanon: The Fractured Country,* (Martin Robertson, Oxford, 1983), £9.95; Sphere paperback, 1984, £2.95

HERZOG, CHAIM, *The Arab-Israeli Wars: War and Peace in the Middle East from the War of Independence to Lebanon,* (Arms and Armour Press, London, 1984), £14.95

HUREWITZ, J C, *Middle East Politics: The Military Dimension,* (Westview Press Boulder, Colorado, 1983), £23.75

LEVINS, H, *Arab Reach: Secret War Against Israel,* (Sidgwick and Jackson, London, 1983), £9.95

MCCULLIN, DON, *Beirut: A City in Crisis,* (NEL, London, 1983), £9.95

MCGHEE, GEORGE, *Envoy to the Middle World,* (Harper and Row, New York, 1984), £15.95

PARSONS, ANTHONY, *The Pride and the Fall: Iran, 1974–1979,* (Jonathan Cape, London, 1984), £8.95

POLLOCK, D, *The Politics of Pressure: American Arms and Israeli Policy Since the Six Day War,* (Greenwood Press, London, 1982), £26.50

TAHIR-KHELI, S and AYUBI, S, *The Iran-Iraq War: New Weapons, Old Conflicts,* (Praeger, New York, 1983), £24.95

MILITARY AVIATION

ALLWARD, MAURICE, *Postwar Military Aircraft 1: Gloster Javelin,* (Ian Allan, Shepperton, 1983), £7.95

ANDERTON, DAVID A, *Republic F–105 Thunderchief,* (Osprey, London, 1983), £8.95

BEAMONT, R and REED, A, *English Electric Canberra,* (Ian Allan, Shepperton, 1984), £9.95

BRAYBROOK, ROY, *Harrier and Sea Harrier,* (Osprey, London, 1984), £8.95

CHANT, CHRISTOPHER, *Aviation: An Illustrated History,* (Orbis, London, 1983), £12.50

CHARTRES, JOHN, *Modern Combat Aircraft 18: Westland Sea King,* (Ian Allan, Shepperton, 1984), £8.95

GETHING, MICHAEL J, *F-15: The Eagle,* (Salamander, London, 1983), £4.95

GETHING, MICHAEL J, *Harrier,* (Arms and Armour Press, London, 1983), £3.95

GODDEN, JOHN, *Harrier: Ski-Jump to Victory,* (Brassey's Oxford, 1983), £9.95 (hardback); £4.95 (paperback)

GUNSTON, BILL, *An Illustrated Guide to Modern Airborne Missiles,* (Salamander, London, 1983), £3.95

GUNSTON, BILL, *An Illustrated Guide to Spy Planes and Electronic Warfare Aircraft,* (Salamander, London, 1983), £3.95

GUNSTON, BILL, *F-111 Electric Fox,* (Salamander, London, 1983), £4.95

GUNSTON, BILL, *Helicopters of the World,* (Newnes Books, London, 1983), £3.99

GUNSTON, BILL, *Modern Combat Aircraft 13: Harrier,* (New Edition), (Ian Allan, Shepperton, 1984), £7.95

GUNSTON, BILL, *RAF Aircraft Today 1: Phantom,* (Ian Allan, 1984), £4.95

HIRST, MIKE, *Airborne Early Warning: Design, Development and Operations,* (Osprey, London, 1983), £11.95

HORSEMAN, MARTIN, *Aircraft Illustrated Annual 1984,* (Ian Allan, Shepperton, 1983), £3.95

JACKSON, PAUL A, *British and European Combat Aircraft,* (Newnes Books, London, 1983), £3.99

KILDUFF, PETER, *Douglas A-4 Skyhawk,* (Osprey, London, 1983), £8.95

MASON, FRANCIS K, *Phantom: A Legend in its own Time,* (Patrick Stephens, Cambridge, 1984), £9.95

MERSKY, PETER B, *US Marine Corps Aviation: 1912 to the Present,* (Patrick Stephens, Cambridge, 1984), £17.95

MILLER, JAY, *The General Dynamics F-16 Fighting Falcon,* (Austin, Texas, Aerofax, 1982), £9.95

POLMAR, NORMAN, *Russian Bombers,* (Patrick Stephens, Cambridge, 1984), £17.95

PAGE, STEVE, *North American XB-70 Valkyrie,* (Arms and Armour Press, London, 1983), £6.60

RICHARDSON, DOUG, *F-16: The Fighting Falcon,* (Salamander, London, 1983), £4.95

RICHARDSON, DOUG, *An Illustrated Technical Survey of the West's Modern Fighters,* (Salamander, London, 1984), £9.95

RICHARDSON, DOUG, *F-4,* (Salamander, London, 1984), £4.95

SULLIVAN, J, *Skyraider in Action,* (Squadron/Signal Publications, Texas, 1983), £3.50

SWEETMAN, BILL and GOULDING, J, *Harrier,* (Jane's Publishing, London, 1983), £7.95

SWEETMAN, BILL and GOULDING, J, *Phantom,* (Jane's Publishing, London, 1983), £7.95

VICARY, ADRIAN, *Naval Wings: Royal Naval Carrier-Borne Aircraft Since 1916,* (Patrick Stephens, Cambridge, 1984), £7.95

WRAGG, DAVID W, *Helicopters at War,* (Robert Hale, London, 1983), £12.50

MILITARY COMMUNICATIONS

MORRIS, D J, *Communication for Command and Control Systems,* (Pergamon, Oxford, 1983), £12.50

RAGGETT, R J (Ed), *Jane's Military Communications 1984,* (Jane's London, 1984), £59.00

WILLCOX, A M, *Command, Control and Communications,* (Brassey's, Oxford, 1983), £15.00 (hardback); £6.95 (paperback)

MILITARY THOUGHT

ARON, RAYMOND, *Clausewitz: Philosopher of War,* (Routledge, London, 1983), £15.00

VIGOR, PETER H, *Soviet Blitzkrieg Theory,* (Macmillan, London, 1983), £25.00

MISSILE TECHNOLOGY

GREEN, WILLIAM, *A Soviet Nuclear Weapons Policy: A Research Guide,* (Westview Press, Boulder, Colorado, 1984), £19.75

HOLM, HANS-HENRIK and PETERSEN, NIKOLAJ, *The European Missiles Crisis: Nuclear Weapons and Security Policy,* (Frances Pinter, London, 1983), £13.95

SORRELS, C A, *US Cruise Missile Program,* (Brassey's, Oxford, 1983), £29.50

TAYLOR, MICHAEL J H, *Missiles,* (Arms and Armour Press, London, 1983), £3.50

WEBBER, PHILIP, (and others), *Crisis Over Cruise: A Plain Guide to the New Weapons* (Penguin, Harmondsworth, 1983), £1.25

MILITARY VEHICLES

AYLIFF-JONES, NOEL, *World Tanks and Reconnaissance Vehicles since 1945,* (Ian Allan, Shepperton, 1984), £11.95

FORTY, GEORGE, *Modern Combat Vehicles No 5: The Scorpion,* (Ian Allan, Shepperton, 1983), £8.95

FOSS, CHRISTOPHER, (Ed) *Jane's Military Vehicles and Ground Support Equipment, 1983,* (Jane's, London, 1983), £55.00

GEARY, LES, *Ford Military Vehicles,* (I. Henry Publications, Hornchurch, 1983), £5.25

HARRISON, P G, *Vehicles and Bridging,* (Brassey's, Oxford, 1983), £15.00 (hardback); £6.95 (paperback)

VANDERVEEN, BART, *World Directory of Modern Military Vehicles,* (Frederick Warne, London, 1983), £14.95

ZALOGA, STEVEN J, *Israeli Tanks and Combat Vehicles,* (Arms and Armour Press, London, 1983), £3.95

ZALOGA, STEVEN J, *Soviet Tanks Today,* (Arms and Armour Press, London, 1983), £3.95

NAVAL VESSELS

CRITCHLEY, MIKE, *British Warships and Auxiliaries, 1984/85,* (Maritime Books, Liskeard, 1984), £2.50

CONWAY'S, *All the World's Fighting Ships, 1947–82: Part Two: The Warsaw Pact and Non-Aligned Countries,* (Conway Maritime Press, London, 1983), £25.00

COUHAT, JEAN LABAYLE, *Combat Fleets of the World, 1982/83,* (Arms and Armour Press, London, 1983), £29.50

GIBBONS, TONY, *The Complete Encyclopaedia of Battleships and Battlecruisers,* (Salamander, London, 1983), £11.95

IRELAND, BERNARD, *Navies of the West,* (Ian Allan, Shepperton, 1984), £9.95

JORDAN, JOHN, *Soviet Warships: The Soviet Surface Fleet, 1960–83,* (Arms and Armour Press, London, 1983), £12.95

LONGSTAFF, REGINALD, *Submarine Command: A Pictorial History,* (Robert Hale, London, 1984), £12.95

MEYER, C, *Modern Combat Ships 1: Leander,* (Ian Allan, Shepperton, 1984), £6.95

MOORE, CAPTAIN JOHN E, (Ed), *Jane's Fighting Ships, 1983/84,* (Jane's, London, 1983), £55.00

MOORE, CAPTAIN JOHN E, (Ed), *Jane's Naval Review, 1983/84,* (Jane's, London, 1983), £7.95

POLMAR, NORMAN, *The American Submarine,* (Second Edition), (Patrick Stephens, Cambridge, 1983), £15.95

ROBERTS, J A, (Ed), *Warship: Volume 6,* (Conway Maritime Press, London, 1983), £12.50

SILVERSTONE, PAUL, *Directory of the World's Capital Ships,* (Ian Allan, Shepperton, 1984), £35.00

NATO

ALFORD, JONATHAN, *Greece and Turkey: Adversity in Alliance,* (Gower, Aldershot, 1984), £11.50 (Adelphi Library No 12)

DINTER, E and GRIFFITH, PADDY, *Not Over By Christmas: NATO's Central Front in World War III,* (Bird/Umbrella, 1983), £8.95

FREEDMAN, LAWRENCE, (Ed), *The Troubled Alliance: Atlantic Relations in the 1980s,* (Heinemann/RIIA, 1983, £16.50 (hardback); £6.50 (paperback)

HENDERSON, SIR NICHOLAS, *The Birth of NATO,* (Routledge, London, 1983), £7.95

LUNN, SIMON, *Burden sharing in NATO,* (Routledge, London, 1983), £3.95

PRESTON, PAUL and SMYTH, DENIS, *Spain, the EEC and NATO,* (RIIA, London, Chatham House Papers Series, 1984), £4.95

STEINKE, RUDOLF and VALE, MICHAEL, *Germany Debates Defence: The NATO Alliance at the Crossroads,* (Greenwood Press, Connecticut/London, 1983), £20.50

NUCLEAR WARFARE

BRACKEN, PAUL, *Command and Control of Nuclear Forces,* (Yale University Press, New Haven/London, 1983), £4.95

EPSTEIN, WILLIAM and LUCY, WEBSTER, *We Can Avert a Nuclear War,* (Oelgeschlager, Gunn and Hain, London, 1983), £17.95

HARVARD NUCLEAR STUDY GROUP, *Living With Nuclear Weapons,* (Harvard University Press, Cambridge, Mass, 1983), £10.00

KISSINGER, HENRY, *Nuclear Weapons and Foreign Policy,* (Westview Press, Boulder, Colorado, 1984), £26.00

KRASS, ALLAN S (and others), *Uranium Enrichment and Nuclear Weapons Proliferation,* (Taylor and Francis, London, 1983), £15.00

NURICK, ROBERT, *Nuclear Weapons and European Security,* (Gower, Aldershot, 1984), £12.50, (Adelphi Library No. 10)

POCHIN, EDWARD, *Nuclear Radiation: Risks and Benefits,* (Oxford University Press, 1983), £17.50

SCHEAR, JAMES, *Nuclear Weapons Proliferation and Nuclear Risk,* (Gower, Aldershot, 1984), £12.50, (Adelphi Library No. 13)

STEPHENSON, MICHAEL and HEARN, ROGER, *The Nuclear Case Book,* (Frederick Muller, London, 1983), £9.95 (hardback); £5.95 (paperback)

SIMPSON, JOHN, *The Independent Nuclear State: The United States, Britain, and the Military Atom,* (Macmillan, London, 1983), £25.00

WILLIAMS, PHIL, (Ed), *The Nuclear Debate,* (RIIA/Chatham House Papers, London, 1984), £4.95

SOUTH EAST ASIA

BLUM, ROBERT M, *Drawing the Line: Origin of American Containment Policy in East Asia,* (W W Norton, New York, 1983), £17.95

KOSAKA, MASATAKA and HUNT, KENNETH, *Asian Security 1983,* (Research Institute for Peace and Security, Tokyo, 1983), £28.00

MORRISON, CHARLES E, (Ed), *Threats to Security in East Asia–Pacific: National and Regional Perspectives,* (Lexington Books, Lexington, Mass, 1983), £22.50

O'NEILL, ROBERT, *Security in East Asia,* (Gower, Aldershot, 1984), £12.50

SEGAL, GERALD, (Ed), *The Soviet Union in East Asia: Predicaments of Power,* (Heinemann, London, 1983), £14.50

WILLIAMS, LEW E, *South East Asia: A History,* (Oxford University Press, 1983), £7.95

SOVIET UNION

BYRNES, ROBERT F, (Ed), *After Brezhnev: Sources of Soviet Conduct in the 1980s,* (Frances Pinter, London, 1983), £15.00 (hardback); £6.95 (paperback)

CRANKSHAW, EDWARD, *Russia and the West,* (Macmillan, London, 1984), £8.95

GARRISON, JIM and SHIVPURI, PYARE, *The Russian Threat: Its Myths and Realities,* (Gateway Books, London, 1983), £9.50 (hardback); £4.95 (paperback)

GOLDMANN, MARSHALL I, *USSR in Crisis: The Failure of an Economic System,* (W W Norton, New York, 1983), $15.00

SCHERER, JOHN L, (Ed), *USSR Facts and Figures Annual Vol 6* (Academic International Press, Gulf Breeze, Florida, 1983), $46.50

VALENTA, JIRI and POTTER, WILLIAM, *Soviet Decision Making for*

National Security, (Allen and Unwin, London, 1984), £27.50 (hardback); £12.50 (paperback)

UNITED STATES OF AMERICA AND CANADA

BERTRAM, CHRISTOPH, *American Security in the 1980s,* (Macmillan, London, 1983), £20.00

GARDNER, LLOYD C, *Covenant With Power: American and World Order from Wilson to Reagan,* (Macmillan, London, 1984), £20.00

HOFFMAN, STANLEY, *Dead Ends: American Foreign Policy in the New Cold War,* (Ballinger Publishing/Harper & Row, New York, 1983), £21.00

IRWIN, W, *America in the World: A Short Guide to United States Foreign Policy,* (Praeger, New York, 1983), £29.95

NYE, JOSEPH S JNR, *The Making of America's Soviet Policy,* (Yale University Press, 1984), £20.00

REGEHR, ERNIE and ROSENBLUM, SIMON, (Eds), *Canada and the Nuclear Arms Race,* (James Lorimer, Toronto, 1983), $16.95 (hardback); £9.95 (paperback)

THOMPSON, W SCOTT, (Ed), *Third World: Premises of US Policy* (Institute for Contemporary Studies/Clio Press, 1983), £18.50 (hardback); £7.25 (paperback)

WILDAVSKY, AARON, *Beyond Containment: Alternative American Policies towards the Soviet Union,* (Institute for Contemporary Studies/Clio Press, 1983), £17.75 (hardback); £7.25 (paperback)

VIETNAM

BELL, DANA, *Air War Over Vietnam, Arms and Armour Vol 3* (Arms and Armour Press, London, 1983), 1983

CARD, JOSEFINA J, *Lives After Vietnam: Personal Impact of Military Service,* (Lexington Books, Lexington, Mass, 1983), £21.00

LUXMOORE, J, *Vietnam: The Dilemmas of Reconstruction,* (ISC, London, 1983), £5.00

WAR AND SOCIETY

BOND, BRIAN, *War and Society in Europe, 1870–1970,* (Leicester University Press, 1983) £12.00 (hardback); Fontana paperback, £3.50

CARROLL, BERNIE A (Ed), *Peace and War; A Guide to Bibliographies,* (ABC-Clio, Clio Press, California, 1983), £32.75

HARRIES, MEIRION and SUSAN, *The War Artists,* (Michael Joseph, London, 1983), £12.95

HARRIES-JENKINS, GWYN (and others), *Armed Forces and Welfare Societies; Challenges in the 1980s; Britain, The Netherlands, Germany, Sweden, and the United States,* (Macmillan, London, 1984), £20.00

ROSENBLATT, ROGER, *Children of War,* (New English Library, London, 1984), £9.95

WORLD HUMAN RIGHTS GUIDE, (Hutchinson, London, 1983), £5.95 (paperback)

WARSAW PACT

FEHER, F (and others), *Dictatorship Over Needs, (Eastern Europe and the Soviet Union)* (Blackwell, Oxford, 1983), £22.50

MCCAULEY, MARTIN, *The German Democratic Republic Since 1945,* (Macmillan, London, 1983), £20.00

WEAPONS SYSTEMS

FARRAR, C L and LEEMING, D W, *Military Ballistics: A Basic Manual,* (Brasseys, Oxford, 1983), £15.00 (hardback); £6.95 (paperback)

HOGG, IAN V, (Ed), *Jane's Infantry Weapons, 1983/84,* (Jane's, London, 1983), £55.00

LEE, R G (and others), *Guided Weapons* (Brasseys, Oxford, 1983), £15.00 (hardback); £6.95 (paperback)

LEWIS, JACK, *"Gun Digest" Book of Single Action Revolvers,* (DBI Books/Arms and Armour Press, London, 1982), £7.00

MYATT, FREDERICK, *An Illustrated Guide to Rifles and Machine Guns,* (Salamander, London, 1983), £3.95

QUIGLEY, CARROLL, *Weapons Systems and Political Stability: A History,* (University Press of America/Eurospan, Washington DC, 1983), £31.95

RODGERS, A L, *Surveillance and Target Acquisition Systems,* (Brasseys, Oxford, 1983), £15.00 (hardback); £6.95 (paperback)

SIMPKIN, RICHARD, *Red Armour,* (Brasseys, Oxford, 1983), £15.00

WESTERN EUROPE

BJOL, E, *Nordic Security,* (IISS, London, 1983), £2.50 (Adelphi Paper No. 181)

FENNELL, DESMOND, *State of the Nation: Ireland Since the Sixties,* (Ward River Press, Dublin, 1983), £4.95

KENNEDY, ROBERT and WEINSTEIN, JOHN M, *The Defence of the West: Strategic and European Security Issues Reappraised,* (Westview Press, Boulder, Colorado, 1984), £21.75 (hardback); £15.75 (paperback)

MAGARELLI, CLYDE, *Crisis of Convergence: Military Professionalism and the Working Class Struggle: Portuguese Case Study,* (University Press of America/Eurospan, Washington DC, 1982), £15.75 (hardback); £7.75 (paperback)

MORETON, EDWINA and SEGAL, GERALD, *Soviet Strategy toward Western Europe,* (Allen and Unwin, London, 1984), £17.50

STOVER, WILLIAM J, *Military Politics in Finland,* (University Press of America/Eurospan, 1982), £15.75 (hardback); £7.75 (paperback)

Chronology of Main Events of Defence Interest, May 1983 — April 1984

ROBERT VAN TOL
Research Assistant, RUSI

1983

1 May: *Norway* Anti-submarine units of the Norwegian Navy conducted an intense search of Hardanger fjord for a suspected trapped foreign submarine. Live anti-submarine Terne rockets were used but the hunt was abandoned on 3rd after a 24 hour absence of contact with the submarine.

1 May: *Poland* The banned trade union Solidarity called on its supporters to demonstrate during the annual May Day celebrations. Several tens of thousands turned out and there were violent clashes in several cities with the riot police. One demonstrator was killed.

1 May: *Lebanon* US Secretary of State George Schultz flew to Jerusalem from Beirut with a proposed agreement for the withdrawal of Israeli troops from Beirut. During discussions with the Lebanese government, Mr Schultz came under rocket attack at the US Ambassador's residence; no one was injured. The attack marked the continued attempt of Syria and the Lebanese Moslem militias to prevent Israel and the Christian Lebanese government signing a *de facto* peace treaty which would leave Israeli troops inside Lebanon.

1 May: *El Salvador* Insurgents destroyed a bridge over the Gascara River, breaking the Pan-

American Highway, the only all-weather road linking North and South America.

1 May: *Nicaragua* Before the UN Security Council Nicaragua accused the US government of 'waging dirty war' against the Sandinista government.

3 May: *USSR* Chairman Andropov proposed to balance warheads, not just launchers, in Intermediate Nuclear Force (INF) talks at Vienna. The Proposal was in line with US demands but was conditional on both the cancelling of the deployment of 572 Pershing–II and Ground Launched Cruise Missiles (GLCM) and on including the nuclear arsenals of the UK and France in the INF balance; these arsenals contain 434 warheads.

4 May: *Sweden* The Swedish Navy reported that a midget submarine in Swedish waters (presumably a Soviet one) was probably destroyed by a remote controlled anti-submarine mine off the island of Alno.

4 May: *Iran — Iraq* 18 Soviet diplomats were ordered to leave Teheran on suspicion of conducting activities against the Islamic Revolution.

10 May: *Israel* The Cabinet of Prime Minister Begin agreed on the proposed withdrawal of Israeli troops from Beirut.

10 May: *Afghanistan* Soviet and Afghan forces mounted a major offensive in Schomadi Valley, 30 miles south of Kabul.

17 May: *Lebanon* President Gemayel of Lebanon and Israel signed accords agreeing to the withdrawal of Israeli troops, in stages, from the Lebanon despite the opposition of Syria and local Moslem factions.

21 May: *PLO* A split in the Al Fateh faction of the PLO threatened the position of Yasser Arafat. Arafat has been leader of the PLO for 14 years and he is also the leader of Al Fateh, the largest organisation within the PLO. On 22nd Arafat visited PLO units in Beirut to quell the rebellion.

23 May: *Zimbabwe* An Air Vice Marshal and an Air Commodore in the Zimbabwe Air Force were accused of conspiring to breach security at air bases to allow saboteurs access to the base. The officers claimed that their statements had been made under torture.

26 May: *UK* In discussing the command and control arrangement for GLCMs deployed in the UK, President Reagan said that the UK has 'sort of cruise veto'. There is no formal dual-key control arrangement on these weapons.

26 May: *Turkey* Two brigades of the Turkish Army advanced up to 20 miles inside Iraq. Iraq and Turkey have agreed to allow 'hot pursuit' operations over each other's border when fighting Kurdish insurgents.

26 May: *Denmark* The Danish Parliament ordered the minority government to ensure that no Pershing–IIs or GLCMs were deployed in Europe, that the UK and French nuclear weapons should be included in the INF talks and that these talks should be prolonged into 1984.

June: *PLO* On 4th fighting between factions loyal to and opposed to Yasser Arafat broke out in the Bekaa Valley in Lebanon. Chairman Andropov sent a message of support to Arafat. On 7th Libya sent an infantry battalion to the Lebanon to join the small group of Libyan 'volunteers' already there. Libya and Syria supported the forces opposed to Arafat in the continued fighting. On 9th, at the insistance of Saudi Arabia, Colonel Gaddafi and Yasser Arafat met in North Yemen. On 20th, the Revolutionary Council of Al Fateh met in Damascus in an effort to resolve the rebellion. But on 24th, Syria expelled Yasser Arafat and began blockading forces loyal to Arafat in the Lebanon. Arafat was escorted from Syria under Soviet protection.

6 June: *USSR* The Soviet government warned that the deployment of Pershing–II and GLCMs would be met by a 'timely and effective reply'.

7 June: *USSR* First reports reached the West that Soviet leader Yuri Andropov was ill.

10 June: *UK* Manpower for the British Armed Forces was published as being 320,623 including 42,394 officers, reduced 7,000 from 1982 and 14,000 from 1981. Individual service totals were: Royal Navy 63,973; Royal Marine 7,754; Army 159,069; RAF 89,827.

11 June: *UK* Following the Conservative Party's victory at the General Election on 10th, Geoffrey Howe replaced Francis Pym as Foreign Secretary.

16 June: *USSR* Yuri Andropov, Chairman of the Communist Party of the Soviet Union, was made President of the Soviet Union.

16 June: *Poland* The state visit of Pope John Paul II sparked off a march of 30,000 in support of Solidarity. It was the largest march since the declaration of martial law.

17 June: *USA* Secretary of State George Schultz told the Senate Foreign Relations Committee that the goal of US foreign policy was to bring about political change in the USSR and Eastern Europe. The statement followed a statement from Soviet Foreign Minister Gromyko reaffirming the Brezhnev Doctrine.

20 June: *UK* The government announced that it spent £17m in improving Civil Defence capabilities and that it would force local authorities opposed to Civil Defence to take part in exercises and build the necessary Civil Defence infrastructure.

20 June: *NATO* The Military Committee of NATO announced that the West could unilaterally reduce its tactical nuclear arsenal without affecting the deterrent capability.

20 June: *Lebanon* The government officially calculated the casualties at the Sabra and Chatila Palestinian refugee camps during the September 1982 massacres at 460.

22 June: *Norway* The assistant military attaché at the Soviet Embassy was expelled for spying.

22 June: *South Africa* The government announced that

it was to build a second nuclear research establishment.

June: *Chad* On 23rd fighting broke out between the forces of ex-President Goukouni, backed by Libya, and President Habre. On 24th the northern provincial capital, Faya-Largeau, was captured by Goukouni's forces. On 28th President Mitterrand of France said that France would honour its agreement with Chad in supporting the government against the rebels.

27 June: *UK* The government announced that it would spend £215m on building a military and civil airport on the Falkland Islands.

29 June: *Norway* The Navy attacked an unidentified submarine within its territorial waters with Terne anti-submarine rockets.

1 July: *West Germany* Chancellor Kohl visited Moscow for talks on arms control. His meeting with President Andropov was delayed on 4th because of the President's ill-health. The meeting took place on 5th in which the Chancellor stressed that UK and French nuclear weapons could not be included in the INF talks.

7 July: *Lebanon* Six French troops of the Multi-National Force (MNF) were killed in a premature explosion.

8 July: *UK* 66 'peace-women' protestors at Green Common were arrested after a forced entry into the air base. The women were mounting a week long 'peace-blockade' and a 600-man infantry battalion was sent to man the perimeter fences of the base.

8 July: *Lebanon* The Israeli Army began handing over its positions in the suburbs of Beirut to the Lebanese Army in preparation for their withdrawal.

8 July: *Chad* The town of Oum Chalouba in western central Chad fell to the forces of ex-President Goukouni. With Libyan backing the rebels continued to advance on the capital, N'Djamena.

12 July: *Chad* The government of Zaire announced

that it would send a further 1,750 troops in support of President Habre's forces. 300 Zairian troops were already stationed in Chad.

14 July: *Poland* Parliament amended the Polish constitution to allow the President to declare a State of Emergency. In the future this will negate the need to suspend the constitution in declaring martial law.

15 July: *Lebanon* The Israeli Army began its withdrawal from Beirut. The withdrawal was followed by the out-break of fighting between the Lebanese Army and the militias of the Shi'ite and Druze communities.

15 July: *Chad* President Habre took personal control of the fighting with rebel forces in order to stabilise the situation.

July: *USA* On 19th President Reagan ordered a Carrier Battle Group (CVBG) to hold exercises off the Pacific coast of Nicaragua. On 21st a second CVBG was ordered to exercise off the Caribbean coast of Nicaragua whilst a third formation, a Surface Action Group centred on the battleship *New Jersey*, was ordered to appear off the Pacific coast on 25th. President Reagan stated that the naval forces were not part of a blockade nor an exercise in 'gunboat diplomacy' and that the US was 'not planning a war'.

18 July: *USA* President Reagan established a bipartisan commission headed by former Secretary of State Dr Kissinger to seek a consensus policy on Central America.

20 July: *Lebanon* Israel announced that its forces would withdraw to the Awali river a few miles north of Sidon and that this would be finished before the end of November, when winter sets in. Fighting between the Lebanese Army and the militias continued in the suburbs of Beirut, at Beirut airport and in the foothills of the Chouf mountains south of Beirut.

21 July: *Poland* After 19 months, General Jaruzelski lifted martial law and declared a partial amnesty for prisoners held without trial.

22 July: *Lebanon* The Israeli Army moved reinforcements into the Bekaa Valley in a threat to Syria not to take advantage of Israel's withdrawal. This follows US Secretary of State George Schultz's visit to Syria on 5th/6th in which the Syrians refused to take part in any talks about the withdrawal of Syrian troops from Lebanon until all Israeli troops were withdrawn.

July: *Sri Lanka* On 22nd 13 troops were killed in an ambush by Tamil separatists. On 25th racial violence in the capital Colombo between rioting Singalese youths and Tamils forced the Army to intervene and impose a curfew. In the northern homeland of the Tamils, government troops were reported to be raiding the country in revenge killings. By 26th one million Tamils were thought to be fleeing to the north as the racial violence spread throughout the island. On 29th President Jayewardene rejected demands for a separate Tamil state as the armed forces began to quell the violence.

26 July: *USA* The Israeli Defence and Foreign Ministers visited US for talks on the withdrawal of foreign troops in the Lebanon.

27 July: *Lebanon* Syrian troops pulled out of the northern city of Tripoli which led to immediate fighting between the opposing factions of the PLO.

30 July: *Lebanon* US Special Envoy to the Middle East, Robert McFarlane, met Lebanese officials to discuss the deployment of the Lebanese Army into the Chouf mountains, homeland of the Druze sect, after Israeli troops had withdrawn from the region.

30 July: *Zimbabwe* The Army's 5th Brigade, trained by North Korean advisers, was withdrawn from Matabeleland following repeated reports of atrocities and intense internal and external pressure for the 5th Brigade's removal.

1 August: *Honduras* 80 military planners from the US southern Command HQ in Panama arrived in the capital Tegucigalpa to prepare them for

the hurriedly announced 6 month series of exercises to be called Big Pine–2.

2 August: *Lebanon* Israel failed to secure US pressure on the Lebanese government of President Gemayel to ratify the 17 May troop withdrawal accord.

August: *Chad* On 2nd, the US delivered Redeye surface-to-air missiles for the protection of the capital N'Djamena and France also announced its intention to supply the forces of President Habre with anti-aircraft weapons. On 3rd the carrier battle group containing the USS *Eisenhower* entered the Gulf of Sirte off Libya and a detachment of E–3 AWACS aircraft and a small fighter escort flew to Sudan to monitor the air activity over Chad following Libyan air raids on northern and central towns in Chad. On 9th the Faya-Largeau, briefly recaptured by government troops, was encircled by rebel forces whilst the first group of French troops, a Foreign Legion detachment stationed in the Central African Republic, arrived at N'Dajmena; reportedly to act as 'specialised instructors'. On 11th, Faya Largeau fell to the rebels as President Habre's troops withdrew back to Um Chalouba and Salal in central Chad. President Reagan stated that there would be no direct intervention in Chad with US forces, saying that the primary responsibility for preventing Chad falling into Libyan hands rested with France. On 13th, further French troops arrived in Chad and began moving northwards from the capital to set up positions (running along the 15th parallel) slightly behind the forward elements of President Habre's forces in central Chad. The last fighting occurred on 15th but French forces, including fighters and helicopters continued to arrive, numbering some 2,000 by the 31st. The French, however, felt that the USA was trying to push them into a fight with Libya, a charge which was refuted in the US on 18th. The rebel forces of ex-

President Goukouni occupied the northern, mainly desert areas, 50 per cent of Chad by the 15th.

3 August: *USA* A US Navy destroyer, on exercise off Nicaragua, stopped a Soviet freighter in international waters to ascertain her cargo. The action was apparently taken to demonstrate that a close watch on arms shipments between Russia (and Cuba) and Nicaragua was being maintained. No arms, however, were found and the USSR immediately protested against the US action.

5 August: *Lebanon* Renewed fighting struck Tripoli after the car bombing of worshippers at a mosque.

7 August: *Honduras* Big Pine-2, the US exercise, started. Activities included joint training of US troops with the Honduran armed forces, the wide scale construction of air bases, the monitoring of movements between Nicaragua and El Salvador and support for the 'Contras', the US-financed Nicaraguan rebel army.

8 August: *Guatemala* A military coup brought down the evangelical President Brigadier General Efrain Rios Montt and installed the former Defence Minister, Brigadier General Oscar Humberto Meija, in the Presidency.

10 August: *USA* The Chief of Staff of the US Army, General John Wickham, complained that with the US's recent commitments to Central America, Chad, the Lebanon and the Horn of Africa US forces were being over stretched.

10 August: *Lebanon* Three Cabinet ministers empowered to intercede in the fighting in the Chouf mountains between the Druze militia and the Christian militia which moved into the area under the Israeli occupation were kidnapped by the Druze. The ministers were later released after the intercession of senior Druze religious leaders.

15 August: *Lebanon* Members of the Shi'ite Amal militia began actively fighting with units of the Lebanese Army as the Amal and Druze militias moved into a closer alliance.

17 August: *USSR* President Andropov warned that if GLCMs were deployed in Europe, the INF talks would be ended.

21 August: *Belgium* One Russian and four Rumanians were expelled for espionage.

21 August: *Philippines* Senior opposition leader Benigno Aquino was assassinated as he got off a plane at Manila after spending three years in exile in the USA. The assassin was killed by government troops at the airport. Popular feeling accused the government of President Marcos of being behind the killing.

22 August: *Lebanon* Intense fighting between Christians and Druze in the Chouf mountains forced the Israeli Army to delay its planned withdrawal to the Awali River. On 29th US Marines of the MNF came under direct attack from the Amal militia fighting in West Beirut, two were killed. Three French soldiers were killed on 30th as they came under similar attack. The Israeli Army further delayed their withdrawal, under US pressure and on 31st the Lebanese Army mounted a major attack on militia positions in West Beirut, recapturing most of this half of the city.

30 August: *Israel* Prime Minister Begin resigned because of ill health despite appeals from his Cabinet to stay on to oversee the withdrawal.

31 August: *Poland* On the 3rd anniversary of the formation of Solidarity, demonstrations in Poland's principal cities of Warsaw and Krakow were broken up by riot police.

1 September: *USSR* After a presumed navigation error, a South Korean Airlines Boeing 747 carrying 269 people was shot down by a Su–15 Flagon fighter from the Soviet's Air Defence Forces (*Voyska PVO*). There were no survivors from the plane which was 310 miles off course and had been flying in Soviet airspace, over sensitive military installations, for 2½ hours before fighters were able to intercept it. USSR claimed that the plane was on a reconnaissance mission but the US, Japan and other

Western countries condemned the Soviets for an inhumane action.

2 September: *Chad* Oum Chalouba, held by government forces in the centre of the country, was attacked by rebel forces. President Habre's troops repelled the attack with French Jaguar strike planes making low passes over the rebel troops in simulated bombing runs.

3 September: *Philippines* The opposition to President Marcos announced a campaign of civil disobedience following the assassination of Benigno Aquino.

3 September: *Pakistan* Demonstrations in Sind Province against the continued rule of General Zia and the provisions of martial law. On 4th some 10,000 para-military troops were deployed to the area to quell the civil disturbances.

4 September: *Lebanon* In a rapid movement the Israeli Army withdrew from the outskirts of Beirut, through the Chouf mountains and behind the Awali River. President Gemayel's government was unable to reach agreement with the leader of the Druze Militia, Walid Jumblat, over the occupation of former Israeli positions in the Chouf mountains. Therefore the Druze militia occupied the positions and intensified their efforts to expell Christian groups which had entered the area, including driving the Lebanese Army out of the foothills of the Chouf at Souk el-Gharb and attacking US and French elements of the MNF, which were seen as propping-up President Gemayel's government.

6 September: *Chad* Following a Libyan air raid on 5th, rebel troops mounted a second attack on the government position at Oum Chalouba, which was unsuccessful. The French build-up in Chad, code-named Operation Manta, consisted of up to 3,000 men, eight aircraft, 15 helicopters, 20 armoured cars, artillery and other equipment.

7 September: *Turkey* It was announced that the air force

would be re-equipped with 160 F–16C/D fighters costing an estimated $4bn.

8 September: *USA* The stance on the negotiation of a Comprehensive Test Ban Treaty changed to considering it to be a long term aim. In the meantime the USA 'specifically required' continued underground nuclear testing for the 'development, modernisation, and certification of warheads, the maintenance of stockpile reliability and the evaluation of nuclear weapons effects'.

8 September: *USA* Chief Negotiator at the INF talks, Paul Nitze, was instructed to offer the Russians greater flexibility over questions about medium range bombers, SS–20s deployed in Asia and the individual weapons systems to be withdrawn under any agreed ceiling. However, UK and French nuclear weapons were not to be included.

8 September: *Greece* US and Greek officials signed a five year agreement extending the US's ability to use military bases in Greece.

13 September: *USSR* During Soviet exercises, four military aircraft penetrated Japanese airspace.

13 September: *Chad* Under emergency military aid programme, two C–130 Hercules transport aircraft were delivered to President Habre's forces.

15 September: *USA* Congress approved the Defense Authorization Bill for Fiscal Year 1984 (FY–84) after a conference of members of the Senate and House of Representatives. The $264.5bn budget, a 5 per cent real increase over FY–83, had an easier passage than expected because of anger caused by the shooting down of the South Korean airliner.

15 September: *Israel* Former Foreign Minister Yitzhak Shamir became the new Prime Minister as Menachem Begin formally left office.

19 September: *Lebanon* The falling position of the Lebanese Army at Souk el-Gharb against the Druze militia brought in the direct intervention of US forces to bolster the front with shelling from warships of the 6th Fleet.

19 September: *Philippines* Imelda Marcos, wife of the President and widely thought of as successor to her husband, announced that she intended to retire from politics.

20 September: *China* It was announced that the UK was to have no part in administrating the colony of Hong Kong after the end of the lease on the New Territories. This caused the confidence in the Hong Kong dollar to fall sharply.

21 September: *Costa Rica* Following an ineffective but dramatic air raid on Nicaragua by light aircraft flown from Costa Rica by members of the Contra organisation, the Costa Rican authorities arrested 80 members of the Democratic Revolutionary Alliance and seized quantities of arms and other equipment.

23 September: *Argentina* The military junta announced a 'self-amnesty' on all those who participated in the so-called 'dirty war' in which thousands of Argentinians disappeared.

25 September: *USSR* Foreign Minister Gromyko cancelled a visit to the UN General Assembly because Aeroflot flights were banned from entering the USA following the shooting down of the South Korean airliner.

25 September: *USSR* The Soviet Union dismissed the new US proposals announced on the 8th as a ploy.

26 September: *Lebanon* Saudi and US mediators managed to get the warring factions around Beirut to agree to a cease-fire, re-open the Beirut airport and attend a Conference of National Reconciliation. As part of the agreement, the Prime Minister, Chafi al Wazzan, and his Cabinet resigned.

28 September: *Greece* Greece withdrew its participation in the NATO exercise 'Display Determination' two days before it was due to start because of a dispute over status of Greek forces on the island of Limnos. Turkey claimed that the island should be demilitarised. NATO avoided including the island in the exercise area, which the Greeks saw as supportive of the Turkish claims.

30 September: *China* It was announced that if no agreement was reached with the UK over the future of Hong Kong by the end of 1984, then China would take a unilateral decision on the colony's future.

1 October: *Lebanon* Druze forces in the Chouf mountain region south of Beirut announced that they were forming their own civil administration independent of the government's structure.

1 October: *Nicaragua* With the increased frequency of attacks by 'Contras' from bases in Honduras and Costa Rica it was announced that the Nicaraguan army would undertake cross-border 'hot pursuit' missions if required. The attacks against economic targets were producing an oil shortage which was endangering the major exports of Nicaragua. On 3rd, it was reported that the US had been attempting to unify the various 'Contra' factions into a government-in-exile. The group under Eden Pastora in Costa Rica, however, refused such a move because the Honduran based 'Contras' contained former supporters of the deposed Samosa regime. In consequence funds from the CIA were withdrawn from Pastora's group.

5 October: *Poland* Lech Walesa, former leader of the Solidarity Trade Union movement, was awarded the 1983 Nobel Peace Prize.

5 October: *USA* The biannual Standing Consultative Committee met to discuss American fears that the Soviet Union was violating several arms control treaties. These included the construction of a new phased-array radar with possible anti-ballistic missile capabilities in Siberia; the testing of a second new intercontinental ballistic missile system; and the encryption of telemetry data from missile flight tests.

6 October: *USA* The Strategic Arms Reduction Talks (START) reconvened with a new set of US proposals known as 'build-down'. This suggests that for every new warhead deployed (during modernisation) two or three old war-

heads (depending on the system) would be withdrawn from service. In addition, air launched cruise missiles were to be considered in the negotiations.

7 October: *USA* The Pentagon's initial request for its Fiscal Year 85 (FY–85) budget was reported to be $321bn, a 22 per cent increase over the $264bn FY–84. The US Congress had cut FY–84 from a 10 to a 5 per cent increase over FY–83 and projected FY–85 at $297bn.

9 October: *USSR* Lieutenant General Grishin, Chief of Staff of the Transcaucasian Military District, was reported to have defected to the West some time in September by walking over the Soviet-Turkish border.

9 October: *South Korea* A bomb in the capital of Burma, Rangoon, killed four South Korean ministers and a number of senior aides in an assassination attempt against President Chum Doo Hwan who was on a state visit to Burma. President Hwan accused the North Koreans of having been behind the bombing.

10 October: *Syria* PLO dissident leaders, Colonels Abu Moussa and Abu Saleh, launched an attack on the PLO's office in Damascus. The Syrians, who increasingly back the PLO dissidents, cordoned off the area but did not intervene. Yasser Arafat warned that Syria would move to destroy loyal PLO forces around the north Lebanese town of Tripoli, which was surrounded by two Syrian Divisions. According to US estimates, Syria received $2.5bn in military aid from the Soviet Union between September 1982 and September 1983 whilst there were some 5,000 Soviet advisers in Syria helping to rebuild the armed forces after Israel's invasion of Lebanon.

12 October: *China* China became the 112th member of the International Atomic Energy Agency (IAEA).

13 October: *USSR* The Chief of Staff of the Warsaw Pact, General Kulikov, stated that if cruise and Pershing missiles were deployed, the USSR

would increase capabilities of its conventional forces, increase tactical and theatre nuclear weapons and take 'corresponding counter-measures against US territory'.

17 October: *Syria* It was confirmed that the USSR had delivered SS–21 short range ballistic missiles, capable of reaching all major static targets, including cities, in Israel.

19 October: *Grenada* Prime Minister Maurice Bishop was killed in an army *coup d'état* when a crowd freed him from house arrest and threatened to restore him to power. General Hudson Austin took over the military junta.

20 October: *Nicaragua* A four point peace plan was offered to the USA. It included the halting of supplies to Salvadorian insurgents if the USA stopped its support for Nicaraguan insurgents; a non-aggression pledge that Nicaragua would not threaten the US or any other Central American country and permission for US inspectors to undertake on-site inspection of Nicaraguan bases. The US State Department said that the proposals did not cover the full range of issues.

23 October: *Iraq* Iraq claimed it had mined the entrance of Bandar Khomeini (formerly Bandar Shahpur) at head of the Persian Gulf.

23 October: *Lebanon* Fundamentalist Shi'ites drove trucks filled with explosives into the compounds of the US Marine Battalion HQ and a French Company position of the MNF in Beirut. They drove into the tower blocks and detonated their explosives manually, killing themselves and 243 US marines and 58 French servicemen.

25 October: *Grenada* 3,000 US marines and US Army Rangers invaded the island of Grenada in an attempt to topple the recently formed military junta. The US forces, which rapidly increased to 5,000, were supported by troops from Jamaica, Barbabos, Antigua, Dominica, St. Lucia and St. Vincent. They were met by unexpectedly stiff resistance from the Grena-

dan Army and Cuban engineers and advisors on the island. The last of the fighting ended on the 31st when the leader of the junta, General Hudson Austin, was captured. The invasion was welcomed by the civil population of Grenada and by most Caribbean countries, though it was condemned by many other countries as being illegal under both the Charter of the United Nations and the Charter of the Organisation of American States.

27 October: *NATO* It was announced that some 1,400 tactical nuclear warheads from NATO's stocks would be withdrawn in a unilateral move. The warheads come mainly from surface-to-air missiles and atomic demolition mines and are in addition to the tactical nuclear weapons which will be withdrawn on a one-to-one basis with the introduction of new nuclear warheads on the cruise and Pershing missiles.

30 October: *Argentina* Raul Alfonsin, leader of the Radical Party, defeated the Peronist Party to become Argentina's first democratically elected President since 1976.

31 October: *Lebanon* The Conference of National Reconciliation between the warring factions in the Lebanese civil war opened in Geneva to discuss its membership, agenda and the cease-fire.

1 November: *USA* Some 10,000 troops involved in the exercise Crisex–83 with Spanish forces were withdrawn as a contingency against further trouble in the Lebanon.

1 November: *USSR* A Victor–III class nuclear attack submarine was spotted motionless between Bermuda and the US coast having become entangled in the AN/SQR–18 towed array sonar of a US FF–1052 Knox class frigate. The submarine was later taken in tow by a Soviet tug out from Cuba.

1 November: *El Salvador* Insurgents inflicted their biggest defeat on the Army following a pitched battle for control of the town of Oiudad Barrios. Insurgent activity was reportedly extended

into nine of El Salvador's fourteen provinces. The Army's major effort in stemming the advance of insurgent activity, the so-called 'pacification program' in San Vincenete province, worked out and coordinated by US advisors, had reportedly 'fizzled out'. The Salvadorian high command was said to be divided over the future course of army operations whilst the forces had poorer mobility, intelligence and morale than the insurgents.

2 November: *Grenada* Hostilities on the island were formally declared to have ended by US Defense Secretary Casper Weinberger. US forces began immediately withdrawing from the island, leaving a garrison of 1,000 troops, mainly engineers and administrators.

3 November: *Iraq* The delivery of French Super Etendard strike planes was confirmed to have taken place during October despite repeated Iranian threats that they would close the Persian Gulf if they were prohibited from using it. A Greek merchant ship, the *Avra,* was attacked and hit by missiles whilst entering Bandar Khomeini at the head of the Gulf. Another Greek ship, the *Antigoni,* was hit by an air attack at the same place on the 21st.

3 November: *Lebanon* After a prolonged period of tension, some 12,000 dissident PLO troops and Syrian forces attacked PLO forces loyal to Yasser Arafat around the city of Tripoli and the two near-by PLO refugee camps Baddawi and Nahr al-Barid. The latter camp fell rapidly and a second offensive, starting on 9th, captured Baddawi on 16th. A surprise counterattack by Arafat's troops recaptured Baddawi on 18th but increased Syrian pressure finally cut-off the refugee camps from Arafat's forces as they withdrew into Tripoli. Following intensive diplomatic pressure on Syria from other Arab countries and the Soviet Union, their forces halted their advance outside Tripoli and talks to remove Arafat and his troops from Lebanon started.

4 November: *Lebanon* An Israeli command post in Tyre suffered a suicide truck bombing similar to that which befell the Americans and French on 23rd October. On 5th, 16th and 21st the Israeli Air Force launched a series of retaliatory attacks for the bombing, which killed some 60 people (including 30 Israelis) against Iranian camps around the town of Baalbek in the Bekaa Valley, from whence the suicide bombers were thought to come. The French mounted a similar air attack with carrier-borne Super Etendards on 17th. It was widely feared that the USA, which temporarily had three aircraft carriers (the USSs *Eisenhower, Independence* and *John F Kennedy*) as well as the battleship *USS New Jersey* and supporting warships in the area, would launch a large retaliatory attack of its own.

6 November: *Turkey* Military government came to end with the election of Turgud Ozal, leader of the Motherland Party. The former junta had wanted the Nationalist Democratic Party to win the election and had put their support behind them; however, they came only third in the elections.

7 November: *Syria* The worsening situation in the Lebanon and the announcement that Israel would hold a full mobilisation exercise on 9th led to the call-up of reservists, strengthening the Lebanese garrison to 62,000. Two additional mechanised divisions were also deployed in the Golan Heights region.

9 November: *USA* Following difficulties with Israel over policy in Lebanon, a new strategic accord was reached between the two countries. In the light of this Congress passed on 11th Israel's FY–84 aid budget of $2.61bn, including $1.7bn in military aid. Despite the objection of the Department of Defense, $550m of the military aid will go to the development of the Israeli Lavi fighter, which is considered inferior to current fighters and will be a direct competitor to the F–20, which was

privately funded without government support.

9 November: *Lebanon* The National Reconciliation talks were adjourned without a date set for their continuation after only general agreement on constitutional issues. President Gemayel began visiting various Arab and Western leaders to discuss the unratified 17th May troop withdrawal accord with Israel, which is seen as a major bar to achieving agreement with the Moslem factions and their chief supporter, Syria.

9 November: *UK* 5 Brigade was converted into 5 Air-Portable Brigade with combined arms support and greater parachute training in order to bolster Britain's out-of-area operations capability utilising the Royal Marine's 3 Commando Brigade.

15 November: *Cyprus* The northern Turkish Cypriot sector of Cyprus unilaterally declared independence from the Greek Cypriot dominated Republic of Cyprus. Turkey, however, was the only country to recognise the self-styled Turkish Republic of North Cyprus.

17 November: *USSR* The Krivak–I class frigate *Razyashchiy* and the US Spruance class destroyer *Fife* collided in the Arabian Sea.

17 November: *UK* It was announced that Great Britain's commitment to increase defence spending by 3 per cent per year would end after the 1985–86 defence budget. The budget for 1984–85 was stated to be £17bn, having suffered a cut of £282m since estimates were published in February. It was claimed, however, that after 'technical adjustments', the cut was only £168m, but some £684m from the 1984–85 budget would be spent on the Falkland Islands.

18 November: *Argentina* Generals Galtieri and Lami Dozo and Admiral Anaya, the members of the junta which began the Falklands War, were ordered to stand courts martial.

20 November: *USA* The CIA announced a revision of its

estimates for defence spending of the USSR between 1976–83. The estimates were revised downwards by 50 per cent from an annual growth rate in defence spending, 1976–83, of 4 to 2 per cent. This compares with a growth rate between 1966–76 of 5 to 6 per cent. A decline in the rate at which the USSR was fielding new major weapons systems was also noted.

21 November: *USSR* The search for wreckage from the South Korean airliner shot down on 1st September officially ended.

23 November: *USSR* The Soviet delegation at the INF talks left without setting a date for resumption of the talks following the vote, on 22nd in the West German Bundestag, endorsing the deployment of cruise and Pershing missiles. The vote is thought to have ended the Soviet campaign to convince Western public opinion to force their representatives to abandon the INF deployments.

23 November: *Lebanon* Yasser Arafat agreed to leave the Lebanon when arrangements for the withdrawal of his loyal troops were completed.

1 December: *USA* A meeting of the National Security Council decided not to undertake a crash programme to develop a Ballistic Missile Defence system. Instead, development was ordered to proceed in a 'prudent' long term research effort.

3 December: *Sweden* Six consignments bound for the USSR were seized after they were found to contain complex modern computers with a potential military utility. The computers, manufactured in the USA, were the 42nd consignment to be seized in Sweden.

3 December: *Lebanon* The United Nations Security Council devised a plan for withdrawing Yasser Arafat's forces from Tripoli.

4 December: *Lebanon* The long expected retaliation for the suicide bombing of 23rd October occurred as 28 attack planes from the carriers USS *Indepen-*

dence and USS *John F Kennedy* of Task Force 60 (under Rear Admiral Tuttle) of the US 6th Fleet attacked Syrian positions east of Beirut. Two of the planes, which flew without any attempt at air defence suppression at medium altitude, were shot down and one of the pilots was captured by Syrian forces. The attack provoked further attacks by the Druze and Shia militias against US marine positions in Beirut which in turn provoked shore bombardment from warships of the 6th Fleet.

8 December: *USSR* The Soviet delegation to the START talks left the talks without setting a date for their renewal.

9 December: *NATO* A NATO Council Meeting stressed the need for a 'long term constructive and realistic relationship' with the USSR involving an 'open, comprehensive political dialogue as well as cooperation: based on mutual advantage'. The call was seen as attempt to redirect East/West relations away from total reliance on arms control talks as the only point of contact between the two power blocs following the collapse of the INF and the START talks and the backing given to the Soviet Union, at a Warsaw Pact meeting on 7th, to counter-deployments.

9 December: *Lebanon* Israeli fast patrol boats began an intermittent bombardment of PLO positions around Tripoli in order to stem public opinion in Israel that Yasser Arafat was being allowed to escape from the Lebanon for a second time.

10 December: *NATO* It was confirmed that former British Foreign Secretary, Lord Carrington, was to be the new Secretary General of NATO.

10 December: *Argentina* The USA ended its ban on arms sales to Argentina, imposed in 1977 by President Carter.

11 December: *USA* Customs officers in the UK seized £500,000 worth of computers bound for the USSR whilst it was announced that Operation Exodus, the US attempt to stop the flow of sensitive high-technology to the USSR, had

stopped 1,444 illegal shipments of goods worth $86m.

11 December: *Bangladesh* Lieutenant General Ershad, the country's military ruler, declared himself President and ordered the release of leading political figures in the hope of getting them to cooperate in forthcoming elections and being an end to recent political violence. The opposition, however, saw the move as cosmetic; as an attempt to give General Ershad's rule legitimacy.

12 December: *Kuwait* Five bombs went off outside Kuwaiti, French and US buildings, killing five and injuring 61 people. The Islamic Jihad movement, which claimed responsibility for the suicide bombing attacks against US, French and Israeli positions in Lebanon, claimed responsibility.

12 December: *Indonesia* Reported that death squads, unofficially supported by the government in its anti-crime programme, were responsible for the deaths of 4,000 'suspected criminals' over the last nine months.

13 December: *USA* Defense Secretary Casper Weinberger stated that 369 SS–20 intermediate-range ballistic missiles had been deployed, 117 of them out of range of Europe in Asia, whilst a further 27 sites were under construction.

13 December: *Argentina* The government announced that all members of the juntas between 1976 and 1983, with the exception of the last junta which oversaw the return to democracy, would face courts martial. All civilians tried by military courts would be given recourse to *habeas corpus* and the self-amnesty declared before the elections would be repealled so that those involved in the so-called 'dirty war' could be brought to trial. The High Command of the armed services was also reformed. The Chiefs of Staff were subordinated to a civilian Minister of Defence. The appointment of relatively junior officers to posts of Chief of

Staff forced the resignation of 26 generals, 16 admirals and two air force generals.

15 December: *USSR* The delegations of the USSR and the six other Warsaw Pact countries to the last remaining arms control negotiation, the MBFR talks, left the conference without setting a date for their renewal in the same fashion as they had left the INF and START talks as a protest to the deployment of GLCMs and Pershing–II missiles.

15 December: *Lebanon* The International Red Cross, under Israeli escort, began evacuating 1,400 Christian militiamen and some 15,000 Christian civilians from the town of Deir el Kamar in the Chouf mountains. The town had been under seige by the Druze militia who are trying to expell Christians from the area since the Israeli withdrawal to the Awali River.

19 December: *Brazil* Following an Argentine announcement on 19 November that they had mastered the techniques of uranium enrichment (necessary for building nuclear reactors for submarines but also a stage in developing atomic weapons), Brazil admitted that it too was engaged in research into nuclear weapons manufacture. It was denied, however, that this meant Brazil was actually developing a nuclear weapon.

20 December: *Lebanon* Yasser Arafat and his loyal troops in Tripoli were evacuated from the city by five Greek merchant ships flying United Nations flags under the escort of the US and French navies. The bulk of the forces, which had to leave their heavy equipment behind, were taken to North Yemen.

21 December: *Sweden* An official report stated that there had been 21 'strong indications' of submarine incursions into Swedish territorial waters since the beaching of a Whiskey class submarine in 1981. These included three within the last three months and evidence that bottom-crawling submarines had been in operation.

22 December: *Egypt* President Mubarak met Yasser Arafat

in a move to reconcile the split which occurred after Egypt signed the 1979 peace treaty with Israel. In a second conciliatory move, Jordan lifted its trade sanctions against Egypt, also imposed in 1979.

24 December: *Lebanon* Intermittent violations of the cease-fire reached a peak of intensity on 24th, 25th and 26th as talks once again foundered.

31 December: *Nigeria* Major General Muhammad Buhari lead a *coup* which toppled the recently elected government of President Shagari. The *coup* met no opposition. The constitution was suspended and political parties banned.

1984

1 January: *El Salvador* Insurgents destroyed Cuscatlan suspension bridge across the Lempa River connecting the capital with the eastern provinces of El Salvador.

4 January: *Lebanon* 16 Israeli Kfir fighters bombed positions around the town of Baalbek in the Bekaa Valley.

4 January: *USA* Paul Thayer, Deputy Secretary of Defense responsible for overseeing the deployment and production of weapons, resigned because of accusations that he had used 'inside information' to benefit selected defence contractors.

9 January: *West Germany* General Günther Kiessling, Deputy Supreme Allied Commander Europe, was dismissed from his post because information ascertained by the security services suggested that he was a potential blackmail victim through homosexual associations. Amid a storm of protests, General Joachim Mack was appointed as his successor. Further investigations, however, cleared General Kiessling completely, forcing resignations within the security services.

9 January: *Lebanon* Talks between Syria and the government of President Gemayel in Saudi Arabia failed to get agreement on the President's

Security Plan. This called for an extension of government authority to all areas of Lebanon not under Israeli or Syrian control (about 40 per cent of the country). Syria insisted that US forces in Beirut should be withdrawn.

10 January: *USA* President Reagan met with Chinese Premier Zhao Ziyang to discuss US relations with Taiwan. The President said he would not abandon economic and technological cooperation, which led to the signing of an agreement on 12th.

10 January: *France* Police mounted over 100 raids in south-west France against the Basque separatist movement ETA. Six leading members of ETA were arrested and deported.

12 January: *Chad* The Organisation of African Unity abandoned efforts to establish peace talks between the warring factions in Chad.

14 January: *Lebanon* Following the release of the US pilot captured after the 4th December raid, the US Special Envoy to the Middle East, Donald Rumsfeld, visited Syria in attempt to capitalise on Syrian gesture of good will. The talks, however, were said to be 'unproductive'.

14 January: *Lebanon* Major Sa'ad Haddad, commander of the Israeli sponsored 'Free Lebanon Forces' on the southern border with Israel, died. Colonel Elias Khalil was appointed as temporary successor, however, President Gemayel hoped to integrate the force with the Lebanese Army, which had equipped and trained three new brigades since the large-scale fighting in September. The Druze and Shia militias had also used the relative lull in the fighting to regroup and expand their forces with Syrian aid.

15 January: *South Africa* Forces involved in Operation Askari, a five week deep penetration into Angola, began to withdraw to their bases in Namibia.

16 January: *South Africa–Mozambique* Talks began between the two countries on possible non-aggression pact. The Frelimo government of

Mozambique would stop supporting the insurgent activities of the African National Congress (ANC) in return for South Africa halting its support of the Mozambique National Resistance insurgent group and economic aid.

16 January: *Jordan* King Hussein opened the first session of the Jordanian Parliament in 17 years with a call to return Egypt to the 'Arab Family' and a move to form a joint approach to the Palestinian problem with Yasser Arafat.

17 January: *UK* A Jaguar strike plane crashed near the Chemical Defence Establishment at Porton Down. The pilot, who ejected, landed safely on the roof of Porton Down's medical centre.

18 January: *Sweden* US Secretary of State Shultz and Soviet Foreign Minister Gromyko met at the start of the Conference on Disarmament and Security in Europe in an effort to get arms control talks restarted. There was, however, no agreement.

19 January: *India* It was reported that India had secured a deal with USSR over the purchase or licence production of a wide range of arms at low prices. These include licence manufacture of the MiG-27 and options to do the same with the MiG-29 and MiG-31 when they become available. The supply of BMP-1s and BMP-2s infantry combat vehicles and T-72 tanks with the option to manufacture the T-72 and T-80 tanks plus delivery of the SA-8 surface-to-air missile system. The navy is to get 21 vessels, including submarines and fast attack craft, in addition to support for India's domestic naval industry.

19 January: *Argentina* Requests from the USA for Argentina to resume training and other assistance for 'anti-communist forces in Central America' were refused, President Alfonsin reportedly having told President Reagan that he favoured trying to find a negotiated settlement.

20 January: *Norway* Arne Treholt, head of the foreign press office and a former junior labour minister, was arrested for spying for the KGB. The

arrest halted a security leak which had been reportedly worrying NATO intelligence services for the last ten years. Treholt is believed to have passed on information regarding NATO's wartime merchant shipping convoy plans, details of Norway's defensive minefields and arrangements for reinforcing Norway with UK, Dutch and US marines, including details of potential landing sites.

21 January: *USA* The US Air Force's anti-satellite system, ASAT, had its first test flight.

22 January: *Poland* The Defence Budget for 1984 was reported to be £1,578m, a 13.9 per cent increase compared with 1983.

25 January: *UK* The Foreign Secretary announced that employees at the Government Communications Headquarters, Britain's signals intelligence centre, were to be banned from being members of trade unions "in the interests of national security'. Employees were given until 1 March to agree to the move and were offered £1,000, tax deductable, in compensation for the loss of their union rights.

25 January: *Chad* A French Jaguar strike plane was shot down in central Chad by a SA-7 man-portable surface-to-air missile as three aircraft attacked a rebel column which had attacked government positions 125 miles south of the *de facto* truce line. The column was reportedly three-quarters destroyed.

26 January: *USA* President Reagan announced a ten year, $8bn programme to place a six-to-eight man space station into a 300 mile high orbit.

20 January: *Egypt* Egypt accepted an invitation to rejoin the Islamic Conference Organisation.

30 January: *El Salvador* Colonel Monterrosa, commander of the Army's forces in the eastern provinces, stated that his forces could not guarantee protection of all polling stations in the region in the forthcoming 25 March elections. The insurgents were reportedly increasing their control of the region by constructing their own

road in the north-east, near the Honduran border.

31 January: *South Africa* South African forces inside Angola began a general disengagement as the prelude for a possible cease-fire between South Africa and Angola.

1 February: *USA* The Pentagon's budget proposals for FY–85 to FY–89 were put before Congress. FY–85 calls for $305bn, a 13 per cent increase over FY–84, and the defence budget would increase to $446bn by FY–89, however, after FY–86 the dramatic increases in the defence budget seen over recent years would diminish to a level of less than 4 per cent per year after inflation. No new major weapons systems were introduced in the budget proposals.

1 February: *Norway* Following the arrest of Arne Treholt, five Soviet diplomats were ordered to leave the country.

1 February: *Iraq* It was reported that Iraq was manufacturing Mustard Gas and other chemical weapons.

2 February: *Lebanon* General fighting in the area of Beirut and the Chouf mountains broke out between the Army and the Druze and Shia militias. The 57 per cent Moslem Army rapidly began suffering a series of reverses leading to demoralisation, desertion and the disintegration of some Army units and the capture of the coast road between Beirut and the International Airport. This cut off the Army from the positions held by US marines.

2 February: *Sudan* Oil exploration work in southern Sudan was stopped because of insurgent activity. Insurgent groups in the non-Islamic south are resisting the imposition of Islamic law throughout the country and have already forced a halt to two other major development programmes: the Jonglei Irrigation canal and the Juba airport.

3 February: *USA* In the wake of the Kissinger Commission's report on Central America, which advocated a continuation of the current policy with

the addition of massive economic and military aid, Congress was asked to approve a $400m increase in economic aid (up to $1.13bn) and a tripling of military aid to $373m over the agreed sums for FY–84, the bulk of this extra aid going to El Salvador.

3 February: *Argentina* British proposals for re-establishing normal relations with Argentina were rejected since they explicitly excluded the possibility of talks on the future of Falkland Islands.

6 February: *Lebanon* The rapid disintegration of elements of the Lebanese Army during the continued fighting allowed the Shia population of West Beirut to stage an insurrection and force the Army out of that area of the city and thus freeing itself from the control of President Gemayel. The government of President Gemayel, the prime minister and his cabinet, had resigned on 5th.

6 February: *Chad* French Foreign Minister Cheysson visited N'Djamena, Addis Ababa and Tripoli in an effort to get negotiations started whilst the French military presence in Chad was strengthened by the arrival of a squadron of 12 attack helicopters.

7 February: *Lebanon* With the disintegration of the government and army of President Gemayel and the isolation of the US marines from the President's remaining forces, the USA announced its decision to withdraw its marines back onto the ships of the US 6th Fleet. Britain and Italy announced the withdrawal of their forces, effectively ending the Multi-National Force's attempt to promote a peaceful settlement in Lebanon. The last member of the force, France, stated that its troops would remain in their positions along the so-called 'Green Line' dividing East and West Beirut (Christian and Moslem quarters of the city respectively) until they were relieved by a United Nations peacekeeping force.

7 February: *USA* Admiral Watkins, the Chief of Naval Operations, announced that the USS *Ticonder-*

oga, the first CG–47 class cruiser carrying the first example of AEGIS, the US Navy's future major air defence system, would be put through a second series of tests during 1984 to resolve the 15 human and systems failures which occurred during its first series of tests in 1983. AEGIS is to be fitted to 26 CG–47 class cruisers and some 60 DDG–51 class destroyers during the 1980s and 1990s.

8 February: *Lebanon* The UK's 115-man element of the MNF was evacuated from Beirut.

8 February: *Honduras* The US exercise, Big Pine II, ended. Another series of exercises, Grenadier I, was set to start in July and a 300-man force will remain in Honduras in the interval between the exercises. In addition USAF OV-1 Mohawk tactical reconnaissance aircraft were deployed to Honduras. These planes are capable of photo-reconnaissance (including using infra-red equipment) and electronic reconnaissance using a sideways-looking radar and can undertake surveillance of both El Salvador and Nicaragua.

9 February: *UK* Geoffrey Pattie, Minister of State at the Ministry of Defence, urged caution in the introduction of Emerging Technology (ET), emphasising the difficulties in speeding the introduction of ET systems, their great cost, the problems they posed for European defence industries and the need to determine fully their feasibility and cost-effectiveness.

9 February: *Pakistan* The head of the atomic energy programme claimed that the technology to produce nuclear weapons had been mastered though foreign assessments believe that Pakistan is still several years from such a capability.

10 February: *Lebanon* Over 1,000 European, American and Commonwealth civilians were evacuated by helicopter from Beirut.

12 February: *Iran* A limited offensive in northern Iraq, operation 'Liberation of Jerusalem', started.

13 February: *USSR* Konstantin Ustinovich Chernenko became General Secretary of Communist Party

of the Soviet Union following the announcement of the death of President Yuri Andropov on 9th. Chernenko was reportedly a close supporter of the late President Brezhnev and had been defeated in the succession battle after Brezhnev's death by Andropov. Chernenko, 73, is seen as an interim leader whilst younger candidates (Grigori Romanov (61), Vitali Vorotnikov (57) and Mikhail Gorbachev (53)) gain experience. During Andropov's funeral, Chernenko briefly met with senior Western leaders including US Vice-President Bush, West German Chancellor Kohl and UK Prime Minister Thatcher.

15 February: *Italy* Leamon Hunt, Director General of the Sinai Multi-national peacekeeping force was assassinated by the Red Brigade. It was the first Red Brigade act since the release of American General Dozier in January 1982.

15 February: *Iran* Limited offensives in the central and southern sectors of the Iraq front line were started, 'Operation Zahra' against Mandali and 'Dawn–56' in the marshy area to the north of the southern city of Basra.

16 February: *South Africa–Angola* A joint commission was established to monitor the disengagement of South African, Angolan, Cuban and SWAPO troops fighting in Angola and Namibia. The USA offered to supervise any cease-fire which resulted from the disengagement.

17 February: *Lebanon* President Assad of Syria rejected an eight point peace plan put forward by President Gemayel despite the fact that it conceded to one of Syria's major demands, the possibility of abrogating the unratified 17th May troops withdrawal accord with Israel whilst a second major demand, that US forces should be removed from Beirut, was about to occur.

19 February: *Lebanon* The Italian contingent to the MNF began its withdrawal, which was completed on 20th, from Beirut and on to two specially chartered ferries under the protection of a

seven warship squadron lead by the *Vittorio Veneto*.

21 February: *Norway* A Vidar class minelayer depth-charged a suspected submarine intruder in Tysfjord, 40 miles from Narvik.

21 February: *Rumania* It was announced that for the first time in ten years, Rumania would take part in a Warsaw Pact exercise, 'Soyuz-84'. The exercise was a command exercise, not involving the use of troops, and covered Hungary, Bulgaria and the south-western USSR.

23 February: *USSR* Konstantin Chernenko assumed the posts of Chairman of the Defence Council and Commander-in-Chief of the Armed Forces.

25 February: *Lebanon* The US Marines were 'relocated' back to the amphibious assault ships of the US 6th Fleet, the withdrawal being completed on 26th as the situation of the Lebanese Army continued to deteriorate. The Druze and Shia militias, however, stopped short of pushing the Army finally out of the Chouf mountains at Souq al-Garb as they regrouped their forces.

26 February: *UK* The Controller & Auditor General recommended that the Naval Staff should be more sensitive to the disruptive effect on the efficiency of the Royal Dockyards of unscheduled repair work which currently takes up 10 per cent of the workload.

27 February: *Iraq* Iraq mounted an air attack on Iran's major oil terminal at Kharg Island.

29 February: *Lebanon* President Gemayel visited President Assad of Syria in an attempt to get Syria to sponsor a renewed peace effort.

1 March: *Iraq* An Indian merchant ship, the *APJ Ambika,* was damaged by an Iraqi air attack as it neared the port of Bushire under Iranian naval escort. The site of the attack, some 200 miles from Iraq, marked an extension of Iraq's offensive to close Iran to merchant shipping. Before, attacks were centred on ships entering Bandar Khomeini, only 30 miles from Iraq.

1 March: *Nicaragua* The 'Contra' movement began a campaign of blockading Nicaraguan ports by

laying minefields off the entrances with, it was learnt later, the support and encouragement of the CIA. A Dutch dredger, the *Geopotes VI,* was the first ship to be damaged, a second ship, the *Los Carides,* being damaged on 4th; both ships being outside the main port of Corinto. On 7th, high speed motor boats with machine guns straffed the port of San Juan del Sur.

8 March: *Greece–Turkey* Greece accused Turkey of firing on a Greek destroyer and a party of fishing boats in the northern Aegean Sea. The incident coincided with the visit of the Greek-Cypriot leader to Greece to discuss defence and a warning from the Turkish parliament to Greece not to send troops to Cyprus. Turkey, however, pointed out that they had warned Greece of the live firing exercise three days before, that the Turkish ships fired landwards to the Turkish shore and that the test was of anti-aircraft shells which represented no danger to the Greek ships — An explanation which Greece accepted on the 9th.

9 March: *Argentina* Hugo Gobbi, Under Secretary for Foreign Affairs resigned because of 'personal differences' with other members of the government. He was responsible for the recent movement in negotiations with Chile over the Beagle Channel dispute and for formulating Argentina's position towards Britain and the Falkland Islands.

12 March: *UK* Minister of Defence, Michael Heseltine, announced plans for a major reorganisation of the top echelon of the ministry to take effect from 1 January 1985. The three service Chiefs of Staff are to lose their policy making functions which will be centralised under a joint civil-military staff headed by the Chief of Defence Staff which, with a new office of management and budget, will provide stronger control over defence policy and spending.

12 March: *Lebanon* The National Reconciliation Conference met again under Syrian sponsorship

and agreed to a cease-fire to stop the fighting which began on 2 February.

13 March: *UK* The cost of the Trident programme was officially admitted to have risen to £8.729bn despite a saving of £500m achieved by not building a plant to refurbish the missiles (sending them to the USA instead). Previous cost estimates for the programme were £4½ to £5bn in 1980 and £7bn in 1981. Unofficial estimates put the cost at £11.5bn.

14 March: *USA* A Congressional report suggested that the MX missile, due for deployment in 1986, will not be fully reliable due to the rushed development programme. The USAF, however, is unwilling to delay deployment lest the controversial project runs into further Congressional opposition.

16 March: *USSR* The Soviet delegation and the six other Warsaw Pact countries returned to the negotiating table at the MBFR talks in the first resumption of a major arms control conference since the deployment of GLCMs and Pershing-II missiles.

16 March: *South Africa–Mozambique* The two countries signed a non-aggression pact which forbade the supporting of any insurgent movement directed at each others country. A joint commission was established to monitor the pact and Mozambique received substantial economic aid for signing the agreement. The African National Council was allowed to maintain a diplomatic mission in Mozambique.

16 March: *Sudan* It was claimed that a Tu-22 Blinder bomber from Libya bombed a radio station on the outskirts of the capital Khartoum.

20 March: *UK* In the reorganisation of the Ministry of Defence it was announced that all operational analysis would be taken out of the control of the services and placed under the responsibility of the Chief Scientific Adviser.

20 March: *Lebanon* The National Reconciliation Conference ended without agreement. Moslem

leaders were said to be unhappy about Syria's insistence that the basics of the constitution should remain unchanged whilst Christian leaders resisted Syrian attempts to diminish the power of the Christian President.

20 March: *Nicaragua* A Soviet tanker, the *Lugansk*, was damaged by a mine whilst entering the port of Puerto Sandino.

22 March: *Lebanon* Fighting broke out in southern Beirut between Druze and Sunni militias. The fighting continued on 23rd and on 25th, a delegation of senior Sunni leaders met with Druze leaders in Damascus in an attempt to avoid future inter-Moslem fighting.

24 March: *USA* Under Israeli pressure, the USA decided not to sell Stinger man-portable surface-to-air missile systems to Saudi Arabia and Jordan.

24 March: *Singapore* The US Pentagon notified Congress of its intention to sell eight F–16s of the less capable export version (F–16/79) in a $200m deal to Singapore. With the purchase of four E–2C Hawkeye early warning aircraft Singapore will, in part, make up for the loss of a squadron of Australian Mirage fighters based in Malaysia.

25 March: *Lebanon* The French contingent of the MNF began withdrawing from Beirut (ending on 31st) despite the absence of a UN force to take its place.

25 March: *El Salvador* The General Election took place amid considerable confusion due to the poor organisation of the polling stations, some of which opened late and some whose location changed at very short notice. The turnout was reported to be 1.6 million of the 5.2m Salvadorian electorate. The insurgents claimed that 89 of the 261 municipalities saw no voting at all though the US Ambassador put the figure at between 40 and 44. A run-off between the two principal opponents had to be organised within 30 days under the constitution.

26 March: *Iraq* The UN General Secretary reported to

the UN Security Council confirmation of Iraq having used chemical weapons against Iran.

26 March: *Iraq* Aeroplanes attacked a Greek tanker and a South Korean offshore support ship, operated by Kuwait and Saudi Arabia respectively. The ships of Iraq's major allies were both well outside the War Zone declared around Iran by Iraq.

27 March: *Angola* The UNITA insurgent movement claimed to have captured the town of Sumbe, less than 200 miles from the capital Luanda. This operation was said to be jeopardising the disengagement of forces since it was felt that UNITA could not undertake such an operation without South African help.

27 March: *El Salvador* The US government admitted that about half the arms used by the insurgents were of US manufacture captured from the Salvadorian Army.

27 March: *Nicaragua* High speed motor boats armed with machine guns were intercepted by the Nicaraguan Navy whilst attempting to attack Corinto. On 28th the Liberian, *Inderchaser* was damaged by a mine when leaving Corinto.

28 March: *UK* First Deputy Foreign Minister of the USSR, Georgi Kornienko, visited the UK for discussions on foreign affairs and trade. Attempts to encourage a return to the INF and START talks failed.

28 March: *USSR* The Baltic and Northern Fleets held a major naval exercise until 5 April. A group of five Krivak frigates were deployed off Jan Mayen Island whilst four Krivaks and a Kynda class cruiser from the Baltic Fleet were deployed off the Shetland Islands. The two groups covered the main force centred on the cruiser *Kirov* north of northern Norway.

2 April: *USSR* The carrier *Minsk* fired flares at the shadowing US warship, the USS *Harold E Holt,* three of which struck the ship. The incident occurred in the South China Sea.

2 April: *China* The Chinese Army began artillery bombardments and cross border attacks

against Vietnamese positions in the now annual Chinese attempt to divert Vietnamese forces away from their spring offensive against Khymer insurgents in Kampuchea.

3 April: *NATO* Defence Ministers of NATO met in Turkey to discuss the US Ballistic Missile Defence programme and the US decision not to seek an arms control agreement with the Soviet Union over the introduction of anti-satellite weapon systems.

3 April: *Lebanon* Israel appointed Major General Antoine Lahd to command the late Major Haddad's militia in southern Lebanon.

3 April: *Guinea* Following the death of President Toure, Africa's longest serving leader, on 27 March the Army staged a bloodless *coup*. The leader, Colonel Lansana, banned the country's sole political party and promised to introduce private enterprise into the country.

4 April: *West Germany* The USA, UK and France, responsible for the air corridors between West Germany and West Berlin over East Germany, protested to the Soviet Union over increased frequency (since February) of restrictions on the use of the corridors due to military exercises. On 6th, a Soviet fighter circled a civil airliner enroute for Frankfurt despite the lack of flying restrictions imposed at that point.

6 April: *Cameroon* Rebels under Colonel Saleh attempted to stage a *coup* against President Biya. Forces loyal to the President were able to defeat the rebels. When the fighting ended on 10th some 500 people had died in what had been thought of as one of Africa's most stable countries.

8 April: *USA* With the revelation that the CIA was behind the Nicaraguan 'Contras' minelaying offensive, the US government announced that it would not accept the verdict of the International Court of Justice when Nicaragua brought a suit against the US.

9 April: *USA* The House of Representatives Armed

Services sub-committee voted to cut the government's defence request for FY-85 by $19bn, reducing the $47bn increase (13 per cent) over FY-84 to $28bn (6 per cent). The defence budget has to pass before the Senate and then a joint House-Senate conference before the final cuts in the budget proposal are worked out.

9 April: *USSR* The helicopter carrier *Leningrad* conducted anti-submarine exercises with the Cuban Navy in the Gulf of Mexico.

9 April: *Lebanon* The Higher Security Committee, formed to oversee the current cease-fire, endorsed a plan to disengage the militias by creating a buffer zone of 100 metres to be observed by the Lebanese police and a group of 150 neutral observers. The plan was put into effect on the 19th.

10 April: *USA* In a vote of censure the Senate voted 82 to 12 forbidding future funds for the mining of Nicaraguan harbours.

12 April: *USA* The Arms Control and Disarmament Agency reported that Soviet defence expenditure rose by 2.3 per cent in 1983, less than the increase in GNP. Future increases are also expected to fall within the increase of GNP hence returning the 1977–82 annual growth rate of about 2 per cent.

13 April: *Nicaragua* Commander Cuadra, Chief of Staff of the armed forces announced that the 'Contras' were mounting their largest offensive yet with attacks both from the north (from Honduras) and the south (from Costa Rica). Both were said to be attempts at establishing permanent bases within Nicaragua. In the south, the insurgents under Eden Pastora captured the small port of San Juan del Norte. Government troops, however, retook it on 17th.

17 April: *UK* Shots fired from the Libyan People's Bureau at an anti-Gaddafi demonstration killed a policewoman and injured eleven of the demonstrators. The building was rapidly

placed under siege by the police. Problems of diplomatic immunity and Libyan threats that they would take counter action against the British Embassy in Libya if the London People's Bureau was entered blocked any attempt to detain the 30 Libyans in the building for questioning over the shooting. On 20th a bomb exploded at Heathrow airport, injuring 22 people. It was suspected to have come from Libya. On 25th the Libyans in the People's Bureau were expelled from the country and diplomatic relations with Libya were broken off.

17 April: *NATO* New proposals were put forward at the MBFR talks which moved away from counting men (the figures are in dispute) and concentrating instead on combat and support formations.

18 April: *USA* Vice President Bush announced a new proposal for a Chemical Weapons Ban at the UN Disarmament Conference.

18 April: *USSR* A naval task group containing the carrier *Minsk* and the amphibious assault ship *Ivan Rogov* conducted a joint Soviet/Vietnamese amphibious assault in the Gulf of Tonkin. This was the first joint exercise between the two countries.

25 April: *Iraq* Aeroplanes attacked and set on fire the super tanker *Safina Al-Arab* 160km north-east of Bahrain.

26 April: *USA* The Director of the CIA, William Casey, formally apologised to the Senate Intelligence Committee for not having kept them informed over the mining of Nicaraguan harbours and assured the committee that all mining operations had stopped.

26 April: *Lebanon* Rashid Karami was appointed as Prime Minister and asked to form a cabinet including the leaders of all the major factions fighting in the Lebanese Civil War.

26 April: *Afghanistan* Soviet forces began a major offensive in the Panjsher Valley utilising some 20,000 troops. The offensive included for the

first time the use of high level bombing by the strategic bombers of Long Range Aviation (DA).

29 April: *Iran* An Egyptian–Yugoslav peace plan for ending the Iran-Iraq War was presented to Iran by India.

29 April: *Sudan* President Nemery declared a general State of Emergency because of the increasing opposition to the 'Islamisation programme'.

20 April: *Costa Rica* The government, which remains neutral in the central American disputes, moved against the 'Contras' based in the country because of damaging reports of CIA involvement in supporting Eden Pastora's 'Contra' group.

30 April: *Lebanon* Prime Minister Karami announced his ten man cabinet which included all major factional leaders. Nabih Berri, leader of the Shia 'Amal' militia, however, refused to take up his seat in the cabinet because his ministerial portfolio did not give him a position from which he could influence events in southern Lebanon, where the great majority of the Shi'ite population live. Walid Jumblatt, leader of the Druze militia supported Berri's claim for an extension of his responsibilities.

Index to Advertisers

For information regarding availability and cost of Advertising Space in this and other Brassey's publications contact your nearest Advertising Office:

(UK and France)

7 Cygnet House
188 Kings Road
London SW3
Contact: Nigel Halliday
Telephone: 01 – 352 2282

(USA and Canada)

Pergamon-Brassey's International Defense Publishers
Maxwell House
Fairview Park
Elmsford
New York 10523
USA
Contact: Art Carlucci
Telephone: 914 – 592 7700
Telex: 13-7328

(Rest of the World)

Brassey's Defence Publishers
Maxwell House
74 Worship Street
London EC2A 2EN
UK
Contact: Rodney Harms
Telephone: 377/4909/4908/4912
Telex: 888804